ASTROLOGY AND POPULAR
MODERN WE

To Wendy

Astrology and Popular Religion in the Modern West
Prophecy, Cosmology and the New Age Movement

University of Wales Trinity Saint David, Wales, UK

Routledge
Taylor & Francis Group

LONDON AND NEW YORK

First Published 2012 by Ashgate Publisher

2 Park Square, Milton Park, Abingdon, Oxon OX14 4RN
711 Third Avenue, New York, NY 10017, USA

Routledge is an imprint of the Taylor & Francis Group, an informa business

First issued in paperback 2016

British Library Cataloguing in Publication Data
Campion, Nicholas.
   Astrology and popular religion in the modern west :
   prophecy, cosmology and the New Age movement.
   1. Astrology – History. 2. New Age movement.
   I. Title
   133.5'09-dc23

Library of Congress Cataloging-in-Publication Data
Campion, Nicholas.
   Astrology and popular religion in the modern West : prophecy, cosmology,
and the New Age movement / Nicholas Campion.
      p. cm.
   Includes bibliographical references (p.   ) and index.
   ISBN 978-1-4094-3514-3 (hardcover)
1. Astrology. 2. Religion. 3. New Age movement. I. Title.

   BF1729.R4C36 2012
   133.5–dc23

                                                                2012005337
ISBN 978-1-4094-3514-3 (hbk)
ISBN 978-1-138-26162-4 (pbk)

Contents

List of Tables

Preface and Acknowledgements

Astrology is a familiar feature of modern culture, yet is widely ignored by the Academy. Our attempts to understand its claims, practices and philosophical context have tended to fall prey to the legacy of the self-defined Enlightenment struggle against superstition, and it has too often been condemned or dismissed, rather than subjected to systematic investigation. This book is an attempt to rectify this situation, to examine the extent and nature of modern belief in astrology, and to place it in its wider cultural environment, in particular in relation to religious and historical themes.

I would like to acknowledge Brian Bocking, Marion Bowman and Michael York, who helped steer me in my present direction, as well as all my students and colleagues in the Sophia Centre.

Nicholas Campion
Sophia Centre for the Study of Cosmology in Culture,
School of Archaeology, History and Anthropology,
University of Wales Trinity Saint David
30 November 2011

Chapter 1

Introduction: A Million-Dollar Business?

Astrology has grown to be a huge worldwide business… It seems that no sector of society is immune to its attraction.[1]

Astrology is … a bizarre survival from pre-scientific times.[2]

Astrology – the study and practice of the presumed relationship between the celestial bodies and events on earth – has millions of fans, a number of vociferous opponents, and is a familiar part of popular culture, but has almost completely escaped examination by modern scholars. Most commentary on the subject, whether by academics or journalists, consults neither astrologers, nor their literature, clients or readers. Both practitioners and users have often been condemned as socially marginal or psychologically deviant and it is therefore usually not considered necessary to examine what they actually say or do. Astrology itself is marked by a relative diversity in its claims. It may be considered, depending on the definition of all these words, to be magic, divination, a psychological tool, a religion, an art or a science; it may be a matter of studying the supposed relationships between celestial and terrestrial events; or it may require practical action. Such is the variety of astrological theories, practices and techniques around the world that some scholars prefer to talk of 'astrologies' than 'astrology'.[3]

In the view of much of the academic literature in the area, astrology, usually, problematically, defined as the belief in the occult influence of the stars, is a religion, nothing more, nothing less. Acceptance of astrology's claims is widespread and, according to Gallup poll data, about 25 per cent of the adult populations of the UK, the US and France subscribe to it. We should put this apparently rather large figure into perspective; the adult population of the UK in 2008 was approximately 48 million, 12 million of whom believed in astrology, 11 million more than attended a church service regularly.[4] In France the proportions are similar. In the US, where

---

[1] Robert Matthews, 'Astrologers fail to predict proof they are wrong', *Sunday Telegraph*, 17 August 2003, p. 9.

[2] John Silber, 'Silliness under Seattle stars', *Boston Herald*, 16 May 2001, at <http://www.bostonherald.com/news/columnists/silber05162001.htm>, accessed 1 June 2001.

[3] Nicholas Campion, *What do Astrologers Believe?* (Oxford, 2006); Nicholas Campion, *Astrology and Cosmology in the World's Religions* (New York, 2012); Nicholas Campion and Liz Greene, *Astrologies: Plurality and Diversity* (Lampeter, 2011).

[4] The population of the UK in 2008 was just over 61 million, of whom around a fifth were children. See the Office for National Statistics, <http://www.statistics.gov.uk/cci/nugget.asp?ID=6>, accessed 5 November 2009. For church attendance see Peter Brierly (ed.), *UK Christian Handbook: Religious Trends no. 3, 2002/3* (London, 2001), p. 2.23.

around 40 per cent of adults claim to attend a church, synagogue or temple service regularly, the number of religious devotees exceeds that of astrology believers, but the latter still represent a sizeable number.[5] These rather startling figures should tell us something about modern religious culture yet are largely ignored by academics and religious specialists. Or, rather, if noticed, they are taken at face value with neither serious comment nor critical investigation.

My intention is to place the discussion of astrology's modern status in a context which is wide enough to allow a better understanding of the recent history and present status of esoteric ideas, occult practices and alternative spiritualities, that potent cultural matrix which alarms evangelical Christians, disturbs sceptical scientists and perplexes many sociologists. As my title suggests, I am concerned with whether astrology is a religion, and particularly whether it is 'New Age'. While my data is mainly from the English-speaking world, there is a recognisable community of astrologers in the modern West who share similar assumptions and the same leading authors. The evidence of opinion polls suggests that public interest in astrology is similar in, say, Germany and France, to the UK and the US, while the network of organised astrologers manages to cross national boundaries, in spite of the language barriers. I also collected data from astrological groups in Serbia and Norway, as well as Brazil and Argentina, and while there are variations in religious attitudes, as one would expect, certain features appear constant: whether in London or Seattle, Oslo or Belgrade, Buenos Aires or Rio de Janeiro, 90 per cent of the audience at astrology meetings are women. Clearly, astrology's appeal is overwhelmingly female, a fact which has never been properly addressed, although the wider female interest in the paranormal has attracted attention.[6] Are women just gullible? Or do they find a mode of expression, a kind of knowing, which compensates for what Tuchman called their 'symbolic annihilation' – their virtual exclusion, except as decorations, from the mass media.[7]

My sub-title is 'Prophecy, Cosmology and the New Age Movement'. The prophecy under investigation is the coming of the often synonymous periods of the Age of Aquarius and the New Age. The cosmology under examination is astrology, especially in its assumption that great historical changes coincide with astronomical movements, and the implications of this for individual lives. Being

---

For a typical report see James Doward, 'Church attendance "to fall by 90%"', *Observer*, 21 December 2008, <http://www.guardian.co.uk/world/2008/dec/21/anglicanism-religion>, accessed 5 November 2009.

[5]   For a summary of figures on religious attendance in the US, see Religious Tolerance, <http://www.religioustolerance.org/rel_rate.htm>, accessed 5 November 2009.

[6]   Susan J. Blackmore, 'Are Women More Sheepish? Gender Differences in Belief in the Paranormal', in E. Coly and R. White (eds), *Women and Parapsychology* (New York, 1994), pp. 68–89.

[7]   Gaye Tuchman, 'The Symbolic Annihilation of Women by the Mass Media', in Lane Crothers and Charles Lockhart, *Culture and Politics: A Reader* (New York, 2000), pp. 150–74.

concerned with the nature of supposed belief in astrology within a wider context of the history of ideas, I will deal with both millenarianism and the New Age chiefly as ideological rather than, say, sociological phenomena. From millenarianism I will consider, briefly, questions of modernism and modernity, both of which are heir to apocalyptic thought in their belief that the 'now' is inherently qualitatively better than the past. My specific examination of contemporary belief in astrology is then intended to illuminate wider contemporary issues concerning the supposed relationship between 'traditional' and 'non-traditional' beliefs, a discussion which can be framed within the context of debates on the place of religion and 'secularisation' in the modern world. As I am concerned with the numbers of people who believe in astrology as well as with the nature of that belief, I draw partly from existing data and partly from my own research.

Having dealt with the problem of the extent of belief in astrology which, as we shall see, is a somewhat complex question, I will address four principal questions concerning astrology's place in modern culture. Firstly, is it a New Age discipline and, if so, what is its relationship with the Western millenarian and apocalyptic tradition? Secondly, if astrology is a New Age discipline, should it be seen as a rival to mainstream Christianity, as so many Christian apologists insist? Thirdly, if astrology is indeed a rival to Christianity, can quantification of belief in it indicate the extent of that rivalry? Fourthly, does astrology's continued existence represent the anomalous survival of a pre-modern superstition in the modern world: is it, as Theodor Adorno claimed, 'basically discordant with today's universal state of enlightenment'?[8] The core of the work is historiographical and I devote a great deal of attention to dissecting the literature to date on the origins of modern New Age and astrological culture. My fieldwork is tentative and preliminary and far from conclusive. It is, rather, suggestive, of possibilities for further work. As my inquiry is partly literary, and as this is the first time that the disparate sources which deal with the topic have been brought together, I have provided copious references, all the more to encourage other scholars to continue this work.

My initial premise is not controversial: that astrology occupies a prominent position in the contemporary popular culture of the modern West is apparent from the ubiquitous presence of the horoscope column in print and, in the last decade, on the web. What is at issue, though, is astrology's character. On this, opinions diverge. It is widely considered to be a feature of the Western esoteric tradition, a New Age belief or practice, paranormal or an 'alternative religion', is seen as a potential contributor to the decline of the mainstream churches in Britain, is regarded as worthy of comment by the cosmologist Stephen Hawking and, even though its function may have changed between medieval and modern times, is arguably connected with the origins of the Western magical tradition in pre-Hellenistic Egypt. It is engaged in a polemical struggle with religious conservatives and scientific sceptics, the roots of which can be traced back around two thousand years to the dual foundations of Christianity and classical scepticism. The sceptics,

---

[8] Theodor Adorno, *The Stars Down to Earth* (London, 1994), p. 36.

in the early twenty-first century, currently have the highest public profile. Richard Dawkins, formerly Professor of the Public Understanding of Science at Oxford University, believes that astrologers should be prosecuted for fraud, while the British television regulatory code prohibits the broadcast of 'horoscopes' except as 'entertainment' or as the subject of 'legitimate inquiry', and forbids transmission of it at times when children are likely to be watching television.[9] Astrology, in this sense, is classed alongside the more traditionally taboo topics, sex and violence. The astronomer and TV presenter Brian Cox regards it as 'new age drivel' which, he claims dramatically, 'is undermining the very fabric of our civilization', and the geneticist Steve Jones adds that 'It is drivel because it flies in the face of four centuries of evidence, from Galileo to the latest space probe'.[10] One may ask why, if it is drivel, it arouses such anger, and why one part of British media regulation regards it as so dangerous. In spite of such opposition, all women's magazines in the UK carry horoscope columns and, in December and January, both they and the 'tabloid' newspapers publish heavily promoted supplements of forecasts for the coming year. The same is true of much of the rest of the world. Moreover, press stories on astrology generally create the impression that it is a multimillion-pound industry. For example, in August 2003, Robert Matthews, science correspondence of *The Sunday Telegraph*, wrote that

> Astrology has grown to be a huge worldwide business ... It seems that no sector of society is immune to its attraction. A recent survey found that a third of science students subscribed to some aspects of astrology, while some supposedly hard-headed businessmen now support a thriving market in 'financial astrology' ... Astrology supplements have been known to increase newspaper circulation figures and papers are prepared to pay huge sums to the most popular stargazers ...[who] can earn £600,000 or more a year. A single profitable web site can be worth as much as £50 million.[11]

Where Matthews found this supposedly £50 million website, and what it was, he did not say. My suspicion is that it did not exist, but this is not the point. What we are dealing with is public perception. In 2009 one TV company expanded the common notion of astrology as a 'million-dollar' business into the unlikely

---

[9]   Richard Dawkins, *Unweaving the Rainbow* (London, 1998), p. 121; Independent Television Commission (ITC), *Paranormal Programming, Consultation Paper*, Programme Code Consultation, 2003, section 1.10.

[10]   Brian Cox, 'Science: A Challenge to TV Orthodoxy', Huw Wheldon Lecture 2011, <http://www.youtube.com/watch?v=QPrdK4hWffo>; Steve Jones, 'A Review of the Impartiality and Accuracy of the BBC's Coverage of Science', *BBC Trust Review of Impartiality and Accuracy of the BBC's Coverage of Science; With an Independent Assessment by Professor Steve Jones and Content Research from Imperial College London* (London, 2011), p. 60.

[11]   Matthews, 'Astrologers fail to predict', p. 9.

figure of a 'billion-dollar' enterprise.[12] Although all such quoted figures are given without reliable sources, they tend to be repeated as journalists base subsequent reports on each other's work.[13] There is, in fact, little in the way of reliable information on astrology's place in contemporary British culture. This book is a preliminary attempt to rectify this situation, particularly in the UK and the US. My study originally arose from my observation that much of the public discourse on astrology is dominated by the assumption that it is overwhelmingly a matter of belief; astrology is classified as a form of 'belief' and students and practitioners of it are characterised as 'believers'.

At this point, let me turn to the question of previous studies. Although astrology is, as has been noted, a subject of considerable journalistic interest, there has been little academic concern with its contemporary cultural nature and function. To put it bluntly, most academics have shunned it. The literature on cultural studies has steered clear of it, largely because it avoids anything which it believes belongs under an existing discipline, such as religious studies; I am grateful to my colleague Sean Cubitt, Professor of Global Media and Communication at Winchester School of Art, for making this simple point. Those attempts to relate religion to popular culture which have been published actually encourage theologians to study popular culture, rather than subject religion to the rigours of cultural analysis.[14]

When we come to the sociology of religion, the English-language literature on the New Age movement includes only one paper in an academic anthology devoted to astrology, while there are a handful of sociological studies which attempt to describe and quantify belief in astrology.[15] Most critiques of astrology tend to concentrate on the veracity of astrology's claims and assume an *a priori* hostile position in which astrology represents either scientific ignorance or religious error, compared to just a few examples of general surveys by sympathetic writers.[16]

[12] 'Supernatural Investigator: It's in the Stars', Sorcery Films 2009.

[13] See, for example, Beth Hale, 'Is astrology bunk?', *Daily Mail*, 18 August 2003.

[14] See, for example, Gordon Lynch, *Understanding Theology and Popular Culture* (Oxford, 2005).

[15] Shoshanah Feher, 'Who Holds the Cards? Women and New Age Astrology?', in James R. Lewis and J. Gordon Melton, *Perspectives on the New Age* (Albany NY, 1992), pp. 179–88. For sociological studies see, for example, Robert Wuthnow, *Experimentation in American Religion: The New Mysticisms and Their Implications for the Churches* (Berkeley CA, 1978); Kurt Pawlik and Lothar Buse, 'Self-Attribution as a Moderator Variable in Differential Psychology: Replication and Interpretation of Eysenck's Astrology/Personality Correlations', *Correlation*, 4/2 (1984), pp. 14–30; John Bauer and Martin Durant, 'British Public Perceptions of Astrology: An Approach from the Sociology of Knowledge', *Culture and Cosmos*, 1/1 (1997), pp. 55–72; Alison Bird, 'Astrology in Education: An Ethnography', DPhil thesis, University of Sussex, 2006; Bridget Costello, 'Astrology in Action: Culture and Status in Unsettled Lives', PhD thesis, University of Pennsylvania, 2006.

[16] For the assumption of scientific error see Roger B. Culver and Philip A. Ianna, *Astrology: True or False? A Scientific Evaluation*, rev. edn (New York, 1988) and Ronny

There is therefore still no wide-ranging work which examines astrology's cultural locus and which may also be classed as academic or rigorous.

My own research was conducted mainly between 1999 and 2003. My interest is with astrology's cultural status, rather than with the truth of its claims. As Gaynard observed in his study of young people's belief in the paranormal, 'it is probably of equal interest to ask, for example, why more people *believe* that they have experienced precognition than OBE [out-of-the-body experience] as it is to question why more people *have* experienced precognition than OBE'.[17] It is important, from a phenomenological perspective, to allow astrologers to speak for themselves and relate their own experiences. This is a goal which I have tried to achieve through surveying the literature with an open mind, reporting on claims and assertions without personal judgement, and through semi-structured interviews. On the grounds that practising astrologers may have specialised knowledge and experience in the field, I therefore conducted the bulk of my fieldwork amongst those active in astrology, particularly attendees at astrology conferences. This may seem obvious, but it is surprising how often statements about astrology's nature are made without any evidence from either practitioners or users. To use Ninian Smart's adaptation of Husserl's phrase, I am concerned with the astrologer's 'I-picture', the definitions astrologers use for themselves, as opposed to those which may be allocated to them by academics or external critics.[18]

Yet the study of astrology's contemporary cultural status may shed light on the condition of modern society as a whole. As Grace Davie has argued, 'by looking at the way that society reacts to new religious movements and the controversy they generate, we can discover more about that society itself'. And what if astrology *is* a religion? In this case, the wider significance of the study of its cultural function is clear, for as Bryan Wilson pointed out, 'Religious change is ... cultural change'.[19] It is, though, not necessary to argue that astrology is a religion in order to make the point that an understanding of the cultural milieu within which it thrives may shed light on contemporary society as a whole. Dale Caird and Henry Law, meanwhile, noted that even in the 1980s there was a substantial lack of

Martens and Tim Trachet, *Making Sense of Astrology* (Amherst MA, 1998). For Christian critiques see Peter Anderson, *Satan's Snare: The Influence of the Occult* (Welwyn, 1988), and Robert A. Morey, *Horoscopes and the Christian: Does Astrology Accurately Predict the Future? Is it Compatible with Christianity?* (Minneapolis, 1981). For non-academic but sympathetic studies see Derek Parker, *The Question of Astrology: A Personal Investigation* (London, 1970) and Neil Spencer, *True as the Stars Above: Adventures in Modern Astrology* (London, 2000).

[17] T.J. Gaynard, 'Young People and the Paranormal', *Journal of the Society for Psychical Research*, 58/826 (1992), p. 179.

[18] Ninian Smart, *The Phenomenon of Religion* (London, 1973), p. 24.

[19] Grace Davie, *Religion in Britain since 1945* (Oxford, 1994), p. 68; Bryan Wilson, *Contemporary Transformations of Religion* (Oxford, 1979), p. 3.

empirical social psychological research into counter-cultural religious beliefs.[20] This has changed, although not much, mainly due to a few studies of modern pagans. There are just a handful of studies specifically devoted to astrology. Of these, there are but three books. One is Marcia Moore's little-known attempt to conduct sociological research amongst astrologers in 1960; the others are Derek Parker's survey published in 1972 and Garry Phillipson's collections of interviews, published in 2000.[21] While there has now been substantial work in some areas, astrology has been generally untouched. Within the academic literature Marcello Truzzi attempted to initiate a discussion of astrology in popular culture in 1975, but his challenge was ignored.[22] Aside from those writers who were concerned with testing astrology's claims, only a few approached anything useful from a sociological point of view. Svenson and White, for example, looked at the content of horoscope columns and Michael Dambrun explored prejudice amongst astrologers.[23] There is, though, little consensus amongst current academic work. In his literature review of 2005, Ivan Kelly concluded that astrology 'offers no valid contribution to understanding ourselves, not our place in the cosmos'.[24] Even Kelly, though, was equivocal: removing the word 'valid' still enables astrology to function as a form of self-understanding, even if one that is scientifically invalid. Geoffrey Dean argued that astrology is useful, if lacking any scientific basis, while Bridget Costello argued that astrology is indeed 'useful in an everyday way', as people deal with the mundane reality of their lives.[25] Judy Pugh, writing on modern Indian astrology, refers to it as a system of 'situation construction' in which therapy is managed through the use of everyday language to 'represent and re-form troublesome situations in the client's life'.[26] While this study cannot tackle the psychological, it does aim to lay the ground for social research by cutting

[20]   Dale Caird and Henry G. Law, 'Non-Conventional Beliefs: Their Structure and Measurement', *Journal for the Scientific Study of Religion*, 21/2 (1982), p. 152.

[21]   Marcia Moore, *Astrology Today: A Socio-Psychological Survey*, Astrological Research Associates Research Bulletin no. 2 (New York, 1960); Parker, *The Question of Astrology*; Garry Phillipson, *Astrology in the Year Zero* (London, 2000).

[22]   Marcello Truzzi, 'Astrology as Popular Culture', *Journal of Popular Culture*, 8 (1975), pp. 906–11.

[23]   Stuart Svensen and Ken White, 'A Content Analysis of Horoscopes', *Genetic, Social and Psychological Monographs*, 12/1 (1995), pp. 7–38; Michael Dambrun, 'Belief in Paranormal Determinism as a Source of Prejudice Towards Disadvantaged Groups: "The Dark Side of Stars"', *Social Behaviour and Personality*, 32/1 (2004), pp. 627–36.

[24]   Ivan W. Kelly, 'The Concepts of Modern Astrology: A Critique', at <http://www.astrology-and-science.com/a-conc2.htm> (2005), accessed 3 September 2011, p. 1.

[25]   Geoffrey Dean, 'Does Astrology need to be True?', in Kendrick Frazier (ed.), *The Hundredth Monkey and Other Paradigms of the Paranormal* (Amherst MA, 1992), pp. 279–319; Costello, 'Astrology in Action', p. 4.

[26]   Judy F. Pugh, 'Astrological Counseling in Contemporary India', *Culture, Medicine and Psychiatry*, 7 (1983), pp. 279–99.

through the polemics which normally dominate public discourse on astrology – whether for or against – and begin to establish a sociological evidence base and context in the history of ideas.

My concerns are partly historical. In particular, I am interested in the problem of origins, in this case of the New Age movement and of contemporary astrology as a language of zodiac signs, personality and psychological potential. While the foundation of my study is historical, this leads directly into an analysis of the contemporary situation, principally from a qualitative standpoint. My use of quantitative data therefore remains indicative of possible areas for future research and is designed mainly to test whether previous and often widely reported figures on 'belief' in astrology are accurate. I am concerned with the nature of the narrative that astrologers themselves weave about their role in society and their place in the cosmos. Even though qualitative and quantitative research are often thought to belong to different research categories, the one focusing on subjective experience, the other on the attempt to establish objective measures of such experience, these contrasting approaches are not mutually antagonistic but, when used together, supportive.[27]

The discussion of astrology's status must revolve around what exactly it is. The descriptions we use tend to condition the kind of conclusions which are reached. For example, if astrology is classified as a form of divination it tends to be more controversial in a Christian context, but often less so to some scientific sceptics on the grounds that it does not make scientific claims. On the other hand, if it is natural philosophy, which is how it would have seemed to many medieval Aristotelians, it is likely to avoid Christian censure but arouse scientific ire. Central to such debates is a useful modern distinction made by some historians, but which can be traced at least back to Isidore of Seville (c. 560–4 April 636), between 'natural' and 'judicial' astrology.[28] Natural astrology required no more than the observation of natural influences deriving from the planets, and was universally accepted in the medieval and Renaissance worlds. Judicial astrology, requiring the astrologer's judgement, depended on complex deductions made from horoscopes and was widespread, but never entirely accepted by theological and sceptical opponents. This distinction is essential for understanding astrology's sometimes contradictory position in the West, especially denunciations of it, which invariably referred to the judicial variety, not the natural. Natural astrology has been generally, although not totally, appropriated by modern materialist science, through such phenomena as gravity, sun-spot cycles and circadian rhythms, and the word 'astrology' has been largely abandoned, with rare exceptions. The astrology I consider in this

---

[27]   Alan Bryman, *Quantity and Quality in Social Research* (London and New York, 2001), pp. 4–5.

[28]   Isidore of Seville, *The Etymologies*, trans. Stephen A. Barney, W.J. Lewis, J.A. Beach and Oliver Berghof (Cambridge, 2007), III.xxvii, p. 99; Nicholas Campion, *A History of Western Astrology* (2 vols, London, 2009), vol. 2, p. 12.

book is therefore of the 'judicial' variety, heavily dependent on the astrologer's judgement. In some versions of judicial astrology, the astrologer is an observer, dispassionately analysing the manifestation of astrological principles in terrestrial affairs. In other versions, which have been carried into the modern world via Neoplatonism, the astrologer is psychically embedded in the cosmos and plays a vital role in the application of astrology to human affairs.[29] Simply, astrology requires the presence of the astrologer. Whichever version of astrology we are discussing, the form with which we are concerned in this book is judicial.

We can also classify astrological practice according to the knowledge of the astrologer, from detailed and sophisticated to simple and crude, as did al-Qabīsī in the mid-tenth century.[30] I have also adopted Patrick Curry's hierarchical model of three forms of astrology forming a rough analogy with the three social groups, upper, middle and lower class.[31] The first, high astrology, is the astrology of the philosophers and theologians, concerned with speculative matters such as whether the theory of celestial influence leaves room for moral choice. The second, middling astrology, is characterised by the casting and interpretation of horoscopes, a practice requiring a considerable level of literary study and mathematical skill. The third, low astrology, is the astrology of street fortune-tellers, of almanacs (after the fifteenth century) and, in the modern world, newspaper and magazine 'sun-sign columns'.

Why, we should ask, is this inquiry important? My argument is that the quest for meaning is a universal human attribute and that in most, if not all, cultures, there is a predisposition to find meaning in the sky. To cite the French philosopher Bruno Latour, 'No one has ever heard of a collective that did not mobilize heaven and earth in its composition, along with bodies and souls, property and law, gods and ancestors, powers and beliefs, beast and fictional beings ... Such is the ancient anthropological matrix, the one we have never abandoned'.[32] According to George Gummerman and Miranda Warburton, who combine expertise in archaeology and anthropology, 'to truly comprehend a culture we must have some sense of its cosmology – the group's conception of themselves in relation to the heavens'.[33] And, in the words of Clive Ruggles and Nicholas Saunders,

---

[29]   Claudius Ptolemy, 'Centiloquium', in John Partridge, *Mikropanastron, or an Astrological Vade Mecum, briefly Teaching the whole Art of Astrology – viz., Questions, Nativities, with all its parts, and the whole Doctrine of Elections never so comprised nor compiled before, &c.* (London, 1679), para. 2, 3.

[30]   Charles Burnett, 'The Certitude of Astrology: The Scientific Methodology of al-Qabīsī and abū Ma'shar', *Early Science and Medicine*, 7/3 (2002), pp. 203–4.

[31]   Patrick Curry, *Prophecy and Power: Astrology in Early Modern England* (Oxford, 1989).

[32]   Bruno Latour, *We Have Never Been Modern* (Cambridge, 2006), p. 107.

[33]   George J. Gummerman and Miranda Warburton, 'The Universe in a Cultural Context: An Essay', in John W. Fountain and Rolf M. Sinclair (eds), *Current Studies in Archaeoastronomy: Conversations Across Time and Space* (Durham NC, 2005), p. 15.

> The study of cultural astronomies is concerned with the diversity of ways in which cultures, both ancient and modern, perceive celestial objects and integrate them into their view of the world. This fact, by definition, illustrates that a society's view of and beliefs about the celestial sphere are inextricably linked to the realm of politics, economics, religion, and ideology.[34]

This sense of cosmology as meaningful is, in modern Western terms, astrological, and the study of astrology's place in the modern world may have implications for our understanding of other aspects of culture which may not be as profound as they were until the seventeenth century but may still illuminate our view of twenty-first-century society.

As Michael Hill wrote, interest in astrology seemed to be considerable 'even in the most technologically advanced areas of Western society',[35] while the astronomers Snow and Brownsberger wrote that 'even today' some people have faith in astrology.[36] Note the use of the word 'even', as if, in the natural scheme of things, astrology should have died out. Glick and Snyder noted that 'belief in astrology ... remains as prevalent today as ever, despite the lack of scientific evidence for such beliefs'.[37] A typical view was expressed by John Silber, President of Boston University. He argued that

> Astrology is in fact a bizarre survival from pre-scientific times. Its theories were worked out when people believed the earth was the center of the universe and that seven planets revolved around it: the Moon, Mercury, Venus, the Sun, Mars, Jupiter and Saturn. Although this view of the universe has been proven false, astrology continues with hardly a wobble.[38]

Silber was following a Tylorian agenda, one which is thoroughly discredited amongst historians and debunked by anthropologists. It was the nineteenth-century anthropologist E.B. Tylor who argued that human culture was subject to an inevitable progression in which primitive magic was succeeded in turn by polytheism, monotheism and atheism.[39] Astrology, Tylor argued, belonged to the earliest, most primitive magical stage and its survival in the modern world is therefore a serious problem. If we accept, though, that Tylorian evolution and progress theory have any validity, this leads us to questions of modernism and modernity. Looking at the context within which astrology thrives, Hess considers

---

[34]   C. Ruggles and J. Saunders, *Astronomies and Cultures* (Boulder CO, 1993), p. 1.

[35]   Michael Hill, *A Sociology of Religion* (London, 1979), p. 247.

[36]   Theodore P. Snow and Kenneth R. Brownsberger, *Universe: Origins and Evolution* (London and New York, 1997), p. 7.

[37]   Peter Glick and Mark Snyder, 'Self-Fulfilling Prophecy: The Psychology of Belief in Astrology', *Humanist*, 46/3 (1986), p. 20.

[38]   Silber, 'Silliness under Seattle stars'.

[39]   Edward Burnett Tylor, *Primitive Culture* (London, 1873), vol. 1.

the New Age movement as a whole to be post-modern, although he offers no explanation for this.[40] Paul Heelas, meanwhile, considers the New Age movement in its counter-cultural aspects, and hence astrology, which he includes as New Age, as an aspect of 'modernity in crisis'.[41]

My purpose is to consider whether astrology's continued existence in the modern world is an anomaly, a legacy of the past which has survived in spite of the Enlightenment and scientific revolution, or whether it may be considered a natural part of the modern world. We therefore arrive at the key historical question, which I hope will play a part in the wider discussion of modern esotericism, new religious movements, New Age culture, alternative spiritualities and questions of the nature of secularism and modernity.

---

[40]   David J. Hess, *Science in the New Age: The Paranormal, its Defenders and Debunkers and American Culture* (Madison WI, 1993), p. 6.

[41]   Paul Heelas, *The New Age Movement* (Oxford, 1996), pp. 23, 24, 138.

Chapter 2

Cosmic Liberation: The Pursuit of the Millennium

Nation will rise against nation, and kingdom against kingdom; there will be great earthquakes and pestilences; and there will be terrors and great signs from heaven.[1]

It is widely argued that the expectation of a coming New Age is millenarian in character, and forms part of a broader cultural tradition which extends from the modern West back to the ancient Near East.[2] The New Age is, in spite of the epithet 'new', part of an ancient matrix of ideas which depend on the notion that human society, the whole world, or even the entire universe, is about to experience a cataclysmic transformation.

The word 'millenarianism' has both narrow and broad definitions. First used in the fifth century CE by St Augustine, it is derived from the Latin *mille*, a thousand, and refers to the Persian and, subsequently, Christian belief that world history is divided into periods of one, two or three thousand years.[3] The classic text of Christian millenarianism, the Revelation of St John, set out a historical template which still exerts a heavy influence in New Age ideology, in which a pervasive moral collapse climaxes in political and military strife, accompanied by the *parousia* (literally 'arrival' or 'presence'), that is, Christ's return. Christ, it was believed, is then due to triumph over Satan and reign in splendour for a thousand years; that is, the millennium, an epoch described in Matthew as the 'age to come'.[4] This period, the prophecy continues, will culminate with Satan's release and the final battle between good and evil, God's victory and the inauguration of a final stage of existence, the 'new heaven', 'new earth' and 'new Jerusalem'.[5] This final state would then complete the prophecy set out in Isaiah 66.22–23: 'For as the new heavens and

---

[1]   Luke 21.10–11.

[2]   See, for example, Elliot Miller, *A Crash Course on the New Age Movement* (Eastbourne, 1990), p. 27; Wouter J. Hanegraaff, *New Age Religion and Western Culture* (Leiden and New York, 1996), pp. 96, 98–103; Stuart Sutcliffe, *Children of the New Age: A History of Spiritual Practices* (London, 2003), pp. 9, 11, 17.

[3]   Augustine, *City of God*, trans. Henry Bettenson (Harmondsworth, 1972), XX.7; Mary Boyce, *Zoroastrians: Their Religious Beliefs and Practices* (London and New York, 1987); Norman Cohn, *Cosmos, Chaos and the World to Come: The Ancient Roots of Apocalyptic Faith* (New Haven and London, 1993); Nicholas Campion, *The Great Year: Astrology, Millenarianism and History in the Western Tradition* (London, 1994).

[4]   Revelation 20.2–7; Matthew 12.32.

[5]   Revelation 21.1–2.

the new earth which I will make shall remain before me'. Some modern Christian theologians retrospectively refer to this new era as 'the New Age'.[6]

There is an additional terminology associated with millenarianism. From the Greek word *eschaton*, the end, we derive the term 'eschatology', which literally means the study of ends, but is also used to imply actual belief in the end of the world. From *apocalypse*, the Greek for 'revelation', we have the word 'apocalyptic', describing the tumultuous vision of the end of the world which was revealed to St John the Divine. Traditions of apocalyptic thought can be traced back to late third millennium BCE Mesopotamia.[7] That they emerge with the earliest written records suggests an origin in pre-literate culture. In the first centuries BCE and CE, apocalyptic ideas permeated the Hellenistic world and formed a part of Gnostic, Jewish and Christian historical theory, and all partook of a common tradition which was shared with the Greek-speaking world.[8]

Even though they may have specific connotations, and some argue that the distinctions are important, the terms 'millenarian', 'millennial', 'eschatological' and 'apocalyptic' are commonly used interchangeably.[9] Although the term 'millenarian' has strictly Christian connotations, it may be applied to all beliefs that the world is about to enter a major new phase. In its looser definition, therefore, any political or religious movement or ideology which expects, prophesies or fights for an imminent historical crisis and a return to, or inauguration of, a golden age or state of purity may be described as millenarian. When the word 'apocalyptic' is added there is often, although not always, an expectation that the coming transformation will be violent.

The key features of millenarianism have been long established – nostalgia for a lost golden age in the past, concern over social and moral decay in the present, and the utopian anticipation of an imminent future crisis, to be followed by the restoration of paradise.[10] Within this scheme there are variations. 'Pre-millennialism', for example, holds that the coming crisis (for example) may be violent and destructive, while 'post-' or 'progressive millennialism' anticipates a calm and peaceful transition to an era of love.[11] The coming age may be of this

---

[6]   See, for example, J. Bradley Chance, *Jerusalem, the Temple, and the New Age in Luke-Acts* (Georgia, 1988); John Ziesler, *Pauline Christianity* (Oxford, 1991), p. 65.

[7]   Helmer Ringgren, 'Akkadian Apocalypses', in David Hellholm (ed.), *Apocalypticism in the Mediterranean World and the Near East: Proceedings of the International Colloquium on Apocalypticism, Uppsala, August 12–17* (Tübingen, 1989), pp. 379–86.

[8]   Paul Hanson, *The Dawn of Apocalyptic: The Historical and Sociological Roots of Jewish Apocalyptic Eschatology* (Philadelphia, 1983); D.S. Russell, *The Method and Message of Jewish Apocalyptic: 200 BC–AD 100* (Philadelphia, 1964).

[9]   See, for example, Hanegraaff, *New Age Religion*, p. 98.

[10]   Campion, *The Great Year*; Norman Cohn, *The Pursuit of the Millennium* (London, 1970); Frank E. Manuel, *Shapes of Philosophical History* (London, 1965); F.E. Manuel and F.P. Manuel, *Utopian Thought in the Western World* (Oxford, 1979).

[11]   Jon R. Stone, *Expecting Armageddon: Essential Readings in Failed Prophecy* (London, 2000); Henri Desroche, *The Sociology of Hope* (London, 1979), pp. 93–4;

world, as in the Marxist paradise, a version rooted in Jewish naturalism and a longing for the restoration of the Kingdom of David. Or it may be supernatural, as in the Kingdom of God anticipated in Revelation.

There are a number of other features of millenarian ideology which are pertinent to the modern New Age. One is an emphasis on education, for which the inspiration is found in the works of the Athenian philosopher Plato. Writing in the early fourth century BCE, Plato argued that schooling in the abstract arts, including astronomy, mathematics and music, all of which revealed the essential order in the cosmos, was essential if the good citizen were to engage with history and delay or prevent political disaster and social decay.[12] Such notions fed into early Christianity via the great Helleniser, St Paul. Another commonly expressed view in the classical world and closely associated with the Stoics and with astrology, of which the Stoics were generally keen supporters, was that time is cyclical, always returning to the same point, usually at regular intervals. It was Mircea Eliade who popularised the term 'the eternal return' to describe this view.[13]

In the Christian tradition, astrology was to be the main predictive tool by which the coming crisis might be predicted, adapting the simple forms of prophecy from celestial signs familiar from the Old Testament. Isaiah, for example, had forecast that, at the Day of Yahweh, when the final reckoning between humanity and God was due, '... the stars of the Heavens and their constellations will not give their light; the Sun will be dark at its rising and the Moon will not shed its light.[14] Such prophecies were repeated or paraphrased in the New Testament, carrying basic Near Eastern celestial divination directly into Christianity. Mark's Gospel, taking up the theme, prophesied that

> In those days, after that tribulation, the sun will be darkened, and the moon will not give its light, and the stars will be falling from heaven, and the powers in the heavens will be shaken. And then they will see the Son of man, coming in clouds with great power and glory.[15]

The simple astrology of the Old Testament prophets and the canonical gospels relied on the observation of unexpected events in the sky which could be interpreted as warnings that God's divine order was about to break down. In scriptural cosmology normal astronomical order expressed through the cycles of Sun and Moon was considered benign, and unpredictable events in the sky therefore warned

---

Catherine Wessinger, 'Millennialism with and without the Mayhem', in Thomas Robbins and Susan J. Palmer, *Millennium, Messiahs and Mayhem: Contemporary Apocalyptic Movements* (London, 1997), pp. 48–9.

[12]   Plato, *Republic*, trans. Paul Shorey (2 vols, Cambridge MA and London, 1937).

[13]   Mircea Eliade, *The Myth of the Eternal Return or, Cosmos and History* (Princeton, 1954).

[14]   Isaiah 13.10. See also Isaiah 61.19–20; Amos 8.9; Jeremiah 4.23; Habakkuk 3.3–6.

[15]   Mark 13.24–26.

of interruptions in the normal political and social order. By contrast, the alternative system, which appeared in Greece by the fourth century BCE, envisioned political or global collapse as integral to the divine order as expressed through predictable, mathematically ordered planetary cycles.[16] Plato developed his model of periodic global destruction in the early fourth century BCE, borrowing from the Egyptians the concept of periodic global conflagrations and formulating the period known as a 'complete' or 'great' year, the period of time which separates the beginning of the world from its end, which occurs when the sun, moon, stars and planets all return simultaneously to their locations at the creation.[17] The planets' Platonic function was not to cause or influence events in earth, but to indicate the changing qualities of the unfolding of the cosmic order and, by inference, the manifestation of divine intent in the material world.[18]

Apocalyptic astrology was provided with a further level of detail and precision in the first centuries CE when the Persian astrologers incorporated the periodic occurrence of conjunctions of Jupiter and Saturn, the slowest-moving of the visible planets, when they met in the same degree of the zodiac once every 20 years. The astrologers noticed that the total sequence of possible Jupiter–Saturn conjunctions took 960 years and, although the real period is somewhat shorter, they regarded it as deeply significant that 960 years is just 40 years short of the significant thousand-year periods which were the basis of Zoroastrian historical periodisation.[19] After this 'conjunctional astrology' was adopted in medieval Europe in the twelfth and thirteenth centuries, there were two principal astrological means of predicting the coming of the millennium. On the one hand, there were signs and wonders in the sky – the disorderly, if divinely ordained, events of the Old Testament, such as comets, which revealed God's changing mood. On the other, the predictable, orderly sequence of planetary patterns understood in classical cosmology allowed corresponding events to be forecast hundreds of years in advance. Order and disorder vied as two contrasting means of using the sky to comprehend affairs on earth: these may be characterised as respectively 'cosmic' on the one hand and 'chaotic' on the other, following Mircea Eliade's two models of the origins of the universe.[20] The belief that God will warn of the End by means of random events is representative of a 'chaotic' cosmology, and of a different nature from the 'cosmic'

---

[16]   Campion, *The Great Year*, pp. 104–31, 186–203.

[17]   Plato, *Timaeus*, trans. R.G. Bury (Cambridge MA and London, 1931), 22B–D, 39D.

[18]   Plato, *Timaeus*, 38C.

[19]   Abu Ma'shar, *On Historical Astrology: The Book of Religions and Dynasties (On the Great Conjunctions)*, ed. and trans. Keiji Yamamoto and Charles Burnett (2 vols, Leiden, 2000); E.S. Kennedy and David Pingree, *The Astrological History of Masha'Allah* (Cambridge, 1971).

[20]   Nicholas Campion, *Astrology and Cosmology in the World's Religions* (New York, 2012); Mircea Eliade, *The Sacred and the Profane: The Nature of Religion* (New York, 1959), pp. 29–32.

notion that great historical changes coincide with the predictable sequence order of astronomical motions.

Significant examples of predictable planetary patterns occurred in 1484, when it was predicted that the Jupiter–Saturn conjunction in Scorpio would bring the demise of Christianity, and the conjunction of 1523 in Pisces which, coming during the first revolutionary wave of the Reformation, was widely used to predict a recurrence of the Biblical Deluge.[21] The search for celestial signs and wonders continued to be a major feature of millenarian Christianity up to the nineteenth century. The Mormons, for example, had their own astrological perspective on the end of the world.[22]

Theories which assume a purpose in history tend to be bound up with concepts of order in nature and the cosmos. From this simple assumption it follows that, if this order can be understood, history's purpose will become clear and once its purpose has been revealed, the future can be prophesied. The relationship between historical and astrological thought was encouraged in the fifteenth century by the translation of the works of Plato, including his crucial cosmological texts, into Latin. So great was Plato's reputation that, as Eugenio Garin put it, in the Renaissance 'the theme of "newness", of a new life, a new age, new worlds, new heavens, new earths – which would run so eloquently through the centuries of the Renaissance … was originally nothing more than an astrological commonplace'.[23]

Ernst Cassirer concurred in this and compared some modern historical literature, such as Oswald Spengler's *The Decline of the West*, to Renaissance astrological theories, making the point that ancient ideas continue to exert a profound effect.[24] Astrology's significance as a model of apocalyptic thought has been acknowledged by New Age writers. David Spangler, understood this well enough when discussing the basis for belief in the coming New Age: 'as the term Age of Aquarius suggests,' he wrote, 'one source was astrology'.[25]

In the modern world, millenarianism has adopted a number of apparently secular forms, including, at its most violent and materialistic, Marxism and Nazism.[26] The most pervasive form of secular millenarianism in the modern West, though, as John Baillie pointed out in 1951, is belief in progress.[27] Progress theory evolved directly out of the Jewish and Christian message of hope that a new world will be born

---

[21]　Lynn Thorndike, *History of Magic and Experimental Science* (8 vols, New York, 1923–58), vol. IV, pp. 438–84, vol. V, pp. 178–233.

[22]　See, for example, John L. Brooke, *The Refiner's Fire: The Making of Mormon Cosmology, 1644–1844* (Cambridge, 1996).

[23]　Eugenio Garin, *Astrology in the Renaissance: The Zodiac of Life* (London and Boston, 1976), p. 18.

[24]　Ernst Cassirer, *The Myth of the State* (New Haven and London, 1967), pp. 291–4.

[25]　David Spangler, *The Rebirth of the Sacred* (London, 1984), p. 18.

[26]　Cohn, *The Pursuit*, pp. 108–9; see also Michael J. St Clair, *Millenarian Movements in Historical Context* (New York and London, 1992), pp. 223–337.

[27]　John Baillie, *The Belief in Progress* (London, Glasgow, Toronto, 1951), pp. 64–5.

but denies the need for violence. Instead the golden age will arise from peaceful cooperation, aided by the sensible use of technology, science and, depending on one's political leanings, either a free or regulated market.[28] In Condorcet's version, there is an optimistic assumption that the condition of the world must necessarily and gradually improve.[29] In the 1940s R.G. Collingwood, considering what he saw as the recent revival of this model, identified three forms of history, two of which he defined as 'quasi-history', the third being 'true history'.[30] Quasi-history came in two forms; firstly, theocratic history, in which the record of events reveals the manifestation of God, or the gods, in nature; and, secondly, myth, in which the characters are often divine and the key events take place outside the normal flow of time. Forms of historiography which impose an *a priori* theoretical structure on history, whether violent and apocalyptic, or peaceful and progressive, are, in Collingwood's terminology, quasi-historical.

Another pervasive feature of millenarian thought, observed by Karl Popper, is the paradoxical belief that active participation in the historical process, rather than passive acceptance, is required in order to bring the inevitable crisis into manifestation. Popper defined this as 'historicism', while he termed the active engagement with the historical process as 'activism'. He saw both as manifested primarily through the historical theories of Plato and Marx. In Marxism, for example, the proletarian revolution may be inevitable, but it is still necessary to form a revolutionary vanguard to ensure that it happens. The New Age movement exhibits the same paradox: while the dawning of New Age is inevitable, it is still vital to encourage it by altering one's lifestyle. Popper also noticed that the practice of astrology is based around the paradox that, although the future is predetermined, knowledge of what is to come enables human beings to amend it. His view was clear and insightful:

> Astrology, it should be realised, shares with historicism the belief in a predeterminate destiny which can be predicted: and it shares with some important versions of historicism (especially with Platonism and Marxism) the belief that, notwithstanding the possibility of predicting the future, we have some influence upon it, especially if we know what is coming ... All astrology, for instance, involves the apparently somewhat contradictory conception that the knowledge of our fate may help us to influence this fate.[31]

---

[28] J.B. Bury, *The Idea of Progress: An Inquiry into its Growth and Origins* (London, 1932), pp. 1–36.

[29] Marquis de Condorcet, S*ketch for a Historical Picture of the Progress of the Human Mind*, trans. June Barraclough (London, 1955).

[30] R.G. Collingwood, *The Idea of History* (Oxford, 1946), pp. 14–15, 18.

[31] Karl Popper, *The Open Society and its Enemies*, rev. edn (2 vols, London and New York, 1986), vol. 1, pp. 210, 244.

Astrology's explanatory power may therefore emerge from the same source as other, similar meta-narratives. In this scheme astrology is sustained by the need for security and order in a world beset by potentially threatening change and instability, a fact on which academics and critics of astrology usually agree. Security is to be obtained through the manipulation of a future which, once forecast, can be turned to human advantage. The fundamental political-astrological belief that the futures of heavenly cosmos and terrestrial state are equally determined can be contrasted with astrology's attempt, via the detailed examination of horoscopes, to manipulate or engage with the future. It is the astrologer's task to enhance human freedom of choice as much as possible within the limits set by historical and cosmic law. Hilary Carey suggested a similar conclusion.[32] Citing Malinowski's theory that one of magic's primary functions is to provide a means of influencing forces and events normally outside human control, she raised the question as to whether astrological forecasting, combined with the rituals which often accompanied it, might be seen as ways of intervening in historical order.[33] Astrology's function, as a particular application of activist divination to the cosmic state, may therefore be understood within the differing frameworks of competing historicist narratives. If the underlying purpose of historicism is to control change then astrology, within the terms set by Karl Popper, may be seen, within the millenarian framework, as a principal activist discipline. Intervention in the historical process can be of different varieties depending of one of three possible eschatons: one is in the mind and involves a personal entry into the Kingdom of God or access to the New Age via personal transformation; another is *in* history – civilisation hits a crisis, but the world continues; the third is *of* history – the entire cosmos comes to an end. Through both the scriptural and classical traditions, each of these three was historically linked to astrological analogues.

[32]   Hilary Carey, *Courting Disaster: Astrology at the English Court and University in the Later Middle Ages* (London, 1992), pp. 3–5.

[33]   Bronislaw Malinowski, *Magic, Science and Religion* (New York, 1954), pp. 25–36.

Chapter 3

The Shock of the New: The Age of Aquarius

We are indeed living just at the time when the Dark Age has run its course and a new epoch is just beginning ... What is beginning at this time will slowly prepare humanity for new soul faculties.[1]

Since the early part of the twentieth century the millenarian terms 'New Age' and 'Age of Aquarius' have often been used as synonyms. They are not, in spite of the many writers who regard them as identical, the same. As an astrological prophecy, the Age of Aquarius is based on the idea of the gradual shift of the stars and constellations in relation to the sun's location at the spring equinox, usually on 21 March, a phenomenon known as the precession of the equinoxes.[2] The consequence is the gradual separation of the so-called 'tropical zodiac', used in Western astrology, from the 'sidereal zodiac', which is based on the actual stars. For example, the Western zodiac sign of Pisces no longer occupies the same portion of sky as the classical Greek constellation of Pisces.

The astronomical details need not concern us here, for they are just a vehicle on which to hang a certain kind of apocalyptic belief. One version of modern astrological theory holds that significant shifts in human civilisation conform to major movements of the constellations or zodiac signs in relation to the equinox. According to the theory, the next age, the Age of Aquarius, will be inaugurated when the Sun rises in Aquarius on 21 March and can therefore, at least in theory, be dated exactly, even if there is considerable disagreement about the exact year. In actuality there is a fair degree of confusion about the precise methodology by which the Age's inauguration should be measured. That said, the astronomical foundation for the theory of astrological ages lends them an aura of objective reality. The New Age, by contrast, is a phase of history whose existence in time is defined by humanity's near-universal psychological inclination to anticipate an imminent transformation in society, the world, or the entire universe. Like the *parousia*, the New Age is always imminent, but never comes.

As we have seen, apocalyptic events were traditionally measured by planetary cycles, chiefly Jupiter–Saturn conjunctions. There is though, not a single extant example of the use of precession of the equinoxes to predict the future by astrologers until the late nineteenth century. There are indeed arguments that precession was used by astrologers in the ancient world, but they are based entirely on the retrospective interpretation of circumstantial evidence and lack any textual support. David

---

[1]   Rudolf Steiner, *The Reappearance of Christ in the Etheric* (Spring Valley NY, 1983), p. 15.

[2]   Jacqueline Mitton, *The Penguin Dictionary of Astronomy* (London, 1993), pp. 306–7.

Ulansey, for example, has proposed that Mithras, the hero of the Roman mystery teachings named after him, was responsible for shifting the constellations.[3] The problem, however, is there is no record that any astrologers of the era mentioned the fact. Literary evidence is not everything but, when it is entirely absent in the works of the people who should have been most concerned with it, the fact does require some attention. Simply, there are no extant classical or medieval astrological texts which attribute any astrological or historical significance to precession. Instead the increasing separation between the tropical and sidereal zodiacs was used to discredit astrology, on the grounds that the planets no longer occupied the parts of the zodiac claimed by Western astrologers. The earliest extant example of precession being used to undermine astrology was penned by the Church father Origen (c. 185–254), evidence that precession was used against astrologers, not by them.[4] During the late Middle Ages and the Renaissance the shift of the constellations away from the signs of the zodiac was regarded by some of the most notable astrologers, such as Guido Bonatti in the thirteenth century and Thomas Campanella in the sixteenth century, as a major problem.[5] At no time was it considered a possible source of astrological forecasts.

The origin of the belief that the Age of Aquarius is imminent is relatively modern and can be traced to three separate but interlinked strands in eighteenth-century European thought.[6] The first was the attempt, central to Enlightenment ideology, to establish a common origin to religion. The means by which this was to be accomplished was the study of comparative religion, the deliberate aim being to diminish Christianity's claim to unique status. The second was the theory that the shared origin of all religion lies in worship of the celestial bodies, especially the Sun, which became a model of all male deities and mythical heroes. The third was the use of the apparent shift of the stars caused by the precession of the equinoxes as a means of dating the history of the Indian sacred texts, the Vedas. The theory that religion and astronomy shared common origins was developed in the revolutionary atmosphere of 1790s France by François Henri Stanislas Delaunaye in his 1791 work, *L'Histore générale at particulière des religions et du Culte*, an attempt to establish the foundation of religion in astral worship. Delaunaye set out for the first time a complete theory of history in which astronomical, and

---

[3]   David Ulansey, *The Origins of the Mithraic Mysteries: Cosmology and Salvation in the Ancient World* (New York and Oxford, 1989).

[4]   Origen, *The Philocalia of Origen*, trans. George Lewis (Edinburgh, 1911), ch. 22, 18 (From Book III of the Commentary on Genesis). See also Jim Tester, *A History of Western Astrology* (Woodbridge, 1987), p. 54.

[5]   For Bonatti see Wayne Shumaker, *The Occult Sciences in the Renaissance: A Study in Intellectual Patterns* (Berkeley, Los Angeles and London, 1972), p. 40; and for Campanella see Tester, *A History*, p. 214.

[6]   Nicholas Campion, 'Prophecy, Cosmology and the New Age Movement: The Extent and Nature of Contemporary Belief in Astrology', PhD thesis, University of the West of England, 2004, pp. 50–8.

hence religious, iconography evolved with the precession of the equinoxes. His scheme commenced in 15,194 BCE, with the Sun in 29 degrees of Libra at the spring equinox. This date, he argued, was the origin of the Egyptian zodiac. After around two thousand years, in 13,079 BCE, the sun rose in Virgo at the spring equinox and it then proceeded in reverse order through the signs until it rose in Aquarius at the spring equinox of 1726. This was too close to Delaunaye's own time for him to specify its cultural correlations. Instead he wrote simply 'Plus de changements'.[7] And so, by the 1960s, after another one-and-a-half centuries, the notion of 'many changes' was to become popularly associated with the coming of the Age of Aquarius.

The twin concepts of the Sun as the origin of all male-anthropomorphised religions (so that all gods and divine saviours are solar deities) and the shift of zodiac signs through precession of the equinoxes as a guide to the changing character of religious observation, circulated amongst both atheists and occultists through the first half the nineteenth century. As a simple example, it was said that when the Sun rose in Taurus, which it did roughly between 4,000 and 2,000 BCE, bull-gods were worshipped. There was, though, a difference in explanations for this phenomenon between the atheists, such as the radical Reverend Robert Taylor, for whom it showed the meaninglessness of religion, and the occultists, such as Geoffrey Higgins, who considered that its very universality indicated a deep stratum of meaning.[8] All could agree that all religion originated in astral worship, but disagree whether all religions were therefore equally false or equally true. The latter proposition was favoured in occult and esoteric circles.

This was the intellectual milieu in which H.P. Blavatsky founded the Theosophical Society in New York in 1875. The society is the most important single institutional influence on the New Age movement, partly because of its global reach, from the US to France, the UK, Germany and India, but also because of the number of leading intellectuals who were members in the late nineteenth and early twentieth centuries.[9] Blavatsky set herself two goals. The first was to recover what she considered to be the lost wisdom of a once-universal human civilisation by bringing together its surviving fragments from Indian, Platonic, Hermetic and Kabbalistic thought. The second was to form a body of people who, by studying and practising ancient wisdom, could prepare the world for the imminent shift into a new historical era. Influenced by the German idealist philosopher George Friedrich Hegel (1770–1831), whose theories of history, she argued, had 'their

---

[7]   Patrick Curry, Nicholas Campion and Jacques Halbronn, *La vie astrologique il y a cent ans* (Paris, 1992), p. 89.

[8]   Godfrey Higgins, *Anacalypsis, an Attempt to Draw Aside the Veil of the Saitic Isis; or an Inquiry into the Origins of Languages, Nations and Religions* (2 vols, London, 1836); Robert Taylor, *The Diegesis; being a Discovery of the origin, Evidences, and Early History of Christianity* (London, 1829).

[9]   See Bruce H. Campbell, *Ancient Wisdom Revived: A History of the Theosophical Movement* (Berkeley, 1980).

application in the teachings of Occult science', Blavatsky set out her theory of cyclical history, in which complex patterns of cycles regulate a cosmos in which physical evolution is dependent on spiritual evolution.[10] In her own words,

> The revolution of the physical world, according to the ancient doctrine, is attended by a like revolution in the world of intellect – the spiritual evolution of the world proceeding in cycles, like the physical one. Thus we see in history a regular alternation of ebb and flow in the tide of human progress.[11]

Blavatsky believed that the Jupiter–Saturn conjunction in Pisces in 7 BCE was a specific sign of the birth of Christ, adding that it 'shines as a symbol of all the past, present, and future Spiritual Saviours who dispense light and dispel mental darkness'.[12] 'The history of the world', she wrote, 'since its formation and to its end "is written in the stars," i.e., is recorded in the Zodiac'.[13]

Blavatsky, though, had no awareness of the concept of the Age of Aquarius and included just one reference to the sign Aquarius, inspired by the poet, Chartist and spiritualist Gerald Massey, and his reading of the 12 tablets of the Nimrod epic as a solar allegory.[14] It was Massey who produced a detailed scheme which explained world history and the evolution of religion according to the precession of the equinoxes. It was Massey who took the step which his predecessors had declined to do and anticipated the Messiah of the next precessional stage, that of the Waterman (Aquarius) though without yet mentioning the phrase 'Age of Aquarius': he wrote that the prophecy that a Messiah will be born again 'will be … fulfilled when the Equinox enters the sign of the Waterman [Aquarius] about the end of this century, to which the Samaritans are still looking forward for the coming of their Messiah, who has not yet arrived for them'.[15] This, from 1887, marks the earliest reference I have found to the Age of Aquarius in the English language.

Astrologers, whom one might imagine would have been eager to adopt the theory of astrological ages as soon as it started circulating, had stood aloof from the new astronomical model of history set out by Delaunaye in 1791. They were either unaware of the conversations taking place, or reluctant to adopt such important information from outside their community. The earliest currently known reference to the precessional ages occurred in the English astrologer A.J. Pearce's *The Textbook of Astrology*, published in 1879, before Massey and 87 years after Delaunaye, but with no mention of the Aquarian Age.[16] Pearce added, with the

---

[10]   H.P. Blavatsky, *The Secret Doctrine* (2 vols, Los Angeles, 1982), vol. 1, p. 641.

[11]   Blavatsky, *The Secret Doctrine*, vol. 1, p. 641.

[12]   Blavatsky, *The Secret Doctrine*, vol. 1, p. 653.

[13]   Blavatsky, *The Secret Doctrine*, vol. 2, p. 438.

[14]   Blavatsky, *The Secret Doctrine*, vol. 2, p. 353.

[15]   Gerald Massey, *The Hebrew and Other Creations* (London, 1887), p. 8.

[16]   Alfred Pearce, *The Text Book of Astrology* (2 vols, London, 1879), vol. 1, p. 10.

same certainty as Massey, that 'from the remotest antiquity there has existed a belief that the world was created at the vernal equinox. It is a remarkable fact that the Christian era is connected with the epoch of the vernal equinox in Aries – the scriptural ram or lamb'.[17]

The general view of the Aquarian Age's nature and characteristics was formed in the 1880s and has changed little since then. A formative description, which directly links nineteenth-century ideas to Renaissance Hermeticism, was given in a text issued to its members by the Hermetic Brotherhood of Luxor.[18] According to the text's anonymous commentator the world had entered the seventh of the latest phase of ages, that of the Archangel Michael, who was related to the Sun, on 21 December 1880, and the Age of Aquarius in February 1881. According to the Brotherhood, the 'Age of Michael'

> will be a period of Imperial Greatness, Empires will shine full of glory, the Human intellect will have full play and all Churches, Religious Creeds and Ecclesiastical Dogmas will fall to the ground and become things of the past. Parsons, Vicars and Bishops will have to work in different fields if they mean to obtain an honest livelihood. Yes, I repeat this prophecy. The Churches and Chapels will fall with a terrible crash, and be destroyed. But from their ashes, Phoenix-like, shall arise a new Religion, whose shining Motto will be: Veritas Excelsior, Truth Above. This era shall proclaim the rights of man. It is essentially the age of reason dreamed of by Bruno and Thomas Paine.[19]

With the exception of the prophecy of imperial greatness, which was at odds with the Age of Aquarius's normal egalitarian character, the Hermetic Brotherhood's statement set the model for all future descriptions of the Aquarian Age, with its expectations of religious and spiritual revolution. The theosophist Max Heindel (1865–1919) gave what may have been the first relatively detailed version of the astrological ages in his book *The Message of the Stars*, first published in the 1900s.[20] The Aquarian Age, he announced, 'will be illuminated and vivified by the solar precession, for the upliftment of the Son of Man (Aquarius), by the Christ within'.[21] Heindel's Christ was '*the* Christ', the cosmic Christ, the great 'Sun spirit' who may manifest in different periods, as he did in around 2,500 BCE when he inaugurated the Arien Age and the religion of the Lamb.[22]

The cosmic Christ, as lord of the Aquarian Age, but with a typically theosophical regard for the East, was the focus of Levi Dowling's 1907 *The*

---

[17]   Pearce, *The Text Book*, vol. 2, p. 15.

[18]   Joscelyn Godwin, *The Theosophical Enlightenment* (New York, 1994), pp. 337, 345, 357–8.

[19]   Cited in Godwin, *The Theosophical Enlightenment*, p. 358.

[20]   Max Heindel, *The Message of the Stars* (London, 1929), pp. 6–29.

[21]   Max Heindel, *The Rosicrucian Cosmo-Conception* (London, 1929), pp. 12–13.

[22]   Heindel, *Cosmo-Conception*, pp. 25, 28.

Aquarian Gospel of Jesus the Christ. This apocryphal gospel was reputedly channelled from the Akashic records, and claimed that Jesus had studied with Buddhists and Brahmins.[23] 'The Christ', as opposed to the Jesus Christ of the canonical Gospels, was defined in another of Levi's channelled texts as the God of Love, the son of the Almighty God, the God of thought. 'The Christ' is the teacher, the 'master spirit' allotted 'to every world and star and moon and sun'.[24] It was from such sources that the twentieth century's two most influential theosophists, Rudolf Steiner and Alice Bailey, borrowed their versions of the Age of Aquarius (although Steiner himself preferred to talk about the Age of Michael). In 1910 Steiner wrote, 'There is much talk about periods of transition … human beings will slowly and gradually develop new faculties and … human souls will gradually undergo a change … What is beginning at this time will slowly prepare humanity for new soul faculties.'[25] Along with Steiner and Bailey, the most influential prophet of the Aquarian Age was C.G. Jung, the founder of analytical psychology. In Jung's theology Christ became a symbol primarily of the self rather than the sun, although his portrayal as a fish in early Christian iconography was indicative of the manner in which human psychic projection onto the universe shifted when the vernal point moved into Pisces.[26] Unlike Steiner and Bailey, Jung did not set out to create a movement of followers whose purpose was to instigate the New Age. He was far more concerned with self-understanding as a prerequisite for subsequent improvements in societal conditions, and he saw the external symptoms of the change of astrological ages, including the collapse of old religious institutions and political divisions, as secondary to the inner process. The transformative crisis, he argued, can be recognised neither by philosophy, nor by economics, nor by politics, but only by the individual being, via his experience of the loving spirit.[27]

The discussion remains a live one amongst astrologers. On 5 December 2009 astrologer Erin Sullivan presented a day-long seminar as a part of the Robert Bateman 'Green Learning Series', on 'Global Transformation: *The Evolution of Consciousness through Mythology and Planetary Archetypes*'. The description included the following:

> Each of us in our own unique way contributes to the collective consciousness. This collective leap has been gestating for about 500 years, but now we are on the threshold of the astronomical closure of a 2,160-year epoch – the Age of

---

[23]   Levi (Levi Dowling), *The Aquarian Gospel of Jesus the Christ* (Chadwell Heath, 1980); see also John P. Newport, *The New Age Movement and the Biblical Worldview: Conflict and Dialogue* (Grand Rapids MI, 1998), p. 161.

[24]   Newport, *The New Age Movement*; Levi, *The Aquarian Gospel*, p. 12.

[25]   Steiner, *The Reappearance of Christ*, p. 15.

[26]   C.G. Jung, 'The Sign of the Fishes', in *Aion*, in *The Collected Works of C.G. Jung*, vol. 9, Pt 2, trans. R.F.C. Hull (London, 1959), pp. 72–102.

[27]   Jung, 'The Sign of the Fishes', p. 87.

Pisces – and the earliest stage of Age of Aquarius. These are creative and critical times where epochal archetypal shifts carry both the dark and the light.[28]

There are two crucial features of Aquarian Age historiography. First, its crisis-laden language, sometimes fearful, but generally hopeful, stands exactly in the lineage of astrological-apocalyptic literature which can be traced back to the ancient Near East, especially to the Old Testament. Second, all the documentary evidence indicates that the use of the shift of the constellations as a technical basis for such prophecies appears to be a product of late eighteenth-century atheism, filtered through theosophy and then adopted by astrologers. We are therefore dealing with a clear example of an 'invented tradition', but one which has deep roots in the Western mentality.

---

[28]   'Global Transformation: *The Evolution of Consciousness through Mythology and Planetary Archetypes*', <http://www.royalroads.ca/continuing-studies/CYGLEL1820-Y09. htm>, accessed 23 September 2009.

Chapter 4
Celestial Enlightenment: The New Age

The New Age is neither a movement nor a religion set apart from others. It is not something one can choose or not to join … It is a mass movement in which humanity is reasserting its right to explore spirituality in total freedom.[1]

The term 'New Age' appeared in the 1790s and 1800s, around the same time as precession of the equinoxes was being adopted by French radicals. Its earliest known occurrence was in the works of the French radical Constantin Volney, who used it in 1795, and the English poet William Blake, who issued the following inspirational challenge to the nation's youth in 1804: 'Rouze up, O Young Men of the New Age!'.[2]

However, the concept of the New Age as one of spiritual enlightenment is directly derived from the teachings of the Christian reformer Emmanuel Swedenborg (1688–1782).[3] Swedenborg argued that the *parousia*, the restoration of Christ's presence on Earth through the Second Coming, had actually occurred in 1757 but only on a spiritual level, which meant that one had to have a certain level of spiritual awareness in order to perceive it.[4] Swedenborg's eschaton was 'of the mind', rather than of history. In the years after Swedenborg's work was published, he accumulated followers amongst radicals who rejected established Christianity but were unwilling to reject religion as a whole. In London the Swedenborgians formed themselves into 'The Theosophical Society Instituted for the Purpose of Promoting the Heavenly Doctrines of the New Jerusalem' and, after 1787, the 'New Church'. They thrived briefly in the millenarian context of late eighteenth-century England in which it was hoped that, as Garrett put it,

---

[1]   William Bloom, *The New Age: An Anthology of Essential Writings* (London, 1991), pp. xiii, xv–xvi.

[2]   Constantin François Volney, *The Ruins, or a Survey of the Revolutions of Empires* (London, 1795), pp. 127–3; William Blake, 'Milton', in Geoffrey Keynes (ed.), *Complete Writings* (Oxford, 1971), preface, line 9, p. 480.

[3]   Michael W. Stanley, 'The Relevance of Emanuel Swedenborg's Theological Concepts for the New Age as it is Envisioned Today', in Robert Larson (ed.), *Emanuel Swedenborg* (New York, 1988); Paul Heelas, *The New Age Movement* (Oxford, 1996), p. 17.

[4]   See Clarke Garrett, 'Swedenborg and the Mystical Enlightenment in Late Eighteenth Century England', *Journal of the History of Ideas*, 45 (1984), p. 69. For Swedenborg's teachings see Emanuel Swedenborg, *The Apocalypse Revealed Wherein are Disclosed the Arcana Foretold Which Have Hitherto Remained Concealed*, Eng. trans. of the Latin edn of 1766, n. d., The Swedenborg Digital Library, at <http://www.swedenborgdigitallibrary.org/contets/AR.html>, accessed 20 June 2009.

'Spiritual enlightenment and human regeneration would come about through events on this earth, including both natural and political, until the wicked had been defeated'.[5] Swedenborg emphasised the transformation of the world rather than, as in traditional Christian millenarianism (at least as a first stage), its destruction, and projected a profound consciousness of the need for inner change as the prerequisite for political and societal improvement. The Church's prophetic ideology was a classic example of Popperian activism. Garrett cites one Swedenborgian, Richard Clarke, who wrote in 1772, 'In our own *inner* man, lies the foundation of the new Jerusalem'.[6] The New Age then becomes an inner condition, not necessarily dependent on external change. In that this particular form of esotericism rejected orthodox religious affiliation we may call it secular, although it is neither materialistic nor atheist. Although Swedenborg is rarely, if ever, acknowledged as a source, this point of view is common in the modern New Age movement. For example, in 1977 David Spangler wrote that 'For each of us the New Age is here now. It has always been here'.[7] In this sense, the New Age constitutes an eternal present which is removed from the world of time and material change, much as in Plato's cosmogony 'Being' was a pure, unchanging condition which underlay the constantly shifting uncertainty of 'Becoming', the material world.[8]

Although the peak of the New Church's popularity passed quickly, Swedenborg became a profoundly influential figure in esoteric circles.[9] That great populariser Helena Blavatsky regarded him as, if not an adept, at least 'the greatest among modern seers', and disseminated his ideas through the Theosophical Society.[10] By the 1870s the term 'New Age' had become an established metaphor for the Swedenborgian spiritual era, and by the 1900s it was being used by Theosophists such as Alfred Orage and Holbrook Jackson, editors of another periodical, *The New Age*.[11] The use of the term 'New Age' crossed the boundaries between mainstream Christianity, Swedenborgianism, spiritualism and psychical research and theosophy.

The erroneous idea that the New Age movement originated in the counter-culture of the 1960s has since become widely accepted in the academic literature, especially

---

[5]   Garrett, 'Swedenborg', p. 67.

[6]   Garrett, 'Swedenborg', p. 68.

[7]   David Spangler, 'Revelation – Birth of a New Age', in William Bloom (ed.), *The New Age: An Anthology of Essential Writings* (London, 1991), p. 29; see also Peter Lemesurier, *This New Age Business: The Story of the Ancient and Continuing Quest to Bring Down Heaven on Earth* (Forres, 1990), p. 232.

[8]   Plato, *Timaeus*, trans. R.G. Bury (Cambridge MA and London: Harvard University Press, 1931).

[9]   Garrett, 'Swedenborg', p. 81.

[10]   H.P. Blavatsky, *Isis Unveiled* (2 vols, Pasadena, 1976), I.73, II.471.

[11]   James Webb, *The Harmonious Circle: The Lives and Work of G.I. Gurdjieff, P.D. Ouspensky, and Their Followers* (Boston, 1980), pp. 195–212.

since Gordon Melton set the launch date as 1971.[12] The first academic works on the new spirituality in the 1970s did not use the term, suggesting that it was only familiar in theosophical circles and was discovered by academics only in the late 1970s or early 1980s.[13] The concept of the New Age as a recent – post-counter-cultural – and hence transient phenomenon has encouraged the view, fuelled by veteran New Agers' anger at the movement's commercialisation in the 1980s, that the New Age is over.[14] Thus, amongst academics Irwin pronounced the New Age 'dead', Melton talked of 'post-New Age', announcing that 'the New Age Movement has passed into history', and Massimo discussed the 'Next Age'.[15] However, the New Age culture of the 1970s–1990s should properly be seen as a popularisation of the theosophical New Age movement, which dates back to the beginning of the twentieth century. The 1960s brought New Age thinking a renewed vigour, but the notion that New Age is a legacy of the counter-culture is contradicted by the historical evidence. The New Age was not invented in the 1970s: it just discovered a wider audience. This is important because if New Age thought is placed within its historical context it can no longer be seen as a fad which is likely to disappear. We can then agree with Paul Heelas and Linda Woodhead that, far from passing away, it is deeply embedded in Western culture: it has not died out but has gone mainstream.[16]

The theosophical prophecy that a New Age was about to begin required, within the framework of Popperian activism, a social and political programme

---

[12]   J. Gordon Melton, Jerome Clarke and Aidan A. Kelly, *New Age Almanac* (London and New York, 1991), pp. xi–xvi, 1. See also James R. Lewis and J. Gordon Melton, *Perspectives on the New Age* (New York, 1992), pp. xi–xii; Patrick Curry, *A Confusion of Prophets: Victorian and Edwardian Astrology* (London, 1992), p. 161; Stuart Sutcliffe, *Children of the New Age: A History of Spiritual Practices* (London, 2003), pp. 11, 28; Wouter J. Hanegraaff, *New Age Religion and Western Culture* (Leiden and New York, 1996), pp. 10–11, 18; Michael York, *The Emerging Network: A Sociology of the New Age and Neo-Pagan Movements* (London, 1995), pp. 1, 21–2, 37–8, 49–50; Heelas, *The New Age Movement*, p. 34.

[13]   For example, the term 'New Age' appears neither in Charles Glock and Robert N. Bellah, *The New Religious Consciousness* (Berkeley, 1976), nor in Robert Wuthnow, *The Consciousness Revolution* (Berkeley, 1976). The volume edited by Edward Heenan preferred a reference to the Aquarian Age: Edward F. Heenan (ed.), *Mystery, Magic and Miracle in a Post-Aquarian Age* (Englewood Cliffs, 1973).

[14]   Lemesurier, *This New Age Business*, p. 185; David Spangler, *A Pilgrim in Aquarius* (Forres, 1996), p. 55.

[15]   William Irwin Thompson, 'Sixteen Years of the New Age', in David Spangler and William Irwin Thompson, *Reimagination of the World: A Critique of the New Age, Science, and Popular Culture* (Santa Fe, 1991), p. 17; J. Gordon Melton, 'The Future of the New Age Movement', in Eileen Barker and Margot Warburg (eds), *New Religions and New Religiosity* (Aarhus, 2001), pp. 142–3, 147; Massimo Introvigne, 'After the New Age: Is There a Next Age?', in Mikael Rothstein (ed.), *New Age Religion and Globalization* (Aarhus, 2001), pp. 61–2.

[16]   Paul Heelas et al., *The Spiritual Revolution: Why Religion is Giving Way to Spirituality* (Oxford, 2005).

in order to enable its smooth inauguration. From the moment of its foundation in 1875 the Theosophical Society fulfilled this purpose, having a clear mission to prepare for the coming of the New Age through organised activity, primarily spiritual activity and education. The term began to spread and, amongst astrologers, the theosophist Max Heindel used the term 'New Age' in 1909.[17] The Theosophical Society's political project, meanwhile, extended to its spin-off groups. In 1928 the Aquarian Foundation, set up by the charismatic leader (and fraudster) Edward Wilson, also known as Brother XII, in British Columbia, had eight thousand devoted members, including Alfred and Annie Barley, the theosophical astrologers and confidantes of Alan Leo, the most influential British astrologer of the early twentieth century.[18] Barley had been the sub-editor of Leo's magazine and propaganda vehicle for theosophical astrology, *Modern Astrology*.[19] The conscious sense of participating in a movement intended to encourage the smooth transition to the New Age extended to the world of theosophical astrology. By 1940 the following slogan had been added to the back cover of the magazine *Astrology*, the quarterly journal of the Astrological Lodge of the Theosophical Society, founded by Leo in 1915:

> Astrology is no mere system of fortune-telling. It is a universal philosophy founded on demonstrable scientific fact. The object of the Lodge is to form a strong body of earnest students, able to study and promulgate astrological truth, and to purify it from unworthy associations of all sorts. In this work we bespeak the help of every serious student, each according to his or her own capacity (The Work of the Astrological Lodge of London, 1940).

Activism is also evident in the wider culture within which much modern astrology is embedded. When Alice Bailey founded her theosophical offshoot, the Arcane School, in 1923, she was quite explicit that she was creating a group of individuals whose purpose was to bring the New Age into being. In 1937 Bailey had discussed the importance of the creation of groups in order to bring God's plan into being, and help inaugurate what she called 'the New Age, the Age of Aquarius'.[20] There are essentially two groups working towards the establishment of the New Age, Bailey argued. On the one hand a select group is engaged in consciousness raising in collaboration with the Christ and, on the other, a greater number are consciously working for greater awareness while remaining unaware of the operations of the spiritual Hierarchy.

---

[17]   Max Heindel, *The Rosicrucian Cosmo-Conception* (London, 1929), pp. 13, 19.

[18]   John Oliphant, *Brother Twelve: The Incredible Story of Canada's False Prophet and His Doomed Cult of Gold, Sex and Black Magic* (Toronto, 1991).

[19]   Alan Leo, 'The Editor's Observatory: Modern Astrology's Coming-of-Age', *Modern Astrology*, New Series, 8/8 (1911), p. 311.

[20]   Alice A. Bailey, 'Seed Groups in the New Age', in Alice A. Bailey, *The Externalisation of the Hierarchy* (New York, 1957), p. 28.

Bailey's work began in 1921 when she and her husband Foster, who was secretary of the Theosophical Association of New York, formed a small meditation group 'to discuss the Plan of the Masters of the Wisdom and to meditate for a while on our part in it'.[21] The volume of correspondence generated by Bailey's first three books, *Initiation Human and Solar* (1922), *Letters on Occult Meditation* (1922) and *The Consciousness of the Atom*, and her classes on the *Secret Doctrine*, resulted in the formation of the Arcane School in April 1923, with the nucleus of the meditation group functioning as collaborators with Bailey herself. The group's apocalyptic mission was clear; it was the spiritual equivalent of the Bolshevik revolutionary vanguard which had seized control of Russia only a few years before. Later, in 1948, Bailey wrote,

> In the age into which we are now emerging, the Aquarian Age, this mode of group work will reach a very high point of development, and the world will be saved and reconstructed *by groups* far more than by individuals ... In them is vested a spirit of construction; they are the builders of the new age ... They are disciples of the Christ, working consciously and frequently unconsciously for His reappearance.[22]

Bailey estimated in 1951 that thirty thousand people had passed through the school and that there were 'many hundreds ... still with us'.[23] Alice Bailey's followers maintain the concept of a political programme. For example, in 1984 an advertisement for the Lucis Trust, the organisation set up to perpetuate Alice Bailey's teachings, announced that the 'Lucis Trust is dedicated to the establishment of right human relations through Education, spiritual discipline, and meditation. The foundations for a new world order can be established ... [through]...group work in preparation for the Aquarian Age' (Lucis Trust 1984).

Bailey's influence on both the New Age movement and the ideological milieu of modern astrology is difficult to overestimate. Her followers amongst New Agers include David Spangler, the prolific author whose books *Festivals in the New Age* (1975) and *Revelation: The Birth of a New Age* (1976) brought the term 'New Age' to wider attention in counter-cultural, esoteric and spiritual groups; also his colleague and collaborator, Sir George Trevelyan, who contributed English upper-class gravitas, and the writer and teacher William Bloom.

The term 'New Age' is used in two ways. It is both the future spiritual era, and the culture which has been promoted by the prophets of the coming era, or has coalesced around their followers. We could say it is both a historical period and a state of mind. One problem is the apparent diversity of New Age beliefs and practices, as several commentators have observed. George Chryssides conceded that 'it is difficult to offer a clear, coherent definition of New Age', and Michael

---

[21]   Alice A. Bailey, *The Unfinished Autobiography* (London, 1951), p. 191.

[22]   Alice A. Bailey, *The Reappearance of the Christ* (New York, 1948), pp. 182–3.

[23]   Bailey, *The Unfinished Autobiography*, p. 193.

York was of the same mind, concluding that 'Even the concept of a New Age is vague'.[24] Wouter Hanegraaff's opinion is that 'New Age' is 'a label' which can be 'attached indiscriminately to whatever seems to fit it'.[25] Michael York described New Age predictions of historical transformation as a 'mnemonic device far more than a prophecy', casting doubt on the need to regard them as literally true.[26] For Stuart Sutcliffe 'New Age' then becomes no more than a 'millennialist' or 'apocalyptic' emblem.[27] As such, anyone who has an instinctive idea of what 'New Age' is can then attach an idea or activity to it. UFOlogy, which is supposedly dominated by women and depends on personal revelation, is therefore 'New Age', while the New Age segment amongst President Obama's supporters in 2009 was instantly identifiable.[28] Writing in *The Sunday Times*, Brian Appleyard identified enthusiasm for the significance of the right-brain/left-brain split as New Age, and the typical reader of *The Times* was expected to understand an unexplained reference to Barbara Ehrenrich's illustration of the dovetailing between capitalism and New Age spirituality, as well as what it meant that the evidence for disruption in teenagers' body clocks was not a 'New Age fad'.[29] However, in spite of Sutcliffe's argument that New Age is just an emblem with no substance, for many users of overtly named New Age services, New Age is real: it has meaning and depth. The readers of the *Llewellyn Journal*, issued by the Llewellyn publishing company, know perfectly well what is meant when they are told that the '*Llewellyn Journal* allows our readers to connect with the various new age and metaphysical topics about which they seek further information'.[30] Shoppers at the online 'New Age Store' know that they can go there to purchase horoscope readings.[31] This confusion between academics, journalists and consumers is highly relevant to the problem of whether astrology is correctly classified as New Age.

There is some academic debate about whether New Age culture constitutes a 'movement' in any meaningful cultural or political sense, and whether, if it is

---

[24] George Chryssides, *Exploring New Religions* (London, 1999), p. 315; York, *The Emerging Network*, p. 22.

[25] Hanegraaff, *New Age Religion*, p. 2.

[26] York, *The Emerging Network*, p. 49.

[27] Sutcliffe, *Children of the New Age*, pp. 9–11.

[28] Robert Sheaffer, 'UFOlogy 2009: A Six-Decade Perspective', *Skeptical Inquirer*, 33/1 (2009), p. 25; Oliver Burkeman, 'New age America is entranced by Obama's electoral aura', *The Guardian*, G2, 3 July 2008, p. 2.

[29] Brian Appleyard, 'Divide and Rule', *The Sunday Times*, Culture section, 29 November 2009, p. 8; Stefanie Marsh, 'Testing positive', *The Times*, Review section, 2 January 2010, p. 9l; Hannah Devlin, 'School finds the secret of exam success: let teenagers have a lie-in', *The Times*, 27 August 2011, p. 4.

[30] *The Llewellyn Journal*, 10 March 2009, <www.llewellyn.com>, accessed 10 March 2009.

[31] The New Age Store, <http://www.newagestore.com/>, accessed 25 August 2011.

not, it is a network.[32] Such arguments are largely ones of semantics which do not alter the substance of the discussion. In any case, Blavatsky, Bailey and Rudolf Steiner all deliberately set out to create organised movements with a common set of goals and, even if we look at wider New Age culture as consisting of series of networks, it is still perfectly possible to talk of a cultural movement. One solution is to distinguish two elements within New Age culture: it is apparent that, as in any cultural group, some individuals have a far greater level of commitment than others, as Steven Sutcliffe correctly recognised.[33] First, there are the small groups of individuals who are well organised, believe that the New Age is coming and that, by their actions, they can actively assist this process. Second, there is the larger community of individuals who may be accustomed to ideas and practices generally included as New Age, whether feng shui, spiritual development, astrology or the use of alternative therapies, but who have either no concept of, or interest in, the approaching entry to the New Age as a major historical shift. It may therefore be possible to identify a New Age Movement on the one hand, and a general cultural phenomenon described as 'New Age' on the other, without the sheer diversity of the latter compromising the existence of the former. As a cultural phenomenon we can therefore distinguish two 'New Age movements', based on the level of intensity of the participants. We may therefore identify a 'narrow' New Age consisting of what Lewis and Melton called 'the phenomena, personalities and events featured in the media since the 1980s'. on the one hand, and a broad New Age consisting of groups who might actually reject the label but still fall inside its scope from an academic point of view, on the other.[34] Wouter Hanegraaff's labels for these two levels of New Age activity and affiliation are New Age *sensu stricto* (in a restricted, narrow sense) and New Age *sensu lato* (in a wide sense).[35] The New Age *sensu stricto* is heavily theosophical and anthroposophical and is concerned with the coming historical transition, the entry into the Age of Aquarius and the resulting urgent need to find means of spiritual transformation in order to prepare for the coming of the World Teacher, ameliorate any violent potential in the approaching crisis and serve the needs of cosmic evolution.

Actually, the situation is not as serious as Sutcliffe imagines, and, while it is true that ideas or activities may be labelled randomly as New Age, just as they might be called Postmodern, or Liberal or Fascist, on the basis of reflexive instinct it is possible to identify key qualities of New Age thought from the primary literature. For example, as a key New Age author, William Bloom identified four

---

[32]   Nicholas Campion, 'Prophecy, Cosmology and the New Age Movement: The Extent and Nature of Contemporary Belief in Astrology', PhD thesis, University of the West of England, 2004, p. 78.

[33]   Stuart Sutcliffe, 'Between Apocalypse and Self-Realisation: "Nature" as an Index of New Age Spirituality', in Joanne Pearson, Richard H. Roberts and Geoffrey Samuel (eds), *Nature Religion Today: Paganism in the Modern World* (Edinburgh, 1998), p. 43, n1.

[34]   Lewis and Melton, *Perspectives*, p. x.

[35]   Hanegraaff, *New Age Religion*, pp. 96–103.

facets of New Age: new science (including new forms of healing), ecology, new psychology and spiritual dynamics.[36] From combining the writing of New Agers with the commentaries of Christian critics of New Age culture and the sociologists who have studied the topic, we can identify the following key qualities of any New Age idea or practice.

1. A belief that the divine exists within each human being, rather than being purely external. The individual is, then, essentially spiritual. There is therefore an emphasis on inner development, whether psychological or spiritual.[37] New Age religion is therefore fundamentally Gnostic, influenced by Blavatsky and, later, by C.G. Jung.[38] God in New Age thought, meanwhile, is more typically the Neoplatonic deist creator, rather than the personal Christian God.[39] The monist nature of New Age theology, its assumption that the divine and the visible universe are one, was summed up by David Spangler when he wrote, 'God is the New Age, the original and only New Age, the Spirit that makes all things new'.[40]

2. Following directly from the idea of the inner divine is the implication that the individual is the highest authority. For Paul Heelas, one of the first sociologists of religion in the field, New Age beliefs can be summed up as 'self-spirituality', and he sees it as based in the 'self-ethic', the need to take responsibility for one's own actions.[41] Heelas refers to 'epistemological individualists', for whom knowledge essentially arises from the self.[42]

3. It follows from this that individual experience, whether of nature or the divine, is the ultimate arbiter of truth.

4. From this in turn is derived a distinct cultural relativism. As the evangelical Christian Elliot Miller wrote, the New Age assumes that belief systems are created to meet cultural needs.[43]

---

[36] Bloom, *The New Age*, p. xvi.

[37] See also Wuthnow, *The Consciousness Revolution*, p. 4; Gillian McCulloch, *The Deconstruction of Dualism in Theology: With Special Reference to Ecofeminist Theology and New Age Spirituality* (Carlisle, 2002), pp. 149–50; Wade Clark Roof, *A Generation of Seekers: The Spiritual Journeys of the Baby Boom Generation* (San Francisco, 1993), pp. 122–3.

[38] See, for example, Blavatsky, *Isis*, I.1–54; C.G. Jung, 'Gnostic Symbols of the Self', in *Aion*, in *The Collected Works of C.G. Jung*, vol. 9, Part 2, trans. R.F.C. Hull (London, 1959), pp. 184–221.

[39] Hanegraaff, *New Age Religion*, pp. 183–9; David Spangler, *Festivals in the New Age* (Forres, 1975), pp. 70–1.

[40] David Spangler, 'The New Age: The Movement Toward the Divine', in Duncan S. Ferguson, *New Age Spirituality: An Assessment* (Louisville KY, 1993), p. 105.

[41] Heelas, *New Age*, pp. 18, 23; see also the previous writing by the Christian critic Elliot Miller, *A Crash Course on the New Age Movement* (Eastbourne, 1990), p. 26.

[42] Heelas, *New Age*, p. 21. See also Christopher H. Partridge, 'Truth, Authority and Epistemological Individualism in New Age Thought', *Journal of Contemporary Religion*, 14/1 (1999), pp. 289–313.

[43] Miller, *A Crash Course*, pp. 25–6.

5. The implication of cultural relativism is, in turn, eclecticism and syncretism, in which ideas from many cultures may be adopted, either individually or combined to create new systems.

6. The tendency to syncretism is then linked to holism, a belief that the entire universe is one interdependent whole. From this idea there develops a concern with the environment.

7. The universe, as Blavatsky argued, is thought to be in a constant process of evolutionary spiritual development.[44]

8. True to the spirit of Popperian activism, it is necessary for each individual to take the necessary steps to encourage the New Age to come into existence. In other words, true or not, the prophecy is a call to action. In the words of David Spangler, 'The New Age offers action' and is a metaphor which galvanises people into action, 'an image of transformation and potential' which can endow people with the power to transform themselves and their society.[45] The astrologer Rupert Gleadow, who was profoundly sceptical of the Age of Aquarius, wrote that 'its only virtue is that it encourages us to look on the future, despite rebuffs, as something for which we must continue to do our best'.[46]

9. The preparation for the New Age is achieved partly via education and any practice designed to facilitate spiritual growth. The literature on correct preparation for the New Age is extensive, from theosophists throughout the nineteenth and twentieth centuries.[47]

10. Linked to activism, meanwhile, is the transformation which will make the inauguration of the New Age possible, as so many evangelical critics (such as Groothuis) pointed out.[48] To quote Michael York again,

> What unites all New Agers, however, is the vision of radical mystical transformation on both the personal and collective levels. In fact, the awakening

---

[44] Irving Hexham and Karla Poewe, *New Religions as Global Cultures* (Boulder CO, 1997), pp. 93–6.

[45] David Spangler, *The Rebirth of the Sacred* (London, 1984), p. 76, 84; Spangler, 'The New Age', p. 88; see also David Spangler, *Revelation: The Birth of a New Age* (Forres, 1976), pp. 180–1; Spangler, *A Pilgrim in Aquarius*, p. 55; Alice A. Bailey, *The Destiny of the Nations* (New York, 1949), p. 36; Sir George Trevelyan, *A Vision of the Aquarian Age: The Emerging Spiritual World View* (London, 1984), pp. 82, 139–47; York, *The Emerging Network*, pp. 34, 39–40, 49, 57.

[46] Rupert Gleadow, *Your Character in the Zodiac* (London, 1968), p. 137.

[47] Alice A. Bailey, *Education in the New Age*, 2nd edn (London, 1954); David Spangler, *Explorations: Emerging Aspects of the New Culture* (Forres, 1980), pp. 12–33.

[48] Douglas R. Groothuis, *Unmasking the New Age: Is there a New Religious Movement Trying to Transform Society?* (Downer's Grove IL, 1986), p. 11; Russell Chandler, *Understanding the New Age* (Milton Keynes, 1989), p. 17; Michael Cole, Jim Graham, Tony Higton and David Lewis, *What is the New Age?* (London, 1990), p. 6; Lemesurier, *This New Age Business*, p. 197; see also Melton et al., *New Age Almanac*, p. 3; Spangler, *The Rebirth*, p. 76.

to the potential abilities of the human self – one's individual psychic powers and the capability for physical and/or psychological healing – is the New Age springboard for the quantum leap of collective consciousness which is to bring about and constitute the New Age itself.[49]

Some argue that New Age culture is also secular, an idea developed by Wouter Hanegraaff, who argued that the New Age is 'characterised by a popular Western culture criticism expressed in terms of a secularised esotericism'.[50] The prime example would be Swedenborgianism, with its combination of esotericism but its rejection of established religion. Others agree – as Joscelyn Godwin has argued, Blavatsky's theosophy was as much a product of the Enlightenment rejection of conventional religion as a reaction against nineteenth-century materialism, which was itself a consequence of Enlightenment thought.[51] Earlier than either Hanegraaff or Godwin, William Braden considered that astrologers who forecast the Age of Aquarius are 'humanists', noting that the key to the prophecy concerns 'long-term prospects for man' rather than, as traditional millenarianism would have it, the inauguration of the kingdom of God.[52] This theme was developed by the Christian writer Elliot Miller, who identified the New Age in the lineage of Western intellectual history, arguing that it is broadly descended from Enlightenment secularism, especially in its humanism, naturalism and existentialism, although in a 'spiritualized' form.[53] Such views reinforce the point I started with in this chapter – that New Age cosmology, although deeply rooted in Western millenarianism, achieved a modern form in the late eighteenth century.

New Age culture is not static. It flourished in esoteric circles in the early twentieth century, combined with counter-cultural radicalism in the 1960s and 1970s, and became commercialised in the 1980s. The label was then simultaneously rejected by many of its proponents while many of its ideas and practices went mainstream. In the first decade of the twenty-first century apocalyptic hopes of a transition to an astronomically derived New Age were transferred from the Age of Aquarius to the supposed end of the Maya Calendar in December 2012.[54] The underlying

---

[49]   York, *The Emerging Network*, p. 39.

[50]   Hanegraaff, *New Age Religion*, pp. 409, 521.

[51]   Joscelyn Godwin, *The Theosophical Enlightenment* (New York, 1994), p. xi.

[52]   William Braden, *The Age of Aquarius: Technology and the Cultural Revolution* (London, 1971), p. 17.

[53]   Miller, *A Crash Course*, p. 4; see also p. 20.

[54]   Nicholas Campion, 'The 2012 Mayan Calendar Prophecies in the Context of the Western Millenarian Tradition', in Clive Ruggles (ed.), *Archaeoastronomy and Ethnoastronomy: Building Bridges between Cultures*, Proceedings of International Astronomy Union Symposium 278 (Cambridge, 2011), pp. 249–54; John Hoopes, 'A Critical History of 2012 Mythology', in Ruggles (ed.), *Archaeoastronomy and Ethnoastronomy*, pp. 240–8; Joseph Gelfer (ed.), *2012: Decoding the Countercultural Apocalypse* (Sheffield, 2011).

cultural patterns, though, continue. New Age-ism is a species of millenarianism, possessing all the characteristics of apocalyptic belief, including messianism, astrology and the expectation of an imminent historical transformation. Combining this with Gnostic notions of the inner divine, it adds other features to the transformational matrix: relativity, personal development and the self-ethic. The New Age movement, as it exists today, has an apocalyptic core (*sensu stricto*) and a wider cultural impact (*sensu lato*). Even though it draws widely on non-Western spiritualities it also has a profoundly Christian dimension, so much so that it may be considered an integral part of a two-thousand-year lineage of Christian apocalyptic thought, although of a more quietist, contemplative form than that favoured by more militant forms of Christian millenarianism. The question I shall consider is whether, as so many commentators assume, it provides an explanatory model for the nature and popularity of modern astrology.

Chapter 5

End Times: The New Age and the Age of Aquarius

Today we stand on the threshold of a new era when, according to zodiacal symbolism, the truth, long hidden, will be revealed – the Age of Aquarius, the Man, the Age of Enlightenment.[1]

The notions of the New Age and the Age of Aquarius share a common origin in the esoteric secularism of the late eighteenth century and a parallel history in the theosophical millenarianism of the 1890s and 1900s, but they are not identical. The New Age may be located sometimes (although not always) imaginatively in the future, but actually occupies a space outside time, located in the apocalyptic imagination, while the Age of Aquarius is a product of the astronomically demonstrable fact of the shift of the spring equinox into Aquarius. The Aquarian Age can be seen as just one more value-free shift of one of an endless series of historical adjustments and so is not necessarily millenarian. It becomes so only when linked to the New Age. The New Age, meanwhile, only assumes a real millenarian force when the coming shift into Aquarius endows it with imminent, objective power. The two ages' power as a mnemonic focus for prophetic expectations comes from the simple formula that the sum is greater than the parts.

The assumption that the New Age and the Age of Aquarius are identical is, though, pervasive. Sociologists certainly tend to assume that this is so. Paul Heelas, whose knowledge of the astrological milieu is slight, allowed for some uncertainty, writing that 'some have supposed that the development of the New Age itself is in the hands of astrological processes'.[2] New Age apologists certainly agree and David Spangler, one of the most prolific of New Age thinkers, was well aware of the mutual reinforcement between the two Ages: 'Now humanity is undergoing another vast evolutionary change which is symbolised both factually and allegorically by the concept of a new age, the age of Aquarius.'[3]

The terms 'New Age' and 'Age of Aquarius' were being used interchangeably from the 1900s. By 1927 the discussion of the New Age as a synonym for the

---

[1] Vera W. Reid, *Towards Aquarius* (New York, 1944), p. 7.

[2] Paul Heelas, *The New Age Movement* (Oxford, 1996), p. 34; see also pp. 1, 43.

[3] David Spangler, *Explorations: Emerging Aspects of the New Culture* (Forres, 1980), p. 78; see also David Spangler, *A Pilgrim in Aquarius* (Forres, 1996), p. 247; William Bloom, *The New Age: An Anthology of Essential Writings* (London, 1991), p. xviii; and Steve Nobel, 'Age of Transition', *Prediction*, 68/7 (2002), pp. 28–30.

Age of Aquarius was accepted amongst astrologers, at least all those who were operating within a theosophical context. The first substantial English-language book to be devoted to the Age of Aquarius, *The Message of Aquaria: The Significance and Mission of the Aquarian Age*, was published in 1921. The book's author, Frank Curtiss, took a theosophical line but, like Heindel and Rudolf Steiner, he emphasised theosophy's Christian content, and gave the astrological Age of Aquarius the spiritual qualities of the New Age. 'Osiris', Curtiss wrote, was 'the Egyptian term for the great Creative Aspect of the Godhead which manifests to the Cosmos as the Cosmic Cause, to our universe as the Sun and to humanity as God.'[4] He also anticipated later goddess-feminism, arguing strongly for the unity of the masculine and feminine aspects of the divine as a characteristic of the beginning of the Age of Aquarius, placing a strong emphasis on the re-emergence of the goddess. Citing Matthew 24.30, he claimed, in his typically prophetic tone, that

> As the new Aquarian Age, so long foretold, dawns for humanity, the outbreathing of the Holy Ghost, the Comforter, again speaks, and in no uncertain tones, to all children who recognise Her, and proclaims to them: 'Behold, it is I, Be not afraid!' At the ushering of this Aquarian Age, She comes under the name of Aquaria. And, true to the promise of Jesus, She brings to our remembrance all that He has told us concerning the New Dispensation when there 'Shall appear the sign of the Son of Man (the sign Aquarius in Heaven)'.[5]

This was the precise literary context within which Alice Bailey began writing about the Aquarian Age: an acceptance of the prediction that the shift into the Age of Aquarius would bring the inauguration of the New Age; that this would bring a dramatic shift towards an enhanced spiritual consciousness, particularly a heightened awareness of the divine within. In spite of the high position given to Eastern teachers, the primacy of the cosmic Christ indicates a strong emphasis on Christian imagery. Bailey did, it is true, disagree with her predecessors on points of detail. Yet her highly influential view of the Age of Aquarius was couched largely in terms of her apocalyptic Christian millenarianism. She confidently identified signs of 'the time of the end' and of 'the reappearance of the Christ and the externalisation of the Kingdom of God'.[6] Bailey's view of the transition to the millennium was that crisis was highly likely but not inevitable, for it depended both on the strength of the spiritual 'Hierarchy of Light' and humanity's willingness to support them.[7] She believed that

---

[4]   Frank Homer Curtiss, *The Message of Aquaria: The Significance and Mission of the Aquarian Age* (San Francisco, 1921), p. vii.

[5]   Curtiss, *The Message of Aquaria*, p. viii.

[6]   Alice A. Bailey, *The Reappearance of the Christ* (New York, 1948), pp. 185, 187.

[7]   Alice A. Bailey, 'The Coming World Order', in Alice A. Bailey, *The Exernalisation of the Hierarchy* (New York, 1957), p. 217.

The functioning of the Law of Loving Understanding will be greatly facilitated and speeded during the Aquarian Age which we are considering; it will eventuate later in the development of a world-wide international spirit, in the recognition of one universal faith in God and in humanity also as the major expression of divinity upon the planet and in the transfer of the human consciousness from the world of material things to that of the more purely psychic.[8]

Just as Blavatsky issued a challenge to Marxist materialism in the 1870s, so Bailey's internationalist, apocalyptic evangelism offered an alternative to revolutionary socialism just as the communist world was approaching its apogee. She also anticipated those philosophers, such as the Frankfurt school, including Theodor Adorno, who were to become disillusioned with the failure of the Marxist prophecy of the proletarian revolution and find solace in notions of inner transformation (in the Frankfurt school's case, to be taken from Freud) as a prerequisite for a successful challenge to capitalism. The notion that the Age of Aquarius is either currently beginning, or will do so sometime in the near future, is a given in most modern astrological literature. The Aquarian Age often occurs in popular works as a hook to the reader. In 1982 American astrologer Debbi Kempton-Smith opened her mass-market paperback *Secrets from a Stargazer's Notebook* with the call to her potential readers, 'Kings and queens of the Age of Aquarius, come on now, I know what you want. You want everything'.[9] Discussion of it occurs regularly in the main astrological periodicals of the English-speaking world and the general impression is that it is taken for granted.[10] That belief in the Aquarian Age is a given amongst astrologers is apparent to many who come into contact with them. As Steve Nobel, of the London-based organisation Alternatives, reported in his discussion of the Age of Aquarius, 'many astrologers I have spoken to agree that we are in an age of transition'.[11]

---

[8]   Alice A. Bailey, *The Destiny of the Nations* (New York, 1949), p. 47.

[9]   Debbi Kempton-Smith, *Secrets from a Stargazer's Notebook: Making Astrology Work for You* (New York, 1982), p. xiii.

[10]   Recent examples include David A. Solté, 'Millennium Watch: The Outer Planets and the Aquarian Age', *Mountain Astrologer*, 85 (1999), p. 77; Ray Grasse, 'Drawing Down the Fire of the Gods: Reflections on the Leo/Aquarius Axis', *Mountain Astrologer*, 89 (2000), pp. 12–21; Ray Grasse, 'Cinema and the Birth of the Aquarian Age', *Mountain Astrologer*, 108 (2003), pp. 9–18; Gary Caton, 'Uranus in Pisces: Birthing the New Age', *NCGR Memberletter*, August/September (2002), pp. 4–5, 20; Theresa H. McDevitt, 'USA and Serbia: The Composite', *NCGR Memberletter* (1999), pp. 1, 9; Theresa H. McDevitt, 'Sharon and Arafat: Axis of Closure to the Pisces–Virgo Age', *NCGR Memberletter* (2002), pp. 1, 16–17; Terry MacKinnell, 'A New Look at the Old Ages', *NCGR Memberletter* (2002), pp. 10–11, 19–20; Robert Zoller, 'The Use of the Archetypes in Prediction', *Astrological Journal*, 44/6 (2002), pp. 6–16; Nobel, 'Age of Transition', pp. 28–30.

[11]   Nobel, 'Age of Transition', p. 28.

A typical account of the essentially progressive millenarian point of view identified by Nobel was submitted to the *ISAR Email Newsletter* by American astrologer Kelly Lee Phipps in 2002: 'We live in the interface period between the Piscean and Aquarian Ages, blending spirituality, institutionalization, and illusion with enlightenment, technology, and cosmic consciousness.'[12] Signs of the Age of Aquarius' approach are widely identified. They may include genetic engineering, multicultural marriages in the US, new technology, jazz music, post-modernism, solar energy, cultural relativism and political organisations exemplified by Jesse Jackson's 'Rainbow Coalition', or American democracy in general.[13] In 2009 the Web buzzed with chatter that Barack Obama's victory in the Presidential election was a symptom of the Aquarian Age's approach.[14] Some Christian evangelicals have even argued that the rising popularity of astrology itself is a sign of the approach of the New Age.[15]

As applied to history, the precession of the equinoxes offers two kinds of statement. One concerns the future, and provides the basis for prophecies of the Age of Aquarius and the identification of the current signs which supposedly provide evidence for the Age's approach. The other relates to the past, and offers a historical cosmology which provides an account of social and religious development, replacing the more conventional scheme based on Jupiter–Saturn conjunctions. The chronological framework is usually based on division into 2,160- (or 2,000-) year periods, the main characteristics of which are derived from the astrological associations of each sign or constellation.

This system of what Collingwood would call quasi-history was given its most comprehensive treatment in Vera Reid's *Towards Aquarius*, published in 1944. Reid's system, in turn, provided the template for most future accounts, including the summary in Margaret Hone's *Textbook of Modern Astrology*, which was first published in 1951 and was to become the most influential student text for almost three decades, from the early 1950s to the late 1970s, going into 13 reprints by 1973.[16] Through *The Textbook*'s pages the notion of 2,000-year astrologically

---

[12]   Kelly Lee Phipps, 'How Not To Collectively Lose Our Minds', *ISAR International Email Newsletter*, 212 (2002).

[13]   J.E. Collins and Carole Wilson, 'Astrology and Extra-Corporeal Fertilization', *Astrological Journal*, 21/3 (1980), p. 125; Joyce Levine, 'Entering the Age of Aquarius', *Horoscope*, February (1997), p. 2; Keith Magnay, 'New Flight in the Age of Aquarius', *Astrological Journal*, 37/3 (1995), p. 162; Grasse, 'Fire of the Gods', pp. 14, 19, 20; Johnny Lister, *The New Age: How Entering the Aquarian Age Affects You and the World Today* (San Francisco, 1984), pp. 249–50; McDevitt, 'USA and Serbia', p. 1.

[14]   See, for example, Nancy Seifer and Martin Vieweg, 'Aquarius Rising: Obama and the Aquarian Age', <http://newagejournal.com/2007/new-age-articles/aquarius-rising-obama-and-the-aquarian-age>, accessed 27 July 2009.

[15]   Michael Cole, Jim Graham, Tony Higton and David Lewis, *What is the New Age?* (London, 1990) pp. 3, 5.

[16]   Margaret Hone, *The Modern Textbook of Astrology* (London, 1973), pp. 278–300; see also Alan Oken, *Astrology, Evolution and Revolution, a Path to Higher Consciousness*

determined periods of history became an unquestioned part of the modern astrology student's education. Two features are obvious in Reid's scheme. The first is that the sequence of Ages is expressed most strongly in religious terms. The second is that there is therefore no idea of absolute truth in terms of human religion, for each Age produces its corresponding religious forms, and all religions are seen as a path to the ultimate truth: there is a profound cultural relativism at the heart of Aquarian Age thinking. In 1951 Hone wrote that 'Each age plays its part in the evolution of the world, which can no more escape its correlation with the cosmic pattern than can the tiny human beings living on its surface.'[17]

Reid took the political situation in 1944 as the starting point for her view of contemporary culture, as well as the past and the future, filtered through the lens provided by Frank Curtiss and Alice Bailey. She wrote that

> Today we stand on the threshold of a new era when, according to zodiacal symbolism, the truth, long hidden, will be revealed – the Age of Aquarius, the Man, the Age of Enlightenment. Response to vibrations of another dimension, which is already beginning to transform our life and thought, can be profoundly disturbing until we catch a glimpse of its purpose. In such circumstances it is inevitable that we ask, 'What is the purpose underlying the present conflict of ideologies? What part has the individual to play in the transformation of his world? What of tomorrow? Does civilisation stand on the verge of collapse or of new life?'[18]

There is a certain apocalyptic concern in her words, but a violent upheaval is posed as a possibility rather than a certain prophecy. In this we can identify the caution necessary to an astrologically based apocalyptic, in which the astrologer reaches a reasoned judgement about the future, as opposed to one in which the millenarian impulse is strongest, and the reality of the imminent upheaval is assured. Although Reid's original purpose was to study zodiacal symbolism in Christian religion, her work relied heavily on quotations from other traditions – Egyptian, Hindu, Buddhist, Taoist, Confucian, Inca: all faiths, it seemed to her and other theosophists, followed a parallel path. As summarised by Hone for a generation of astrology students, Reid's account envisaged the division of history into 2,000-year epochs, in each of which

---

through Astrology (New York, 1976), pp. 3–44; Lorna St Aubyn, *The New Age in a Nutshell: A Guide to Living in New Times* (Wellow, 1990), pp. 6–11; Marjorie Orr, *The Astrological History of the World: The Influence of the Planets on Human History* (London, 2002), pp. 18–19; Gordon Strachan, *Christ and the Cosmos* (Dunbar, 1985); Peter Lemesurier, *Gospel of the Stars: The Mystery of the Cycle of the Ages* (London, 2002); Luella Sibbald, *The One With the Water Jar: Astrology, the Aquarian Age and Jesus of Nazareth* (San Francisco, 1978).

[17] Hone, *Textbook*, p. 279.

[18] Reid, *Towards Aquarius*, p. 7.

the complexities, subtleties and richness of human development, not to mention the evidence, are compressed into a couple of lines.

> 10,000 BCE. Age of Leo, corresponding to Atlantean civilisation and solar monotheism.
> 8,000 BCE. Age of Cancer, corresponding to the Deluge, lunar and fertility goddess cults.
> 6,000 BCE. Age of Gemini, corresponding to cults of twins, such as Romulus and Remus.
> 4,000 BCE. Age of Taurus, corresponding to stable civilisations, such as Egypt, and bull worship.
> 2,000 BCE. Age of Aries, corresponding to military empires, exploration, discovery, and the use of the ram and lamb as religious symbols.
> 1 CE. Age of Pisces, corresponding to Christianity and the fish as a religious symbol.
> 2,000 CE. Age of Aquarius, corresponding to humanity, peace, justice and equality.

The appeal of such a system is very similar to that offered by the major apocalyptic alternatives, Marxism and Christianity, in that simplicity provides for certainty: a simplified account of the past provides evidence that prophecies concerning the near-future 'must' be true. The uncertainty lies in the detail: while the future transition to the Age of Aquarius is not open to question (for it must happen as assuredly as the constellations move), whether it will be peaceful or violent and whether we are in a pre- or post-millennial phase are not known. The scheme remains very popular and is regularly revisited in the specialist astrological journals.[19]

One question is how, if at all, Aquarian Age prophecies fit into the pre-millennial/post-millennial dichotomy. Pre-millennialism is more inclined to assume an imminent crisis, post-millennialism a gradual induction into the coming Age. Opinion on the matter in relation to the New Age is uncertain. Wouter Hanegraaff argued that, while the New Age *sensu stricto* tended originally to be pre-millennial and passive, awaiting the coming crisis, it subsequently became post-millennial and inclined to actively work for a smooth transition to the promised earthly utopia.[20] However, pre-millennial and post-millennial points of view are actually inseparable in the astrological literature. A pre-millennial version of the future was summarised by the society astrologer Count Louis Hamon in 1925, writing under the pseudonym Cheiro.[21] He forecast a violent combination of political revolution, global war and natural catastrophe that would be sufficient to destroy the known

---

[19]   For example, Robert Fitzgerald, 'Astrological Ages as an Accurate and Effective Model of History', *Astrological Journal*, 51/5 (2009), pp. 55–62.

[20]   Wouter J. Hanegraaff, *New Age Religion and Western Culture* (Leiden and New York, 1996), p. 100.

[21]   Cheiro, *The Book of World Predictions* (London, 1931), pp. 178–9, 184.

world. The promise, or fear, of a violent crisis, is certainly evident in maintaining a pre-millennial, apocalyptic point of view amongst some astrologers. However, inherent in the theosophical vision of the future is the prophecy, promoted by both Rudolf Steiner and Alice Bailey, that the approach of the New Age (and, in Bailey's view, the Aquarian Age) will be accompanied by spiritual evolution, a process which may offset the risk of catastrophe. There is a widespread view, then, that a shift of consciousness may convert a pre-millennial disaster into a post-millennial paradise. This is precisely why astrology is seen as so important, as a means of preparing humanity for the inevitable.

Various astrologers have proposed their own solutions for the conversion of a potential crisis away from violence and into peaceful transformation. Amongst contemporary American astrologers we find the following: for Ray Grasse the key is knowledge, while Kelly Lee Phipps calls for unspecified 'immediate action' and Gary Caton for love.[22] What distinguished New Age astrologers from other New Agers, as Marc Lerner (an astrologer as well as a follower of Alice Bailey) argued, is their emphasis on astrology as a primary means of raising consciousness and engineering the peaceful transition into the New Age.[23] However, that the New Age and the Aquarian Age are not the same is evident in a strong resistance to New Age utopianism by astrologers who fully accept that, as the spring equinox sunrise shifts against the background of the stars, so historical phases begin and end, but with no apocalyptic, millenarian expectations. There is no progress, no qualitative improvement, just more change. Stoic repetition is emphasised and hopes of cosmic salvation are regarded as, at best naive, at worst, stupid.

A classic anti-New Age position was set out in 1947 by Charles Carter, the President of the Astrological Lodge of the London-based Theosophical Society from 1920 to 1952, and one of the most influential astrologers in the twentieth-century English-speaking world. At first sight we might imagine Carter, being a theosophist, would be anticipating the New Age with great excitement. Far from it. His blunt opinion was that 'It is probable that there is no branch of Astrology upon which more nonsense has been poured forth than the doctrine of the precession of the equinoxes.'[24] In 1951 he followed this up with another burst of contempt for the New Agers, declaring that

> In the West we have heard about the so-called Aquarian Age, which is to follow that of Pisces and for some unexplained reason is to be so much pleasanter to inhabit, until the very mention of this term fills the careful astrologer with apprehension. For it is questionable whether many who talk about it, and even some of those who write about it, understand what is meant.[25]

---

[22]   Grasse, 'Fire of the Gods', p. 20; Phipps, 'How Not To Lose Our Minds'; Caton, 'Uranus in Pisces', p. 4.

[23]   Mark Lerner, editorial comments in *Welcome to Planet Earth*, 14/10 (1995).

[24]   Charles Carter, 'Editorial', *Astrology*, 21/2 (1947), p. 111.

[25]   Charles Carter, *An Introduction to Political Astrology* (London, 1951), p. 73.

For Carter, only the highbrow elite are able to understand the subtleties of astrological historiography. Ordinary astrologers might get it wrong. As a warning against any tendency to make simplifications based in apparent ideological affiliation, we should understand that Carter may have been a theosophist, yet he clearly had no time at all for the vague idealism and revolutionary spirituality of Alice Bailey and her followers: not all theosophists think alike and Carter's Neoplatonic inclinations were better served by his membership of the discrete Universal Order, than of the Theosophical Society. Yet, while condemning popular belief in astrological ages, Carter did acknowledge that the Age of Aquarius was an actual phenomenon, and produced his own detailed historical scheme in which each astrological age was in turn divided into 12 sub-ages.[26] When he considered the nature of the Piscean sub-age, which he thought was to begin in 1980 and to conclude the 2,000-year Piscean Age in preparation for the Age of Aquarius, he predicted that it might be only 'different' from the outgoing Aquarian phase. There is not much advance here of Delaunaye's vague prediction of 'changements' and, in any case, human agency would shape the outcome: as a Popperian activist, Carter wrote 'whether it will be better and more agreeable (which is what most people mean when they say "better") depends chiefly upon Man himself'.[27] Carter's anti-New Age view has struck a chord with a number of prominent astrological authors and there is a small but little-noticed group for whom the notion of the New Age is an unwelcome import of an alien and unnecessary millenarian doctrine into astrological historiography.

The Age of Aquarius and the New Age therefore do not offer identical views of the future, in spite of the widespread assumption, propagated by sociologists, critics of astrology and some astrologers, that they are one and the same. The former depends on a value-free prediction that history is tied to the precession of the equinoxes and postulates endless change, but not necessarily an imminent breakthrough to a wonderful new blissful phase of existence, while the latter is rooted in the Swedenborgian prophecy that the coming age is to be more spiritual than the last, and the Blavatskyan notion that it will begin the ascent to humanity's final reintegration with the cosmos. For Blavatsky the coming of the New Age, though, was a matter of a cosmically determined evolutionary law and it was therefore natural for theosophical astrologers to time its beginning according to precession of the equinoxes, hence the overlap between New and Aquarian Ages. New Agers in the tradition of Bailey and Steiner then regard the New and Aquarian Ages as identical. The dominant mode of discourse within the New Age *sensu stricto* sees the astronomical fact of the Age of Aquarius as validation of its own prophetic future, while the dominant discourse amongst astrologers sees the spiritual qualities of the New Age as those which will be introduced when the Aquarian Age dawns. The minority view amongst astrologers, as advocated by Charles Carter, is that the Age of Aquarius will be different from the Piscean

---

[26]   Carter, *Political Astrology*, pp. 76–86.
[27]   Carter, *Political Astrology*, p. 86.

Age, but not necessarily better or more spiritual. There is therefore a plurality of views on the matter. Pre- and post-millenarianism occur throughout astrological and New Age historiography, but are difficult to distinguish precisely. The future is not settled, on account of the insistence that individual participation can shape the future. The historicist/activist assumption holds that the pre-millenarian apocalypse is inevitable if not action is taken but that the future transformation will be peaceful if the right steps are taken. At any rate, what is clear is that assumptions that the Age of Aquarius and the New Age are one and the same are incorrect, and the belief that astrologers are New Agers (in the sense that they believe the New Age is coming) is not the case. Simply, the critics who assume that astrologers are all New Agers and that the Aquarian and New Ages are identical, are guilty of the cardinal academic sin: a failure to consult the primary sources.

Chapter 6
The Writing of Heaven: New Age Astrology

> Astrology is a science as infallible as astronomy itself, with the condition, however, that its interpreters must be equally infallible … In astrology one has to step beyond the visible world of matter, and enter into the domain of transcendent spirit.[1]

The literary roots of astrology's role in apocalyptic thought date back to Plato's *Timaeus* in the fourth century BCE, were reinforced by Biblical expectations that the End of Days would be preceded by extraordinary celestial events, and sought predictive detail in Persian theories of the Jupiter–Saturn cycle and the cosmic drama of Zoroastrian religion.[2] That Near Eastern and Western astrology has long served apocalyptic and millenarian purposes is apparent. On the grand scale it was concerned with the eschaton of history – the complete breakdown of cosmic order. However, it also had other immediate applications, the function of which was to maintain stability, staving off personal crisis and political upheaval in the short-term – the eschaton in history – but were not overtly concerned with warding off the cosmic millennial trauma. Astrology could be simultaneously concerned with the management of daily affairs, and with the ultimate forces which were one day to sweep daily life away altogether. However, such mundane matters as finding one's runaway slave or lost treasure, which mattered profoundly to the wealthy clients of Greek astrologers such as Vettius Valens, have no connection even with maintaining one's personal harmony with the cosmos, let alone historical transformation.[3] Astrology could be apocalyptic, but was not necessarily so. We can therefore identify four kinds of Hellenistic astrology, based on their relationship to eschatology.[4] First, the prediction and preparation for the next apocalyptic crisis transcended all personal affairs. Second, the management of political matters was designed to mitigate the effects of cyclic repetition in historical affairs: critical moments – eschatons in history – could be delayed and minimised. Third, individual astrology concerned the ascent of the soul to the stars, fulfilled a soteriological function and could be seen as a means to prepare for the cosmic crisis: this was certainly how some Christians interpreted it. Fourthly, one application of astrology was concerned with purely personal interests such as

---

[1]   H.P. Blavatsky, *Isis Unveiled* (2 vols, Pasadena, 1976, facs. of 1877 edn), I.259.

[2]   Nicholas Campion, *A History of Western Astrology* (2 vols, London, 2009), vol. 1, chs 5, 8, 10, 15.

[3]   Vettius Valens, *Anthologarium*, ed. David Pingree (Leipzig, 1986).

[4]   Campion, *A History of Western Astrology*, vol. 1, chs 10–13, 15, 16; Nicholas Campion, *The Great Year: Astrology, Millenarianism and History in the Western Tradition* (London, 1994), chs 6, 9–10.

marriage and financial fortunes, and had no connection with historical matters or cosmic annihilation. To move to the present, then, we may ask whether modern astrology is any more necessarily New Age and millennial than its classical ancestor.

Many astrologers assume that astrology is indeed New Age, although the use of the word is sometimes nuanced. In 2011, the small but resilient British Astrological and Psychic Society announced on its Facebook page that 'it exists to provide a means of bringing together those actively working in, or interested in, the many different aspects of esoteric, spiritual and "New Age" teachings, such as Psychic Perception, Astrology, Palmistry, Tarot, Numerology and Healing'.[5] The use of quotation marks around the words 'New Age' indicates an awareness that, while the use of the term is common, there is a slight discomfort around the problem that all the 'new' disciplines listed have ancient origins. There is in such language a suggestion that while 'New Age' is a useful description with wide public recognition, it does not tell the whole story.

However, that modern astrology is in its entirety a New Age discipline, with no question over the meaning of the term, is assumed by most external commentators whether evangelical, historical or sociological.[6] Amongst sociologists, Paul Heelas and Linda Woodhead saw the introduction of astrology classes in the English town of Kendal in 1985 as evidence for the emergence of a spiritual revolution (code for New Age) there. Daren Kemp assumes that the rise of astrology is a symptom of New Age culture.[7] This proposition, though, is to extend Steven Sutcliffe's view of certain perceptions of New Age thought, an 'etic', or outsider, formulation. In other words, astrology's inclusion as a New Age discipline is taken for granted by academics who have not engaged either with astrologers or their works, and there has, to date, been no study of astrology's nature in any commentary on New Age culture, with the sole, and brief, exception of Shoshanah Feher's study in the

---

[5] British Astrological and Psychic Society, Facebook, accessed 15 June 2011.

[6] For evangelical views of astrology as New Age, see Peter Anderson, *Satan's Snare: The Influence of the Occult* (Welwyn, 1988), p. 39; Walter Martin, *The New Age Cult* (Minneapolis, 1989), p. 15; J. Yutaka Amano and Norman L. Geisler, *The Infiltration of the New Age* (Wheaton, 1989), pp. 32–3; Michael Cole, Jim Graham, Tony Higton and David Lewis, *What is the New Age?* (London, 1990), p. 6; Elliot Miller, *A Crash Course on the New Age Movement* (Eastbourne, 1990), p. 19; John P. Newport, *The New Age Movement and the Biblical Worldview: Conflict and Dialogue* (Grand Rapids MI, 1998), p. 8. For historical see Patrick Curry, *A Confusion of Prophets: Victorian and Edwardian Astrology* (London, 1992), p. 161. For sociological views see John A. Saliba, *Perspectives on New Religious Movements* (London, 1995), p. 23; Steve Bruce, *Religion in Modern Britain* (Oxford, 1995), p. 105; Robin Gill, *Churchgoing and Christian Ethics* (Cambridge, 1999), pp. 50–1, 81, 135.

[7] Paul Heelas, Linda Woodhead, Benjamin Seel, Karin Tusting and Bron Szerszynski, *The Spiritual Revolution: Why Religion Is Giving Way to Spirituality* (Oxford, 2005), p. 43; Daren Kemp, *New Age: A Guide* (Edinburgh, 2004), p. 47.

early 1990s.[8] Feher reported on her survey of the 1989 United Astrology Congress in New Orleans, in which she broadly distinguishes a New Age astrology mainly represented by women and concerned with personal growth, and an 'Old Age' astrology mainly represented by men and concerned with event prediction. However, Feher's was a brief sociological foray lacking either a substantial literature review or an awareness that her categories are contradicted by many personal examples. The notion of a divide between 'New Age' and 'Old Age' astrologers is, though, one supported by various leading New Age apologists, including, as we shall see, some of the twentieth century's most influential astrologers, so Feher's finding does indeed conform to certain dominant 'insider' perspectives.[9] It has been noted elsewhere that there are 'two basic forms of astrology', one 'outward', based on traditional techniques and concerned with behaviour, and the other 'inner' and psychological.[10] There is no mystery about this, and the distinction is drawn straight from the work of some of the most prominent of overtly New Age astrologers, for whom outer, event-oriented astrology is known as 'exoteric', inner, spiritual and psychologically based is defined as 'esoteric'.[11] However, there is unpublished ethnographic research which indicates that this is not so, and that the distinction is far from clear. Yet, while the sociological view that *all* astrology is New Age is very difficult to sustain, it is clear that there is *a* New Age astrology which is millennial in origin and which has had a wide impact on the discipline as a whole, and hence on the popular culture within which astrologers exist. The evidence suggests that the notion that all astrology is New Age is a careless generalisation and that it is only the esoteric variety, and its offshoots, that might genuinely be called New Age.

Obviously, it is essential to explore the textual evidence, examining the attitudes of at least some leading astrologers and their impact on astrology in the English-speaking world, and to consider Paul Heelas's proposition that, along with other ancient or pre-modern practices, astrology in the hands of New Agers has adopted a 'detraditionalised' nature, dislocated from its past form. He notes the paradoxical

---

[8]   Shoshanah Feher, 'Who Holds the Cards? Women and New Age Astrology', in James R. Lewis and J. Gordon Melton, *Perspectives on the New Age* (Albany NY, 1992), pp. 179–88; and Shoshanah Feher, 'Who Looks to the Stars? Astrology and Its Constituency', *Journal for the Scientific Study of Religion*, 31/1 (1992), pp. 88–93.

[9]   For 'Old Age' see Alice A. Bailey, 'The Period of Transition', in Alice A. Bailey, *The Externalisation of the Hierarchy* (New York, 1934), p. 35; Dane Rudhyar, *The Astrology of Transformation: A Multilevel Approach* (Wheaton IL, 1984), p. 27; Alan Oken, *Alan Oken's Complete Astrology*, rev. edn (New York, 1988), p. 43; Peter Lemesurier, *This New Age Business: The Story of the Ancient and Continuing Quest to Bring Down Heaven on Earth* (Forres, 1990), p. 5; David Spangler, 'The New Age: The Movement Toward the Divine', in Duncan S. Ferguson, *New Age Spirituality: An Assessment* (Louisville KY, 1993), p. 102.

[10]   Liz Greene and Howard Sasportas, *The Development of the Personality: Seminars in Psychological Astrology* (London, 1987), p. xi.

[11]   Alan Leo, *Esoteric Astrology: A Study in Human Nature* (London, 1925).

New Age devotion to the past and aversion to traditional dogma which leads to traditional practices being first adopted and then transformed.[12] In a sense, there is a process of invention, not out of nothing but on the basis of an existing tradition, a phenomenon explored by Eric Hobsbawm, Terence Ranger and Stephen Bann, and introduced to the study of religion by Steven Vertovec.[13]

Whether they approve of it or not, those few astrologers who have considered the recent history of their discipline generally agree that astrology in the twentieth century underwent a substantial change, moving from a rigid medieval concern with prediction to a more flexible and reliable concern with personality and self-knowledge.[14] The seminal moment which produced this change in astrology was its encounter with the Theosophical Society from 1875 onwards. This is not to say that the Society was exclusively responsible, for it was itself part of a wider cultural current, theosophical with a small 't', including such esoteric figures as the French occultists Eliphas Levi and, in the UK, groups such as the Golden Dawn. Esoteric currents in astrology certainly pre-dated the formation of the Theosophical Society, and can be traced directly back to classical Platonism. However, Blavatsky's charismatic presence loomed large and presented a challenge to the prevailing concern of much nineteenth-century astrology with the prediction of external affairs. Blavatsky herself set the tone for theosophical attitudes to astrology when she stated that

> Astrology is a science *as infallible* as astronomy itself, with the condition, however, that its interpreters must be equally infallible; and it is this condition, however, *sine qua non*, so very difficult of realization, that has always proved a stumbling block to both. Astrology is to exact astronomy what psychology is to exact physiology. In astrology one has to step beyond the visible world of matter, and enter into the domain of transcendent spirit.[15]

Infallibility was in the air – Papal infallibility had become official dogma in 1870 – and in two sentences Blavatsky had set out a manifesto for what was to become New Age astrology – at least, one particular version of it. The core argument was that astrology, as what Blavatsky's successor Annie Besant called a 'Department

[12]   Paul Heelas, *The New Age Movement* (Oxford, 1996), p. 23. See also p. 27.

[13]   Eric Hobsbawm and Terence Ranger (eds), *The Invention of Tradition* (Cambridge, 1983); Stephen Bann, *The Inventions of History: Essays on the Representation of the Past* (Manchester, 1990); Steven Vertovec, 'Inventing Religious Traditions', in Armin W. Geertz and Jeppe Sinding Jensen (eds), *Religion, Tradition and Renewal* (Aarhus, 1991), pp. 79–97.

[14]   Geoffrey Dean and Arthur Mather, *Recent Advances in Natal Astrology: A Critical Review 1900–1976* (Subiaco, 1977), p. 5; Robert Hand, 'Foreword', in Olivia Barclay, *Horary Astrology Rediscovered* (West Chester PA, 1990), pp. 13–18; Oken, *Complete Astrology*, pp. 11–13; Jeff Mayo, *Teach Yourself Astrology* (London, 1981), p. 7; Garry Phillipson, *Astrology in the Year Zero* (London, 2000), p. 76.

[15]   Blavatsky, *Isis*, I.259.

of the Divine Wisdom', is infallible but that astrologers, being only human, are all too fallible.[16] Astrology, in Blavatsky's universe is always true, but astrologers, being human, err. However, by moving beyond the realm of the visible into the transcendent, they can become, in effect, infallible. Blavatsky thus established a requirement for those astrologers with a deep commitment to the theosophical vision of New Age to condemn the fallible astrologers they saw all around them and instead set out to create an astrology which would be, as she hoped, infallible. It was this simple command which was later to be taken up by two influential theosophists, Alan Leo and Dane Rudhyar.[17]

Blavatsky's attitude to astrology was infused with her belief in the esoteric universe and angelic cosmology of the Platonists, Hermeticists, Zoroastrians, Kabbalists, Hindus and Sufis, together with the assumed existence of transcendent spiritual masters, humanity's spiritual evolution and reincarnation. Thus, there is a purpose to each human life, which is to work to purge one's self of the 'dross' of one's nature working towards a gradual improvement in each incarnation until one can finally secure the chance of escape to nirvana at the end of the sequence of zodiacal ages.[18] Blavatsky's astrology then, was teleological, based on the theory of a final state into which all individuals were to evolve, and designed to promote the shift into the new historical era.[19]

The pivotal figure in the incorporation of New Age ideology into astrology was an English commercial traveller called William Frederick Allen (1860–1917), who is generally known under his pseudonym, Alan Leo. In Leo's own account he discovered astrology as a teenager in 1877 although other versions make him 21.[20] In either case, his discovery of the ancient discipline was precocious, and over the next forty years he worked ceaselessly to study it and understand its principles. From around 1890 until his death in 1917 Leo was to be one of the dominating figures in UK astrology, a verdict on which his contemporaries, future astrologers and later historians would all agree.[21] Annie Besant, Blavatsky's successor as President of the Theosophical Society, and an intimate friend of Leo (he never

[16]   Annie Besant, 'An Appreciation', in Bessie Leo, *The Life and Work of Alan Leo* (London, 1919), p. 8.

[17]   Alan Leo, 'The Editor's Observatory', *Modern Astrology*, New Series, 8/5 (1911), p. 180; Alan Leo, 'The Editor's Observatory', *Modern Astrology*, New Series, 8/3 (1911), p. 95; Dane Rudhyar, *The Planetarisation of Consciousness* (New York, 1977), p. v.

[18]   Blavatsky, *Isis*, II.456.

[19]   H.P. Blavatsky, *The Secret Doctrine* (2 vols, Los Angeles, 1982, facs. of 1888 edn), II.437.

[20]   Leo, *Esoteric Astrology*, p. vii; Ellic Howe, *Urania's Children: The Strange World of the Astrologers* (London, 1967), p. 358.

[21]   Besant, 'An Appreciation', p. 8; Margaret Hone, *The Modern Textbook of Astrology* (London, 1973), p. 295; J. Gordon Melton, Jerome Clarke and Aidan A. Kelly, *New Age Almanac* (London and New York, 1991), p. 274; Curry, *A Confusion*, pp. 122–59; Howe, *Urania's Children*, pp. 56–7.

appears to have become close to Blavatsky herself) stated that 'Mr Alan Leo is so well known among all who are interested in Astrology, and he has done so much to raise Astrology from the position of a superstition to that of a science'.[22] The feeling was mutual and, repaying the complement, Leo called Besant 'without a doubt the most remarkable woman of the twentieth century'.[23] After his untimely demise at the age of 57, Leo's colleague F.W. Lacey recalled how his astrology had originally been of the standard event-oriented, character-describing variety typical of the nineteenth century, dealing with such matters as infant mortality and the horoscopes of ships.[24] In the late 1880s, though, Leo began reading theosophical material, and around 1890 he was invited by the theosophist and astrologer, Sepharial (1864–1929), to the Theosophical Society's headquarters at Avenue Road in London. There he was introduced to Blavatsky and her fellow heads of the movement, Henry Olcott and William Q. Judge. Leo had found his calling: he became a devout theosophist and began to study Blavatsky's major works, *Isis Unveiled* and *The Secret Doctrine*, which he later claimed were two of the only books he ever read deeply.[25] If anything, he loved theosophy more than astrology although, as Anne Besant reported, he believed that the two were so intertwined that they were almost indistinguishable.[26] Even though Sepharial was always much closer to Blavatsky than was Leo, Besant was much closer to Leo. He became her personal astrologer and performed tasks such as the election of the moment to lay the foundation stone for the new Theosophical Society headquarters in London.[27]

The 'great upheaval' in his social life occasioned by his introduction to Blavatsky, Olcott and Judge prompted Leo to begin an empirical study of all the horoscopes in his possession, which by then represented up to 13 years' work. The result, of this study, Leo reported, was 'to establish beyond all question the permanent value of Esoteric Astrology, itself defined as the combination of astrology with the 'eastern teachings concerning Reincarnation and Karma'.[28] Leo was no relativist, though. He wrote that the 'laws which guide the evolution of the world are infallible laws which work incessantly for the ultimate good of humanity' and 'are capable of demonstration to all who apply themselves thoughtfully to the methods required to obtain first-hand knowledge'.[29] He added,

---

[22]   Annie Besant, *The Theosophist*, February (1911), cited in Alan Leo, *The Art of Synthesis* (London, 1936), p. viii.

[23]   Alan Leo, 'The Editor's Observatory', *Modern Astrology*, New Series, 8/10 (1911), p. 399.

[24]   F.W. Lacey, 'Early Days in Astrology', in *The Life and Work of Alan Leo*, (ed.) Bessie Leo (London, 1919), pp. 50, 54.

[25]   Besant, 'An Appreciation', pp. 7–8; Lacey, 'Early Days', p. 43.

[26]   Besant, 'An Appreciation', p. 8.

[27]   Alan Leo, 'An Historic Event', *Modern Astrology*, New Series, 8/10 (1911), p. 402.

[28]   Leo, *Esoteric Astrology*, p. vii.

[29]   Leo, *Esoteric Astrology*, p. v.

Today my whole belief in the science of the stars stands or falls with Karma and Reincarnation, and I have no hesitation in saying that without these ancient teachings, Natal Astrology has no permanent value. The law which gives to one soul a nativity of good environment in which refinement, opportunity, and sound moral training are uppermost; and to another poverty, disease, and immoral training, is manifestly unjust to say the least, apart from its being without any apparent purpose.[30]

Leo's insistence that the soul was central to astrology was to become the orthodoxy amongst some of the most influential astrologers of the twentieth century. Charles Carter, who, as we have seen, scathingly dismissed the notion of a spiritual Aquarian Age, wrote a series of standard works on the relationship between astrology and the soul, issued the following statement of his views on astrology, phrased deliberately as an article of faith, not unlike the Christian creed:

I BELIEVE, and many believe with me, that the Zodiac portrays the pathway of the soul of man and humanity. On the other hand, there are, at the present time, very many more who either do not believe in any soul at all, either of individual or of race, or who are entirely agnostic as to its nature, origin and destiny ... Man has a purpose and that this is an eternal purpose we see, analogically, in the circular Zodiac, which has no real beginning or end, when viewed as a whole and not as so many signs.[31]

For Leo, reincarnation was seen as liberating, and as a means of escaping one's destiny. However, the positive negotiation of one's future incarnations was dependent on management of the present, and this in turn was dependent on alteration of one's behaviour patterns which, itself, required self-understanding. Such an astrology is humanist in the true Renaissance sense of the word: the individual and his or her values and interests become the focus of attention in the universe. Leo argued that understanding one's character and past, including past lives, was therefore central to the control of one's future, adapting the Heraclitian aphorism 'Man's character is his daemon' to the more accessible 'character is destiny'.[32] The statement that 'character is destiny', caught a particular strand of modern ideology in which, it is assumed, individuals make their own futures, and is still widely quoted by astrologers.[33] As Leo put it,

---

[30]　Leo, *Esoteric Astrology*, p. vii.

[31]　Charles Carter, *The Zodiac and the Soul* (London, 1948), p. 13.

[32]　R.S. Kirk, J.E. Raven and M. Schofield, *The Presocratic Philosophers*, 2nd edn (Cambridge, 1983), p. 211; Leo, 'The Editor's Observatory', 8/3, p. 95; Leo, *The Art of Synthesis*, pp. 134–41.

[33]　Alan Leo, *How to Judge a Nativity* (London, 1922), p. 35; Leo, 'The Editor's Observatory', 8/3, p. 95; Leo, *The Art of Synthesis*, pp. 134–41; Howard Sasportas, *The Gods of Change: Pains, Crisis and the Transits of Uranus, Neptune and Pluto* (London,

Sooner or later it must be realised that character is destiny. That is why so much stress is always laid upon the fact that the nativity must be fully understood before 'directions' [a form of predictive technique] can be interpreted. We each bring our character with us as a result of past efforts, aspirations and opportunity.[34]

We should pause for a moment to absorb the implications of Leo's statement. He was issuing an absolute, unconditional manifesto that the function of astrology is self-knowledge, and that prediction of the future only makes sense once the individual's level of self-knowledge has been established. Leo enrolled two other traditional aphorisms in support of his free-will hypothesis; the first was 'the stars incline, they do not compel', the second, 'the wise man rules his stars, the fool obeys them', announcing himself to be a believer in free will.[35] Astrology's immediate purpose, he argued, must therefore be self-understanding, the goal being, as Annie Besant helpfully put it, to 're-act … on circumstances, remoulding and reshaping them', changing the world and introducing 'far-reaching changes into the life-map drawn from the horoscope at birth'.[36] Prediction, by inference, is useless, at least for individuals who have developed self-awareness and free will. Paradoxically, the pursuit of astrology-as-spiritual-awareness therefore assists liberation from the universe of astrology-as-fated-causes. Blavatsky's infallible astrology dealt with spiritual truths, which it could identify with absolute certainty, but not with predictive accuracy. The absolute confidence in astrology as an aid to spiritual growth was linked to the idea that spiritual certainty was necessarily matched by uncertainty in one's normal daily affairs. Besant helpfully explained that,

> as the power of the Spirit, the Inner Ruler Immortal, passing in ever increasing measure out of latency in potency, so did the future become more and more inscrutable by means of ordinary rules, since the emergent new forces brought about their necessary results in fashions well nigh incalculable by most Astrologers.[37]

Accurate prediction of the future is therefore, to all intents and purposes, not just useless, but impossible. This is not a complete break with astrological tradition. Far from it. The Neoplatonic astrologers of the late classical period and the Renaissance would all have understood this well enough, and Guido Bonatti, perhaps the most important of medieval astrological authors, insisted that accurate astrological judgement was impossible without a combination of self-awareness and divine

---

1989), pp. 4–5; Arthur Mee, 'The Divine Use of Astrology', in Bessie Leo (ed.), *The Life and Work of Alan Leo* (London, 1919), p. 156.

[34] Leo, *How to Judge a Nativity*, p. 35.
[35] Leo, 'The Editor's Observatory', 8/3, p. 95.
[36] Besant, 'An Appreciation', pp. 8–9.
[37] Besant, 'An Appreciation', p. 9.

intervention.[38] In the philosophical sense, then, Heelas' detraditionalisation hypothesis has to be questioned: there was a direct continuity between Leo's theosophy and the tradition of esoteric, Hermetic thought, extending in a direct literary lineage back to Hellenistic Egypt and located in Orphic and Gnostic concepts of the inner divine. The theosophical revolution in astrology saw the restoration of a previous status quo. Yet, having been restored, its previous truths were transformed and the consequences of Leo's promotion of reincarnation (which had been unacceptable to Renaissance Neoplatonists) produced an entirely new genre of astrology in which one's past and future lives might be described in precise detail.[39]

The new esoteric, spiritual-psychological astrology, Leo believed, represented the future of the discipline, and it was his urgent task to create it. Leo announced his historically driven millenarian task: 'I am actuated by the primary motive of expressing what I believe to be the true Astrology, for the new Era that is now dawning upon the world'.[40] He could not have been clearer in setting out his reforming, modernising mission. Yet his modernity looked back to the past and cannot be understood without it. To build a new future which incorporated imagined, long-past Utopias is, of course, a standard feature of millenarianism. Leo followed Blavatskyan Neoplatonic, Gnostic cosmology in every detail. All souls, he wrote, are a 'Divine Fragment' of 'the great Being whom men ordinarily call God – the God of this system – and whom theosophists often refer to as the Solar Logos', and of whom they were once part.[41] Through successive incarnations, souls then descend lower and lower into matter and, as they do, so the inner light becomes so blurred that the memory of the soul's origin is almost obscured. Following Blavatsky, he believed that humanity was at the lowest, half-way point of its evolutionary cycle, the fifth sub-race of the fifth root race. The Age of Aquarius, he argued, would begin with the messianic arrival of the new world Teacher.[42] This would then inaugurate the evolutionary shift back to spirituality and humanity's long-term return to God, the Neoplatonic Solar Logos. Urgency was added by the fact that the souls of future eras were already beginning to incarnate.[43] In addition, what the theosophical astrologer Oliver Lowe called the 'Intelligences at the back of things', Besant the 'the Great Beings who are the Guardians of Humanity and the Teachers of the individual Souls', and Leo 'devas and planetary spirits' were

---

[38]   Campion, *A History of Western Astrology*, vol. 1, ch. 16; and ibid., vol. 2, ch. 7; Guido Bonatti, 'The One Hundred and Forty-Six Considerations of the Famous Astrologer Guido Bonatus', trans. Henry Coley, *The Astrologer's Guide* (London, 1986), nos 1 and 2, pp. 1–2.

[39]   Steven Forrest and Jeffrey Wolf Green, *Measuring the Night: Evolutionary Astrology and the Keys to the Soul* (Boulder CO, 2000).

[40]   Leo, *Esoteric Astrology*, p. v.

[41]   Leo, *The Art of Synthesis*, p. 1.

[42]   Leo, *Esoteric Astrology*, p. 116.

[43]   Oliver Lowe, 'Astrology as an Aid in the Education of Children', *Modern Astrology*, New Series, 8/10 (1911), p. 406.

encouraging the use of astrology to guide humanity through the current crisis.[44] The higher beings, those who knew what was best for humanity, understood that astrology could help ease the transition into the New Age and minimise the risk of violent crisis. The crucial stages in the historical process might therefore be better understood within the context of his essentially spiritual understanding of precession of the equinoxes: the zodiac, Leo wrote with a deliberate invocation of Christian imagery, 'is the book of life that is read on Judgement Day'.[45] Leo was actually present in India for the Theosophical Society's foundation of the Order of the Star in the East under the leadership of Jiddu Krishnamurti, in order to make preparations for the great spiritual Teacher's arrival, and he became convinced that the Age of Aquarius was to begin on 21 March 1928.[46]

The core features of Leo's esoteric astrology were drawn partly from Neoplatonism: the doctrine of correspondences (as expressed in the Hermetic maxim 'as above so below') was a revival of Hermetic angelology mediated through theosophy, in which humanity is surrounded by invisible beings with superior powers and the zodiac provides a 'book' in which divine plans can be read, using astrology as a language.[47] His primary contribution to practical astrology was his maximising of the importance of psychological delineation and his minimising of the relevance of prediction, in the process dramatically simplifying the technical procedures of interpretation.[48] Relying on the notion that the soul is superior to the body and that the planets have essentially spiritual natures, he argued that planets therefore 'manifest', as they would in a Neoplatonic model, through the individual life.[49]

Alan Leo was not alone. There were other esoterically minded astrologers in both the UK and the US, but his influence can only be matched by two other individuals, Alice Bailey and her student, Dane Rudhyar. Like Alan Leo, Bailey came from a profoundly conservative UK Christian background. In 1915 she came into contact with theosophy, began studying works such as *The Secret Doctrine* and Annie Besant's *A Study in Consciousness*, and began teaching for the Theosophical Lodge in Pacific Grove, California.[50] In 1917 she moved

---

[44]   Lowe, 'Astrology as an Aid', p. 406; Besant, 'An Appreciation', p. 9; Leo, *Esoteric Astrology*, pp. 122–8, see also p. 63.

[45]   Leo, *Esoteric Astrology*, p. 63.

[46]   For Leo on Krishnamurti see Leo, 'The Editor's Observatory', 8/10, pp. 397–8. See also Leo, 'The Editor's Observatory', 8/3, pp. 92–3; Alan Leo, 'The Editor's Observatory', *Modern Astrology*, New Series, 8/5 (1911), pp. 133–5. For the Age of Aquarius see Alan Leo, 'The Age of Aquarius', *Modern Astrology*, New Series, 8/7 (1911), p. 272.

[47]   For 'as above so below', see Leo, *Esoteric Astrology*, p. 122. For angelology see Leo, *Esoteric Astrology*, pp. 63, 120, 122–8; and for the zodiac as a book see Leo, *Esoteric Astrology*, p. 63.

[48]   See Maurice McCann, *The Sun and the Aspects* (London, 2002), pp. 60–70.

[49]   Leo, *Esoteric Astrology*, p. 187.

[50]   Alice A. Bailey, *The Unfinished Autobiography* (London, 1951), pp. 7–8.

to Krotona, near Hollywood, at the Theosophical Society's main cultural and missionary centre. There she met Foster Bailey, her second husband, long-term collaborator and, in 1919, National Secretary of the Theosophical Society. However, Bailey became disillusioned with what she found to be the authoritarian atmosphere at Krotona and she and her husband then embarked on the process of separating from the Theosophical Society and setting up their own classes which, in April 1923, became formalised as the Arcane School.[51]

Bailey had immense respect for esoteric astrology, which she regarded as 'one of the keys to *The Secret Doctrine*' and 'the purest presentation of occult truth in the world'.[52] She argued that it was absolutely essential to understand and prepare for the New Age, and hence for the entire great evolutionary shift in consciousness which she believed was then taking place.[53] Ultimately, she thought, esoteric astrology would reveal the true karma of the Heavenly Man, the incarnation of a Planetary Logos itself. Astrology, though, is not just one of a number of disciplines that might facilitate the individual's entry into the New Age. More than any other, it is crucial to the whole success of the apocalyptic enterprise. She wrote that 'The sequence of the Mysteries which each of the signs of the Zodiac embodies will be clarified for us by the Christ, because the public consciousness today demands something more definite and spiritually real than modern astrology, or all the pseudo-occultism so widely extant.'[54] Bailey, though, appears to have had little or no grasp of technical astrology and developed her own version based on a notion of spiritual rays and the inclusion of hypothetical planets.[55] It was left to her fellow theosophist and student in the Arcane School, Dane Rudhyar, to articulate her vision within mainstream astrology. Rudhyar was arguably the second most important astrologer in the twentieth-century English-speaking world after Leo, and certainly the most significant to emerge from the US. In the tribute published in the British *Astrological Journal* in 1985 to mark his ninetieth birthday, Layla Rael, Rudhyar's student, collaborator and wife, wrote that 'virtually no astrologer practising today is unaffected by Rudhyar's work'.[56] Aidan Kelly described Rudhyar as 'the leading figure in the movement that reoriented twentieth-century astrology from the prediction of events to its present emphasis on the analysis of personality'.[57] Others saw him as a prophet,

---

[51]   Bailey, *The Unfinished Autobiography*, pp. 158, 161, 193.

[52]   Alice A. Bailey, *A Treatise on Cosmic Fire* (London, 1925), p. 625; Alice A. Bailey, *Initiation, Human and Solar* (London, 1933), p. 19.

[53]   Alice A. Bailey, *Esoteric Astrology* (London, 1973), p. 5.

[54]   Alice A. Bailey, *The Reappearance of the Christ* (New York, 1948), p. 127.

[55]   Bailey, *Esoteric Astrology*.

[56]   Layla Rael, 'Happy Birthday, Rudhyar, and Thanks', *Astrological Journal*, 27/2 (1985), p. 77.

[57]   Aidan Kelly, 'Dane Rudhyar', in James R. Lewis (ed.), *The Astrology Encyclopaedia* (Detroit, London and Washington, 1994), p. 458.

as the 'seed man for the New Age'.[58] For his followers he was himself one of the souls who incarnated in order to guide humanity to its glorious future.

If only because of its sheer scope – some twenty books and around a thousand articles – Rudhyar's published work constitutes as great an application of theosophy's broad principles to astrology as do Leo's. He was driven by the same sense of urgency as Leo, a sense of mission which arose from his belief that the upheavals of the twentieth century were the final prelude, the Baileyite 'seed period', necessary to prepare for the New Age which, as the Age of Aquarius, he thought was to finally commence in 2162.[59] They are also influential in the wider New Age movement, partly through the writings of David Spangler and Jose Arguelles (who was almost single-handedly responsible for stating the apocalyptic fervour over the supposed end of the Mayan calendar in 2012), who endorsed Rudhyar's 1974 book, *An Astrological Mandala*. Arguelles wrote that the book was 'invaluable ... for every person seriously interested in symbols as a medium for achieving the kind of transformation necessary to bring about the "new age"'. Rudhyar was also one of the few astrologers to be recommended in the wider literature of the New Age *sensu stricto*, receiving an endorsement in 1976 from David Spangler, who recommended two of his books, *The Planetarization of Consciousness* and *Occult Preparations for a New Age*.[60]

Rudhyar's major contribution was to take Leo's theosophical astrology forward by one important logical step. While Leo believed he was developing a psychological astrology, writing in the 1890s and 1910s prior to the translation into English of the emerging work on psychoanalysis, he lacked the language of depth psychology. As we have seen, his psychology, like Blavatsky's, concerned the psyche as soul rather than as a set of internal processes. Jung, who did so much to create a psychology that could be applied to astrology, was studying the subject only in 1910, close to the end of Leo's career.[61] By the time Rudhyar began writing in 1930, though, Jung's early works were available in English.

[58]   Alexander Ruperti, 'Dane Rudhyar (March 23, 1895 – September 13, 1985): Seed-Man for the New Era', *Astrological Journal*, 33/2 (1986), p. 55; see also Stephen Arroyo, *Astrology, Karma and Transformation: The Inner Dimensions of the Birth Chart* (Davis CA, 1975), p. 41; Barbara Somerfield, 'To Dane Rudhyar, Who Inspired my First Steps on the Path with Loving Gratitude for his Sustainment, In Memorium', *Welcome to Planet Earth*, 14/10 (1995), p. 56; Greg Bogart, 'Rudhyar's Astrology in Plain Language', *International Astrologer*, 31/4 (2002), p. 30. Also see Deniz Ertan, *Dane Rudhyar: His Music, Thought, and Art* (University of Rochester Press, 2009).

[59]   Dane Rudhyar, *Astrological Timing: The Transition to the New Age* (San Francisco, New York and London, 1972), p. 135.

[60]   Daivd Spangler, 'Revelation – Birth of a New Age', in William Bloom, *The New Age: An Anthology of Essential Writings* (London, 1991), p. 180. See also p. 211.

[61]   C.G. Jung, 'Jung to Freud, 12 June 1911', in Gerhard Adler et al. (eds), *Letters 1906–1950* (Princeton, 1992); Roderick Main, *Jung on Synchronicity and the Paranormal* (London, 1997), p. 79.

Rudhyar's early articles, from 1931 onwards, represent the first comprehensive application of Jungian principles and depth psychology to astrology in the English-speaking world. These were then read by Alice Bailey, who suggested that her Lucis Trust publish them in book form as *The Astrology of Personality* in 1936. Paul Clancy, *American Astrology*'s editor, described this book as 'the greatest step forward in Astrology since the time of Ptolemy'. Echoing Leo's reference to the 'new aera', Rudhyar claimed, with an astonishing faith in his own powers, that it 'represented the birth of a new epoch'.[62] More cautiously, the *Larousse Encyclopaedia of Astrology* considered that the book 'is generally acknowledged to be a classic'.[63]

In 1974, 38 years after its publication, the book was voted second in 'a survey of 100–200 opinions on "The 7 Best Books in Astrology"'.[64] In 1970 Rudhyar himself remarked that his outlook in 1934–35 had been so heavily theosophical that, had he written *The Astrology of Personality* in 1970, he would have formulated some of his interpretations differently. Yet the publication of *Occult Preparations for a New Age* in 1975 stood as the enduring testimony of Blavataskyan eschatology as a central theme in his thought. There is no real evidence in his writing that his adherence to theosophical teachings ever diminished. Rudhyar's importance lies not in his incorporation of theosophical principles into astrology, for Leo had been there first, but in his use of depth psychology to reinforce the importance of self-awareness, and his role as a propagandist and populariser of the notion that astrology's primary function is as a spiritual preparation for the New Age. So successful was he that by the 1980s he was revered by astrologers throughout the Western world.

Rudhyar's impact was described by his late wife, Leyla Rael, in terms of the extent of the widespread acceptance of his ideas by astrologers in the 1980s. She wrote that 'Today, even the most event-oriented astrologer ... *counsels* clients – that is to say, points out the client's responsibility, indeed purpose in life, to grow and learn from whatever happens, however dire or sublime.'[65] There was one further implication of Rudhyar's work for astrology: a profound relativism. 'Each individual', he wrote, 'is in a very real sense the center of his own universe. It is the way he orients himself to the universe as a whole that matters.'[66] The individual's concerns in Rudhyar's new 'person-centred astrology' were more important than the rules of astrology.[67] While there was, Rudhyar conceded, an astrology which might govern people's lives and might therefore be subject to scientific proof, this

---

[62]   Dane Rudhyar, *Occult Preparations for a New Age* (Madras and London, 1975), p. 77.

[63]   Jean Louis Brau, Helen Weaver and Allan Edmunds, *Larousse Encyclopaedia of Astrology* (New York, 1982), p. 244.

[64]   Dean and Mather, *Recent Advances*, p. 3.

[65]   Rael, 'Happy Birthday', p. 77; see also Greene and Sasportas, *Development*, p. xii.

[66]   Dane Rudhyar, *The Astrology of Personality* (New York, 1970), p. xii.

[67]   Dane Rudhyar, *Person Centered Astrology* (New York, 1980).

applied only to people who were not in control of their lives. The astrology which he advocated consisted of a set of symbols which could be used to encourage spiritual evolution. In 1936 he wrote:

> Astrology of itself has no more meaning than algebra. It measures relationships between symbols whose concreteness is entirely a matter of convention, and does not really enter into the problems involved – just as the symbols of algebra, x, y, n, are mere conventions ... In other words, the astrological realm of moving celestial bodies is like the realm of logical propositions. Neither one nor the other has any real content. Both are purely formal, symbolical, and conventional ...[68]

The legacy of the two devout New Agers Alan Leo and Dane Rudhyar is evident throughout modern astrological literature.[69] Rudhyar's legacy, though, has followed different paths, and there is a fundamental difference between the ideas of leading contemporary American astrologers such as Alan Oken and Stephen Arroyo, both of whom are deeply influenced by Rudhyar and both of whose books were regarded as seminal texts in the 1970s and 1980s – and still are.[70] Both Oken and Arroyo follow the tradition set out by Rudhyar, but Oken's emphasis is more theosophical and Baileyite, while Arroyo leans to the psychological and Jungian, although both would recognise the shared description 'spiritual'. The psychological form tends to be, as Curry observed, dominant, and most contemporary astrology may be better described as psychological rather than spiritual because it deals with the question 'what am I like?' rather than 'what is the state of my soul?'[71] That said, modern astrological literature is awaiting academic scrutiny. The primary philosophical distinction between the two models is that, whereas in spiritual, esoteric astrology the soul is represented in the birth chart, and may be described in great detail, in psychological astrology the soul is converted into the 'Self' and is regarded as being a higher faculty, the source of free will, and may be outside the chart.[72] That

[68] Rudhyar, *The Astrology of Personality*, p. 48.

[69] Nicholas Campion, 'Prophecy, Cosmology and the New Age Movement: The Extent and Nature of Contemporary Belief in Astrology', PhD thesis, University of the West of England, 2004, pp. 124–8.

[70] Stephen Arroyo, *Astrology, Psychology and the Four Elements: An Energy Approach to Astrology and its Use in the Counselling Arts* (Davis CA, 1975); Arroyo, *The Inner Dimensions*; Alan Oken, *As Above, So Below: A Primary Guide to Astrological Awareness* (New York, 1973); Alan Oken, *The Horoscope, the Road and its Traveller: A Manual of Consciousness Expansion through Astrology* (New York, 1974); Alan Oken, *Astrology: Evolution and Revolution, a Path to Higher Consciousness through Astrology* (New York, 1976); Alan Oken, *Soul-Centred Astrology: A Key to Your Expanding Self* (New York, 1990).

[71] Curry, *A Confusion*, p. 116.

[72] Liz Greene, *Relating: An Astrological Guide to Living with Others on a Small Planet* (London, 1977), pp. 25–6; Mayo, *Teach Yourself Astrology*, p. 6; Sasportas, *The*

is, there is a source of individual free will which cannot be described, influenced or pressurised by the planets.

It is clear, then, that there is no one single entity as 'New Age' astrology. Rather there are two types, one that emphasises spiritual evolution and another that concentrates on personal development. The former is devoted to the coming of the New Age as an imminent, real event, whereas, for the latter, the New Age is primarily a motif for the current historical shift or, in Sutcliffe's terms, an 'emblem'.[73] Within Hanegraaff's typology, esoteric astrology may be considered New Age *sensu stricto*, while psychological astrology begins to move towards the New Age *sensu lato*. There is also a distinction to be made between a psychological astrology which is more descriptive, which talks of the way people are, and one which is more dynamic, presupposing personal growth and what people can become.[74] Yet the two can recognise each other. For example, Margaret Hone, a prime representative of the former, and Dane Rudhyar, the principle advocate of the latter, were friends and admired each other's work.[75] We might also consider that while Leo and Rudhyar were absolutely concerned with facilitating individual preparation for the New Age, those influenced by them may not be.

The core task of the Aquarian Age astrologer was outlined by Melanie Reinhart in 1987. She argued that,

> in order to relate with feeling to a client and to follow the lead of the healing process itself, one needs to … simply be with someone, listen carefully to what they say, observe carefully how they are and what they do without the need to 'make it better', interpret, or change anything. This depends not on a large vocabulary of astrological concepts and psychological techniques, but on the astrologer's self-knowledge, self-acceptance and continuing relationship with his or her own unconscious.[76]

Gods of Change, pp. 6–7.

[73] For New Age as an imminent, real event see, for example, Oken, *As Above, So Below*; Oken, *The Horoscope*; as a motif for the current historical shift see for example Greene, *Relating*; Stuart Sutcliffe, *Children of the New Age: A History of Spiritual Practices* (London, 2003), p. 9.

[74] For a descriptive psychological astrology see, for example, Charles Carter, *An Encyclopaedia of Psychological Astrology* (London, 1977), and for a dynamic psychological astrology see, for example, Greene and Sasportas, *Development*; Liz Greene and Howard Sasportas, *The Dynamics of the Unconscious: Seminars in Psychological Astrology* (London, 1988).

[75] Hone, *Textbook*, pp. 19–20; Dane Rudhyar, *The Practice of Astrology as a Technique in Human Understanding* (New York, 1975).

[76] Melanie Reinhart, 'In the Shadows of the Age of Aquarius', *Astrological Journal*, 29/3 (1987), p. 113.

At the heart, then, of the ideology of New Age astrology lies Heelas's 'self-ethic'.[77] The penetration of New Age ideology – its eclecticism, universalism, use of magic and emphasis on the soul – into astrology, including books aimed at a mass market, is profound. For example, Terry Lamb's *Born Together: Love Relationships, Astrology and the Soul* defines the purpose of astrology as 'to help us know our True Self, to find our connection with the Divine, and to know ourselves as part of the source', while 'Aries goes to the deepest of levels – back to the Source itself' and 'Capricornians are looking for the keys to the cosmos'.[78] Liz Greene's *Astrology for Lovers* couched sun-sign readings in terms of the psychological interpretation of myth and the development of one's future potential, and her introduction of such concepts into the mass sun-sign literature was followed by a series of imitators.[79] Typical were Sheila Geddes's *Self-Development with Astrology* and Janice Huntley's *The Elements of Astrology*, a guide to learning astrology, which was aimed at the popular market, both published in 1990. Huntley wrote that the sun 'rules our ego and individuality, often the deepest, innermost part of our character, which can be hidden from view. We relate to our Sun sign as being our true self, and should strive to achieve the positive characteristics of this sign in order to be living a fulfilled life.'[80]

The activist view, in a Popperian sense, meanwhile, was summarised by Donna Cunningham in 1978:

> To believe that you are being buffeted by Pluto or held back by some bad aspect is very short-sighted ... every difficult thing in the chart can lead us to positive, constructive insights and actions that will help us move along on the spiritual path. We generally grow through the mastery of the adverse circumstances, inner conflicts and difficult times that we go through. With that in mind, you can regard difficult aspects, transits, and sign placements as opportunities to grow. The true usefulness of a chart, as I see it, is to get a better perspective on yourself, to appreciate your own individuality and potential, and to work toward your most positive expression of self. Your chart is only an instrument panel where you take readings on the course of your life. YOU ARE THE PILOT.[81]

In Cunningham's astrology, the Self is everything. Two questions necessarily arise from consideration of astrology's relationship to the New Age movement. The first is whether astrology in itself can be considered a New Age discipline. The second is whether astrology's contemporary popularity is a function of the rise of the New Age movement. There are subtleties, though, in these questions. For

[77]	Heelas, *New Age*, pp. 18, 23.
[78]	Terry Lamb, *Born to be Together: Love Relationships, Astrology, and the Soul* (Carlsbad, 1998), pp. 15, 63, 87.
[79]	Liz Greene, *Astrology for Lovers* (London, 1986).
[80]	Janice Huntley, *The Elements of Astrology* (Shaftsbury, 1990), p. 52.
[81]	Donna Cunningham, *An Astrological Guide to Self-Awareness* (Reno, 1978), p. 9.

example, Michael York points out that astrology's philosophical roots are classical, yet that it is the 'lingua franca' of New Age movement, which 'establishes itself on astrological nuance, metaphor and interpretation'.[82] Sutcliffe, meanwhile, acknowledges astrology's significance as the popular wing of the occult and esoteric revival of the early twentieth century.[83]

There is, though, no consensus amongst astrologers either on the date or desirability of the coming of the Age of Aquarius, and within the prevailing belief in the Age, there is also an overt anti-New Age tendency, as identified by Shoshanah Feher. That is, if there is a New Age astrology, there may also be a non-New Age one. For example, James Holden argued that although 'throughout the ages some people who were devotees of a particular philosophy or religion, and some who practiced magic have also been interested in astrology', he concluded that 'this does not mean that astrology itself has anything to do with religion or magic, or, for that matter, with "New Age" thought'.[84] There was opposition to Leo's theosophical reform programme from its inception in the 1900s from astrologers who resented what they saw as his entirely inappropriate attempt to impose his theosophical conceptions on astrology.[85] In addition, some theosophical astrologers, notably Sepharial, considered that astrology was self-sufficient and had no need of theosophical input; a point of view represented more recently by Dennis Elwell.[86] The distinction between two types of astrology was also recognised in the astrological literature in 1987 by Liz Greene and Howard Sasportas, who were of the opinion that the psychological branch was expanding at the expense of the event-predicting, character-describing version.[87] However, the 1980s saw a reaction against the dominance of post-New Age psychological astrology in the so-called 'traditional revival' which harked back to the apparent technical certainties, although not the esotericism, of medieval and Hellenistic astrology.[88] Nevertheless, even amongst those who reject New Age

---

[82] Michael York, *Historical Dictionary of New Age Movements* (Lanham MD, 2003), pp. 25–6.

[83] Sutcliffe, *Children of the New Age*, pp. 28, 36–7.

[84] James Herschel Holden, *A History of Horoscopic Astrology* (Tempe AZ, 1996), p. 261.

[85] Alan Leo, 'The Editor's Observatory: Modern Astrology's Coming-of-Age', *Modern Astrology*, New Series, 8/8 (1911), p. 310; Margaret Matthews, 'Dogmatism', *Modern Astrology*, New Series, 8/6 (1911), p. 263; Daniel Naylor Smith, 'Astrology and Theosophy', *Modern Astrology*, New Series, 8/9 (1911), p. 396.

[86] Dennis Elwell, 'Astrology: An Alternative Reality', *Astrological Journal*, 28/4 (1986), pp. 143–9. For Sepharial see Kim Farnell, *The Astral Tramp: A Biography of Sepharial* (London, 1998), pp. 34–5; Curry, *A Confusion*, p. 161.

[87] Greene and Sasportas, *Development*, p. xi.

[88] Nicholas Campion, 'Editorial', *Astrological Journal*, 36/1 (1994), p. 3; Olivia Barclay, 'Memoirs of a Horary Astrology', *Astrology Quarterly*, 'Chapter 1', 69/1 (1998/99), pp. 6–11; 'Chapter 2', 69/3 (1999), pp. 36–44; 'Chapter 3', 69/4 (1999), pp. 23–8; 'Chapter 4', 70/1 (1999/2000), pp. 42–50.

affiliation there is strong evidence of an adherence, if not to New Age ideology, to its Neoplatonic ancestry. Elwell, for example, cited Rudolf Steiner while Olivia Barclay, one of the leading figures of the traditional revival, argued for the unity of the 'Inner Spirit' with the universe and claimed that astrology demonstrated the 'Oneness of Life'; however, she insisted that such ideas had nothing to do with practical astrology.[89] Thus the issue would appear to be primarily one of rhetorical positions adopted in order to show hostility to the New Age, rather than any real philosophical distinction. As Robert Wallis has observed, 'neo-Shamans and Pagans often use New Age as a derogatory term, denoting a shallow, woolly approach to spirituality, with one Pagan suggesting "newage" be pronounced "rather unkindly, as in 'sewage'"'.[90] The same tendency may be evident amongst astrologers who have nevertheless adopted aspects of New Age ideology, or who share the esoteric currents from which New Age thought is descended.

The position is complex. However, the bold statement that astrology is New Age is quite simply wrong. Instead we encounter a plurality of views and positions. Alan Leo's devout belief in the coming of the New Age encouraged him in his development of a 'New Age' astrology which was philosophically Neoplatonic and Hermetic, so hardly new at all. His simplified technical astrology, though, was innovative, and can be termed New Age, for want of a better term. Charles Carter, though, who bought into Leo's Neoplatonic Hermeticism, despised belief in the New Age. Then there is a third group, like Olivia Barclay, who rejected all modern astrology on both philosophical and technical grounds, yet shared Leo and Carter's Neoplatonism. For the sake of argument, though, if there is such a creature as New Age astrology, embodied in Leo and Rudhyar's teachings, it has the following distinctive theoretical qualities: it holds that spiritual realities are more important than material ones, that humanity is evolving spiritually as the New Age approaches, and that individuals are obliged to assist this evolutionary process by developing self-awareness and responsibility for their actions. Self-spirituality is present, but limited, for ultimately the purpose of self-development is submission to the forces of cosmic evolution. The development of the self is a transformational stage towards its ultimate loss through its absorption into the universe.

---

[89]   Dennis Elwell, *Cosmic Loom: The New Science of Astrology* (London, 1987), pp. 40–2, 54–5, 106–7; Olivia Barclay, *Horary Astrology Rediscovered* (West Chester PA, 1990), p. 19.

[90]   Robert J. Wallis, *Shamans/Neo-Shamans: Ecstasy, Alternative Archaeologies and Contemporary Pagans* (London, 2003), p. 29; see also Joanne Pearson, 'Assumed Affinities: Wicca and the New Age', in Joanne Pearson, Richard H. Roberts and Geoffrey Samuel (eds), *Nature Religion Today: Paganism in the Modern World* (Edinburgh, 1998).

Chapter 7

Oracles to the Vulgar: Sun-Sign Astrology

There is but One Life within the Universe – The Supreme Life of God, streaming through the Sun.[1]

The main vehicle for the transmission of popular astrology is the horoscope column, the familiar feature of popular newspapers, women's magazines and now the World-Wide-Web, consisting of 12 paragraphs, one for each of the approximately 30-day periods when the sun occupies each of the signs of the zodiac.[2] The zodiac sign occupied by the sun at birth is known as the 'sun-sign' by astrologers, or frequently as the 'birth-sign' or 'star-sign' in public discourse. Hence the star-sign or sun-sign column has become a seemingly ubiquitous feature of modern popular culture. The existence of sun-sign columns has been a matter of some discomfort amongst many astrologers, and they have either been roundly condemned by the few, or dismissed as not 'proper' astrology by a considerable number (which begs the unanswered question – what is 'proper' astrology?).[3] Although the tensions appeared to have diminished in the twenty-first century, from the 1950s to 1990s the accusations were often bitter, with those who wrote columns being accused of prostituting their art, and many astrologers blamed such columns for astrology's poor public reputation.[4] Whatever the case, sun-sign columns are generally taken as representative of astrology as a whole in the public mind.[5] Within astrological

---

[1]   Alan Leo, *The Art of Synthesis* (London, 1936), p. xix; see also pp. 126–7.

[2]   Nicholas Campion, 'Horoscopes and Popular Culture', in Bob Franklin (ed.), *Pulling Newspapers Apart: Analysing Print Journalism* (Oxford, 2008), pp. 253–61.

[3]   See the summary by Geoffrey Dean and Arthur Mather, 'Sun Sign Columns: An Armchair Invitation', *Astrological Journal*, 38/3 (1996), pp. 145–6, 150–2; see also Robin Heath, 'To Sun Sign or not to Sun Sign? (Is that Really the Question?)', *Astrological Journal*, 38/3 (1996), pp. 129–32.

[4]   Nicholas Campion, 'Prophecy, Cosmology and the New Age Movement: The Extent and Nature of Contemporary Belief in Astrology', PhD thesis, University of the West of England, 2004, pp. 132–3. See also Bernard Eccles, 'The Radical Nature of Sun-Sign Astrology', *Astrological Journal*, 38/5 (September/October 1996), pp. 306–310; Roger Elliot, 'Notes', *Astrological Journal*, 32/2 (March/April 1990), pp. 87–88; Michael Harding, 'Response to Roger Eliot's Views in "Notes"', *Astrological Journal*, 32/2 (March/April 1990), pp. 89–91; Ronald Harvey, 'Scientists and Sun-Signs', *Astrological Journal*, 38/5 (September/October 1996), pp. 339–340.

[5]   Charles Harvey, 'Town v Gown', *Astrological Journal*, 16/1 (1973–74), p. 39.

discourse as a whole, sun-sign columns are best understood as a modern form of what Patrick Curry termed 'low astrology', the astrology characterised by the simplified advice and dramatised predictions of the seventeenth-century almanacs, or what he pithily called 'oracles to the vulgar'.[6]

There are two types of sun-sign astrology which need to be distinguished, even though they are not unrelated. First there are the sun-signs as descriptions of character, as encouraged and developed by Alan Leo as part of his simplifying, modernising mission. Leo, Kim Farnell has shown, was working within a nineteenth-century tradition, but he was undoubtedly responsible for embedding the notion of the 'sun-signs' and their personalities in modern astrological consciousness.[7] It is rare to find an astrologer who does not talk publicly in terms of such generalisations, however complex the work they might do in private. All astrologers refer to their friends and colleagues by the zodiac shorthand of 'Arien', 'Taurean' and so on, even though, when criticised, they respond that there is far more to astrology than just the Sun: rhetoric and practice do not always coincide. Second, and more controversially, are the sun-sign columns. These 'horoscopes' are based on brief readings for individuals born with the sun in the respective signs of the zodiac and consisting of a combination of generalised advice and prediction. Both sun-sign character delineations and sun-sign forecasts are simplifications of astrology which allow it quickly and simply to relate to large groups of people, each individual being able to easily identify their astrological type from their date of birth. They are a highly effective means of communicating astrology to the general public, as admitted even by many of those astrologers who are uncomfortable with their existence. The wide dissemination of these columns has led to a popular identification of astrology as a whole with the birth-, sun- or star-sign; that is, the zodiac sign containing the sun at birth.[8] The question 'what's your sign?' was to become a classic 'chat-up' line in the 1960s, as even Dane Rudhyar, by then safe in his reputation as the leading New Age astrologer, acknowledged.[9]

However, the concept of the sun-sign would have been meaningless to any astrologer prior to the early twentieth century. My evidence suggests it did not catch on amongst the general public, at least in the UK, until the 1950s. The standard technical procedure for interpreting birth charts prior to Alan Leo's reform assigned the planets significance on the basis of series of complicated technical considerations which were derived from Hellenistic Egypt, had changed little since medieval times, and were reproduced as late as 1882.[10] Under this system the sun might actually turn out to be the most insignificant 'planet'. The dominant planet at

---

[6]   Patrick Curry, *Prophecy and Power: Astrology in Early Modern England* (Oxford, 1989), p. 157.

[7]   Kim Farnell, *Flirting with the Zodiac* (Bournemouth, 2007).

[8]   Harvey, 'Town v Gown', p. 39.

[9]   Dane Rudhyar, *The Astrology of Personality* (New York, 1970), p. viii.

[10]   Zadkiel, *Lilly's Astrology* (London, 1882).

birth might instead be Mars, say, or Saturn, or whatever planet 'ruled', according to classical dogma, the zodiac sign rising over the eastern horizon at the time of casting a horoscope. It was Alan Leo who radically reformed the interpretative procedures for the judgement of birth charts, making a series of revisions which were designed to simplify the techniques of interpretation, such as the planetary aspects, and moving the sun to the centre of astrological interpretation.[11]

The qualities of the zodiac signs themselves in Western astrology appear to have originated in Mesopotamia, the Near East and Hellenistic Egypt in the last four centuries BCE.[12] The earliest extant records date to the first and second centuries CE, particularly in the work of the Alexandrian astronomer Claudius Ptolemy in the second century. Ptolemy was primarily concerned with the systematic attribution of particular qualities to the zodiac signs in order to allow their use either in the analysis of individual horoscopes, or in the prediction of the consequences of specific actions. Aries was, for example, hot, dry and masculine, attributes which might be applied to description of character, the diagnosis and treatment of disease or the prediction of general events for the year.[13] The same accounts were repeated time and again in subsequent literature, as generations of astrologers copied each other. One typical nineteenth-century description of Aries was provided by Zadkiel, the leading British astrologer of the time, in his 1849 *Grammar of Astrology*. His account of the sign was brief, but what he did include was almost entirely physical, and contained only seven words of psychological delineation: 'This sign produces a dry, lean body, middle stature, strong limbs, large bones, long and meagre face, sharp sight, neck rather long and scraggy, dark eyebrows, swarthy complexion, hair reddish and wiry, thick shoulders; disposition, angry and violent as the ram.'[14]

Of the various aspects of Leo's reformed astrology, the most dramatic, in terms of the interpretation of the zodiac signs, was his discarding of almost the entire list of zodiacal attributes which had been accumulated from the first to the seventeenth century. In his opinion, these were of no use at all if people were to prepare for the New Age. He therefore set out to create a zodiacal astrology which would fulfil this purpose by encouraging people to reflect on their inner character, rather than measure the extent to which they conformed to a set of externally imposed criteria. Leo's description of Aries was typical. At almost four times the length of Zadkiel's version, Leo's completely ignored physical characteristics and set the tone for all future descriptions of the sign. Aries, he wrote,

---

[11]   For Leo's simplification of astrological technique see Maurice McCann, *The Sun and the Aspects* (London, 2002), pp. 66–70.

[12]   Nicholas Campion, *A History of Western Astrology* (2 vols, London, 2009), vol. 1, chs 5, 11, 13.

[13]   Claudius Ptolemy, *Tetrabiblos*, trans. F.E. Robbins (Cambridge MA, 1940), I.11–16.

[14]   Zadkiel, *The Grammar of Astrology* (London, 1849), p. 359.

represents undifferentiated consciousness. It is a chaotic and unorganised sign, in which impulse, spontaneity, and instinctiveness are marked features. Its vibrations are the keenest and most rapid, but without what may be called definite purpose, except towards impulsiveness and disruption. It signifies explosiveness, extravagance and all kinds of excess. Its influence is more directly connected with the animal kingdom, in which life is full and without the directive power of fully awakened self-consciousness.[15]

Such language was entirely innovatory. Certainly, Leo's description does contain the recognisable legacy of the classical and medieval canon, but was psychologised to the extent that Aries' traditional rulership of the head becomes 'a desire to be at the head and command'. The rulership of Aries by Mars, classical god of war, meanwhile, is responsible for the strong dose of martial qualities, 'force, combat, energy, strength and vigour ... enthusiastic, pioneering, ambitious, militant, enterprising, independent, assertive, and self-willed'. Blavatsky's physics are evident in the notion that the sign has 'vibrations', and her theory of evolution is represented by the concept that Arien consciousness is 'undifferentiated' and that its lack of 'fully-awakened self-consciousness' signifies its closeness to the animal kingdom. Leo had adapted Blavatskyan evolution to the notion of the tropical zodiac as a developmental cycle, commencing with Aries, the first sign and hence the point of creation and lowest point of evolution, and then rising to Pisces, the highest point. The concept of psychological growth was thereby written into the zodiac. If we examine Leo's astrology then, it overtly rejected classical astrology but retained some of its interpretative notions – such as Mars and Aries being aggressive; it is, in Heelas's terms, detraditionalised.

Leo's formulation of the zodiac signs' characters were to become the basis of most subsequent 'sun-sign' descriptions and, arguably, every description within the English-speaking world after 1945, with the exception of those associated with the 'traditional revival' of the 1980s onwards. Leo's description of the Arien character, for example, was repeated in most of the standard texts.[16] The Arien passage in Linda Goodman's best-seller from the 1970s, *Linda Goodman's Sun Signs*, illustrates the point. Leo's forceful impulsiveness and spontaneity became Goodman's 'forceful manner [and] firm handclasp' together with an imaginative warning to prepare for 'a dizzy dash around the mulberry tree', and his adaptation of Blavatskyan spiritual evolution to the zodiac cycle was evident in Goodman's statement that Aries 'represents birth, as Pisces represents death and consciousness of the soul. The ram is only conscious of himself'.[17] Thus theosophical cosmology, mediated through Leo's astrology as New Age

---

[15]   Alan Leo, *How to Judge a Nativity* (London, 1922), p. 17.

[16]   See, for example, Derek Parker and Julia Parker, *The Compleat Astrologer* (London, 1971), p. 106; Margaret Hone, *The Modern Textbook of Astrology* (London, 1973), pp. 48–50; Jeff Mayo, *Teach Yourself Astrology* (London, 1981), pp. 41–2.

[17]   Linda Goodman, *Linda Goodman's Sun Signs* (London, 1970), p. 3.

sensu stricto, was embedded into the text of what claims to be the biggest-selling sun-sign book of the twentieth century and therefore the principle work of late twentieth-century popular astrology. It does not follow from this that Goodman had any interest in the coming of the Age of Aquarius or, if she did, whether she considered it to be important. She was a vehicle for the transmission of New Age thought into the general population, converting astrology *sensu stricto* to *sensu lato*. Through Goodman New Age astrology became mainstream, as Heelas and Woodhead have argued that New Age as a whole has become mainstream.[18] She also established, en route, the potential profitability of the sun-sign books which dominated popular astrology publishing from the 1970s to 1990s.

However, although Leo's sun-sign astrology may be characterised as New Age without too much argument, like other forms of New Age discourse it is also deeply rooted in a continuous lineage which, in this case, can be traced directly back to the ancient world. Leo's insistence on the importance of the sun-sign was derived from Egyptian solar religion via the Hermetic teachings developed in Egypt in the second and third centuries CE, and filtered through Blavatsky. Hermetic cosmology held that God's benevolent powers flowed through the sun, the *Demiurge* ('craftsman'), described as the creator of our world, 'a mighty deity ... who is posted in the midst of the universe and watches over all things done on earth by men' and without whom there would be no physical life.[19]

When Blavatsky referred to the 'Central Spiritual Sun' she was, as she explicitly states, harking back to the Hermetic teachings.[20] 'In the shoreless ocean of space', she wrote, 'radiates, the central, spiritual and *Invisible* sun'.[21] The 'Hermetic axiom', she continued, maintains that our 'spirits ... incorruptible and eternal' both emanate from the 'eternal central sun' and 'will be reabsorbed by it at the end of time'.[22] She added that the material sun then 'shines for bodies' as 'the spiritual sun shines for souls'.[23] The sun, she added, drawing on Jowett's recent translation of Plato's *Timaeus*, neither emits heat nor exerts gravitational influence, but instead operates according to magnetism and becomes the lens through which the spiritual light of the invisible sun, or God, becomes visible.[24]

---

[18]   Paul Heelas, Linda Woodhead, Benjamin Seel, Karin Tusting and Bron Szerszynski, *The Spiritual Revolution: Why Religion is Giving Way to Spirituality* (Oxford, 2005).

[19]   Libellus XVI.17–19, in Walter Scott (trans.), *Hermetica: The Ancient Greek and Latin Writings which contain Religious or Philosophic Teachings Ascribed to Hermes Trismegistus* (4 vols, Boulder CO: Shambala, 1982), vol. 1, p. 273. Excerpt VII: Hermes to Tat.1, in Scott, *Hermetica*, vol. 1, p. 421. See also Asclepius 3b–4, I.10, in Scott, *Hermetica*, vol. 1, pp. 291, 305. For a summary see Garth Fowden, *The Egyptian Hermes: A Historical Approach to the Late Pagan Mind* (Princeton, 1986), p. 77.

[20]   H.P. Blavatsky, *The Secret Doctrine* (2 vols, Los Angeles, 1982), I.100.

[21]   H.P. Blavatsky, *Isis Unveiled* (2 vols, Pasadena, 1976), I.302.

[22]   Blavatsky, *Isis*, I.502.

[23]   Blavatsky, *Isis*, I. 324.

[24]   Blavatsky, *Isis*, I. 270–1; see also I.258.

The planets are also, being fragments of light, equivalent to the sun. Thus, when Blavatsky deliberately evoked Christian imagery, punning on the words 'sun' and 'son', she stated that the 'Sun-Sons', the stars and planets, are, like the sun, children of the 'Spiritual Sun'.[25]

Alan Leo's solar astrology, the foundation of all modern sun-sign psychology, was derived directly from Blavatsky's reformulation of Hermetic cosmology. In one of his most important works, *Esoteric Astrology*, Leo stated plainly that 'There is but One Life within the Universe – The Supreme Life of God, streaming through the Sun'.[26] Again following Blavatsky, he wrote that the planets are fragments of the sun and hence, like it, parts of the body of the 'Great Logos'.[27] The sun, as the 'life-giver' is the most important single factor in the birth chart, and the zodiac, Leo argued, should be seen less as the sun's path through the sky than a circle surrounding it; the sun's rays permeate the entire circle at once as its rays but pass through one particular sign at birth.[28] Then relying on Blavatsky's sun-son analogy, Leo laid the spiritual foundation for a new psychological astrology. He wrote that

> It is these rays of light and consciousness sent forth from the Sun that form the individualities of men and that make of them in very truth the Sons of God. For the Sun represents the great Sacrifice and sends forth individualities that will afterwards be drawn back in full self-consciousness to share that Bliss which is the essence of the Divine Nature.[29]

It was in another passage in *The Art of Synthesis*, published in 1904, though, that Leo set out the foundations for a technical revolution in twentieth-century astrology. He began by paraphrasing Blavatsky and then moved straight to the direct statement that the sun is the most important single feature in astrological interpretation:

> The Sun, then is a representative of our Solar Logos, whose sacrifice on a lower plane is a reflection of that on higher planes above.
>
> The Sun is the giver of the life-principle, or the breath of life, and when manifesting in the physical world the Sun represents the specialised life or 'Prana' in each separate individual. In all degrees of manifestation the Sun is the giver of life, spiritually, mentally, and physically, and it is therefore of vital and primary importance in all study of Astrology. It is the representative of the

---

[25]   Blavatsky, *Isis*, I.50, II. 463; Blavatsky, *The Secret Doctrine*, I.100, 400.

[26]   Leo, *The Art of Synthesis*, p. xix; see also pp. 126–7.

[27]   Alan Leo, *Esoteric Astrology: A Study in Human Nature* (London, 1925), pp. 126–7.

[28]   Leo, *The Art of Synthesis*, pp. 30–1.

[29]   Leo, *The Art of Synthesis*, p. 30.

One Life that permeates all things; and therefore careful study of the Sun and all that it denotes in a nativity is necessary before a sound judgment can be given.[30]

This single passage marked a profound shift in the technical procedures of astrological interpretation, perhaps as great a change as any since the development of the horoscope in the Hellenistic world. When Margaret Hone in 1951 described the Sun, she was deeply indebted to Leo. In the standard British astrological textbook of the 1950s–1980s, she wrote of the Sun:

> This is the most powerful of all the horoscopic factors. When considering a personal chart, the judgment of the type of person will depend largely on his solar characteristics ... The real underlying *self* will be largely shown by the placing of the Sun ... it is understood as the creative principle, the power-giving body, the personal self-expression. Its symbol is that of Eternity, and of the power of primal motion, from whence all else issued and was created.[31]

The use of the Sun for character analysis is, as we have seen, the first variety of sun-sign astrology. The second is its use for forecasting. Here again, there are ancient antecedents. It has been argued, for example, that there is a continuous practice of using the position of the sun 'as propitious or appropriate for various activities' dating back to Hellenistic astrology, around the fourth century BCE up to the nineteenth century.[32] The practice may be partly understood in terms of the so-called 'Egyptian days', a tradition imported into the Hellenistic world from Egypt in which days were considered variously lucky or unlucky.

From around 1850, the primary UK exemplar of 'low astrology', Raphael's *Prophetic Almanak*, included forecasts for the year ahead for individuals born on each day of the year, but not grouped together by zodiac sign.[33] By the early twentieth century, Cheiro, the society astrologer, was producing character descriptions and forecasts but with the different types grouped by month of birth, with absolutely no mention of zodiac sign.[34] By the 1940s, the English astrologer Edward Lyndoe was producing equivalent books in which knowledge of the zodiac signs was taken for granted.[35] Sometime between these two dates, the language of the signs had entered popular culture, even if it was not yet universally established.

The first such columns appear to have been published in the US, although the date is uncertain. A weekly feature of the type written by Naylor may have

---

[30]   Leo, *The Art of Synthesis*, pp. 30–1.

[31]   Hone, *Textbook*, pp. 24–5.

[32]   Ulla Koch-Westenholtz, *Mesopotamian Astrology: An Introduction to Babylonian and Assyrian Celestial Divination* (Copenhagen, 1995), p. 170.

[33]   Dean and Mather, 'Sun Sign Columns', p. 144.

[34]   Cheiro, *When Were You Born?* (London, 1913).

[35]   Edward Lyndoe, *Plan with the Planets* (London, 1949).

appeared in the *Boston Record* in 1931.[36] However, what is known is that the first regular 12-paragraph horoscope columns appeared in *American Astrology* magazine, written by the editor Paul Clancy (though published anonymously), from the first issue onwards.[37] Ken Irving, then editor of *American Astrology*, suggested to me in 2003 that it was Dane Rudhyar, on the basis of his own philosophical inclinations, who actually suggested the 12-paragraph format to Clancy.[38] Rudhyar had certainly inherited Blavatsky's respect for the spiritual sun. In 1938 he opened his second book, a detailed account of the planets and horoscope houses in terms of their potential for spiritual development, with a proclamation of the change of the ages:

> Today is a new birthday for the ancient gods ... New men call for new symbols. Their cry rises, beyond their logical intellects ashamed of mystical longings, for new gods to worship and to use in order to integrate their harrowing mental confusion and to stabilize their uprooted souls. Young gods, fresh and radiant with the sunshine of a new dawn, glorified with the 'golden light' of a new Sun of Power, ecstatic with virgin potentialities after the banishment of ancient nightmares.[39]

To rely on a mass market magazine as his first major vehicle was also consistent with the claim by Alexander Ruperti, Rudhyar's leading advocate, that Rudhyar used astrology much as Blavatsky used spiritualism – to reach the greatest number of people.[40] And the more people who could be reached through astrology, the more would be prepared for the New Age, all the better to convert the coming crisis into a peaceful transition. Clancy himself, according to Irving, had been producing such columns in his previous magazine, the Detroit-based *Modern Astrology*.[41] The format clearly had an immediate appeal. According to Carl Weschke, the president of Llewellyn, one of the largest publishers of New Age and popular astrology titles in the US, '"American Astrology" magazine's start was entirely based on Clancy's conviction that sun sign astrology would prove popular'.[42] Benedict Anderson's notion of imagined communities may also provide an insight. Anderson observed that the newspaper, being based on

---

[36]   Penelope McMillan, 'Horoscopes: Fans Bask in Sun Sign', *Los Angeles Times*, 5 July 1985.

[37]   'Personal Forecast', *American Astrology*, 1/1 (1933), pp. 11–15.

[38]   Ken Irving, personal communication, 10 October 2003.

[39]   Dane Rudhyar, *New Mansions for New Men* (New York, 1938), p. xiii.

[40]   Alexander Ruperti, 'Dane Rudhyar (March 23, 1895 – September 13, 1985): Seed-Man for the New Era', *Astrological Journal*, 33/2 (1986), p. 55.

[41]   Interview, Ken Irving, 8 September 2001. Clancy himself referred to a second previous magazine as *Popular Astrology*. See 'The Message of the Stars', *American Astrology*, 1/1 (1933), p. 6.

[42]   Personal communication, Carl Weschke, 4 May 2002.

a calendar date, one among an endless series of such dates, provides a sense that events reported on a particular date, however diverse, possess an imagined linkage.[43] The horoscope reader then finds a special relationship with the date, which is perceived to possess special significance, even more so because the reader becomes one of a 'family' born under a particular zodiac sign – as a family of Ariens, or Taureans, and so on. Horoscope columns then spread from the astrological media to the national press, including *The New York Post* in 1936 and the *Los Angeles Times*, whose columns for 1952–53 were critiqued by Theodor Adorno.[44] Whereas in the UK the publication of horoscope columns was hit by wartime newsprint shortages, the same problems were absent in the US. As Margaret Hone wrote, while the UK suffered, in the US 'great strides took place, because of the comparative ease with which astrological knowledge could be spread to the vast magazine reading public'.[45]

Aside from war-time disruption, though, developments in the US were paralleled in the UK, where the first modern newspaper astrology column was published in the *Sunday Express* on 24 August 1930, written by R.H. Naylor, an astrologer with no theosophical interests and no recorded interest in the New Age.[46] The *Express* had approached Cheiro and asked him to provide an analysis of the horoscope of the infant Princess Margaret, daughter of the Duke of York, later George VI, and younger sister of the future Elizabeth II. Cheiro, being too grand and too busy, declined and the feature was actually composed by his assistant, R.H. Naylor. Naylor included, along with an analysis of the Princess's birth chart, general political predictions and about fifty words per day of birthday predictions for each day of the coming week. The column, though, was not based on the 12-paragraph scheme apparently devised by *American Astrology*, a significant fact, for mention of the zodiac signs was absent: for a birthday prediction the reader need only know their date of birth, and not the relevant zodiac sign.

The newspaper was clearly delighted. The public response was immediately appreciative and the result was a repeat of the column on the following Sunday. An accompanying editorial note reported that 'enormous interest was aroused' in Naylor's predictions and treatment of the Princess's birth chart.[47] The potential increase in circulation clearly guaranteed support from the paper's editor and

---

[43]   Benedict Anderson, *Imagined Communities* (London, 2006).

[44]   McMillan, 'Horoscopes', p. 3; Theodor Adorno, *The Stars Down to Earth* (London, 1994), pp. 34–127.

[45]   Hone, *Textbook*, p. 296. See also Ellic Howe, *Urania's Children: The Strange World of the Astrologers* (London, 1967), p. 69.

[46]   R.H. Naylor, 'What the stars foretell for the new Princess and a few hints on the happenings of this week', *Sunday Express*, 24 August 1930, p. 11; Campion, 'Prophecy', pp. 142–5.

[47]   R.H. Naylor, 'Were you born in September?', *Sunday Express*, 31 August 1930, p. 7.

owner: the exercise was repeated a month later after which the column was published weekly, and only war-time pressures caused a break in publication.[48]

Arthur Christiansen, the entertainment editor of the *Express* who hired Naylor, later added his personal testimony. He wrote that 'Naylor and his horoscopes became a power in the land. If he said that Monday was a bad day for buying, then the buyers of more than one West End store waited for the stars to become more propitious.'[49] Naylor himself was in no doubt that he had initiated a popular revolution in astrology, claiming that his first column in August 1930 had been both 'the only worthwhile forward step in Astrology this century' and had 'entirely altered the orientation of the public mind towards astrology'.[50] The result, he added, was 'a widespread willingness to admit that there is or might be something in Astrology. An enormous potential market for horoscopes and Astrological literature was created.'[51] He was not the only astrologer to identify a change. In 1938 Charles Carter reminisced on developments in the astrological world since 1926, writing that 'The science itself has since then undergone a great change. A new race of astro-journalists has sprung up, popular astrological periodicals have come into existence, and the very small, but enthusiastic astrological world of my young days is no more.'[52]

In 1936 Naylor himself referred to the number of imitators in other newspapers, adding that, as a consequence, a 'flood of astrological literature … swept throughout the bookshops'.[53] It was clear though, that the language of the zodiac birth-signs was still unfamiliar as recently as the early 1930s. Initially Naylor did not use them and, in one of his first features, he gave a brief but painstaking introduction to the zodiac and its division into 12 sections.[54] By 1934 Naylor was introducing his readers to the sun-sign as a character type, including profiles for the sign of the month, featuring 'Mr' and 'Mrs Taurus' on 29 April 1934 but it is clear that the process of mass education was slow.

What is clear, though, is astrology's popularity, even if some editorial staff were slow to realise it. The *Daily Express* launched a daily column in 1934, four years after the Sunday version started, but with a much lower profile. It was anonymous and consisted of about 100 words for the birthday of the day and 20 words to sum up the day as a whole for all other readers. The feature, though, was regarded in some quarters as a major success. James Leigh, the editor of

---

[48]   R.H. Naylor, 'Were you born in October?', *Sunday Express*, 5 October 1930, p. 11; Howe, *Urania's Children*, p. 69.

[49]   Arthur Christiansen, *Headlines all my Life* (London, 1961), p. 65.

[50]   R.H. Naylor, 'What is the Future of Astrology', *Prediction*, 1/4 (1936), p. 151.

[51]   Naylor, 'What is the Future of Astrology', p. 151.

[52]   Charles Carter, 'Editorial', *Astrology*, 12/1 (1938), p. 1.

[53]   Naylor, 'What is the Future of Astrology', p. 151; R.H. Naylor, 'Star-Lore (1)', *Prediction*, 8/8 (1943), p. 24.

[54]   R.H. Naylor, 'What the stars foretell for this week', *Sunday Express*, 26 October 1930.

Prediction, reported on the public storm that took place when the paper went to press without its horoscope:

> The *Daily Express* will never again doubt the interest which its readers take in Astrology ... From 1 a.m. the newspaper was besieged by 'phone and personal enquiries indignantly demanding to know what had happened to the horoscope! A special staff team was delegated to deal with these queries. It spent several working days reading the horoscope over the telephone and sending proofs to readers who lived in the provinces ... the day when the horoscope was omitted will always be remembered, for it caused endless inconvenience in the office, and disturbed the peace of thousands of readers.[55]

Naylor himself wrote his first 12-paragraph sun-sign columns in 1936 when he became astrologer to *Prediction*. It was clear, however, that even amongst the readers of such a specialised magazine, there was little awareness of the zodiac signs. In the very first issue, in February, Naylor headed each paragraph as 'Sun in Aquarius', 'Sun in Pisces' and so on, adding the dates when the sun was in that sign. Yet in March the 12-paragraph column was dropped.[56] When it was revived in August the paragraphs were headed with the dates of birth, such as 'Born anywhere between January 21st and February 19th inclusive', followed by the zodiacal subheading in parentheses, such as '(THE AQUARIUS TYPE)'.[57] It seems clear that the language of birth-signs was not familiar and required a few words of explanation.

However, even this hesitant progress in the UK was aborted by war-time paper shortages, which seriously restricted the size of newspapers, and the sun-sign format was not fully adopted in the British press until 1955, a highly significant fact because it illustrates just how recently the language of zodiac signs entered vernacular culture.[58] While astrology, through almanacs and cunning folk had long been an established feature of the popular world view, the zodiac sign as a guide to one's personal destiny was not. One of my interviewees, a keen horoscope reader who was born in 1925, told me that she was not aware of birth-signs until 1955: she was a *Daily Express* reader and this was the year that the *Express* restored its regular horoscope column, restored after 14 years of paper rationing.

My conversations with editors of women's magazines in the UK in the 1980s and 1990s suggest that the horoscope column is considered an essential feature, and I was told on several occasions that the first freelance contributor to be hired for the launch of a new women's magazine is the astrologer. Even if this latter claim is an exaggeration, every single magazine aimed at women

---

[55]   James Leigh, 'Editorial', *Prediction*, 1/3 (1936), p. 98.

[56]   R.H. Naylor, 'Born in February?', *Prediction*, 1/1 (1936).

[57]   R.H. Naylor, 'Horoscopes for all Months', *Prediction*, 1/7 (1936), p. 16.

[58]   Howe, *Urania's Children*, p. 69; Hone, *Textbook*, p. 296; John Anthony West and Jan Gerhard Toonder, *The Case for Astrology* (London, 1973), p. 115.

and teenage girls in the UK carries a horoscope column. The U.K. mass-market 'tabloid' newspapers, the *Daily Mail*, the *Daily Express*, the *Daily Mirror*, the *Daily Star* and *The Sun* all carry daily horoscopes and, as print media move to the Web, so cyberspace has been colonised by horoscopes, often offered free as hooks for commercial services. In the 1990s, the greatest space devoted to any astrologer was given to Jonathan Cainer who was allocated a whole page in the *Daily Mirror* to publish his column and its associated features. On Sunday the publication of horoscopes in the UK extends periodically from the tabloids to the upmarket 'broadsheets' including *The Sunday Times*, the *Independent on Sunday*, the *Sunday Telegraph* and *The Observer*. The latter three papers, though, have an uneasy relationship with astrology, either giving it minimal space and promotion (*Independent on Sunday*), running a spoof column to compete with the genuine one (*Telegraph*) or periodically cancelling their column (*Observer*). Only *The Sunday Times* has taken advantage of the web to further promote its astrologer. At the level of mass popular culture represented by the tabloid newspapers and women's magazines, though, sun-sign astrology is considered an essential ingredient. The question is partly one of gender, but also of class.

Little attention has been paid to the appeal of horoscope columns. The claim that they are read 'for a laugh' doesn't really stand up because, as Richard Dawkins observed, they are not funny. Carl Weschke, interviewed in 2002, reflected a New Age perspective, considering that sun-sign astrology's mass appeal 'was all part of the adventure of self-knowledge. That is what was really new in the 20th century. Never before had there been any system that could be applied on a mass market basis that "revealed" one's self to oneself'.[59] The authority on the subject, though, has to be Dane Rudhyar, the format's possible inventor. In his view,

> The 'solar astrology' of popular astrology magazines and newspaper columns is oracular in that it is meant to convey to human beings, categorized according to the twelve Sun signs, general value judgments concerning the character of those responses to everyday circumstances which would be most suited to their basic temperament.[60]

Another leading theosophical astrologer, meanwhile, echoed Rudhyar and pointed to the sun-sign column's appeal as being to 'focus on the need to clarify one's individual identity'.[61] Shelley von Strunckel, who writes for *The Sunday*

[59]   Interview, Carl Weschke, 3 May 2002, 4 May 2002.

[60]   Dane Rudhyar, *An Astrological Mandala: The Cycle of Transformation and its 360 Symbolic Phases* (New York, 1974), p. 20.

[61]   Alan Oken, *Soul-Centered Astrology: A Key to Your Expanding Self* (New York, 1990), p. 11.

Times and the London *Evening Standard*, argues that astrology fulfils an unsatisfied public need for a contemplative, philosophical perspective:

> In our culture today, what we are pleased to call education doesn't go anywhere near anything about philosophy ... simple education doesn't teach people to observe how they think or to pause and be still. Therefore, part of the process in their ... reading a column, even something as short as an entry in the *Standard* ... is that an individual is introduced to this new way of being with their mind in which they step outside of themselves ... because most people don't know how to pause, so their appointment with their astrology column ... may be their only time in their life when they have stillness.[62]

This all somewhat mirrors Stuart Sutcliffe's sociological verdict that astrology addresses personal concerns while providing a metaphysical framework, converting the 'vast occult cosmologies' of Blavatsky, Jung and Gurdjieff into a form which 'could travel socially and speak both to everyday concerns of love and happiness and grand theories of meaningful coincidence'.[63] Different horoscope columns, though, have different styles. I asked Jonathan Cainer, current astrologer for the *Daily Mail* and past columnist for a series of UK newspapers, *Today*, the *Daily Mirror* and the *Daily Express*, about the source for his popularity. He replied,

> It's a cocktail. There's not one ingredient. It's a cocktail. That's how I think of it ... I meditate every day and that takes a bit of a discipline. Enough to leave me with this feeling of 'what do I do?' In that hour I spend my time trying not to be on the planet. Trying to be ... at one with the one single thing that goes on forever and ever and then I come out of it, generally speaking, with a sense of optimism and I think that's where my optimism comes from ... I am, one way and another, relentlessly optimistic ... So I can't bring myself to write a forecast that has got an edge of gloom to it and I think that's the one thing that people like. So somewhere between my spiritual view of life, which is 'stand back from everything, let it go and it will be alright', and my Sagittarian ebullience is that. And that I think is the factor that people like.[64]

As David Spangler wrote, 'The idea of the new age, as I see it is – and must be – an optimistic vision. It cannot be anything other.'[65] The key, though, for editors, is not philosophical content but popularity. Ken Irving, then *American Astrology*'s editor, who was in a position to evaluate the appeal of sun-signs as

---

[62] Interview, Shelley von Strunckel, 31 October 2002.

[63] Stuart Sutcliffe, *Children of the New Age: A History of Spiritual Practices* (London, 2003), p. 6.

[64] Interview, Jonathan Cainer, 8 September 2001.

[65] David Spangler, *The Rebirth of the Sacred* (London, 1984), p. 76.

opposed to a more detailed interest in astrology, estimated that when I spoke to him in 2001, around 75 per cent of the 110,000 who bought the magazine every month purchase it for the sun-sign columns. He added,

> The other 25% is perhaps three-fourths people who are mostly interested in sun signs but who know something about other aspects of astrology and are interested in reading about those, and then there is a very small portion, maybe from 5–10%, who are people who would read the magazine just for astrology. Learning about astrology. Finding out things they didn't know about it. And those people ... sort of tolerate the fact that the sun signs are there.[66]

Irving works in the specialist press. In the wider media Gill Hudson's view is typical. She has extensive experience of editing magazines both for women and men. She was the editor of *Company* from 1987 to 1991, *New Woman* from 1991 to 1994 and, later, *Radio Times*. When I spoke to her, she volunteered the opinion that, while the dominant modern religion is undoubtedly the 'consumer religion', 'there's a real need to find something more: "Is life only shopping?"'. People are still looking. You want to know that there's something more than the IKEA sofa. Astrology might offer a path to that "something more"'.[67] So, from one of the most successful UK editors of the late twentieth and early twenty-first centuries we have a powerful statement on the role of the horoscope column in women's magazines. From her perspective, astrology's popularity represents a clear reaction to consumerist religion, one which seeks an alternative to materialism in a quest for personal meaning. This takes us to another possible – and debateable – point: that astrology empowers disempowered groups. This is an adaptation of John Fiske's view that popular culture, far from being a means for ruling elites to keep the masses in a state of subservience, which is how Adorno saw astrology, provides a mean for ordinary people to assert their own identity against the dominant culture.[68] A feminist analysis would therefore see women's dominance as both providers and users of astrological services as a form of resistance against male-dominated culture.

A study of sun-sign astrology presents us with the same paradoxical narratives as we found in astrology as a whole. On the one hand sun-sign delineations are philosophically rooted in the religious context of sun-worship, and in Hermetic notions of the central spiritual sun, but they have little basis in the astrological interpretive tradition, being based largely on Alan Leo's self-conscious reform of astrology in the 1890s and 1910s. Sun-sign columns in turn were developed by astrologers out of the new astrology of sun-sign delineation, drawing its inspiration from the classical Hermetic texts. In this we need to distinguish Naylor, the inventor of the newspaper astrology column, from Rudhyar, the presumed inventor of the

---

[66]   Interview, Ken Irving, 8 September 2001.

[67]   Personal communication, Gill Hudson, 21 March 2000.

[68]   John Fiske, *Understanding Popular Culture* (London, 1989).

sun-sign format. Naylor's work can be located in an ancient tradition of lucky and unlucky days, but the sun-sign format, through Rudhyar, is theosophical. Certainly, some its high-profile authors, such as Shelly von Strunckel, appeal to a theosophical rationale. Both sun-sign delineations and sun-sign forecasts thus conform to Heelas's definition of New Age disciplines as 'detraditionalised' and, if we accept Gill Hudson's view, advocate 'self-spirituality'.[69] Indeed, it was this very break with the tradition that Charles Harvey, then President of the UK-based Astrological Association, used in his attack on sun-sign forecasts.[70] Further, in that Leo's reform of astrology was devoted to the need, as he saw it, to prepare for the Age of Aquarius, sun-sign astrology as a whole may be seen as a feature of New Age culture. Leo's entire body of work may be identified as belonging to Hanegraaff's New Age *sensu stricto*. However, in that neither sun-sign delineations post-Leo nor horoscope columns require any adherence to, or even knowledge of, the millenarian aspects of New Age culture, they may be better identified as belonging to Hanegraaff's New Age *sensu lato*. And lastly, if we refer back to Karl Popper, sun-sign columns, for Rudhyar, are a means of raising popular consciousness: they are, for the New Age activist, a means of converting pre-millennial chaos into post-millennial peace. This lofty purpose may be lost in the mundane drip-feed of lucky numbers, love and 'loot', but the intent remains. And there is also, we need to observe, a parallel with Ronald Hutton's account of the construction of Wicca as a deliberately invented religion with no relationship in either dogma or practice to any presumed early, organised, witchcraft religion but, instead, an affiliation with a magical tradition which can be traced back to ancient Egypt.[71] We can therefore see both sun-sign delineation and sun-sign columns as New Age in the wide, *sensu lato* meaning of the term, yet neither is necessarily so. Naylor, the great British populariser, certainly had no New Age sympathies and, even if Leo and Rudhyar were motivated entirely by the need to prepare for the New Age, there is no reason why either sun-sign delineations or columns need be directed to New Age purposes. Instead the remarkable feature of the recent history of sun-sign astrology is the speed with which it became a part of modern popular culture. In the UK we should shrink the period to ten years, from 1955 when the horoscope column became a regular and permanent feature of the post-war popular press, to the mid-sixties when the question (and frequently chat-up line) 'what's your sign' achieved widespread currency.

We need to make one more observation, though, that there is a coincidence in time between the rise of the sun-sign column in the 1930s and the popular awareness of the now apparently infinite size of the universe as a result of the discoveries of the 1920s. We can not draw a cause-and-effect relationship

---

[69]   Paul Heelas, *The New Age Movement* (Oxford, 1996), pp. 18, 23.

[70]   Harvey, 'Town v Gown', p. 39; see also Harding, 'Response'.

[71]   Ronald Hutton, 'Astral Magic: The Acceptable Face of Paganism', in Nicholas Campion, Patrick Curry and Michael York (eds), *Astrology and the Academy* (Bristol, 2004), pp. 10–24.

between these two phenomena, but as Edwin Hubble created a universe in which humanity was utterly insignificant, so Naylor domesticated it, bringing it down to such personal terms as the routine affairs of Mr and Mrs Taurus.[72] This was the point made by the novelist Martin Amis. After putting into one of his character's minds a series of thoughts about the incomprehensible magnitude of the universe, he asked, 'And what was astrology? Astrology was the *consecration* of the homocentric universe. Astrology went further than saying that the stars were all about *us*. Astrology said the stars were all about *me*.'[73]

[72] Campion, *A History of Western Astrology*, vol. 2, p. 262.
[73] Martin Amis, *The Information* (London, 1996), p. 437.

Chapter 8

An Evolutionary Paradox: The Survival of Belief in Astrology

Is there in this whole monstrous farrago no truth or value whatsoever? It appears that there is practically none.[1]

In 2001, the historian and cultural theorist Patrick Curry received an email from a journalist at *Time* magazine, who was preparing a major feature on astrology. Curry is not a practising astrologer. He knows how to calculate and read a horoscope but he has never taught astrology, does not write on it, and does not see clients. Far from it – the reason he was contacted is because he is the author of a number of respected academic works on the history and culture of astrology. The journalist's words are therefore telling: 'Please tell me a bit about yourself – background, career, your interest in astrology (are you a believer?). How did you initially get involved in astrology?'[2] We can see the absurdity of this question if we consider a historian of romantic literature, Islamic science, the nineteenth-century penal system or the Second World War being asked 'Do you believe in it? And yet the question is frequently asked of historians of astrology, with no suspicion on the part the questioner of why. In October 2010 I was called in my office at the University of Wales by a science journalist from a well-known UK Sunday newspaper who said: 'Let me put it bluntly. Do you BELIEVE in astrology?' The capitals are mine, but they convey the emphasis in the journalist's voice. My refusal to answer on the grounds that the question is inappropriate met with incomprehension and anger. The notion of astrology as inseparable from belief is deep and persistent, yet is in urgent need of critical examination. The question of why people should believe is also largely ignored, with rare exceptions.[3]

In spite of the lack of research in the area, most sociologists invariably consider astrology as a matter of 'belief', while astronomers tend to consider it as the product of 'faith' rather than, say, knowledge.[4] Yet there is currently no detailed consideration of the function of belief in astrology, or even whether it

---

[1] Edward Burnett Tylor, *Primitive Culture* (London, 1873), vol. 1, p. 133.

[2] Personal communication, Patrick Curry, 18 April 2001.

[3] See, for example, Rudolf Smit, 'Moment Supreme: Why Astrologers Keep Believing in Astrology', translated and updated from the original Dutch article in *Skepter*, March 1993, at <http://www.rudolfhsmit.nl/a-mome2.htm>, accessed 6 July 2008.

[4] For sociology see, for example, Stephen J. Hunt, *Alternative Religions: A Sociological Introduction* (Aldershot, 2003), p. 173; and for astronomy see Bart J. Bok and Margaret W. Mayall, 'Scientists Look at Astrology', *Scientific Monthly*, 52 (1941), p. 244.

should be considered a matter of belief at all: the entire issue is taken for granted. Throughout, though, we can identify certain general assumptions. Michael Hill, for example, suggests that 'astrology provides an "alternative source of self-definition" among groups of individuals who are searching for such "definition"'.[5] It is not clear, though, why such individuals should have found this function in astrology: what is it about astrology that provides such self-definition? Does science, for example, provide an 'alternative source of self-definition'? The question is simply not asked, and until it is, any conclusions concerning supposed alternative spiritualities exist in a vacuum. We should continue to gather such data, but in the knowledge that our conclusions are necessarily limited by the absence of any control groups. Elsewhere, claims are made but little independent argument offered. For example, Hexham and Poewe mentioned astrology briefly, but offered no independent reasons for belief in astrology, preferring to cite Eliade, though without a reference, as the source for their claim that belief in astrology arises out of belief in karma and reincarnation, and vice versa.[6]

The greatest concern with belief in astrology is found not amongst sociologists, who tend to mention it only in passing, but in literature written by Christian evangelicals and scientific sceptics. Some of the Christian evangelical literature on belief in astrology includes the argument that astrology's claims are true, but originate in the satanic realm: the issue is primarily political, a matter of a historical dislike for anything considered to be a rival spirituality.[7] The major part of the debate on belief in astrology is based on the sceptical premise that science has disproved it.[8] Such information is cited in the literature on the sociology of religion. For example, Hexham and Poewe cited sceptical writers such as John McGervey and Ralph Bastedo as their source for their statement that 'astrology has been thoroughly discredited by scientific testing' and conclude, consequently, that it must therefore be magical and irrational.[9] Some astrologers may agree, but

---

[5]   Michael Hill, *A Sociology of Religion* (London, 1979), p. 247.

[6]   Irving Hexham and Karla Poewe, *New Religions as Global Cultures* (Boulder CO, 1997), p. 104.

[7]   See, for example, Doug Harris, *Occult Overviews and New Age Agendas: A Comprehensive Examination of Major Occult and New Age Groups* (Richmond, 1999); Doug Harris, *Occult Dangers Explained – Safely* (Richmond, 2000).

[8]   For sociologists see Richard A. Crowe, 'Astrology and the Scientific Method', *Psychological Reports*, 67 (1990), p. 163; see also Peter Glick and Mark Snyder, 'Self-Fulfilling Prophecy: The Psychology of Belief in Astrology', *Humanist*, 46/3 (1986), p. 20. For sceptics see George O. Abell, 'Astrology', in George O. Abell and Barry Singer (eds), *Science and the Paranormal: Probing the Existence of the Supernatural* (London, 1981), p. 89; Richard Dawkins, *Unweaving the Rainbow* (London, 1998), p. 122; Susan Blackmore, *The Meme Machine* (Oxford, 1999), p. 184; Geoffrey Dean and Ivan Kelly, 'Is Astrology Relevant to Consciousness and Psi?', *Journal of Consciousness Studies*, 10/6–7 (2003), p. 175.

[9]   Hexham and Poewe, *New Religions*, p. 104, citing sceptical writers such as John D. McGervey, 'A Statistical Test of Sun-Sign Astrology', *Zetetic*, 1/2 (1977); Ralph W.

the point is that there is a naivety amongst some sociologists, which leads to an inclination to accept scientific claims uncritically, unaware of their contentious nature; this is combined with a substantial failure to actually investigate astrology's claims, talk to astrologers or consider astrological literature. The need to explain belief in astrology, therefore, arises directly out of the view that its claims are so patently false that those who take it seriously are suffering from a series of failures of judgement.[10] They may even be suffering from psychological weakness or disorder.[11]

When sociologists do speak to astrologers they immediately find that the whole notion of belief is a highly problematic one, and that many astrologers resist the proposition that they even believe in astrology. I was alerted to this issue by Jane Ridder-Patrick, a well-known medical herbalist and author of *A Handbook of Medical Astrology*, a standard work on the subject. When the question 'Do you believe in astrology?' was put to her when she was addressing a meeting of students in the astronomy department at Glasgow University on 1 March 1990, Ridder-Patrick replied simply, 'No, I don't believe in astrology. I know from more than ten years of almost daily hands-on experience that astrology is a valid and useful tool for understanding our world and our relationship with it.'[12] She later added that

> Belief for me is a leap of faith which is not based on concrete personal experience. When working with any tool or system, including astrology, I need some kind of PROOF that makes sense to me. It doesn't have [to] be formal scientific proof which is so often, in any case, a complete non-sense for looking at astrology. However, I would add that I have the working hypothesis that astrology can be used to examine, quite literally, anything under the Sun. When venturing into new territory, as I am at the moment, I keep an open mind, constantly testing if a proposition is 'true' or not either literally or symbolically and rejecting whatever doesn't pass the stringency test. If I have any belief in relation to astrology it is that life is meaningful and purposeful, and that astrology has a part to play in illuminating this meaning and purpose.[13]

Ridder-Patrick's understanding of 'belief' is that it is inherently false. She concedes belief only in astrology's function, not its existence, and considers that its validity is based in empirical observation. The key determinants of her attitude to astrology are knowledge and experience. Later I had a conversation with British astrologer Ronald Harvey, then in his nineties – and so with a longer memory than

Bastedo, 'An Empirical Test of Popular Astrology', *Skeptical Inquirer*, 3/1 (1978).

[10] Theodor Adorno, *The Stars Down to Earth* (London, 1994).

[11] Geoffrey Dean, Ivan Kelly and Arthur Mather, 'Astrology', in Gordon Stein (ed.), *The Encyclopaedia of the Paranormal* (New York, 1996), pp. 86–93.

[12] Personal communication, Jane Ridder-Patrick, 5 December 2000a.

[13] Personal communication, Jane Ridder-Patrick, 5 December 2000b.

most of the debates within British astrology. I asked him how he would respond to the question 'Do you believe in astrology?' His answer was unequivocal and, as I have found, typical in its irritation: 'It's a stupid question. What does it mean? There are phases of belief, from belief in sun-signs to more complex belief in astrology. What does astrology claim? It's not about facts but clues, pointers. It provides clues, not absolute truth. The truth is fuzzy.' Astrologers, as I found in my fieldwork, justify their use of astrology overwhelmingly on the pragmatic grounds that it is not a matter of belief but of knowledge based on personal experience, often citing C.G. Jung who, when asked whether he believed in God, replied 'I don't believe, I know'.[14] Astrologers who say they believe in astrology justify their belief by knowledge and positive experience of it, and those who say they do not believe in it cite in their support the proposition that, as it is matter of knowledge derived from daily experience, it cannot be contained by belief.

Such attitudes occur widely in popular discourse. In a BBC discussion on balance in science in 2011, the comedian Katy Brand said that she read her horoscope not, she emphasised, because she believed in it, but because it made her feel better and gave her a sense of purpose; she went through the day looking to see if life reflected astrology.[15] To this the geneticist Steve Jones replied that 'We all know that astrology is silly', to which Katy Brand responded that 'Actually, we don't know that'. We have to understand how such conversations are heard: the notion of astrology as matter of belief is denied by the horoscope-reader, and the scientist who attempts to attack astrology is heard resorting to ridicule rather than evidence, and is firmly put in his place. The scientist relies on certainty ('we all know'), while the apparent 'believer' expresses sceptical doubt ('actually, we don't know'). To the ordinary person who has no particular view that scientists automatically know more than anyone else, why should Brand not sound more reasonable than Jones? The proposition is that the need to explain belief in astrology as if it is some strange, unreasonable condition fails because it just does not take into account the complex, uncertain nature of language and public discourse.

Strictly speaking, the definition of belief is neutral, meaning 'trust or confidence' in the object of belief and, in the examples given in the *Oxford English Dictionary*, the objects of belief can be either religious or intuitive, a matter of opinion or an accepted fact. Thus it is possible to 'believe' both in the Virgin Birth and the existence of gravity, without the use of the word 'belief' implying that one is more true than the other. In this sense a belief does not have to be true but neither is it necessarily false: it is the perception of the believer which counts. Allen Edwards, speaking as a statistician, defined belief as a 'psychological concept' and added that, 'By a person's beliefs about a psychological object we shall mean all those statements relating to the object that he agrees with or accepts. By a person's

[14]   Cited in David Cox, *'I Don't Need to Believe in God – I Know'* (London, 1985).

[15]   'The Infinite Monkey Cage', Series 5, 'A Balanced Programme on Balance', BBC Radio 4, 28 November 2011.

disbeliefs about a psychological object we mean all of those statements about the object that he disagrees with or rejects.'[16]

This kind of definition is value-free: belief requires no more than acceptance or rejection of a set of propositions. In the strict definition of the word one can believe in science, or that a particular phenomenon is scientific, including astrology, as did Colin Wilson, well known for his popular writings on the occult, when he headlined an article in the UK newspaper, the *Daily Mail*, 'Why I now believe astrology IS a science'.[17] In Wilson's strictly grammatical use of the term, belief does not carry religious connotations. The same applies to much popular discourse in which scientists are also regularly described as believers. For example, on the same day as Wilson's piece, *The Independent* newspaper reported that 'scientists... believe that they have found the gene' responsible for a 'sweet tooth' and that 'some scientists believe [that evolution] has come to a standstill'.[18] In popular usage, then, scientists 'believe' and scientific propositions can themselves be a matter of belief. This renders the isolation of particular practices as a matter of belief as somewhat problematic.

It is commonly assumed that everyone knows what is meant by 'belief', but this just is not the case, and the failure to acknowledge this is the cause of a huge amount of academic confusion, Theological discussions of 'belief' tend to concentrate on its relationship with faith for which, according to the classic *Dictionary of the Bible*, it is a synonym.[19] Yet, having noted the two words' shared meaning as 'loyalty', or 'to hold dear', Wilfred Cantwell Smith argued that, due to shifting usage, 'belief' has lost its spiritual connotations to the extent that 'belief in God' no longer carries the same power as 'faith in God'.[20] Are faith and belief, then, different? The confusion is evident. Anthony O'Hear defined faith as 'an all-encompassing set of attitudes to human life and the world', as opposed to mere 'scientific', 'historical' or 'psychological' beliefs (allowing for the existence of scientific beliefs); yet he went on to argue that 'for believers faith is overwhelmingly a matter of living and of acting', as if faith were a natural attribute of believers.[21] This uncertainty is not new. In 1910, James Lindsay argued that belief might (although might not) be based on some kind of actual evidence,

---

[16]   Allen L. Edwards, *Techniques of Attitude Scale Construction* (New York, 1957), p. 10.

[17]   Colin Wilson, 'Why I now believe astrology IS a science', *Daily Mail*, 22 March 2001.

[18]   Steve Connor, 'Scientists identify "the sweet tooth gene"', *The Independent*, 23 April 2001, p. 3; Steve Connor, 'Human evolution is heading in a new direction claims study into childbirth', *The Independent*, 23 April 2001, p. 9.

[19]   'Belief' in James Hastings (ed.), *A Dictionary of the Bible* (2 vols, Edinburgh, 1910).

[20]   Wilfred Cantwell Smith, *Faith and Belief* (Princeton, 1998), pp. 104, 116–17.

[21]   Anthony O'Hear, *Experience, Explanation and Faith: An Introduction to the Philosophy of Religion* (London, 1984), p. 2.

whereas faith was always derived from personal feeling.[22] The result, simply, is confusion, and the attempt to separate faith from belief, as if they are distinct cognitive states, is clearly next to impossible.

In much of the sceptical scientific literature, the discussion of belief becomes value-laden, as opposed to value-free, and a 'belief' is automatically defined as false unless, in rare cases, it is proved otherwise. The default assumption that beliefs are, by definition, false is a common one amongst sociologists and psychologists. For example, in his summary of the psychological reasons for belief, David Meyers generally treats beliefs as false but regards them as dangerous only when 'belief perseverance' (the tendency for individuals to retain beliefs when they have been disproved) occurs and leads to 'self-defeating behaviour'.[23] Later, though, he contradicts himself and concedes that a false belief may be countered by a true one, suggesting uncertainty over the word's precise use. Other discussions – in relation to the placebo effect – suggest that 'positive' beliefs can be helpful, negative ones dangerous.[24] Again, a general confusion is evident: what if a necessarily dangerous belief, such as belief in placebo effect, leads to a benevolent result? Even if we all agree that belief is necessarily false, opinion divides on whether the consequences must be harmful or can be harmless.

In scientific usage, then, the word 'belief' can be used either neutrally or pejoratively at one and the same time and, in the literature on paranormal phenomena, the term 'believe' is applied to both sympathetic and sceptical opinions of paranormal phenomena.[25] Some beliefs, in this usage, can be false but others, if they are verified by observation, true. If some beliefs are true and others false, what would explain Ridder-Patrick's denial of belief in astrology?

The problem derives from popular discourse amongst modern sceptics, in which belief is automatically regarded as false, in contrast to science, which is, *a priori*, the source of truth – in fact, the *only* certain source of truth (putting disciplines such as history on a less reliable footing).[26] Belief and falsity, belief and disbelief are, then, in this perspective, contrasted in a kind of Manichaean polarity akin to black and white, good and evil.[27] For example, discussing the granting of a PhD to Elizabeth Teissier, President Mitterand's astrologer, by the

---

[22]   James Lindsay, *The Psychology of Belief* (Edinburgh and London, 1910), p. 5.

[23]   David G. Myers, *Social Psychology*, 3rd edn (New York, 1990), pp. 102, 109–11.

[24]   Helen Pilcher, 'Beware Witchdoctors: Are you a Victim of Placebo's Evil Twin', *New Scientist*, 202/2708 (2009), pp. 30–9.

[25]   See, for example, Rupert Sheldrake, 'Research on the Feeling of Being Stared At', *Skeptical Inquirer*, 25/2 (2001), p. 58; see also David Marks and John Colwell, 'Fooling and Falling into the Feeling of Being Stared At', *Skeptical Inquirer*, 25/2 (2001).

[26]   Glick and Snyder, 'Self-Fulfilling Prophecy', p. 22; Stanley Krippner and Michael Winkler, 'The Need to "Believe"', in Gordon Stein (ed.), *The Encyclopaedia of the Paranormal* (Amherst NY, 1996), pp. 441–54.

[27]   See, for example, Carl Sagan, *The Demon-Haunted World: Science as a Candle in the Dark* (New York, 1995).

Sorbonne, the journalist Magnus Linklater commented in *The Times* that the core problem of the incident was that 'In short, the woman really *believes* in astrology. And there is the rub. If you seriously believe that the stars rule our lives, you have abandoned the most basic tenet of science which is knowledge obtained by observation and experiment.'[28] In Linklater's scenario the believer becomes an ontological criminal: what mattered for Teissier's academic qualification was not the quality of her work but her private beliefs. When the *Time* journalist asked Patrick Curry whether he 'believed' in astrology, she was really attempting to gauge his state of mind. Teissier's thought crime was so great that she deserved to fail her PhD no matter what the quality of her work. In such a world we would return to the early nineteenth century when, in Britain, the Test Acts ensured that only Anglicans could study at university; Catholics, Nonconformists and atheists were excluded on the grounds that their religious affiliation invalidated any claim they might have to education. Also, for Linklater, the only source of knowledge can be science; the social sciences and humanities are automatically inferior explanatory models. Such an approach, of course, is borne of scientism, the blind faith in the ability of science to answer all questions, rather than science itself, as evidence-based rational inquiry. If applied more widely, many universities would close. Even science departments would be hit by the prohibition of scientists with Christian backgrounds. We could say this is an example of liberalism masquerading as fundamentalism, but then really what we are looking at is an example of the failure of public discourse in such areas.

If belief, according to this point of view, is a thought crime, what are its origins? Here the cognitive psychologists step into the argument. Stephen Pinker regards metaphorical thought as an essential means for humans to make sense of the world, a notion which might actually lead straight to an understanding of astrology as a metaphorical system (as in Dane Rudhyar's version) as a natural way to think.[29] This function of astrology, to provide a metaphorical sense of meaning and to connect humanity with the divine, particularly in the context of the current historical crisis, is the foundation of contemporary psychological astrology, especially when it is closely linked to psychoanalysis, psychotherapy or counselling.[30] 'Meaning', wrote Liz Greene and Howard Sasportas in relation to astrology, 'is essential for life'.[31] When life is devoid of meaning, they add, the very psychological problems may develop which are typically those which prompt clients to visit astrologers. The astrologers' view, in this respect, is close to

---

[28] Magnus Linklater, 'An academic dispute that is out of this world', *The Times*, 30 August 2001, p. 12.

[29] Brian Appleyard, 'Bryan Appleyard meets Steven Pinker', *Sunday Times*, News Review, 14 October 2007, p. 5.5.

[30] Howard Sasportas, *The Gods of Change: Pain, Crisis and the Transits of Uranus, Neptune and Pluto* (London, 1989), p. 3.

[31] Liz Greene and Howard Sasportas, *The Development of the Personality: Seminars in Psychological Astrology* (London, 1987), pp. xi–xiii.

that of the cognitive psychologists. For example, in an interview in 1999 Steven Pinker claimed that 'We have meaning and purpose here inside our heads, being the organisms that we are. We have brains that make it impossible for us to live our lives except in terms of meaning and purpose.'[32] Meaning is therefore necessary for survival. Ed Krupp, director of Los Angeles' Griffith Observatory, related the human survival instinct to the stars, arguing that the projection of meaning and order onto the heavens originated as a survival tool.[33] This is a view favoured by some astrologers; when Jane Ridder-Patrick stated that 'If I have any belief in relation to astrology it is that life is meaningful and purposeful, and that astrology has a part to play in illuminating this meaning and purpose', she may be pointing to astrology's satisfaction of a need which is essentially and unavoidably human.[34] For Stephen Arroyo, whose writing on astrology was amongst the most influential of the 1970s, this was the key to astrology's contemporary popularity:

> I have often been asked why astrology has witnessed such renewed popularity in recent years. I think part of the answer lies in the fact that Western culture no longer has any viable mythology to sustain it. Myth always serves as a vitalizing force in any culture by showing man's relationship to a larger, more universal reality. People have always needed a pattern of order to guide their collective lives and to infuse their individual experience with meaning. In this sense astrology comprises within itself an entire mythological framework.[35]

There is in such statements, born of the evolutionary spirituality of theosophy, a profound parallel with contemporary evolutionary psychology. However, this connection does not seem to be made.

Pinker, still defaulting to the problematic assumption that belief is both an identifiably distinct and inferior cognitive state, defined beliefs as 'information, incarnated as configurations of symbols'; symbols, in his view, are 'physical states of bits of matter' which correspond to beliefs and are 'triggered' by 'things in the world'; when two of these bits of matter 'bump' into each other, he argues, the symbols to which they correspond combine to form a new belief.[36] In Pinker's model the brain is a kind of pool table, with thoughts as billiard balls, bumping into each other, not unlike an old-fashioned view of atoms. Pinker's views may be idiosyncratic but are influential by virtue of his reputation as a brilliant and original thinker. The assumption that a belief is a distinct cognitive state arising from

---

[32]   Ed Douglas, 'Stephen Pinker: the mind reader', *Guardian*, Saturday Review, 6 November 1999, pp. 6–7.

[33]   E.C. Krupp, 'Night Gallery: The Function, Origin and Evolution of Constellations', *Archaeoastronomy: The Journal of Astronomy in Culture*, 15 (2000), pp. 43–4.

[34]   Personal communication, Jane Ridder-Patrick, 8 December 2000.

[35]   Stephen Arroyo, *Astrology, Psychology and the Four Elements: An Energy Approach to Astrology and its Use in the Counselling Arts* (Davis CA, 1975), pp. xv–xvi.

[36]   Steven Pinker, *How the Mind Works* (New York, 1997), p. 25.

physiological processes was combined with a summary of the sceptical arguments on the nature of belief by Robert Park, Professor of Physics at the University of Maryland. Using a mechanical analogy, Park argued that brains are 'belief engines'.[37] According to Park's line of reasoning, belief has physiological causes and occurs when the believer mistakenly infers a causal connection in two unconnected events. Park argues that when 'the chemical messengers of emotion cause the thalamus to bypass the sensory cortex and route the information directly to the amygdala', a belief then becomes a 'personal superstition'.[38] Park acknowledges belief's positive function in encouraging survival strategies and social cohesion but, he argues, when carried to extremes, it can become destructive – as in the mass suicides at Jonestown and Heaven's Gate.[39] However, Park continued:

> If this sounds hopelessly gloomy, be patient, we are coming to the good news: we are not condemned to suffer the tyranny of the belief engine. The primitive machinery of the belief engine is still in place but evolution didn't stop there. It provided us with an antidote, namely science.[40]

Again, like Pinker's view, Park's may be untested and lacking in evidence, but what concerns us here is the influence he achieves through this his public roles, such as Director of Public Information at the Washington office of the American Physical Society and Fellow of the Committee for Sceptical Inquiry, and his journalistic profile through such periodicals as *The New York Times* and *Scientific American*. Between them, journalists such as Linklater, psychologists such as Pinker and physicists such as Park combine to build up a value-laden picture of 'belief' as not just false but a result of a potentially dangerous physical malfunction in the brain. The result is an inclusion of astrology in a history of abnormal behaviour.[41] In this view, the Manichaean struggle between truth and falsehood actually has a biological basis, and the assumption is that the study of science will then produce physiological consequences which can minimise the tendency to belief. However, for Bruce Lipton, whose view straddles biological science and New Age metaphysics, the very biological basis of belief provides a mechanism for changing beliefs from negative and restrictive to positive and life-enhancing.[42] This is an important argument for those geneticists for whom

---

[37]   Robert Park, *Voodoo Science: The Road from Foolishness to Fraud* (Oxford, 2000), p. 35.

[38]   Park, *Voodoo Science*, p. 36.

[39]   For Heaven's Gate see John R. Hall, *Apocalypse Observed: Religious Movements and Violence in North America, Europe, and Japan* (London and New York, 2000).

[40]   Park, *Voodoo Science*, p. 37.

[41]   Leonard P. Ullman and Leonard Krasner, *A Psychological Approach to Abnormal Behaviour*, 2nd edn (Englewood Cliffs NJ, 1969), p. 125.

[42]   Bruce H. Lipton, *The Biology of Belief: Unleashing the Power of Consciousness, Matter and Miracles* (London, 2008).

women (who constitute the highest number both of producers and consumers of astrology, to adopt market terminology) are biologically conditioned to believe, whereas men are physiologically inclined to scepticism.[43]

The question was clarified by Richard Dawkins when contrasting astrology with science; he said that 'for a scientist to believe something, there has to be evidence'.[44] If we marry this argument with the genetically-conditioned hypothesis, then male scientists are more inclined to believe the evidence and female scientists less so. That is, women make worse scientists, a somewhat problematic proposition for many who would prefer to focus on cultural influences. Dawkins's theory that scientists believe, but in a different way from non-scientists, is often found in science journalism, and a recent review of Isaac Newton's theories included the telling phrase, 'We can believe them; they're science'.[45] So, if scientists believe, then Park's notion of belief as a peculiar cognitive condition or brain-disturbance has no value. Dawkins does not really solve the problem, however, for astrologers do have evidence, even if it remains experiential, anecdotal and non-verifiable. The inherent absurdity of the biological argument is simply revealed: if, according to Park, the scientist who believes, regardless of whether they do so on the basis of the evidence, is suffering from a neurological disorder, then so is the scientist who, in Dawkins's terms, believes.

Nevertheless, the consequences of this kind of attitude – that astrology is automatically false and belief in it therefore explicable only as a form of psychological inadequacy – became clear in a brief exchange in the journal *Sexuality, Reproduction and Menopause* in May 2009. Pat Harris, reporting on her recent PhD at Southampton University, gave a positive account of possible astrological factors in the success of IVF treatment, which elicited a particularly instructive response from Jackie Boivin of the School of Psychology at Cardiff University, and signed by five of her students.[46] After a brief discussion, Boivin made some methodological criticisms of Harris's study, but concluded with the following point, which departed from scientific criticism and entered theological realms: 'Frankly, we were surprised that a scientific journal would devote any space to a question that is outside the domain of science since it requires faith in a phenomenon that cannot be tested using the scientific methods of evidenced-

---

[43]   James E. Kennedy, 'The Roles of Religion, Spirituality and Genetics in Paranormal Beliefs', *Skeptical Inquirer*, 28/2 (2004), pp. 39–42.

[44]   Richard Dawkins, 'Newsnight', BBC2, 3 January 1996.

[45]   Ann Finkbeiner, 'What Newton Gave Us', review of Edward Dolnick, *The Clockwork Universe: Isaac Newton, the Royal Society, and the Birth of the Modern World* (San Francisco, 2011), *New York Times*, Sunday Book Review, 27 March 2011, p. BR19, available at <http://www.nytimes.com/2011/03/27/books/review/book-review-the-clockwork-universe-by-edward-dolnick.html?nl=books&emc=booksupdateema4>, accessed 3 September 2011.

[46]   Pat Harris, 'Managing Fertility Treatments and Stress with Astrology', *Sexuality, Reproduction and Menopause*, 6/3 (2008), pp. 43–4.

based medicine.'[47] We need to quote Harris's response, for clarity: 'The fertility treatment data were historical data – the outcome had occurred prior to both of the studies. Patients had no knowledge of the absence or presence of astrology in relation to timing of treatment when they underwent the process.'[48]

We should be quite clear about what is happening in this exchange. Whatever conclusions we might read into Harris's thesis, her data is clear and published. Yet Boivin's crucial argument was that, regardless of Harris's conclusion, the only reasonable *a priori* view on astrology dictates that it cannot be used to demonstrate an astrological relationship, and positive results must therefore, of necessity, be spurious and should not be published. This is not so much scepticism as negative dogmatism and is derived from the Freudian point of view – that even to mention the word 'astrology' is to risk endowing the practice with credibility.[49] It is easy to see how such reasoning leads to a circular argument which runs as follows: astrology is a matter of belief; belief is false and therefore dangerous; astrology is false and therefore dangerous; positive results from tests of astrology must therefore result from error; there is therefore no evidence for astrology; astrology, therefore, is a matter of belief; publication of positive research results is dangerous; positive results must therefore not be published; and, in the absence of published positive results, it can be concluded that there are none, and astrology is false. Paradoxically, this is an example of anti-science and we might example that the correct procedure in such circumstances is to publish positive results and then critique them on scientific grounds. Scepticism then becomes based in *a priori* assumptions rather than evidence, a position which Marcello Truzzi defined as pseudoscepticism.[50] In that much of the criticism of astrology emerges from an *a priori* position (that is, the proposition that it *should* be false) it is pseudosceptical. The reason that this is important is that the statement of *a priori* positions, as in the exchange between Jones and Brand, appears weak when faced with the word of experience. The issue is not the stubborn persistence of belief in astrology in the face of overwhelming scientific disproof, but the failure of science communication.

However useful astrology is, the arguments that it is inherently false are reminiscent of the notion of religion as 'primitive error'.[51] By association, then,

[47]   Jackie Boivin, 'Pat Harris, "Astrology and Fertility: Where is the Evidence?"', *Sexuality, Reproduction and Menopause* (2009), at <http://www.srm-ejournal.com/>, accessed 3 September 2011.

[48]   Pat Harris, 'Response to Jacki Boivin, "Pat Harris, 'Astrology and Fertility: Where is the Evidence?'"', *Sexuality, Reproduction and Menopause* (2009), at <http://www.srm-ejournal.com>, accessed 24 September 2009.

[49]   Sigmund Freud, 'Psychoanalysis and Telepathy', in *The Complete Psychological Works of Sigmund Freud*, trans. James Strachey, vol. 18 (London, 1955), pp. 177–94. For negative dogmatism see R.J. Hankinson, *The Sceptics* (London, 1995), p. 14.

[50]   Marcello Truzzi, 'On Pseudo-Skepticism', *The Anomalist*, repr. from the *Zetetic Scholar*, 12–13 (1987), atv<http://www.anomalist.com/commentaries/pseudo.html>.

[51]   James Thrower, *Religion: The Classical Theories* (Edinburgh, 1999), pp. 99–125.

astrology is also condemned by Linklater, Park and their associates as primitive error. The evolutionary position in religion was summarised comprehensively by Jevons, who argued that progressively, over the millennia, as humanity evolved, it used its reason to correct false beliefs and identify true ones so that religion, even though fundamentally false, became progressively less so.[52] Broadly speaking, the evolutionist perspective holds that religion originates as 'primitive' totemism, animism or magic (in which natural forces are animated or anthropomorphised), evolves through polytheism into monotheism and finally, in line with the law of progress, into atheist materialism.[53]

The anthropologist E.B. Tylor set the tone for cultural-evolutionist discussions of astrology in strident tones, following his discussion of magic. Forgetting that notions of 'truth' are beyond the remit of the anthropologist, he wrote:

> Looking at the details here selected as fair examples of symbolic magic, we may well ask the question, is there in this whole monstrous farrago no truth or value whatsoever? It appears that there is practically none, and that the world has been enthralled for ages by a blind belief in processes wholly irrelevant to their supposed results, and which might as well have been taken the opposite way.[54]

Somehow astrology's survival represented a grand paradox, as if, somewhere in central London, men were still living in caves, killing each other with flint axes. Astrology, in this sense was barbaric. If it can be argued that magic is a primitive form of religion, and that religion itself results from primitive error, then astrology can be deemed false purely by defining it as magic. This was the basis of Boivin's case that Harris's work should not have been published as a matter of principle. Yet Tylor's evolutionary hypothesis is no longer taken seriously outside that small group of anti-astrology sceptics. Peter Pels has comprehensively demonstrated Tylor's context within the nineteenth-century confusion between theory and data, and the extent to which, from allowing data to generate theory, he moved to allowing theory to manipulate data.[55]

Even so, the evolutionary model remains the basis of the attempt to 'explain' why people believe in astrology. For example, Lawrence Jerome, one of the driving forces behind the 1975 'Objections to Astrology' argued that 'astrology is false because it is magic' and that, consequently, 'to bow to the magical "dictates of the stars" is to abandon free will and rationality'.[56] Statements such as those of the

---

[52]   Frank Jevons, *Introduction to the History of Religions* (London, 1896), pp. 402–3.

[53]   E.E. Evans-Pritchard, *Social Anthropology* (London, 1967), pp. 31–3; Hill, *A Sociology of Religion*, pp. 19–43.

[54]   Tylor, *Primitive Culture*, vol. 1, p. 133.

[55]   Peter Pels, 'Spirits of Modernity: Alfred Wallace, Edward Tylor and the Visual Politics of Fact', in Birgit Meyer and Peter Pels (eds), *Magic and Modernity: Interfaces of Revelation and Concealment* (Stanford, 2003), p. 216.

[56]   Lawrence E. Jerome, 'Astrology: Magic or Science?', *Humanist*, 35/5 (1975), pp. 10, 16; Bart J. Bok, Lawrence E. Jerome and Paul Kurtz, 'Objections to Astrology: A

sceptic, George Abell, for whom belief in astrology is necessarily 'incredible and absurd', can therefore be understood in their historical context as a manifestation of the positivist proposition that all religious belief is patently false.[57]

However, although the idea that there are such mutually exclusive categories as magic, religion and science is still popular amongst most sceptics, many scientists and some academic theologians, it is generally regarded as untenable amongst historians of ideas.[58] Rodney Stark, the sociologist, argued that the evolutionist point of view, based in what he regarded as the erroneous notion of the 'primitive mind', was 'incorrect, extremely misleading, and often simply fabricated', and had been discredited once anthropologists began to conduct rigorous fieldwork rather than rely on theory.[59] The entire attempt to demonstrate that astrology is a form of historical error – pseudoscience in some sceptical language – is actually pseudohistory – history pursued in the absence of evidence.[60] We might equally call it quasi-history. This has no bearing on astrology's truth or validity, only on the poor quality of critiques of it.

For the sake of argument, if we follow the sceptical (or pseudosceptical) hypothesis, it is necessary to explain just why people end up believing in astrology. Stephen Hawking took a functional view, seeing the desire for control as crucial: 'The Human race has always wanted to control the future', he wrote, 'or at least to predict what will happen. That is why astrology is so popular.'[61] Bernulf Kanitscheider advanced what we may call the 'gullibility hypothesis', blaming publicity through the media, an argument which may explain how belief spreads but not why it spreads.[62]

Belief in astrology, then, arises from a series of 'reasoning errors'.[63] Of these errors, one is self-attribution, the natural tendency to agree with what one is

---

Statement by 186 Leading Scientists', *Humanist*, 35/5 (1975), pp. 4–6.

[57]   Abell, 'Astrology', pp. 73, 94.

[58]   Stanley Jeyaraja Tambiah, *Magic, Science, Religion and the Scope of Rationality*, Lewis Henry Morgan Lectures (Cambridge, 1990); Charles Webster, *From Paracelsus to Newton: Magic and the Making of Modern Science* (Cambridge, 1982); Frances Yates, *The Occult Philosophy in the Elizabethan Age* (London and Boston, 1983); Frances Yates, *The Rosicrucian Enlightenment* (London, 1986); J. Milton Yinger, *The Scientific Study of Religion* (New York, 1970), p. 77.

[59]   Rodney Stark, 'Atheism, Faith, and the Social Scientific Study of Religion', *Journal of Contemporary Religion*, 14/1 (1999), p. 47.

[60]   Douglas Allchin, 'Pseudohistory and Pseudoscience', *Science and Education*, 13 (2004), pp. 179–95.

[61]   Stephen Hawking, *The Universe in a Nutshell* (London, 2001), p. 103.

[62]   Bernulf Kanitscheider, 'A Philosopher looks at Astrology', *Interdisciplinary Science Reviews*, 16/3 (1991), pp. 259–60. See also Lucy Sherriff, 'Women are NOT from Gullibull', *Skeptic*, 14/3 (2001), p. 7; see also Geoffrey Dean and Arthur Mather, *Recent Advances in Natal Astrology: A Critical Review 1900–1976* (Subiaco, 1977), pp. 7, 15.

[63]   See Garry Phillipson, *Astrology in the Year Zero* (London, 2000), pp. 136–7; Dean et al., 'Astrology', pp. 89–90; Glick and Snyder, 'Self-Fulfilling Prophecy', p. 50.

told about oneself.[64] However, gullibility is itself only a plausible explanation if astrology is patently false, while self-attribution may equally explain belief in psychology or science.[65] It is then unclear why such arguments should apply particularly to astrology. Geoffrey Dean and his collaborators, including Ivan Kelly, an educational psychologist at the University of Saskatchewan, proposed four reasons for belief, all assuming gullibility; 'reading sun-signs', 'reading astrology books', 'visiting an astrologer' and 'being an astrologer', their argument being that 'astrology seems to work, so we become believers'.[66] Regarding Dean and Mather's third reason, 'visiting an astrologer', Edgar Wunder argued that this was a marginal consideration when compared to more active engagement through personal study of astrology: one studies and, as a result, one believes.[67] There is a shift away from Kanitscheider here, though, and Dean emphasises the personal validation that comes from an experience of astrology 'working', whether through reading horoscope columns or visiting or working as an astrologer. This much is acknowledged by sceptics. For example, Robert Basil conceded that there is an experiential basis for many New Age beliefs; the distinction, though is between experience and explanation, and the former does not constitute version of the latter.[68] According to Ivan Kelly, a sceptic, although its claims are false, 'many people appear to be attracted to astrology because it seems simple and speaks to their lives'.[69] Paradoxically, then, Kelly then agrees with Arroyo: astrologer and sceptic are of one mind.

Inextricably tied to the notion that astrology represents the survival of magical, primitive religion is the theory that it originates as a means of providing security to people who are naturally insecure, fearful and unable to deal with their environment or responsibilities without a crutch: this is an argument made extensively in

---

[64]   Donald L. Mosher, 'Approval Motive and Acceptance of "Fake" Personality Test Interpretations Which Differ in Favorability', *Psychological Reports*, 17 (1965), p. 400; D.R. Babbage and H.R. Ronan, 'Philosophical Worldview and Personality Factors in Traditional and Social Scientists: Studying the World in our own Image', *Personality and Individual Differences*, 28 (1998), p. 418.

[65]   James E. Alcock, *Parapsychology: Science or Magic? A Psychological Perspective* (Oxford, 1981), p. 61; see also C.R. Snyder and Glenn R. Larson, 'A Further Look at Student Acceptance of General Personality Interpretation', *Journal of Consulting and Clinical Psychology*, 38/3 (1972), p. 388.

[66]   Geoffrey Dean, 'Discourse for Key Topic 4: Astrology and Human Judgement', *Correlation*, 17/2 (1998/99), pp. 26–8, 47–51; see also Dean et al., 'Astrology', pp. 86–8.

[67]   Edgar Wunder, 'Erfahrung, Wissen, Glaube – ihr Beziehungsgeflecht bezuglich der Astrologie', *Zeitschrift fur Anomalistik*, 2/3 (2002).

[68]   Robert Basil, 'New Age Thinking', in Gordon Stein (ed.), *The Encyclopaedia of the Paranormal* (Amherst NY, 1996), p. 458.

[69]   Ivan Kelly, 'Why Astrology Doesn't Work', *Psychological Reports*, 82 (1998), p. 542.

relation to the origins of astrology in the ancient Near East.[70] The assumption that insecurity produces, in stages, fear, low self-esteem, 'persuasability' (that is, gullibility) and, ultimately, belief in astrology, has entered the psychological literature as a rationale for contemporary belief in astrology.[71] The astronomer Bart Bok, for example, cited a statement put out by the Society for Psychological Study of Social Issues (SPSSI), which claimed that

> The principal reason why people turn to astrology and to kindred superstitions is that they lack in their own lives the resources necessary to solve serious personal problems confronting them. Feeling blocked and bewildered they yield to the pleasant suggestion that a golden key is at hand – a simple solution – an ever-present help in time of trouble.[72]

The problem with such assertions is that they are taken as a given. Neither Bok nor the SPSSI had any evidence: they were taking a faith – pseudosceptical–position.[73] Simply, there had been no studies and, for both, the political imperative of condemning astrology took priority over the normal evidential requirements of science. Most astrologers would agree that astrology provides assistance in times of trouble. The issue is that there is no evidence to suggest that those who use astrology to provide answers are any more psychologically disadvantaged than anyone else. The problem was identified by Carl Sagan in 1975: when invited to sign that year's manifesto, 'Objections to Astrology', he refused on the grounds that none of the signatories had any knowledge of astrology, that the experimental data was absent and that the whole exercise represented an authoritarian and fundamentally dishonest attempt to impose one group's set of values on another.[74] Sagan had no time for astrology, which he dismissed impatiently as a 'pseudoscience', yet he regarded the position of the organised sceptics as untenable.[75] There is actually a dialogue about such attitudes amongst sceptics, with some expressing the view that, as one cannot prove a negative, it is not possible to claim that all astrology is false.[76] From within

---

[70]   Nicholas Campion, *A History of Western Astrology* (2 vols, London, 2009), vol. 1, p. 83.

[71]   See for example Glick and Snyder, 'Self-Fulfilling Prophecy', p. 50; I.L. Janis, 'Personality Correlates of Susceptibility to Persuasion', *Journal of Personality*, 22 (1954); I.L. Janis, 'Anxiety Indices related to Susceptibility to Persuasion', *Journal of Abnormal and Social Psychology*, 51 (1955); Adorno, *The Stars Down to Earth*, p. 3.

[72]   Bok and Mayall, 'Scientists Look', p. 244; see also Bok et al., 'Objections to Astrology'.

[73]   Nicholas Campion, 'Do Astrologers Have to Believe in Astrology?', *Sceptic*, 15/2 (2002), pp. 20–2.

[74]   Sagan, *The Demon-Haunted World*, p. 285.

[75]   Carl Sagan, *Cosmos: The Story of Cosmic Evolution, Science and Civilisation* (London, 1994), p. 66.

[76]   Wendy Grossman, 'Bang!', *Skeptic*, 22/3 (2011), p. 9.

sceptical ranks we see calls for moderate scepticism as genuine doubt and a rejection of the irrational excesses of dogmatic, radical sceptics.[77]

In spite of its wide currency, the 'insecurity' rationale for the development of ancient astrology should not be taken for granted. It has been notably challenged by Ulla Koch-Westonholtz on the grounds that, firstly, it represents the inappropriate projection of modern concerns onto an ancient society, and secondly, that the Babylonian omen literature (from which Western astrology is descended) indicates a society which was very certain of its worldview.[78] In addition, other evidence suggests that, far from religion appealing to the inadequate and insecure, religious people enjoy better than average mental and physical health.[79] Moreover, those attracted to New Age beliefs tend to be more educated than the average.[80] Under these circumstances, it becomes difficult to sustain the insecurity argument.

A number of other explanatory models are linked to the notion that astrology is an evolutionary hang-over. The 'deprivation theory' maintains that paranormal beliefs 'provide people with the means to cope with the psychological and physical strains and disadvantaged social and economic status', and predicts that 'socially marginal people will be more likely to believe in classic [paranormal] phenomena'.[81]

It has also been argued that 'innate and learned personality characteristics' may play a greater role in belief in astrology than do social factors.[82] Plug found that belief in astrology may be correlated with emotionality, as measured in the Eysenck Personality Inventory of suggestibility and persuasability, while Belter and Brinkmann found a higher probability that believers in 'magical... supernatural powers' such as 'luck, chance, fate, superstition and astrology' would be more likely to locate control in their lives in external forces.[83] However, as most publicly accepted definitions of astrology posit the existence of external forces, this is not surprising. On the extreme of the psychological hypothesis lies the

---

[77]   Mario Bunge, 'Absolute Skepticism Equals Negative Dogmatism', *Skeptical Inquirer*, 24/4 (2000), pp. 34–6.

[78]   Ulla Koch-Westonholtz, *Mesopotamian Astrology: An Introduction to Babylonian and Assyrian Celestial Divination* (Copenhagen, 1995), pp. 17–18.

[79]   Stark, 'Atheism, Faith', p. 56.

[80]   Wade Clark Roof, *A Generation of Seekers: The Spiritual Journeys of the Baby Boom Generation* (San Francisco, 1993).

[81]   Tom W. Rice, 'Believe It or Not: Religious and Other Paranormal Beliefs in the United States', *Journal for the Scientific Study of Religion*, 42/1 (2003), pp. 95, 104; Robert Wuthnow, *Experimentation in American Religion: The New Mysticisms and their Implications for the Churches* (Berkeley, 1978), p. 45.

[82]   Rice, 'Believe It or Not', p. 105.

[83]   C. Plug, 'An Investigation of Superstitious Belief and Behaviour', *Journal of Behavioural Science*, 2/3 (1975), pp. 172–4.

claim that belief in astrology is pathological and a warning sign of possible fascist tendencies.[84]

This was developed in the pioneering work of the Freudian Marxist Theodor Adorno (1903–69). Adorno identified a personality type which he termed 'authoritarian', distinguished by excessive conformism, bullying and submission to higher authority, of which two varieties were provided by astrology and fascism.[85] Belief in astrology then becomes a warning sign of possible fascist tendencies: astrologers, like Nazis, both need to bully those weaker than them and be bullied, in turn by those stronger than them, and where astrology raises its head, there we should fear a new holocaust. Comparing readers of horoscope columns to willing supporters of both Nazism and Stalinism, Adorno wrote:

> People even of the supposedly 'normal' mind are prepared to accept systems of delusions for the simple reason that it is too difficult to distinguish such systems from the equally opaque one under which they actually have to live out their lives. This is pretty well reflected by astrology as well as by the two brands of totalitarian states which also claim to have a key for everything, know all the answers, reduce the complex to simple and mechanical inferences, doing away with anything that is strange and unknown and at the same time fail to explain anything.[86]

It was in this context that the sceptical astronomer George Abell, in his own attack on astrology, cited Voltaire's aphorism that 'Men will cease to commit atrocities only when they cease to believe absurdities', and that the 'use of astrology' is considered an indication of neurotic or psychotic behaviour, along with alcoholism, use of illegal drugs, being a victim of sexual abuse or 'having horrible thoughts'.[87] The latter indications of abnormal behaviour are used to diagnose psychiatric problems by the Piedmont Psychiatric Clinic, established as recently as 1980 in Atlanta, Georgia. Adorno's critique of astrology can only be understood in its context: astrology, he thought, had to be attacked because, as a representative of the 'culture industry', it was necessarily involved in the oppression of the working class. Whatever astrologers

---

[84]   Adorno, *The Stars Down to Earth*, p. 115; see also Cary J. Nederman and James Wray Goulding, 'Popular Occultism and Critical Social Theory: Exploring Some Themes in Adorno's Critique of Astrology and the Occult', *Sociological Analysis*, 42/4 (1981), pp. 325–32.

[85]   Theodor Adorno, Else Frenkel-Brunswick, Daniel J. Levinson and R. Nevitt Sanford, *The Authoritarian Personality*, abr. edn (New York and London, 1982).

[86]   Adorno, *The Stars down to Earth*, p. 115; see also Nederman and Goulding, 'Popular Occultism and Critical Social Theory'.

[87]   Abell, 'Astrology', p. 94; Lorraine Welsh, 'Fear Abandonment, Use Astrology, Cut Wrist', *AFAN Newsletter* Winter 13 (2000), citing the 'Piedmont Psychiatric Clinic's Symptom Checklist': see Piedmont Psychiatric Clinic, 'Patient's Check List', at <http://www.piedmontpsychiatricclinic.com/forms.html>, accessed 30 November 2009.

said or did, no matter what the evidence might suggest, astrology was, *a priori*, an agent of repression. Dominic Strinati summarised Adorno's perspective well: 'The power of the culture industry to secure the dominance and continuity of capitalism resides, for Adorno, in its capacity to shape and perpetuate a "regressive" audience, a dependent, passive, and servile consuming public.'[88] Astrology, being often accused of fatalism, seemed to be an ideal fit for the passivity required of the mass media's audience. Adorno was profoundly anti-democratic and contemptuous of the working class for its failure to overthrow capitalism. When he analysed the *Los Angeles Times* horoscope column he was doing more than deconstructing its language; he was attributing to it a share of blame for the failure of the entire Marxist project. Opposition to the claim that popular culture was necessarily a hegemonic tool of capitalism was developed by those cultural theorists such as Raymond Williams, who saw the media as a vehicle for democratic aspirations, and Stuart Hall, who recognised culture as a political battleground, including struggles over the politics of knowledge, and questions of who has the right to decide what kinds of knowledge are legitimate.[89] The democratic legacy of Williams and Hall allows popular culture to be empowering rather than repressive, in which case Adorno's view of astrology's function as necessarily repressive and readers of horoscope columns as inevitably inclined to authoritarianism fails. Popular astrology, along with rock and roll and teen-fashion, becomes potentially empowering rather than disempowering.

Scientific illiteracy is also cited as a cause of gullibility, and hence belief in astrology. One aspect of this ignorance, it is argued, is public confusion between astronomy and astrology, with the latter, according to this hypothesis, benefiting in the public mind from the credibility of the former.[90] At its most extreme, the sceptical argument continues, public perceptions are not so much a matter of ignorance as of outright hostility to science. If such hostility can be diminished through a rise in scientific knowledge, so, the argument runs, belief in astrology, of necessity, must decline.[91] However, the supposed negative correlation between belief in science and either the paranormal in general or astrology in particular has been challenged or reversed by a series of studies.[92] The position is complex and

[88]   Dominic Strinati, *An Introduction to Theories of Popular Culture* (London, 1995), p. 64.

[89]   Raymond Williams, *Culture and Society 1780–1950* (London, 1971); Stuart Hall, 'Cultural Studies: Two Paradigms', *Media, Culture and Society*, 2 (1980), pp. 57–72.

[90]   Bok and Mayall, 'Scientists Look', p. 233; Theodore P. Snow and Kenneth R. Brownsberger, *Universe: Origins and Evolution* (London and New York, 1997), p. 7.

[91]   Kanitscheider, 'A Philosopher', p. 259; Jerome Tobacyk and Gary Milford, 'Belief in Paranormal Phenomena: Assessment Instrument Development and Implications for Personality Functioning', *Journal of Personality and Social Psychology*, 44/5 (1983), pp. 1029–37.

[92]   Robert Wuthnow, *The Consciousness Revolution* (Berkeley, 1976), pp. 164–8, 173, 181; Richard N. Williams, Carl B. Taylor and Wayne L. Hintze, 'The Influence of Religious Orientation on Belief in Science, Religion, and the Paranormal', *Journal of Psychology*

different samples of data produce variable results.[93] As Steve Bruce pointed out in relation to the decline of mainstream Christianity, there is no reason to suggest that 'modern people, the beneficiaries of science and technology, are incapable of believing in the supernatural'.[94] The evidence is confused and contradictory and, quite simply, there is no established correlation between educational attainment, on the one hand, and belief in theories which some scientists find unacceptable, on the other.

For some religious theorists the supposed rise in belief in astrology can be explained by secularisation theory, the widespread belief that religion in the Western world is in a state of long-term decline. One accepted working definition of secularisation is 'the erosion of belief in the supernatural – a loss of faith in the existence of otherworldly forces'.[95] The obvious initial criticism of such a simple historical theory is that, if astrology's popularity is increasing, and if astrology is supernatural, then belief in the supernatural is not declining. There are, of course, substantial criticisms of secularisation theory, which we do not need to deal with here.[96] However, the debate now recognises variations in the theory, of which the most applicable to the case of astrology is privatisation, in which religious affiliation becomes increasingly diverse, pluralistic and a matter of individual choice.[97]

Three models (at least) can be identified for the supposed impact of modernity on religion.[98] First, modernity is characterised by increasing secularisation and a corresponding growth of scepticism about religion which is therefore in decline, perhaps inevitably, as in the six variants discussed above. Second, modernity has had little effect on religious belief, which persists relatively undiminished, obscured by the decline in official church attendance. This argument was proposed influentially by Andrew Greeley, Milton Yinger, who coined the phrase 'hidden' religion, and Thomas Luckmann, who devised the term 'invisible religion' in order to describe the religiosity of those who retain traditional beliefs but no longer attend

---

and Theology, 17/4 (1987), pp. 356–8; Roof, *A Generation of Seekers*; Henri Broch, 'Save our Science: The Struggle for Reason at the University', *Skeptical Inquirer*, 24/3 (2000); Erich Goode, 'Education, Scientific Knowledge, and Belief in the Paranormal', *Skeptical Inquirer*, 26/1 (2002), p. 27; and Rice, 'Believe It or Not', p. 101.

[93]   E. Haraldsson, 'Representative National Surveys of Psychic Phenomena: Iceland, Great Britain, Sweden, USA and Gallup's Multinational Survey', *Journal of the Society for Psychical Research*, 53 (1975), pp. 150–1.

[94]   Stephen Bruce, *Religion in Modern Britain* (Oxford, 1995), p. 55.

[95]   Rodney Stark and William Simms Bainbridge, *A Theory of Religion* (New Brunswick NJ, 1987), p. 429.

[96]   See Andrew Greeley, *Unsecular Man: The Persistence of Religion* (New York, 1974).

[97]   Bryan Wilson, *Religion in Secular Society: A Sociological Comment* (Harmondsworth, 1969).

[98]   Paul Heelas, *Religion, Modernity and Postmodernity* (Oxford, 1998).

a regular church service.[99] Stark and Bainbridge relate this theory to their view that secularisation is not only not new but is a continuous and natural process within 'religious economies' in which the tendency of religious institutions to become more worldly is both continuous and is automatically balanced by countervailing tendencies to revival (producing 'sects') and innovation (which results in the development of 'cults').[100] The very concept of the decline of the church, the triumph of science and the shift towards a 'religionless' future is therefore, in their view, contradicted by the historical evidence. And third, modernity is characterised by increasing fragmentation of established religious forms and greater pluralism, an argument which is, perhaps, most congenial to the inclusion of new religious movements and New Age beliefs within the framework of the contemporary religious world. Davie has coined the phrase 'believing without belonging', a direct reference to Michael Hornsby-Smith's consideration of the joint questions of 'beliefs and belonging' in relation to modern English Catholics, in order to describe those individuals for whom religious experience is no longer found in one of the mainstream churches.[101] She adds that 'the sacred does not disappear – indeed in many ways it is becoming more rather than less prevalent in contemporary [British] society'; in Europe as a whole, she reports, the increase of 'other-faith categories' represents a growth area in religiosity since 1945, contrary to the decline predicted by secularisation theory.[102]

The central theme, then, of most of the literature on modern belief in astrology is that it is a phenomenon in urgent need of explanation. However, a counter-argument is to be found within the literature on the sociology and phenomenology of religion. Andrew Greeley, for example, launched a substantial critique of Adorno and argued that the definition of the paranormal as abnormal is unsustainable.[103] Instead, he claimed that 'the paranormal is normal' and that people who have paranormal experiences are not only 'not kooks…deviants…social misfits', but may actually 'be more emotionally healthy than those who do not have such experiences'.[104] Actually, other evidence suggests that paranormal ideas are widespread, frequently appeal to educated people and that attempts to label such notions as bizarre or marginal are misleading and unhelpful.[105] The situation is

---

[99] Greeley, *Unsecular Man*; J. Milton Yinger, 'A Structural Examination of Religion', *Journal for the Scientific Study of Religion*, 8 (1969), p. 90; Thomas Luckmann, *The Invisible Religion* (New York, 1967).

[100] Rodney Stark and William Simms Bainbridge, *The Future of Religion: Secularizaton. Revival and Cult Formation* (Berkeley, 1985), pp. 429–31.

[101] Davie, pp. 93–116; Michael Hornsby-Smith, *Roman Catholic Beliefs in England: Customary Catholicism and Transformations in Religious Authority* (Cambridge, 1991), p. 4.

[102] Grace Davie, *Religion in Britain since 1945*, p. 43; see also p. 27.

[103] Andrew M. Greeley, *The Sociology of the Paranormal* (London, 1975), p. 7.

[104] Greeley, *Sociology*, p. 7.

[105] Harvey J. Irwin, *The Psychology of Paranormal Belief: A Researcher's Handbook* (Hatfield, 2009).

complex and Stephen Hunt observed the evidence that while university-educated middle-class people may be more attracted to New Age ideas, better educated people are less likely to believe in astrology.[106] Where does this then leave astrology's classification as New Age?

The tendency to regard adherence to non-conventional religions, in which Caird and Law included theosophy and spiritualism, as a form of social deviance, arises from a flawed model of Western religion in which a stable society is said to be currently meeting a unique challenge from new ideological sources which it is obliged to resist.[107] Thus the labelling of astrology as deviant may be no more then a device to confirm what Glock and Stark called the 'humanistic value-orientation', or what Herbrechtsmeier termed the 'imperial' attitudes of modern science.[108] It is an application of 'methodological scientism', the imposition of inappropriate scientific methodologies on questions which they cannot answer.[109]

From a phenomenological standpoint, the nature of belief is difficult to understand if it is assumed, *a priori*, to be false. As David Hufford has argued, the investigation of belief traditions has itself been distorted by the *a priori* assumption that those beliefs are false, even when researchers make ritual declarations of their own neutrality. As he summarised the situation, the essentially misguided question that such researchers ask is 'Why and how do some people manage to believe things which are so patently false?'; he added that 'the interpretations that follow often obtain most or all of their explanatory force from the assumption that the beliefs under study are objectively incorrect'.[110] Further, he argued that attempts to debunk supernatural beliefs, or to subject them to rational explanations, may be equally based on statements of faith and that, therefore, 'traditions of disbelief should be recognised as such and no more accepted uncritically than are traditions of belief'.[111]

We need to consider just how such debates impact on astrologers. The sceptical, positivist point of view, that belief is essentially false no matter what the evidence in its favour, is well known to astrologers, and has been disseminated through literature familiar to them. Astrologers who are members of astrological societies for a number of years will become aware of such sceptical arguments, particularly when applied to astrology by sceptical scientists, because they are summarised in the specialist literature, as by John Bowles in the newsletter of the

---

[106]   Stephen Hunt, *Religion and Everyday Life* (London, 2005), p. 96.

[107]   Dale Caird and Henry G. Law, 'Non-Conventional Beliefs: Their Structure and Measurement', *Journal for the Scientific Study of Religion*, 21/2 (1982), pp. 151–2.

[108]   Charles R. Glock and Rodney Stark, *Religion and Society in Tension* (Chicago, 1966), pp. 10–11; William Herbrechtsmeier, 'Buddhism and the Definition of Religion: One More Time', *Journal for the Scientific Study of Religion*, 32/1 (1993), p. 15.

[109]   Mikael Stenmark, *Scientism: Science, Ethics and Religion* (Aldershot, 2001), pp. 2–3.

[110]   David Hufford, 'Traditions of Disbelief', *Talking Folklore*, 1/3 (1987), p. 19.

[111]   Hufford, 'Traditions of Disbelief', pp. 25, 27.

US-based Association for Astrological Networking (AFAN).[112] Geoffrey Dean's point of view, regarded as hostile by many astrologers was also given prominent space, supported by some sceptical colleagues, in a volume of interviews with contemporary astrologers, produced by an astrological publisher and targeted specifically at the astrological market.[113]

In case we should imagine that not all astrologers are aware of Dean's work, those in much of the English-speaking world are certainly aware of Richard Dawkins. The following exchange between Dawkins and the BBC journalist Jeremy Paxman on British television in 1996 occurred as part of a larger discussion which attracted a huge amount of attention amongst astrologers in the UK:

> *Jeremy Paxman:* Richard Dawkins, where would you put astrology on the scale of belief?
>
> *Richard Dawkins:* Somewhere with fairies.[114]

The issue is not whether Dawkins is right, but of the nature of the public debates and their impact on notions of what it is to 'believe'. Every astrologer familiar with this exchange was aware that, according to an influential body of opinion, their interest in astrology equates to infantile belief in fairies and Father Christmas. Astrologers in the UK and US vigorously respond to such perceived attacks. In 2011, when the physicist Brian Cox and the comedian Dara O'Briain made dismissive remarks about astrology on the BBC, the British Astrological Association organised a petition, seeking support for a response.[115] O'Briain encouraged followers of his Twitter account to sabotage the petition, and abusive comments were duly posted, of which this is an example (misspellings in the original):

> They called astrology rubbish because it IS rubbish you fucking reatards. I hope you none of you have kids. We don't need any more additions of the fucking moron gene to the gene pool. THank you and have a good day. PS the BBC and Cox et al. are laughing their asses off at you dumbcunts right now.

Another email to Frances Clynes, a member of the Astrological Association council, warned her that she would feel the 'side of my fist'.[116] The AA publicised

---

[112]   John A. Bowles, 'Astrology and the Skeptics', *AFAN Newsletter*, Winter (2001).

[113]   Phillipson, *Astrology in the Year Zero*, pp. 124–66.

[114]   Dawkins, 'Newsnight'.

[115]   Astrological Association, 'AA Response to Anti-Astrology Propaganda', at<http://astrologicalassociation.blogspot.com/2011/01/aa-response-to-anti-astrology.html>, accessed 19 January 2012; Deborah Houlding, 'The Backstory of the AA's Petition and how Twitter-Chums Stick Together when the Beeb makes a Boob, 07/02/2011', <http://www.astrologicalassociation.com/pages/bbc/petition.pdf>, accessed 28 July 2011.

[116]   Personal communication, Frances Clynes, 13 January 2012.

the dispute to its members, while there was also some wider media comment.[117] This, then, is how sceptics are often experienced by astrologers, as far from scientific and rational. Most of the high-profile sceptics are polite and courteous, but astrologers are aware of the intolerant and sometimes violent tone which is stirred up by the legacy of the Tylorian statement that astrology is a monstrous farrago which is destructive of modern civilisation. This induces amongst some sceptics a sense that astrologers pose a threat to the modern world, as Miller concluded when he argued that astrology undermines democracy. The generally apocalyptic mythology which gives the organised sceptic movement its sense of urgency finds it justification in the claim that the enlightenment itself is under threat from a rise in obscurantism and superstition.[118] There may be no evidence for this proposition but lack of evidence is not the issue. Rather, the founders of organised scepticism issued a call to arms as powerful as that which drove Blavatsky, Bailey and Steiner, and which was based on an equally profound sense of historical danger.

Some sceptical attacks on astrologers may be unpleasant, but the point is made again that the problem of the discourse between astrologers and sceptics is often one of science communication, rather than science education. The issue is not who is in the right, but the nature of the discourse and its impact on astrologers' perceptions, and the experience that sceptical criticism is based not only on science but also on jeers and threats. The petition controversy was widely discussed within astrological networks, and reinforced the conclusion that the anti-astrology position rests not in science but rhetoric. This was precisely Ivan Kelly's complaint in 1999; that astrologers respond to sceptical attacks as if they are all equally rhetorical and hence devoid of real substance.[119] But when sceptical attacks on astrology really are rhetorical and devoid of substance, the astrologers' complaint seems to be reasonable.

Secondly, the sceptical proposition, that belief in astrology requires explanation because scientific evidence does not exist, is contradicted by the existence of positive research results, as in Pat Harris's doctoral research into fertility. Notable in this respect is the so-called 'Mars Effect', which has been refuted by sceptics but nevertheless remains a part of the pro-astrology literature.[120] The French

---

[117]   Martin Robbins, 'Astrologers angered by stars', *Guardian*, 24 January 2011, at <http://www.guardian.co.uk/science/the-lay-scientist/2011/jan/24/1>, accessed 20 January 2012.

[118]   Bok et al., 'Objections to Astrology'.

[119]   Ivan Kelly, '"Debunking the Debunkers". A Response to an Astrologer's Debunking of Skeptics', *Skeptical Inquirer*, 23/6 (1999), p. 42. For the astrological position see Valerie Vaughan, 'Debunking the Debunkers: Lessons to be Learned', *Mountain Astrologer*, 80 (1998), pp. 35–42, 122.

[120]   Michel Gauquelin, *Written in the Stars* (Wellingborough, 1988); Suitbert Ertel and Kenneth Irving, *The Tenacious Mars Effect* (London, 1996); Nicholas Campion, 'The "Mars effect" that refuses to go away', *Independent*, Thursday Review, 21 October 1999, p. 7.

statistician Michel Gauquelin (1928–91) demonstrated, amongst a series of results, that Mars tends to be either rising or culminating at the birth of sports champions. Astrologers are aware that the sceptical critiques of Gauquelin's work have been refuted in some cases, and are subject to allegations of fraud by the sceptics themselves in others. The Mars Effect and other positive results may be challenged and undermined. Their conclusions may be false, but that does not remove them from the literature, and astrologers respond to sceptical critiques by referring to positive scientific results.[121] Another well-known example concerns astrologers' rebuttal of one of the most famous of anti-astrology papers, the Carlson research of 1985, which concluded that astrologers were unable to distinguish one birthchart from another.[122] Carlson's conclusions are regularly cited in sceptical literature as conclusive that astrology does not work, but astrologers' rebuttals are never mentioned.[123] Astrologers are aware of the situation, and that, if Carlson does not respond then, in their view, there is good reason to doubt his work. The argument that astrologers are somehow suffering from a psychological disorder which inclines them to believe in something they know to be false, is therefore deeply flawed, as are all the explanatory models which flow from it. In the view of many astrologers, it is they who take a scientific stance, again an argument to which Ivan Kelly drew attention.

The problem, then, of how astrologers respond to the word 'belief' and their response to the question 'Do you believe in astrology?' is therefore an important one. The evidence suggests that the word is widely held to have negative connotations. Neil Spencer, who writes the horoscope column in the UK Sunday newspaper, *The Observer*, described 'belief' as a 'troublesome word', while when Margaret Hone, speaking with all her authority, addressed the problem in 1951, she advised students to sidestep the question of belief by stating, rather, that they observe 'that certain traits of character and certain types of events appear to correlate with certain planetary relationships'.[124]

A critical study of the sociological and psychological literature suggests that the various explanations advanced for modern belief in astrology emerge primarily from the positivist assumption that astrology, *a priori*, must be false precisely because it conflicts with the positivist worldview. The argument is therefore fundamentally one of epistemology, and of competition between

---

[121] See, for example, Ingrid Lind, *Astrology and Commonsense* (London, 1962), pp. 17–21; Arthur Mather, 'Correlation', *Astrological Journal*, 18/1 (1975/76), pp. 28–30; Mary Downing, 'Media Watch – "Astrology is rubbish, says new research"', *AFAN email digest*, 530 (2003).

[122] Shawn Carlson, 'A Double-Blind Test of Astrology', *Nature*, 318 (1985), pp. 419–25.

[123] For a summary of the rebuttals of Carlson see Ken McRitchie 'Support for Astrology from the Carlson Double-Blind Experiment', *International Astrologer*, 40/2 (2011), pp. 33–8, at <http://www.theoryofastrology.com/carlson/carlson.htm>.

[124] Spencer, *Truce as the Stars Above*, p. 14; Margaret Hone, *The Modern Textbook of Astrology* (London, 1973), p. 15.

different approaches to knowledge. Further, amongst scientific sceptics, the term 'belief' is automatically used to indicate propositions which are false. Thus, the argument continues, the presumed problem of astrology's existence in the modern world can be explained if, first, belief in it can be explained. All such explanations, emerging from the automatic assumption that astrology is false, therefore, assume psychological disorder or weakness, or social deviancy, as explanations. However, the challenge to secularisation theory, questioning the evolutionist view of religion, opens the way to another possibility: that astrology may exist as part of the process of privatisation, the increasing pluralism of religiosity which is a feature of modernity, and that individual affiliation to it may be a consequence of rational choice rather than superstition. The consequence, though, of the debate on the nature of belief in the sceptical, psychological and sociological literature, and the frequent assumption that beliefs are automatically false, may have made both astrologers and members of the public reluctant to admit to belief in astrology. Simply, the perceived need to explain belief in astrology is based on a series of discredited evolutionary ideas, and measurements of it are highly suspect.

With this in mind I set out to ask astrologers whether the simple question 'Do you believe in astrology' is likely to elicit reliable information. In view of the problems surrounding public reaction to the word 'belief', I devised a questionnaire asking students and practitioners of astrology (defined as attendees at the 2000 British Astrological Association conference) how they would respond to the question 'Do you believe in astrology?' and invited them to explain their reasons. I sought a quantitative result, but one which could be further examined in the light of qualitative material, the respondents' justification of their answers.

This questionnaire was distributed at the Astrological Association Conference in Reading on 1–3 September 2000 and I received 47 replies out of a total of 220 questionnaires distributed. All were anonymous and each questionnaire was numbered. The numbers are given in brackets in the text below. Correspondents were offered four answers to the question, 'If you were asked whether you believe in astrology, would you answer: A; Yes, B: No, C: Don't Know and D: Other'. The responses were as follows:

Yes: 27 (57 per cent).

No: 3 (6 per cent).

Don't Know: 1 (2 per cent).

Other: 14 (30 per cent).

Of the remainder one ticked both 'yes' and 'no', and one ticked both 'yes' and 'other'. Although the percentages, rounded to the nearest whole figure, are meaningless when applied to a figure of one, it is useful to note that only 57 per cent ticked 'yes', and that 30 per cent ticked 'other', disputing the terms in which the question was asked. The 'no' figure is so small as to suggest that the alternative to 'yes, I believe' is not 'no, I don't believe' but a search for alternative words to 'belief'. While it may be objected that we cannot extrapolate the results of a survey of astrologers' attitudes to astrology in order to draw conclusions concerning studies of the general public's attitudes to astrology, the nature of those attitudes forms only part of this study. The key consideration concerns responses to the word 'belief'. In that respect we should examine the reasons given for the various answers. Of the respondents who ticked 'yes', most defined astrology as something they find useful. Only one stated that astrology 'has now become my way of life'. Of the 27 who ticked 'yes', 25 gave further reasons. Of these 17 (36 per cent of the total sample, 63 per cent of those who ticked 'yes') cited personal experience, the fact that astrology 'works' and that they have studied it. Only one of those addressed the question of whether astrology is a religion and specifically stated 'It is not a religion'. For these respondents, experience and empirical observation precede belief.

Only one respondent tackled the question of the claim made by some astrologers that 'I don't believe in astrology. I use it', arguing that they use it *because* they believe in it and that belief therefore precedes experience. The concept of pure knowledge was important for some. One wrote, citing Jung, 'I don't believe, I know'.[125] Some of those who gave experience as a reason for belief also pointed to the truth of astrology: 'I am convinced of the truth of astrology', 'The planets don't lie. The truth is out there for us to learn'. In addition some people may be astrologically disinclined to believe: 'So many predictions are true. But not everyone has the chart to see! Or the inclination to watch.'

Of those who cited other reasons, a number discussed problems of terminology. One argued that astrology is more a matter of faith in a predetermined destiny than belief in a possible future. Only one other respondent mentioned faith – and then as a lack of faith in newspaper horoscopes. Only a handful cited reasons for belief which may be considered overtly religious. Of those who claimed that their belief is based on experience, one stated that astrology is also 'very much a spiritual matter' and another that 'it is a personal spiritual pursuit'. Only three gave religious reasons without claiming that experience of astrology preceded belief. One wrote that 'there exist correlations between events on earth and planetary positions. The universe is more like a great thought than a great machine. The heavens declare the glory of God. Rather, as the mind rules the body, the mind of God rules the universe.' Another compared belief in astrology to belief in God: 'I believe astrology works – it is almost as vague as being asked "Do you believe in God?" Well, yes I do – but from within and I "feel" astrology comes from within also.' A third stated that 'I believe in astrology because my feeling for God's work in my life and lifes[*sic*] or existence of all other things and humans is more clear and my faith is stronger.' It is clear that for respondents who believe in astrology, belief is seen as primarily based on empirical evidence – the observation and

---

[125]   Spencer, p. 14; Hone, p. 15.

experience of astrology working either in the sense of giving correct predictions or being helpful. There would seem to be no grounds for arguing that belief in astrology is an alternative to belief in Christianity. Of the three who cited religious reasons for their belief in astrology, there seems no reason to suspect an anti-Christian attitude.

Then we should consider the negative answers. Of the three respondents who answered 'no', two gave further reasons. One of these claimed that 'astrology is not a belief system', but otherwise gave reasons which have elsewhere been cited as evidence for belief – 'astrology…works'. The third posed the question 'Do you believe in television? Do you believe the sun rises in the morning?', arguing that astrology is self-evident in much the same way as the 'yes' respondent's rhetorical question 'Do you believe in music'. The remainder of the reasons given for not believing – astrology is 'immensely useful…satisfying and stimulating' – could equally well have been cited as reasons for believing by the 17 who cited this same explanation as a basis for belief.

A number of respondents refused to answer either 'yes' or 'no'. Of the two respondents who answered 'don't know', one stated that astrology is not a religion and that it is better to say that it can be used, and that '"I know" astrology maintains truths that are inherent in the human condition', both grounds given for belief for those who ticked 'yes'. The other claimed that belief would only come with irrefutable proof, agreeing with the 'yes' camp that experience precedes belief, but that there is at present insufficient evidence. Most of the reasons given by those who answered 'other' overlap with those given by those who ticked 'yes', 'no' and 'don't know'.

The rhetorical questions 'Do you believe in music' and 'Do you believe in television' or 'that the sun rises' which were used to justify 'yes' and 'no' respectively were repeated five times in different forms with variations such as 'Do you believe in art? … geography?… mathematics? … science? …cat food?' One respondent actually said that this could be a reason to answer 'yes'. The statement 'I don't believe, I know', cited as a reason for belief, now becomes a reason why the question cannot be answered. Eight respondents cited as reasons their personal experience of astrology working; hence astrology is not a matter of belief and therefore that the question cannot be answered. One respondent even ticked both 'yes' and 'no', citing as reasons 'faith in Astrology's meaning and value' and 'experience' of it working. The other ticked both 'yes' and 'other', arguing that the issue is less about belief than about astrology 'working in practice'.

It is notable that whatever the answer given to the question, astrologers frequently cited analogies with other commonly accepted phenomena to justify their opinion. This is consistent with other reported opinions. In a report on students at Kepler College of the Astrological Arts it was reported that:

Student Karen Hawkwood, who moonlights as an astrological counsellor, says it makes her laugh when people ask, 'Do you believe in astrology?' 'Because that's like asking, "Do you believe in biology?" Of course this thing exists. The question is, what do you believe it can or cannot do?' She says she 'violently disbelieves that the planets *cause* anything'. But she thinks astrology 'can show us patterns, how the pattern in the sky represents synchronistically the pattern in the human being. I don't know how this works. The microcosm reflects the macrocosm. We see patterns in things that there's no objective way to explain. I believe astrology is one of the best ways to see those patterns.'[126]

It is apparent that the different answers may be based on different reactions to the word 'belief'. Simply, if the reasoning behind the answers is similar, then the difference between the actual answers may be based on a sense amongst those who answer 'no' that the object of belief of necessity does not exist. This opinion is not shared by those who answer 'yes'.

This exercise confirmed the profound suspicion surrounding the concept of belief. Of the sample of practitioners and students of astrology just over half admitted to belief in astrology. The principle reason – that it works – is also the dominant reason cited by the slightly less than half who answered 'no', 'don't know' or 'other'. Thus the reasons cited for sharply conflicting answers to the question do not fundamentally differ. The reasons why individuals respond positively to questions concerning belief in astrology may therefore have little do with their opinions as to the nature of astrology and a great deal to with personal experience. The overwhelmingly pragmatic justifications for respondents' attitudes to astrology are therefore unlikely to be affected by any religious or theological criticism. Such criticism may, though, affect astrologers' religious affiliation by alienating them from the church.

I need to offer one further thought for discussion at this point. I repeated this exercise at the Norwegian Astrological Conference in November 2001. A similar range of justifications for astrology's efficacy were given; it is a tool which clearly works, as experience demonstrates. However, only one respondent denied belief in astrology, five answered 'other' and 19 answered 'yes'. The problem with the word 'belief' may therefore be one which only afflicts the English-speaking world. Still, as the English-speaking world is the focus of my research, it is a problem with which we must deal.

The probable solution to the problem of 'belief' is now clear: the presumed necessary relationship of the word to religious ideas, or to a range of practices considered unacceptable to some modern scientists or sceptics, results from a narrow and anachronistic understanding of religion as defined by Christianity and its articles of faith. In most religious traditions practice is more important than belief. In India, for example, religious devotion is a matter of practice. Clifford Ando has recently made the point in his study of Roman divination, including astrology, that practice was crucial.[127] One practises divination and it either works or it does not. If it does, one continues. If it does not, there is a choice: one can

[126]   David Cox, *I Don't Need to Believe in God – I Know* (London, 1985).
[127]   Clifford Ando, *The Matter of the Gods* (Berkeley, 2008).

either give up or refine one's practice. Without making any point about modern astrology being defined as divination, the principle holds: astrologers work at it and either experience it working or not. This is orthopraxy, correct practice, as opposed to orthodoxy, correct belief. Dean and his colleagues almost reached this conclusion when they insisted that belief in astrology is based on the perception that it works, but they failed to realise that the word 'belief' itself is the problem.

Chapter 9

Salvation and the Stars: Astrology, Religion and Belief

Consulting horoscopes [and] astrology, conceal(s) a desire for power over time, history, and, in the last analysis, other human beings, as well as a wish to conciliate hidden powers. They contradict the honor, respect, and loving fear that we owe to God alone.[1]

The discussion of astrology as a matter of belief is closely associated with the proposition that it is a religion. When this assumption is made it is rarely substantiated, any more than claims that astrology is New Age or postmodern are justified. Generally it is enough that the statement is made and accepted with the need neither for a statement of what religion is (or isn't) nor for evidence. Now, some astrology may well be a religion, if we can match the right definition of astrology to the appropriate understanding of religion but, astrology's practices and truth claims being diverse, it is frankly unlikely that *all* astrology is a religion. The only plausible way that we could define all astrology as a religion would be to take a sufficiently broad definition of religion itself, such that we might include sport, or economics, or socialism, as religious, in which case the discussion becomes meaningless. However, much of the literature on astrology by non-astrologers is clear on this point: astrology *is* a religion. This is hardly surprising, for it is often listed as a religion in dictionaries and encyclopaedias.[2]

Astrology's ancient religious connections are used by evangelical Christians as evidence for their argument that it remains a pagan practice.[3] According to the astronomer George Abell, for example, 'astrology is the polytheistic religion of ancient Babylonia and Greece and is based in symbolism – a magical correspondence between the gods and the planets that bear the same names'.[4] For Mircea Eliade, the distinguished historian of religion, it is not quite religious, but 'parareligious'.[5] The sociologist of religion Stephen Hunt argued that astrology is

---

[1] Catechism of the Catholic Church 1994, para. 2116: Divination and magic. Online at <http://www.usccb.org/catechism/text/pt3sect2chpt1.htm>, accessed 30 July 2011.

[2] See, for example, John R. Hinnells (ed.), *A New Dictionary of Religions* (Oxford, 1995), pp. 52–4.

[3] See, for example, Charles Strohmer, *What Your Horoscope Doesn't Tell You* (Wheaton IL, 1988), pp. 15–26.

[4] George O. Abell, 'Astrology', in George O. Abell and Barry Singer (eds), *Science and the Paranormal: Probing the Existence of the Supernatural* (London, 1981), p. 73.

[5] Mircea Eliade, *Occultism, Witchcraft and Cultural Fashions* (Chicago, 1976), p. 61.

'popular religion' and, following Rodney Stark and William Bainbridge, that those 'committed' to it constitute a 'cultist' movement.[6] There is also general agreement within the academic literature that contemporary astrology may be characterised as a 'new religious movement'.[7] Eileen Barker, though, takes a more cautious line, suggesting that some such new religious movements merely draw on astrology which is, therefore, itself not necessarily religious.[8] The argument that astrology is a religion has various subsidiary forms, one of which is that it is a substitute religion.[9] Some astrologers, critical of what they see as deficiencies in the general condition of modern astrology, call it a 'substitute religion', as did the influential German astrologer Walter Koch.[10] Some astrologers, though, regard the word 'religion' in a positive light, and agree, at least, that astrology can be a religion. This is from one recent online newsletter: 'Astrology becomes a religion when one worships the stars. For the past thirty years I have been a member of The Church of Light which was incorporated to teach, practice and disseminate the Religion of the Stars. My religion is – The Religion of the Stars'.[11]

Of course, no statement that astrology is a religion makes sense unless we know what a religion is, a point on which there is no consensus. There is actually no single accepted definition of religion, a fact of course much debated and well known to scholars in the field, but curiously not familiar to those outside it. As William Herbrechtsmeier, who was struggling to make sense of academic attitudes to Buddhism, realised: 'The definition of religion continues to be a matter of dispute among scholars. And I suspect that disagreement about the topic will persist so long as religion is studied in academic circles'.[12] Engagement with the literature on astrology which emerges from the sociology of religion, brief as it is,

[6]   Stephen J. Hunt, *Alternative Religions: A Sociological Introduction* (Aldershot, 2003), p. 173; Rodney Stark and William Simms Bainbridge, *The Future of Religion: Secularization, Revival and Cult Formation* (Berkeley, 1985).

[7]   Steve Bruce, *Religion in Modern Britain* (Oxford, 1995), p. 105; Irving Hexham and Karla Poewe, *New Religions as Global Cultures* (Boulder CO, 1997), pp. 85–6, 104; J. Gordon Melton, 'The Emergence of New Religions in Eastern Europe Since 1989', in Eileen Barker and Margot Warburg (eds), *New Religions and New Religiosity* (Aarhus, 2001), p. 53.

[8]   Eileen Barker, 'New Religions and New Religiosity', in Eileen Barker and Margot Warburg (eds), *New Religions and New Religiosity* (Aarhus, 2001), p. 18; see also Nils G. Holm, 'The Indian Factor in New Religious Movements: A Religio-Psychological Perspective', in Eileen Barker and Margot Warburg (eds), *New Religions and New Religiosity* (Aarhus, 2001), p. 103.

[9]   Bernulf Kanitscheider, 'A Philosopher Looks at Astrology', *Interdisciplinary Science Reviews*, 16/3 (1991), pp. 259–60.

[10]   Walter Koch, 'Vernal Point and Era of Aquarius', *In Search*, Winter 1958/59 and Spring 1959, 2/1 and 2/2, p. 81.

[11]   Dee Wynne, 'Astrology as a Religion', *AFAN Interactive Digest*, 1281 (2010).

[12]   William Herbrechtsmeier, 'Buddhism and the Definition of Religion: One More Time', *Journal for the Scientific Study of Religion*, 32/1 (1993), p. 1.

leads to a slightly different conclusion – that the vigorous debates on the nature of religion are ignored and that some unspecified version of it is applied to astrology as if no further consideration were required. We need, then, to consider which varieties of religious dogma, experience or belief might be usefully applied to astrology.

A useful distinction between different theories of religion was provided by Brian Zinnbauer and his colleagues, who distinguished the 'substantive' approach, which focuses on 'beliefs, emotions, practices, and relationships of individuals in relation to a higher power or divine being', from the 'functional', which emphasises 'the function that religiousness serves in the life of the individual [and] how they are used in dealing with the fundamental problems of existence such as life, death, suffering and injustice'.[13] As Zinnbauer recognised, the arguments over the nature of religion in general concern such matters as whether belief in spiritual beings is necessary, as E.B. Tylor argued, whether all that is required is a sense of the numinous, of something greater and sacred outside one's self, as Rudolf Otto suggested or whether social function, rather than supernatural belief, is the vital ingredient, as Emile Durkheim argued.[14] The latter position leads naturally to the proposition that ideologies which have no supernatural component, such as science or Marxism, may be considered religions.[15] In their response, though, Stark and Bainbridge pointed out that such inclusive definitions inevitably make it difficult to establish conceptual tools for the study of religion.[16] Simply, if everything is a religion, then nothing is not.

Nevertheless, inclusive approaches such as Thomas Luckmann's and Milton Yinger's may be seen as a necessary response to the previous attitude that religion is expressed primarily through Christianity or the church, and allow the study of wider forms of religiosity in society.[17] Thus, for Luckmann, religions generate 'symbolic universes [which] are objectivated meaning-systems that relate the experiences of everyday life to a "transcendent layer of reality"'.[18] Such a definition sounds very appropriate for astrology, especially in view of astrologers' tendency

---

[13] Brian J. Zinnbauer et al., 'Religion and Spirituality: Unfuzzying the Fuzzy', *Journal for the Scientific Study of Religion*, 36/4 (1997), p. 550.

[14] Edward Burnett Tylor, *Primitive Culture* (London, 1873), p. 491; Rudolf Otto, *The Idea of the Holy* (Oxford, 1958), pp. 1–7; Emile Durkheim, *The Elementary Forms of Religious Life*, trans. Karen E. Fields (New York, 1995), pp. 41, 206–8.

[15] J. Milton Yinger, *The Scientific Study of Religion* (London, 1970), pp. 11–12, 196–200.

[16] Stark and Bainbridge, *The Future of Religion*, p. 5; see also Peter Berger, *The Sacred Canopy: Elements of a Sociological Theory of Religion* (New York, 1969), p. 177.

[17] Thomas Luckmann, *The Invisible Religion* (New York, 1967); and J. Milton Yinger, 'A Structural Examination of Religion', *Journal for the Scientific Study of Religion*, 8 (1969), p. 89.

[18] Luckmann, *The Invisible Religion*, p. 44.

to focus on symbol and meaning in their discussions of astrology's nature and appeal.

Yinger's solution is a useful one: to treat as religions 'those phenomena labelled religious by the individuals or societies in question', yet to recognise that 'some groups labelled religious, may deny the appellation'.[19] The question, simply, is whether 'outsiders', academics in this case, have the right to impose categories on 'insiders' which those insiders reject. That is, by defining a practice or belief-system as a religion, how do we avoid the pejorative associations which many sociologists have of the term 'religion'? The same problem applies to astrology as to Buddhism, namely that any description of it as a religion is bound to carry inferences which distort an understanding of what practitioners and users of astrologers actually do and claim.[20]

The debate on the problems of defining religion reached their final stage with Jonathan Z. Smith's statement that, while people have wondered about their relationship with the ultimate for millennia, Western academics have pondered the nature of religion for just two centuries.[21] Religion, then, is an ontological category devised by Enlightenment philosophers who were concerned to restrict the power of the Christian church as an institution, an exercise which also meant challenging its dogma, function and very existence: religion could not be destroyed until it was first identified as a distinct form of activity, unrelated to the rest of mundane existence. For eighteenth-century radicals such an exercise followed naturally from several centuries' worth of Protestant assault on Catholic theology. As the power of the church was pushed back, so religion, as a category of experience, knowledge and activity, became separated from the other routine affairs of daily life. Therefore, to argue about whether astrology *is* or *is not* a religion only makes sense within a peculiar set of typologies devised in the modern West. In India, the question makes no sense at all: the response of Indians I have asked is one of perplexity.

The associations of ancient astrology with religion are not in doubt – if we take a conventional view of religion as submission to higher cosmic powers and the worship of deities. That, of course, requires us to forget that religion in the ancient world, especially the Near East and eastern Mediterranean from where Western astrology emerged, was not the discrete category which it has become in the modern West. If we accept that religion was such a discrete, recognisable social and ontological category then, that astrology relied heavily on the planets which themselves were agents of the divine, meant that an association between astrological interpretation and religious practice was inevitable.[22] Different scholars couch the relationship between astrology and religion in a variety of terms. Lester

---

[19]   Yinger, 'A Structural Examination', p. 90.

[20]   Herbrechtsmeier, 'Buddhism', p. 1.

[21]   Jonathan Z. Smith, *Imagining Religion: From Babylon to Jonestown* (Chicago, 1982), p. 3.

[22]   See the arguments in Nicholas Campion, *A History of Western Astrology* (2 vols, London, 2009), vol. 1.

Ness referred to astrology as an 'adjunct' to the Mesopotamian religion of the third to second millennia BCE.[23] Max Weber argued that astrology was a 'consequence' of astral religion while Franz Cumont proposed the reverse, claiming that the development as astral religion in the sixth century BCE was instead a consequence of the rise of astrology.[24] According to modern scholarship, the Babylonians saw the movement of the stars as, in the words of C.J. Gadd, 'the writing of heaven', the means by which divine wishes were expressed, and it is therefore commonly understood that Mesopotamian astrology should be categorised as divination, and as a form of language.[25] To summarise a half a millennium of cultural exchange, Babylonian astrology was imported into the Greek world where it was to be intimately linked to Hellenistic astral theology, and was closely tied to Gnostic theories of the salvation of the soul.[26]

Yet, having religious origins does not mean that modern astrology is necessarily a religion any more than modern science's descent from magic, if we accept Charles Webster's thesis, means that it is itself necessarily magic.[27] If to classify astrology as a religion can be perceived as pejorative, how much more is it to describe it as not even a real religion at all, but a mere substitute. The very notion of a substitute religion is, of course, impossible to sustain, for it suggest that religions can be tested in order to establish which are genuine and which not. This makes sense to Jewish, Christian or Islamic mentality, but not to the historian or anthropologist. We can, though, take a different slant on this concept by arguing that astrology might be a 'religion' in the sense that it slips into the social or conceptual space left by the decline of mainstream, organised religion, in other words by the established Christian churches. In this sense it would be what Michael Hill considered a 'God of the Gaps', that is, one of many popular responses to the supposed 'disenchantment', or loss of sacred character, of the modern world.[28] That this argument follows naturally from popular accounts of secularisation theory is indicated by the related media reports. For example, in an article by Derek Draper in *The Times*, the question was posed: 'As religious belief dies in Britain, is it being replaced with a tendency towards superstition, magic or obscure cults?'[29]

---

[23]   Lester Ness, *Written in the Stars: Ancient Zodiac Mosaics* (Warren Center PA, 1998), p. 81. See also Franz Cumont, *Astrology among the Greeks and Romans* (New York, 1960), pp. 12–21.

[24]   Max Weber, *The Sociology of Religion*, trans. Ephraim Fischoff, 4th edn (Boston, 1963), p. 22; Cumont, *Astrology*, p. 16.

[25]   C.J. Gadd, *Ideas of Divine Rule in the Ancient East*, Schweich Lectures of the British Academy (Munich, 1980).

[26]   Campion, *A History of Western Astrology*, vol. 1, esp. chs 3, 12, 17.

[27]   Charles Webster, *From Paracelsus to Newton: Magic and the Making of Modern Science* (Cambridge, 1982).

[28]   Michael Hill, *A Sociology of Religion* (London, 1979), p. 247; Roy Willis and Patrick Curry, *Astrology, Science and Culture: Pulling Down the Moon* (Oxford, 2004), p. 77.

[29]   Derek Draper, 'I used to live a shallow life', *Times*, 21 February 2001, p. 3.

Nigella Lawson, citing the 1996 Church of England report, *The Search for Faith*, argued that 'star-signs' and 'the cult of the clairvoyant' are replacing the Church as 'the new religion'.[30] This view is also echoed in the sceptical literature.[31] We need to make a simple point here about these three writers: they are all educated and influential. Of the two who found a voice in *The Times*, Derek Draper was, in the 1990s, a Labour Party insider very close to Tony Blair, and TV chef Nigella Lawson is the daughter of former British Chancellor of the Exchequer, Nigel Lawson. The notion that one can distinguish a sensible religion from a nonsensical one, and that the former's current decline allows the rise of the latter are both, I argue, impossible to sustain when subjected to the evidence, yet are prevalent and unquestioned assumptions amongst many educated and influential people. The prevailing hypothesis is therefore that religious and classical paranormal beliefs should be negatively correlated, because they are naturally competing sets of beliefs, and this view does certainly have its supporters, suggesting that belief in astrology correlates inversely with church attendance.[32]

However, such arguments exist in a simple Manichaean world in which 'good' religion is pitted against 'bad' and devotees are obliged to choose one or the other, exactly as in pseudoscepticism. Such a scenario is frankly implausible, however widely it circulates. Here again, Stark and Bainbridge point to a solution. They identify a more complex position suggesting that, while, in their words, 'traditional religious affiliation' may inhibit 'the acceptance of occult practices and cult movements' including astrology, those who claim no religious affiliation are not secular rationalists, but show a high acceptance of occultism and cults and hence of astrology.[33] Thus, modernity, in their view, proceeds via a shift in the forms of religiosity rather than a decline. The notion of a rivalry between astrology and traditional religion, is, to be sure, retained in such a model, but the simple notion that a decline in one form of religious belief is matched by an equivalent rise in another is at least abandoned.

An alternative proposition, one that is also not necessarily incompatible with the notion of a rivalry between astrology and Christianity, is that religiosity and belief in astrology might actually be positively correlated on the grounds that they both appeal to anti-scientific sentiments. There is some evidence for the latter hypothesis, concluding that strong belief in the paranormal, including astrology,

---

[30]   Nigella Lawson, 'Astrology and the need to believe: Why are we going to New Age cranks for old-style cures?', *Times*, 13 November 1996, p. 17.

[31]   See, for example, Wendy Grossman, 'Skeptic at large', *Skeptic*, 15/3 (2002), p. 7.

[32]   C. Plug, 'An Investigation of Superstitious Belief and Behaviour', *Journal of Behavioural Science*, 2/3 (1975), pp. 176–7; Robert Wuthnow, *Experimentation in American Religion: The New Mysticisms and their Implications for the Churches* (Berkeley, 1978), pp. 58–9; Robin Gill, *Churchgoing and Christian Ethics* (Cambridge, 1999), pp. 42, 51; and Hunt, *Alternative Religions*, p. 17; see also M.A. Persinger and K. Makarec, 'Exotic Beliefs may be Substitutes for Religious Beliefs', *Perceptual and Motor Skills*, 71 (1990).

[33]   Stark and Bainbridge, *The Future of Religion*, pp. 384–6.

is likely to correlate with strong belief in either religion or science, or both.[34] In other words, the unifying principle is belief and the object of belief may be irrelevant. However, that a committed advocate of science is as likely to be a strong proponent of astrology as is an evangelical Christian completely challenges the assumption in both scientific and evangelical literature. There is, though, an obvious complication in this data: it completely demolishes the ontological distinction between science and religion, and between both of them and astrology, and instead focuses on 'belief', a concept which is deeply problematic. Again, the situation which emerges is one of confusion and complexity.

This is where Tom Rice makes a useful intervention. He argued that there are many 'belief patterns', and that attempts to distinguish religion, science and the paranormal as if they are mutually exclusive categories are therefore deeply flawed.[35] Supporting evidence for this proposition was found by Glenn Sparks in a survey of two hundred randomly selected individuals. He found that there was no relationship between belief in astrology and religious affiliation, a conclusion which receives a certain amount of backing from Gallup Polls in the 1970s, which found that there is no relationship between either churchgoing or Christian belief and belief in astrology in the US.[36] Under these circumstances we need to abandon the notion that there is any necessary correlation between religious ideology (or even scientific commitment) and belief in astrology. The evidence is mixed but strong enough to suggest that most of the simple statements which populate the sociological literature have to be abandoned.

A further subset of the astrology-as-religion argument is the astrology-as-cult hypothesis. The typology of church, sect and cult has been widely debated and the definitions of each seriously challenged, particularly in view of the pejorative associations attached to 'cult' as opposed to 'church'. Notably Stark and Bainbridge include discussion of astrology in their influential work *The Future of Religion* and they define it and its organisations as 'cults'. For example, they state that 'Personalized horoscopes cast for specific clients represent pure cult activity; impersonal mass media horoscopes are pure audience cult communications'.[37] Given Stark and Bainbridge's description of cults it has to be doubtful whether their assessment is correct. They state that cults are 'deviant religious bodies – that

---

[34]   Richard N. Williams, Carl B. Taylor and Wayne J. Hintze, 'The Influence of Religious Orientation on Belief in Science, Religion, and the Paranormal', *Journal of Psychology and Theology*, 17/4 (1989), pp. 356–8.

[35]   Tom W. Rice, 'Believe It or Not: Religious and Other Paranormal Beliefs in the United States', *Journal for the Scientific Study of Religion*, 42/1 (2003), p. 101; see also p. 105.

[36]   Glenn G. Sparks, 'The Relationship Between Paranormal Beliefs and Religious Beliefs', *Skeptical Inquirer*, 25/5 (2001), pp. 50–6; George H. Gallup, *The Gallup Poll: Public Opinion 1972–1977* (2 vols, Wilmington DE, 1978), I.574; George H. Gallup, *The Gallup Poll: Public Opinion 1978* (Wilmington DE, 1979), p. 184.

[37]   Stark and Bainbridge, *The Future of Religion*, p. 227.

is, they are in a state of relatively high tension with their surrounding sociocultural environment'.[38] Indeed, in their opinion, 'astrology is most commonly a limited client or audience phenomenon': the typical audience cult

> most closely resembles a very loose lecture circuit. Persons with a cult doctrine
> to offer rely on ads, publicity, and direct mail to assemble an audience to
> hear their lectures. Efforts almost invariably are made at these lectures to sell
> their ancillary materials – books, magazines, souvenirs and the like – but no
> significant efforts are made to organize the audience.[39]

This describes the world of organised astrology well enough, but it could also to any group activity, so it is unclear whether the word 'cult' in this sense has any value. Even so, 'Visiting an astrologer or actually being one,' Stark and Bainbridge continue, 'is a public cult activity rather than a private belief." A client cult is defined as a 'service and therapy occupation', and est, Scientology, Rolfing and psychoanalysis are given as examples.[40] The weakness of Stark and Bainbridge's typology, though, is that anything can be defined as a cult; if a visit to a therapist is a cult activity, then so must be a visit to a doctor for reassurance. The UK National Health Service may then be a cult organisation. Stark and Bainbridge's inclusive typology can be applied to almost any public activity, which renders it useless as an analytical tool. If every form of public behaviour can be cultic then the argument about what is or is not a cult breaks down. Ironically, having criticised inclusivist definitions of religion, they then fall into exactly the same trap in relation to cults.

To return to astrologers' own attitudes, when the still-influential English astrologer William Lilly, in his 'Epistle to the Student in ASTROLOGY', published in 1647, defined astrology as 'this heavenly knowledge of the Stars, wherein the great and admirable works of the invisible and all-glorious God are so manifestly apparent', or Olivia Barclay, an influential modern student of Lilly, states that the rules of astrology come from God, is astrology then an 'adjunct to religion', to adapt Lester Ness's phrase or actually religious?[41] The theosophical astrologer Alan Leo was convinced that astrology was itself a religion. By the end of the twentieth century, he predicted, 'Astrology [will] once again [be] established as a bright facet in the diamond of the coming World Religion.' In the meantime, Leo claimed that the subscribers to *Modern Astrology*, his 'true friends' and 'valued supporters', backed his view that 'Astrology was a religion and a hope for the

---

[38]   Stark and Bainbridge, *The Future of Religion*, p. 25.

[39]   Stark and Bainbridge, *The Future of Religion*, p. 227.

[40]   Stark and Bainbridge, *The Future of Religion*, p. 230.

[41]   William Lilly, *Christian Astrology* (London, 1647); Olivia Barclay, 'Will the Astronauts have to Abandon the Mir Space Station?: A Horary Judgement', *The Astrological Journal*, 41/6 (1999), p. 30; Ness, *Written in the Stars*, p. 81.

betterment of human life'.[42] For Leo, astrology's identification with religion was positive, but for others it is quite the opposite. When David Hamblin, former Chair of the British Astrological Association, became disillusioned with astrology after failing to find controlled, reliable evidence, he concluded that it was, instead, a religion.[43]

However, there is currently a strong rhetorical resistance amongst astrologers to astrology's categorisation as a religion. For example, in his discussion of belief in astrology, former *Observer* astrological columnist Neil Spencer considers that 'Astrology is not a religion – as we have seen, attempts to turn it into one annoy even astrologers'; this is so in spite of the fact that, he adds, they often regard it as having a high spiritual value.[44] Demetra George, author of a number of influential astrological texts, argues that 'most astrologers today would deny that astrology is a religion', even though she personally considers that it has religious origins.[45] There is, then, amongst astrologers, a profound antipathy to its categorisation as a religion. James Holden was most emphatic on the matter:

> Horoscopic astrology itself has little or nothing to do with religion. It was not 'revealed' in remote antiquity to priests of a particular religion or to leaders of mystical societies by divinities or 'transcendental masters.' It is not 'occult' in the usual sense of the word. It is a clear-cut empirical science that was invented by human beings and that operates on the basis of definite rules that have been established by experience ... It is independent of religion and independent of philosophy.[46]

However, while Holden separates astrology from religion on account of its origins, his argument is based on astrology's cultural context as much as its intrinsic nature. In India, he adds, where there is no conflict between religion and astrology, there is no need to make the distinction.

Astrology is frequently identified as a rival to Christianity by fundamentalist Christians, who regard it as overtly satanic, and liberals, whose discomfort may be mild, but is still evident. The UK-based Reachout Trust spoke for the fundamentalists when it claimed that, 'If God condemns astrology then we are left

---

[42]   Alan Leo, 'The Editor's Observatory: Modern Astrology's Coming-of-Age', *Modern Astrology*, New Series, 8/8 (1911), p. 311.

[43]   David Hamblin, 'Astrology as Religion: The Spiritual Dimension of Astrology', from his letter in *Astrological Journal*, 32/6 (1990), pp. 406–7, <http://www.rudolfhsmit. nl/p-reli1.htm>, accessed 6 July 2008.

[44]   Neil Spencer, *True as the Stars Above: Adventures in Modern Astrology* (London, 2000), p. 245.

[45]   Demetra George, Kepler College first year draft syllabus notes, email 5 April 2001.

[46]   James Herschel Holden, *A History of Horoscopic Astrology* (Tempe AZ, 1996), p. 261.

with no alternative but to conclude that this power is from the demonic realm'.[47] The Roman Catholic catechism of 1994 is unequivocal in its condemnation of astrology on the grounds that it is a form of divination which contradicts 'the honor, respect, and loving fear that we owe to God alone'.[48] The opinion of liberal Christian commentators on Christianity's current sociological and political status is often less harsh, though still hostile. This was evident in the Church of England report, *The Search for Faith*, published in 1996.[49] The report's problem with astrology is not that it is actively anti-Christian but only that it makes a sin of omission by failing to acknowledge the primacy of Christ in all matters.

It is precisely the definition of astrology as divination which prompted the UK Independent Television Commission to investigate its possible dangers.[50] The ITC found itself in the curious position of bracketing astrology with the more usually taboo topics of sex and violence and, in effect, sharing the evangelical Christian perspective. However, as far as astrology's possible New Age identity is concerned, serious questions are raised concerning its historic relationship with Christianity. For example, although the influential American astrologer Dane Rudhyar's theosophy owed more to Alice Bailey's esoteric Christianity than to Blavatsky's anti-clericalism, he strongly supported the argument that the coming of the Age of Aquarius will see the eclipse of the traditional churches by the new theosophical Christianity. In this sense Rudhyar saw astrology and the established churches in direct competition. In his opinion,

> Men question the stars because they [men] are in chaos, in darkness, in a bewildering fog. Astrology must answer for men the question of the existence of order. The known order of the earth and of human society is shattered. Souls that are dark and anguished turn to the stars – others turn to God and his supposed representatives among men.[51]

Blavatsky's profound hostility to the Christian church was matched by the fact that her respect for Christ was based only on his identity as one of a series of great teachers, along with Krishna and Buddha. However, the Theosophical Society attracted many adherents of existing traditions of Christian esotericism, including Alice Bailey and Rudolf Steiner, both of whom placed a huge emphasis on the coming of the 'Christ' at the beginning of the Aquarian Age. Rudhyar followed in this tradition, being a friend and student of Alice Bailey: he believed that the

---

[47]   *Astrology* (Richmond, n.d.), p. 5.

[48]   Catechism of the Catholic Church 1994, para. 2116.

[49]   *The Search for Faith and the Witness of the Church: An Exploration by the Mission Theological Advisory Group* (London, 1996), pp. 85–6.

[50]   Jane Sancho, *Beyond Entertainment?: Research into the Acceptability of Alternative Beliefs, Psychic and Occult Phenomena on Television* (London, 2001).

[51]   Dane Rudhyar, *The Practice of Astrology as a Technique in Human Understanding* (New York, 1975), p. 23.

established Christian church was incapable of satisfying the spiritual hunger that resulted from the historical crisis of the post-war world.[52] What was needed, he argued, was a new, revitalised Christianity which might generally manifest the 'Christ-impulse' and end its stale obsession with Jesus the man and the worn-out institutions, dogma and rituals of the church. Thus, in a curious anticipation of evangelical Christian attacks on the New Age, Rudhyar argued that the coming of the New Age was actually necessary if the Eastern religions were to be prevented from overwhelming Western civilisation. He argued that

> The challenge we must meet goes far deeper than to be merely 'good Christians' in the usual taken-for-granted manner. What one takes for granted, that one loses spiritually. One does not create a new world, a new society, with values taken for granted; with images, idols, or ideas worn thin and pale by familiarity and an unquestioning, unthinking sense of superiority … no one can truly and dynamically be a *Christian* leader who has not experienced in some measure the reality of the Christ.[53]

Rudhyar's words are a profound statement of Christian faith. Even if their context is his Gnostic emphasis on the Christ-within. They are a direct continuation of that first century CE 'Christian Gnosticism [which] emerged as a reaffirmation, though in somewhat different terms, of the original stance of transcendence central to the very beginnings of Christianity'.[54] The key, then to evangelical Christianity's hostility to the New Age is, as I noted in Chapter 4, New Age culture's Gnosticism. The clash between the two, when the Western theosophical tradition is considered, is not one of Christianity versus anti-Christianity, but of the competition between two Christianities. The question, then, is to what extent Christianity features in astrologers' religious attitudes.

There is also a debate amongst some mainstream Christians, who question the definition of astrology as a matter of belief. Father Lawrence Cassidy, Professor of Philosophy and teacher of astrology at Saint Peter's Jesuit College in New Jersey, is one of the most prominent. In response to the new Roman Catholic Catechism's criticism of astrology in 1994, he argued that if astrology-as-divination was condemned then, by implication, astrology-as-natural philosophy was permissable, concluding, as only a Jesuit theologian could, that the debate depended on how you understand the two general names, Christianity and astrology.[55]

---

[52]   Dane Rudhyar, *Fire out of the Stone: A Reinterpretation of the Basic Images of the Christian Tradition* (The Hague, 1963), p. 11.

[53]   Rudhyar, *Fire out of the Stone*, pp. 8–9.

[54]   James M. Robinson, 'Introduction', in James M. Robinson (ed.), *The Nag Hammadi Library in English* (Leiden and New York, 1988), p. 4.

[55]   Lawrence Cassidy, 'The Believing Christian as a Dedicated Astrologer', *Astrology Quarterly*, 64/3 (1994), p. 3.

At the end of all this we are none the wiser regarding whether astrology in its very nature is a religion, save to say that academics argue about what exactly religion is. The way that the word is used in relation to astrology is both ill-defined and suggests that everyone knows not just what astrology is, but what religion is. My suggestion is that they do not, for nobody has yet argued that astrology might suit some definitions of religion but not others. Neither has anyone until now recognised that astrologers' attitudes may be as diverse and complex as those within any other cultural group. The tendency to assume a monolithic identity is persistent. The only discussions that take into account the nature of astrology are those conducted by astrologers, whereas those which take place amongst sociologists and practising Christians all assume that we all agree on the basic terms of the debate. Our concern, then, is with the realm of perceptions – perceptions on whether astrology is a religion and, if so, whether it is a rival to Christianity. For these purposes it is not necessary to know what a religion is, but how people respond to the word.

Chapter 10

Superstitious Times: The Extent of Belief in Astrology

We are living in a scientific, largely post-religious age in which faith is presented as unscientific superstition. Yet paradoxically, we have replaced such faith by belief in demonstrable nonsense.[1]

Attempts to measure the extent of belief in astrology are beset by methodological muddle, compounded by confusion over what exactly it is that is being measured – and how. The consequence is a massive disparity in the published figures. It is generally agreed, though, that astrology is popular.[2] 'There is no doubt about the popularity of astrology,' wrote Hans Eysenck and David Nias in 1982, citing opinion polls to support their assertion that a third of the adult population of the UK believes in it, a third is sceptic and the last third is interested enough to read their horoscopes, but without 'believing'.[3] So much for public belief. But what about the numbers of actual astrologers? The quoted figures are vague. In 1994 Kepler College (which awarded degrees in Astrology and the Liberal Arts from 2000 until 2011) announced as support for its launch that 'no one knows the exact number of practicing astrologers and serious students there are in the United States. We do know, however, that they number in the tens of thousands'.[4]

It is also widely assumed that belief in astrology is not just widespread, but is growing. This assumption was certainly shared by astrologers in the 1980s and 1990s (in 1980, Dane Rudhyar himself claimed simply that 'astrology is becoming widely accepted'[5]), even if such confidence took a knock in the 2000s, when an apparently aging demographic at astrology conferences caused concern, especially in the US, that astrology was dying out.[6] A few years later, in 2011, the electronic

---

[1] Melanie Phillips, 'The Age of Unreason', *Daily Mail*, 6 August 2007.

[2] For much of what follows see also Nicholas Campion, 'The Extent of Contemporary Belief in Astrology in the UK and USA', *Correlation* (2011), forthcoming.

[3] Hans Eysenck and David Nias, *Astrology: Science or Superstition?* (London, 1982), p. 1.

[4] 'A Degree in Astrology: A Long-Standing Dream Comes True', *The Kepler College of Astrological Arts and Sciences, Notes*, 1/4 (1994).

[5] Dane Rudhyar, *Person Cantered Astrology* (New York, 1980), p. 67; see also Stephen Arroyo, *Astrology, Karma and Transformation: The Inner Dimensions of the Birth Chart* (Davis CA, 1978), p. xv.

[6] For a pessimistic view see Bernard Eccles, 'The Death of Astrology', paper presented to the Astrological Association of Great Britain conference, Plymouth, August

memberletter of the International Society for Astrological Research (ISAR) reported that 31 per cent of American adults (67 million individuals) believe in astrology and just over 1.25 million Americans say they 'like' it on Facebook.[7] The article went on to contrast this with other, much lower figures. The largest-selling 'serious' American astrology magazine, *The Mountain Astrologer*, distributed 17,000 copies in 2009; the combined membership of all national US astrological societies is currently 3,000; and fewer than 500 US astrologers claim to make a living from astrology. The gap between these figures – public interest huge, the numbers of students and professionals tiny – was such that (the article concluded) a massive marketing opportunity was opened up, with great scope for attracting students and clients. It also raises a serious research problem. For many astrologers the primary concern, though, is that growing popularity should be complimented by an end to centuries of rejection by their educated peers. For many astrologers the perceived growth of belief in astrology is also a symptom of the decline of traditional religion, which itself, it is argued, accompanies the transition to the Aquarian Age.[8] In this logic both belief in and educated acceptance of astrology *has* to be on the increase because astrology is a vital tool of self-development required for the smooth transition to the New Age and the coming of the New Age is both inevitable and imminent. The cultural-evolutionist theory that astrology should have died out (because it properly belongs in a former era) is reversed and many astrologers argue that it necessarily belongs in the future.[9]

Amongst sociological commentators on astrology, Peter Underwood's statement that 'there is probably a greater interest in the subject than there has been for centuries' and that its study 'has never been more widespread and popular than it is today', are typical, but clearly exaggerated;[10] if the present is compared to the Renaissance, imperial Rome or eighth-century BCE Assyria, for example, when astrology was either part of the state apparatus or of the prevailing worldview, to pretend that it is now more popular than ever is nonsense; if more people do now

---

1999; and Bernard Eccles, 'Astrology in England in the Twenty-First Century', *Journal for the Study of Religion, Nature and Culture*, 1/2 (2007), pp. 237–58.

[7]   Donna Woodwell, 'Marketing Astrology 2.0', *ISAR Memberletter*, 637 (2011).

[8]   Dane Rudhyar, *The Practice of Astrology as a Technique in Human Understanding* (New York, 1975), p. 23; see also Margaret Hone, *The Modern Textbook of Astrology* (London, 1973), p. 272; Joyce Levine, 'Entering the Age of Aquarius', *Horoscope*, February (1997), p. 4; Ray Grasse, 'Drawing Down the Fire of the Gods: Reflections on the Leo/Aquarius Axis', *Mountain Astrologer*, 89 (2000), p. 20; Gary Caton, 'Uranus in Pisces: Birthing the New Age', *NCGR Memberletter*, August/September (2002), p. 20; Theresa H. McDevitt, 'Sharon and Arafat: Axis of Closure to the Pisces–Virgo Age', *NCGR Memberletter*, June/July (2002), pp. 1, 16; Steve Nobel, 'Age of Transition', *Prediction*, 68/7 (2002), pp. 1, 28–9.

[9]   John Addey, *Astrology Reborn* (London, 1971).

[10]   Peter Underwood, *Into the Occult: A Survey for the Seventies* (London, 1972), pp. 1, 34.

'believe' in astrology than in the past, it is surely only because more people are alive now than in the past. Amongst scholars of the New Age, the tone is set by Melton, Clarke and Kelly who, writing in 1991, regarded the 'growth of interest in astrology' as 'the most widespread indication of the modern renewal of interest in all manner of things occult'.[11] The argument that belief in astrology is growing is also shared by astrology's sceptical critics. Indeed, the assumption that astrology's popularity is increasing, and needs to be resisted, was a major factor in the development of the organised sceptic movement in 1976, and the foundation of the Committee for the Scientific Investigation of Claims of the Paranormal (CSICOP).[12] The sceptical journalist Catherine Bennett introduced her 1996 BBC2 TV programme on the esoteric, occult and paranormal, including astrology, 'Strange Days', with the following apocalyptic announcement: 'We live in superstitious times and reason is on the retreat. The remarkable rise of Feng Shui shows that nowadays people will believe anything, no matter how strange or ludicrous'.[13] Another UK journalist, Melanie Phillips, expressed similar opinions. In 2008 she described astrology as 'mumbo-jumbo ... which goes to prove the truth of the old adage that when people stop believing in God, they will believe in anything'.[14] Both, of course, were repeating a familiar claim attributed to G.K. Chesterton that 'When people stop believing in God, they don't believe in nothing – they believe in anything'.[15] According to this hypothesis, church attendance is declining; therefore belief in astrology, as part of a package of strange or ludicrous beliefs, *must* be increasing, because the two exist in a close relationship: the fall in mainstream religious devotion is inversely related to a rise in non-mainstream religion.

Actually, research in 2000 suggested that belief in conventional Christian claims correlates positively with belief in angels, Heaven and the Devil.[16] Further, a close look at the claim that, as mainstream religion declines, unorthodox beliefs increase, suggests that they are historical nonsense. Quite simply, Bennett and Phillips are giving voice to a classic statement of golden-age nostalgia, in this case that there was a point in the past in when either true reason ruled (Bennett) or true religion (Philips), and that the rise of superstition presents a threat to social order and/or correct faith. The concept of a recently lost past coupled with a present cultural decline forms part of modern pseudoscepticism's mythic

---

[11]   J. Gordon Melton, Jerome Clarke and Aidan A. Kelly, *New Age Almanac* (London and New York, 1991), p. 277.

[12]   Bart J. Bok, Lawrence E. Jerome and Paul Kurtz, 'Objections to Astrology: A Statement by 186 Leading Scientists', *Humanist*, 35/5 (1975), p. 4.

[13]   'Strange Days', BBC2, 18 June 1996.

[14]   Melanie Phillips, 'The False Faith of Scientific Reason', *Jewish Chronicle*, 17 October 2008.

[15]   Elizabeth Knowles (ed.), *The Oxford Dictionary of Quotations* (Oxford, 2004), p. 217.

[16]   Erich Goode, 'Two Paranormalisms or Two and a Half? An Empirical Exploration', *Skeptical Inquirer*, 24/1 (2000), pp. 29–35.

culture: superstition is on the rise; people who 'believe' in it are in error and need to be saved from themselves.[17] However, the assumption that interest in astrology has recently undergone a major increase is not confined to the 1970s to 1990s. It was remarked on by the astronomer Bart Bok in 1941, also the astrologer F.B. Marsom, quoting an unnamed American astronomer, and Charles Carter in 1939.[18] As long ago as 1911 Alan Leo identified a 'revolution in astrologic thought' which he thought had begun in 1891, using very much the same evidence, the increasing publication of astrological periodicals, as did Bok in 1941.[19]

Two major problems may therefore be identified in the argument that the popularity of, or belief in, astrology is increasing. First is that the assumption that this is the case appears to have been taken for granted throughout the twentieth century, mainly on the basis of recent impressions. Secondly, it depends on the concept of a previous decline. Jim Tester represented the typical historical view when he concluded his history of astrology with the assumption that it died out at the end of the seventeenth century.[20] However, Patrick Curry argued that the situation was more complicated and depended on the distinction between three varieties of astrology, high, middling and low.[21] Curry argued convincingly that it was only 'high', philosophical, astrology which died out in the mid- to late seventeenth century, while 'middling' survived in isolated examples of professional horoscope casters, and 'low' continued to thrive in the form of mass-market almanacs. I would add to this the suggestion that 'high' astrology only died out as a public enterprise and went underground into esoteric Masonry.[22] The public collapse of 'high' astrology' and, to an extent, the 'middling' form, was associated, as Ann Geneva has pointed out, with the dismantling (except in private, esoteric circles) of the Neoplatonic universe, which had provided astrology with a sympathetic cosmological framework, in the face of the Galilean and Newtonian discoveries in astronomy.[23] Such philosophical changes, though, had no relevance for popular

[17]   Nicholas Campion, *The Great Year: Astrology, Millenarianism and History in the Western Tradition* (London, 1994), pp. 59–60.

[18]   Bart J. Bok and Margaret W. Mayall, 'Scientists Look at Astrology', *Scientific Monthly*, 52 (1941), p. 233; F.B. Marsom, 'Astrologers and Astronomers', *Astrology Quarterly*, 13/1 (1939), p. 20; Charles Carter, 'Editorial', *Astrology*, 13/1 (1939), p. 2.

[19]   Alan Leo, 'The Editor's Observatory: Modern Astrology's Coming-of-Age', *Modern Astrology*, New Series, 8/8 (1911), p. 265; see also Ellic Howe, *Urania's Children: The Strange World of the Astrologers* (London, 1967), p. 67.

[20]   Jim Tester, *A History of Western Astrology* (Woodbridge, 1987), p. 243.

[21]   Patrick Curry, *Prophecy and Power: Astrology in Early Modern England* (Oxford, 1989), pp. 95–152.

[22]   Nicholas Campion, *A History of Western Astrology* (2 vols, London, 2009), vol. 2, ch. 13.

[23]   Ann Geneva, *Astrology and the Seventeenth-Century Mind: William Lilly and the Language of the Stars* (Manchester and New York, 1995), p. 281; Bernard Capp, *Astrology*

culture. There is therefore ample evidence of a continuation of a consistent popular astrological tradition throughout the eighteenth century and up to the latter part of the nineteenth century, represented mainly by the almanacs, whose content was based around astrological forecasts for the coming year.[24] The tradition continued and in 1972 Derek Parker recorded sales in the UK of eight million copies of the annual *Horoscope Purse Books*, which breaks down to an average of 666,000 per zodiac sign.[25]

The proposition that astrology has enjoyed a substantial revival in the nineteenth and twentieth centuries is therefore dependent on the notion that it died out in the seventeenth century. If the notion of decline must be qualified, as Curry indicates, then so must the nature of the revival. While Curry's 'high' astrology was scarcely to be found in the public sphere in post-seventeenth-century Britain with the exception of a few thinkers such as C.G. Jung (in the twentieth century) whose astrological writings were all translated into English from the 1950s onwards, 'middling' astrology has enjoyed a measurable revival since the late eighteenth and early nineteenth centuries. The evidence for this is to be found in the successful publication of magazines and books devoted to the casting and interpretation of horoscopes in the early nineteenth century and the organisation of sustained societies and schools of astrology since the early twentieth century.[26] However, most journalistic interest in astrology's contemporary popularity is concerned with 'low' astrology in its modern form of newspaper and magazine columns which fill the place once occupied by almanacs. In the UK, the US and much of the Western world, horoscope columns are carried by most of the popular press and women's magazines. According to the pollsters Gallup, in 1978, 'Attesting to the popularity of astrology in the United States today is the fact that astrology columns are carried by 1,200 of the nation's 1,750 daily newspapers'.[27] The journalist and religious commentator Anne Atkins stated in 1999 that, in her opinion, the horoscope column is the most popular piece in any newspaper, with the agony aunt coming a close second.[28] A more recent development is the spread of astrology to the internet, a medium which can expand the print formula of the standard 12-paragraph horoscope

---

and the Popular Press: English Almanacs 1500–1800 (London and Boston, 1979), pp. 238–69; and Maureen Perkins, *Visions of the Future: Almanacs, Time, and Cultural Change* (Oxford, 1996).

[24]   Capp, *Astrology and the Popular Press*, pp. 238–69; and Perkins, *Visions of the Future*.

[25]   Derek Parker, *The Question of Astrology: A Personal Investigation* (London, 1970), p. 114.

[26]   Patrick Curry, *A Confusion of Prophets: Victorian and Edwardian Astrology* (London, 1992); Campion, *A History of Western Astrology*, vol. 2, chs 14–16.

[27]   George H. Gallup, *The Gallup Poll: Public Opinion 1978* (Wilmington DE, 1979), p. 185.

[28]   Anne Atkins, 'The Message', BBC Radio 4, 4 June 1999.

column to the supply of downloadable computerised readings based on the customer's exact birth data. In 2001 Jonathan Cainer, then the *Daily Mirror* astrologer, reported that his website (<www.Cainer.com>) received 100,000 'unique' visits per day; each page the visitor then looks at constitutes a 'hit' so, if each visitor looks at between three and six pages, the site received between 300,000 and 600,000 hits per day which made it Britain's fourth most popular website.[29]

Cainer also reported that when he worked on *Today* newspaper in the late 1980s, when the first horoscope phone lines, running pre-recorded tapes, were launched, the weekly call figures were 25,000 out of a circulation of 500,000, representing 5 per cent of the circulation. By 1999 he was working for the *Daily Mail* where his lines were receiving around 17,000 calls a week, less than 1 per cent of the circulation of 2,500,000, bringing in a gross income of approximately £1,000,000 per annum. While the headline figure of a £1,000,000 turnover can make for dramatic headlines, the actual percentage of readers calling was very small. Even then, Cainer's earnings dwarfed those of earlier astrologers. Writing in 1972, Derek Parker reported that 'an editor will pay at least £30 for a week's predictions', with extra funds provided by syndications; he calculated that the total amount paid to their astrologers by all the newspapers and magazines in the UK totalled £20,000, a figure which, he estimated, rose to £150,000 in the US.[30] When we consider that when he retired as the *Daily Mail* astrologer in 1986, John Naylor (R.H. Naylor's son) was earning £120 per week for providing six days' worth of copy, for Monday to Saturday, the scale of some astrologers' earnings in the 1990s becomes clear.

The problem with such figures is a certain novelty value in the technology on which they are dependent. Already in the early 1990s companies were introducing call-barring technology to block their employees using all commercial '0800' numbers, not just astrology. By the late 1990s the delivery of free horoscopes on the Web made the horoscope phone lines next to redundant and the newspapers themselves lost interest as revenues plummeted. In April 2008 Mick Ellis of the Total Features press agency, who had considerable experience in the field, described his view: 'My feeling is that premium rate phone numbers are no longer important to newspapers because of their minimal earnings. Nobody seems to want to be responsible for them unlike about 5–10 years ago when every paper had a department dealing with premium rate revenues'.[31]

However, the public view of astrology as a hugely profitable business continues. The Channel 4 TV programme 'Witness', broadcast in the UK in 2000 when astrological phone line revenue on all but a few of the most popular magazines and newspapers had already sharply declined, assumed that it had caught the upwave of a recent surge of interest in astrology:

---

[29]   Interview, Jonathan Cainer, 8 September 2001.
[30]   Parker, *The Question of Astrology*, p. 114.
[31]   Personal communication, Mick Ellis, 7 April 2008.

For centuries astrology has been languishing in the dark ages, undermined by the relentless advance of its relationship with science. But we're witnessing a comeback, an astrological Renaissance. A new astrology is emerging that is modern, practical and business-minded. An ancient belief system is being reinvented for the 21st century.[32]

Journalists are fond of repeating large statistics to justify their stories on astrology. As we already noted, in 1981 Eysenck and Nias claimed that two thirds of adults read horoscope columns, of whom half believed their truth. This is plausibly the basis of the journalist Catherine Bennett's unsourced claim in 1996 that 'In Britain at least half the population regularly read horoscopes, about half of whom think they are really true'.[33] Different, equally unsourced figures were provided by the TV presenter Esther Rantzen on the 'Esther' discussion show in 1997: 'They say that four million people pick up a newspaper and turn first to read their own horoscopes. And yet, 80 per cent of the population, when asked, said it was all a load of rubbish'.[34]

The figures on horoscope readership show a wide range of variation. In 1977 Dean and Mather summarised previous surveys in the UK, Germany, France and the US. They estimated that 70 per cent of the adult population read horoscopes, while only 20 per cent 'believe that there is something in it'.[35] To take these figures at face value, 50 per cent of the adult population read horoscopes while believing that there is nothing in them. The question, then, is why so many people should do something that is apparently so meaningless. A simple explanation is that the figures are distorted by the problems noted by the psychologist Gustav Jahoda. When he considered the problems arising from direct questions concerning belief he observed that adherents of 'superstitious beliefs' in England 'are apt to be somewhat shamefaced about superstition and liable to deny holding any such beliefs when faced with a strange interviewer'.[36] If they are influenced by critiques of beliefs such as Park's (above), they may well answer in the negative even when their position is ambivalent. The consequence, as Gillian Bennett noted, is that questionnaires which seek simple yes/no answers to questions of belief are liable to elicit misleading responses. She reported that respondents

very often like to phrase their answers with a little face-saving ambiguity. In these circumstances, if they are pushed to say whether 'I think there may be

---

32   'Witness', Channel 4, 18 June 2000.

33   Catherine Bennett, 'Strange Days', BBC2, 18 June 1996.

34   'Esther', Esther Rantzen Discussion programme, BBC1, 1997, n.d.

35   Geoffrey Dean and Arthur Mather, *Recent Advances in Natal Astrology: A Critical Review 1900–1976* (Subiaco, Australia, 1977), pp. 79, 83.

36   Gustav Jahoda, *The Psychology of Superstition* (London, 1969), pp. 25–6.

something in it' means 'definitely yes' or 'definitely no', they will probably say 'no', even though that is far from their real opinion.[37]

Leaving aside the question of astrology students and professionals, we turn to wider levels of public belief. Here again, the picture is confused. The existing research is based mainly on large-scale surveys and often relies on simple yes/ no questions: 'Do you believe in astrology, yes or no?' Gillian Bennett identified the obvious weakness in such questions in her studies of folklore. She found that, when respondents are asked to make simple yes/no judgements about matters on which they may have no clear view, they tend to be influenced by reluctance to admit to belief in 'superstition'.[38] We are back to the corruption of the word 'belief' in the service of positivist scepticism – that any object of belief is considered to be necessarily false. In addition, the types of questions in the various surveys vary, which can make comparison difficult. Some surveys pose direct questions about belief, others about readership of horoscope columns.[39] Others inquire into respondents' opinions on matters such as connections between birth-signs and character.[40] The results are then used to infer levels of belief of astrology, a problematic exercise, as we shall see.

However, in the academic literature the most quoted sources for statistics on belief in astrology are the Gallup Polls, which have been asking related questions on the subject since 1962. The questions asked are a mixture of direct (overtly concerning belief) and indirect (seeking information about attitudes from which belief may then be inferred). The questions are often confused. The question, 'Do you believe in horoscopes?' (which resulted in positive figures amongst UK adults of 14 per cent in 1975 and 20 per cent in 1978) could mean 'Do you believe horoscopes exist, are useful or are true?'[41] The 1975 question 'Do you believe in astrology or not?' found positive responses amongst 22 per cent of American adults.[42] The equivalent

---

[37]   Gillian Bennett, *Traditions of Belief: Women, Folklore and the Supernatural Today* (London, 1987), p. 27.

[38]   Bennett, *Traditions of Belief*, p. 26.

[39]   Jon D. Miller, 'The Public Acceptance of Astrology and Other Pseudo-Science in the United States', paper presented to the 1992 annual meeting of the American Association for the Advancement of Science, 9 February 1992.

[40]   Kurt Pawlik and Lothar Buse, 'Self-Attribution as a Moderator Variable in Differential Psychology: Replication and Interpretation of Eysenck's Astrology/Personality Correlations', *Correlation*, 4/2 (1984), pp. 14–30.

[41]   For 1975 figures see George H. Gallup, *The Gallup International Public Opinion Polls: Great Britain 1937–1975* (2 vols, New York, 1976), vol. 2, p. 1417; and for 1978 figures see George Gallup, *The International Gallup Polls: Public Opinion 1978* (Wilmington, 1980), p. 329.

[42]   George H. Gallup, *The Gallup Poll: Public Opinion 1972–1977* (2 vols, Wilmington DE, 1978), p. 573.

figure for American adults was 29 per cent in 1978.[43] In 1995 and 1996 the question was extended as follows: 'Do you believe in astrology, or that the positions of the stars and planets can affect people's lives?' Positive responses of 23 per cent were obtained in the first year and 25 per cent in the second.[44]

The public polling figures remain pretty constant (see Table 11.1). A Harris Poll in 2009 reported that 'What may be surprising is that a third of [adults in the US] believe in astrology', by which was meant 26 per cent.[45] A Gallup poll in 2005 reportedly found that 22 per cent of UK adults – or 25 per cent of Americans – believe in astrology, using the same parameters as in 1995 and 1996, and both this and the Harris figures have made their way into the public domain via both astrological and sceptical websites, as well as online press and the ubiquitous Wikipedia.[46] The problem with the way that Gallup phrases its question, though, is that it is nonsensical. Of course the position of the celestial bodies can affect our lives: all life on earth is sustained by the Sun and, of the planets, Jupiter acts as a gravitational vacuum cleaner, diverting potentially devastating comets away from collision with the Earth. The only logical answer to Gallup's question is 'yes', even if traditional notions of planetary 'influence' are denied, and the fact that it is not is testimony to widespread confusion over what exactly astrology claims, and a reluctance to answer in the affirmative to questions concerning belief in widely ridiculed subjects. Gallup's apparently rigorous figures form the basis of most considerations of the extent of belief in astrology in the academic literature.[47] The American National Science Foundation relied on Gallup's 1996 figure in its discussion of the extent of 'pseudoscience' in 2002.[48]

Meanwhile, Christian evangelicals such as Russell Chandler and Doug Harris both depended on Gallup statistics to indicate that belief in astrology is rising and

---

[43] Gallup, *The Gallup Poll: Public Opinion 1978*, p. 184.

[44] George Gallup Jr, *The Gallup Poll: Public Opinion 1995* (Wilmington DE, 1996), p. 10; George Gallup Jr, *The Gallup Poll: Public Opinion 1996* (Wilmington DE, 1997), p. 205.

[45] Harris Poll, 'What People Do and Do Not Believe in', at <http://www.harrisinteractive.com/vault/Harris_Poll_2009_12_15.pdf>, accessed 1 September 2011.

[46] Linda Lyons, 'Paranormal beliefs come (super)naturally to some: more people believe in haunted houses than other mystical ideas', Gallup, 1 November 2005, at <http://www.gallup.com/poll/19558/paranormal-beliefs-come-supernaturally-some.aspx>, accessed 24 September 2009.

[47] Rodney Stark and William Simms Bainbridge, *The Future of Religion: Secularization, Revival and Cult Formation* (Berkeley, 1985), pp. 228–30.

[48] National Science Foundation, 'Science and Technology: Public Attitudes and Public Understanding Science Fiction and Pseudoscience', at <http://www.nsf.gov/sbe/srs/seind02/c//c/s5.htm>, accessed 6 May 2002. For Gallup's 1996 figure see Gallup, *Public Opinion 1996*.

is a threat both to Christian belief and society.[49] Gallup's simple and inherently inaccurate yes/no questions have made it into the sociological and evangelical and Christian literature, becoming the basis of conclusions which are also, therefore, misleading. Gallup's figures also become the basis on which policy is made by concerned institutions. Accordingly, Robin Gill interpreted Gallup poll results in the light of what he sees as the essential rivalry between 'traditional' and 'non-traditional' belief and the decline in mainstream church attendance.[50] If both the history and the statistics are unreliable then the whole notion of a clash between old and new religious cultures becomes little more than a fiction, yet policy on relations with those of new religions or none are made partly on this basis.

The relationship between experience and belief is a far from a simple one. For example, in a study of students' belief in paranormal phenomena, Gaynard found that experience of a phenomenon is not necessary for belief.[51] Other measures of 'belief' in astrology have included readership of horoscope columns and knowledge of one's own birth-sign. Yet here we have material issues to contend with. For example, one limit on the readership of horoscope columns is the circulation of the titles which carry them. In the UK in October 2003, the total circulation of daily national newspapers carrying horoscopes was just under 10 million and, of Sunday papers, just over 10 million.[52] Beyond this figure there are a number of imponderables. For example, while it may be calculated that four people read each newspaper sold, most people will not read every section. In addition, some newspapers give their astrologer a very high profile, whereas others provide only a lesser one. In general the space occupied by astrology columns is driven by revenue. It expanded in the late 1980s as income from horoscope phone lines boomed, and shrank in the late 1990s when it declined.

Indirect questions posed by Gallup include those on the readership of horoscope columns. In 1975 15 per cent of French adults claimed to read a horoscope column 'regularly' and, in the same year, 23 per cent of American adults gave a positive answer.[53] However, as Stark and Bainbridge noted, the same poll indicated that 17

---

[49]   Russell Chandler, *Understanding the New Age* (Milton Keynes, 1989), p. 21; and Doug Harris, *Occult Overviews and New Age Agendas: A Comprehensive Examination of Major Occult and New Age Groups* (Richmond, 1999), p. 23.

[50]   Robin Gill, *Churchgoing and Christian Ethics* (Cambridge, 1999), pp. 51, 80, 126, 128, 135.

[51]   T.J. Gaynard, 'Young People and the Paranormal', *Journal of the Society for Psychical Research*, 58/826 (1992), p. 179.

[52]   Figures from ABC, <http://abc.co.uk>, accessed 12 December 2003. See also <http://udel.edu/~semmel/Circulation.htm>, accessed 12 December 2003; <http://www.telegraph.co.uk/pressoffice/graphics/research/nrsjul02jun03.pdf>, accessed 29 November 2003.

[53]   George H. Gallup, *The Gallup International Public Opinion Polls: France 1939, 1944–1975* (2 vols, New York, 1976), vol. 1, p. 309; Gallup, *Public Opinion 1972–1977*, vol. 1, p. 572.

per cent of those who claimed not to believe in astrology also read a horoscope column regularly.[54] Their conclusion was that what they call 'actual belief' in astrology is held by members of a 'client cult' in which the members, or 'clients', have faith in the astrologer's ability to provide real results.

Other questions have concerned knowledge of one's birth-sign: research conducted by the French Public Opinion Institute in 1963 found that 58 per cent of the population knew their birth-signs, 53 per cent 'regularly read their horoscopes in the press', 38 per cent 'have at one time or another wished to have a personal horoscope made', 37 per cent believe 'that there is a relationship between the character of persons and the sign under which they were born' and 23 per cent believe that predictions come true.[55] However, there is still the matter of the discrepancy between the number of people who regularly read their horoscopes and those who admit to belief in the relationship between character and birth-sign; an excess of 16 per cent of the former over the latter in the French figures.

Later surveys added to the picture, though not consistently. In Germany Pawlik and Buse asked a series of questions about astrology, from which they then deduced that 38 per cent of their sample were 'strong believers', 32 per cent were 'believers' and 30 per cent non-believers.[56] In the UK John Bauer and Martin Durant inferred levels of belief from the frequency with which their subjects read newspaper and magazine horoscopes and obtained the following figures:[57]

'Serious believers' (read horoscopes often or fairly often and take them seriously or fairly seriously) 5 per cent.

'Non-serious believers' (read horoscopes often but take them not very seriously) 18 per cent.

'Non-serious believers' (read horoscopes fairly often but take them not very seriously) 21 per cent.

'Non-serious believers' (read horoscopes not very often and take them not very seriously) 29 per cent

'Non-believers' (do not read horoscopes) 27 per cent.

Bauer and Durant's attempt to convert attitudes to horoscope columns into belief in astrology led to conclusions differing sharply from those obtained by Pawlik

---

[54]   Stark and Bainbridge, *The Future of Religion*, p. 230.

[55]   Cited in Michael Gauquelin, *The Cosmic Clocks* (London, 1969; San Diego, 1982), pp. 37–8.

[56]   Pawlik and Buse, 'Self-Attribution'.

[57]   John Bauer and Martin Durant, 'British Public Perceptions of Astrology: An Approach from the Sociology of Knowledge', *Culture and Cosmos*, 1/1 (1997), pp. 55–72.

and Buse. Although figures for non-believers in both studies (27 per cent and 30 per cent) roughly coincide, Bauer and Durant's 'serious believers' number 5 per cent, while Pawlik and Buse's 'strong believers' are almost eight times as numerous at 38 per cent, providing yet more evidence that both methodology and terminology may make a substantial difference to the eventual reporting on the conclusions of such surveys.

The linear concept of strength of belief on a single scale suggested by both Pawlik and Buse and Bauer and Durant is unlikely to take account of countless individual variations, let alone the possibility that a daily reader of sun-sign columns, rated as a weak believer, might be considered far more devout than a professional astrologer for whom their work may be primarily a money-making activity. Meanwhile, readership of horoscope columns is not necessarily an indicator of belief in astrology. Lucy Sherriff, writing in *The Skeptic*, remarked that most people, including her, read horoscope columns 'for a laugh'.[58] No evidence was offered other than the anecdote and we really have to query statements such as this: why would anyone read horoscope columns 'for a laugh' any more than the weather forecast, stock prices or the court circular for the day? As Richard Dawkins pointed out, horoscopes are just not funny. The psychologist Richard Crowe agreed and challenged claims that horoscope columns are read 'for entertainment value only' and concluded that 'the evidence suggests otherwise'.[59] An alternative explanation for the discrepancy between relatively high figures for readership of columns and relatively low figures for belief in astrology is therefore that a proportion of those who read columns react negatively to the word 'belief', as Bennett and Hufford both suggested.

Shelley von Strunckel, astrologer for *The Sunday Times* and the London *Evening Standard*, is likewise sceptical that the word 'belief' has any value when applied to the readership of horoscope columns:

> When people are asked if they believe in astrology, we are really discussing two questions. How they hold the art/science of astrology is one thing but what they get out of a column may be quite another and it may be that it is their only moment of stillness in the day or week. Now if that column is written by someone who has some degree of spiritual content in their own life, then what they are going to get is not just something to read but it is going to take them to some place within themselves that they don't have the skill to visit on their own. Patrick[60] had that as well. He was an altar boy as a kid ... So when we are talking about what goes on in reading a column, we are talking about the astrological skill and the astrological structure but we are also talking about the content. And the reason I bring this up, particularly in context of what you are writing, is

---

[58]   Lucy Sherriff, 'Women are NOT from Gullibull', *Skeptic*, 14/3 (2001), p. 7.

[59]   Richard A. Crowe, 'Astrology and the Scientific Method', *Psychological Reports*, 67 (1990), p. 181.

[60]   Patrick Walker, former astrologer to the *Mail on Sunday* and *Evening Standard*.

that it is important to discuss what we consider to be belief today because when people say 'Do you believe in astrology?' I would propose that people don't actually know what the term belief means.[61]

If a large number of people are aware of the argument that a belief is automatically false, and even potentially dangerous, we may assume that they are likely to take this into account when questions of belief arise. For example, if the question 'Do you believe in God?' is regarded as hostile, it can be interpreted as assuming ignorance on the part of the person being questioned and will not elicit an accurate response.[62] We can therefore expect defensiveness amongst subjects when the question 'Do you believe ...?' is asked by a questioner who is perceived to be critical.

It is possible, therefore, that respondents are afraid to answer 'yes' to questions which they fear might expose them to ridicule. The fact that individuals may be embarrassed to admit to an interest in astrology in public situations was noted by Laurel Sanford who, at the time, was a student on the BA programme in Astrology and the Liberal Arts at Kepler College in Seattle. Sanford, who works as a 'personal coach,' says, 'If I'm talking to an individual client and say, "Well, how about if I read your chart?" they'll say, "You can do *that*?" But if they're in a group with other co-workers, no way'.[63]

The most accurate measurement of the current extent of Curry's 'middling astrology' may be the number of professional astrologers. There has been, though, no measurement of this number, in spite of the figures cited by Kepler College. At the high end, the Christian evangelical writer Peter Anderson estimated that there were 60,000 'fortune-tellers, clairvoyants and astrologers' in France in 1988.[64] In 1991 Melton, Clarke and Kelly estimated that there were '10,000 professional astrologers in the United States serving more than 20 million clients'.[65] However, there is no indication of how they arrived at this figure. It is, though, double the figure of 5,000 astrologers catering for 10 million customers given by the poet Louis MacNeice in 1964, suggesting that it may be a simple extrapolation from MacNeice's estimate.[66]

The earliest data was collected by Marcia Moore, an astrologer, in her study of US astrologers in 1960. She found that, of her sample of 250 'serious' astrologers, only 50, or 20 per cent, earned any money from astrology, and of those only 11, or

---

[61]   Interview, Shelley von Strunckel, 31 October 2002.

[62]   Interview, Kathleen Quigley, 25 March 2001.

[63]   Mark D. Fefer, 'Battle of the stars: if religion is, why isn't astrology a legitimate subject for study?', *Seattle Weekly*, 23–29 August 2001, at <http://www.seattleweekly.com/features/0134/news-fefer2.shtml>, accessed 6 September 2001.

[64]   Peter Anderson, *Satan's Snare: The Influence of the Occult* (Welwyn, 1988), p. 9.

[65]   Melton et al., *New Age Almanac*, p. 277.

[66]   Cited in Gauquelin, *The Cosmic Clocks*, p. 36.

4 per cent, claimed to earn all their income from it.[67] This is surely a tiny number, and far less than the previous wild estimates. I was interested in whether the situation had changed forty years later. When I distributed a survey at the Northwest Astrology Conference (NORWAC) in Seattle in 1999, 40 individuals (49 per cent of my sample – there were around 200 delegates in total at the conference) claimed to be professional astrologers, a small number out of a high proportion of delegates at such a specialist gathering. When I visited the Norwegian astrology conference in Oslo in 2001, the figures were comparable: 14 individuals, or 46 per cent of my respondents, claimed to be professionals. However, the NORWAC figure gave no indication of the real demand for professional services. How many clients did these astrologers see and how much could they charge? I looked for more detailed information at the British Astrological Association conference in 1999 and the United Astrology Congress (UAC) in Orlando, Florida, in 2002. The figures for the AA Conference were very low. Of the three astrologers who claimed to earn 100 per cent of their income from astrology, two were American keynote speakers, leaving just one British astrologer earning their entire income from astrology. In total 75 delegates claimed to be professional but, in order to gain a better measure of astrology in the UK, non-British respondents were excluded. Of the British astrologers at the conference, 45 claimed to be professional and ten claimed to be full time, but only the one keynote speaker claimed to earn all his/her income from astrology. Of the remainder, just three earned 75 per cent of their income from astrology, a further three earned between 60 per cent and 70 per cent and the rest below 30 per cent, of which 15 earned less than 10 per cent of their income from astrology. Four even stated that they earned none of their income from astrology, which calls into question exactly what is meant by 'professional'. As a guide to earning potential, based on my interviews, it may be estimated that those who claimed they earned 30–50 per cent of their income from astrology would earn a total of around £2,500 to £5,000 a year from their astrological activities. Five saw more than ten clients a week, eleven saw one a week, three saw less than one a week and one saw none. Most, 16, saw two to four clients a week. These figures are an indication that astrological consultancy is neither a popular or profitable activity in the UK.

At the 2002 United Astrology Congress in Atlanta, 54 delegates (35.5 per cent) stated that they were full-time astrologers and 50 (32.8 per cent) part-time. The majority claimed to do around five readings per week, although some do one and 13 do ten or over. Of these one claimed to do 50 readings a week, a figure which may be explained by working for a '0900' phone line service in which clients phone astrologers for short consultations. Taking all these figures at face value, the total number of clients is approximately 440 per week, or an average of four per astrologer. From information gleaned from my interviews a common rate for a reading is $150 for a session lasting an hour-and-a-half. At this rate the

---

[67] Marcia Moore, *Astrology Today: A Socio-Psychological Survey* (New York, 1960), p. 101.

gross income earned from ten readings per week will be $1,500 and from four it will be $600. When the percentage of income earned from astrology is analysed, 20 astrologers earn 100 per cent of their income from astrology and an almost equivalent number, 18, earn under 10 per cent. Twenty-nine earn under 50 per cent. Although stronger than in the UK, these figures certainly do not indicate a thriving profession. Sixty-six (63 per cent) of the total number of professionals, though, were also teaching astrology, suggesting that this is a means by which potential clients are approached but also that the total income received from clients is only a proportion of that which they earned from astrological activities as whole. While the opportunities for professional astrology consultancy in the US appear to be greater than in the UK, the scope still appears to be limited. Taken together, the figures from both the UK and US contradict the widespread journalistic view, discussed in Chapter 1, that astrology is 'a huge worldwide business'.[68] In fact, the business of astrology is so marginal that it scarcely exists, with the exception of a few spectacularly successful individuals

Another source of data is membership of the astrological societies which stand at the hub of the floating networks of those whose interest in the subject, often temporarily, leads them to connect with like-minded individuals. In the UK, the Astrological Association (AA) had 1,422 members in October 2001 and 1,302 in October 2003, of which around a third were international.[69] In July 2011 the AA had 595 members. Does this fall represent a decline in interest in astrology? The more likely reason is the emergence of cyberspace as a challenge to the AA's main raison d'être (apart from its annual conference) – its bi-monthly journal. The largest astrological gathering in the UK, the annual AA conference, usually attracts between 250 and 300 delegates: the 2010 conference figure was apparently down at 162 attendees (of whom 117 were paying delegates), which is actually similar to the 1995 figure of around 150.[70] A recent dip in attendance is not so much evidence of decline as a return to status quo. Whether such figures are indicative of any real underlying trend is doubtful. What they do reveal is that the appeal of institutional astrology in the form of societies and organised groups is both miniscule and that there is little change over the last twenty years. Similar conclusions are revealed elsewhere. The 2002/03 edition of the *Guide to Worldwide Astrology* listed 73 local astrology groups in the UK.[71] Yet even a flourishing group such as the Suffolk Astrological Society, which has been meeting continuously since 1981, has around '20–30 paid up members' and holds 22 meetings per year which may attract 'between 8 and 12 members/non-members' or 'around 18 on a good evening'.[72] We may extrapolate from this figure to estimate that between 650 and

---

[68]   Robert Matthews, 'Astrologers fail to predict proof they are wrong', *Sunday Telegraph*, 17 August 2003, p. 9.

[69]   Personal communication, Roy Gillett, 26 October 2003.

[70]   Personal communication, Wendy Stacey, 17 July 2011.

[71]   *Guide to Worldwide Astrology* (2002/03), pp. 111–17.

[72]   Personal communication, Andy Gray, 15 December 2003.

1,300 individuals attend meetings of local astrology groups in the UK. That is hardly a great number.

By comparison, in the US, the National Council for Geocosmic Research (NCGR) had 2,225 members in November 2003, of whom 115 were outside the US.[73] (Its nearest rival, the International Society for Astrological Research (ISAR) had 984 members, of whom 830 were in the US and 154 international.[74] In 2011, the figure had increased slightly to 1,299.[75] The ISAR conference in Anaheim in October 2003 attracted around 600 delegates while the ISAR education conference in Minnesota in November 2003 was attended by almost 200 delegates. If we turn to education, the largest private school of astrology in the UK, The Faculty of Astrological Studies, had 474 students in 2003, working for the basic qualification, the Certificate, and 163 studying for the Diploma, a total of 637 which was boosted to 809 when students at occasional seminars and the annual summer school were added.[76] Of the 637 active students, 578 were based in the UK and 165 attend classes in London.

To summarise, the attempt to measure astrology's popularity, and assess whether it is increasing, stable or declining, is afflicted by anachronistic historical models, simplistic models of the nature of belief, and the naive use of data which is fluid, malleable and unstable. The model of astrology which posits a decline of astrology in the seventeenth century followed by a revival in the nineteenth applied only to what Curry called 'high' and 'middling' astrology and not to the popular astrology of almanacs and, in the twentieth-century, sun-sign guides. I have also shown that the figures for belief in astrology are highly variable, ranging from less than 20 per cent to over 70 per cent. The larger context is an absence of data. For example, Robert Wuthnow argued that, in the absence of similar questionnaires asking the same question over long periods, it is possible to assess neither trends nor the rate of change in belief.[77] With reference to the specific question of whether belief in astrology is increasing, I am suggesting that, after comparing data from the 1970s to 1990s to that gathered by Gorer in 1950, the natural fluctuations in the figures do not suggest a pronounced trend.[78] In spite of anecdotal evidence it cannot, therefore, be shown that belief in astrology is increasing. In terms of Curry's 'middling' astrology, the evidence from membership of astrological societies and number of students on courses, is that numbers are tiny. The argument over whether contemporary belief in astrology is anachronistic, and that it therefore represents some of difficult-to-explain cultural anomaly, may therefore be answered in part

[73] Personal communication, Linda Fei, 13 November 2003.

[74] Personal communication, Margueritte dar Boggia, 5 November 2003.

[75] Personal communication, Margueritte dar Boggia, 16 July 2011.

[76] Personal communication, Clare Martin, 28 October 2003. See Campion, 'Contemporary Belief in Astrology', for other figures.

[77] Robert Wuthnow, *The Consciousness Revolution* (Berkeley, 1976), pp. 9, 172.

[78] Gill, *Churchgoing*, pp. 80–1; Geoffrey Gorer, *Exploring English Character* (London, 1955).

by the conclusion that Curry's 'low' astrology is fundamentally a normal part of popular culture.

If we can generalise from the specific example of astrology, the conclusions for wider discussion of modern religion's social status are somewhat damning for a great deal of literature in the sociology of religion. The indiscriminate use of inaccurate statistics, combined with unjustified notions of trends in religious affiliation, render much that has been published frankly unreliable. We can just draw two general conclusions, though. First, somewhere between half and three quarters of the adult population of the US and UK accept the validity of astrology. Second, it is not a million-dollar business. Rather, in spite of its wide public appeal, as a money-making profession it scarcely exists. It is part of the general mentality of the modern West, not an organised force. It is ideology rather than business, lived experience rather than commerce.

Chapter 11
Belief in Astrology: A Public Survey

It is therefore unclear what the statement that '*x* percent of the population believe in reincarnation' means.[1]

There are a number of distinct features of many critical studies of astrology's appeal, religious identity and popularity. First, they are based on discredited, anthropological theories of intellectual evolution which decree that, as a hangover from a distant, dark, superstitious past, so-called 'belief' in astrology is not only a problem to be explained in terms of the psychological inadequacy of the believer but, for the most hostile of astrology's critics, poses a danger to society as a whole. For Jon Miller, astrology might actually undermine the entire fabric of American democracy: by surrendering choice to cosmic forces, Miller reasoned, astrologers would be less able to participate in the democratic process.[2] Second, when they rely on statistics, these are often inadequate and the conclusions reached are therefore misleading. These results are used to contribute to debates on secularisation, the decline of traditional religion, the need for increased scientific literacy, the rise of alternative spiritualities and the condition of New Age culture. However, as Tony Walter and Helen Waterhouse pointed out in their study of modern belief in reincarnation, statements such as that a certain percentage of the population believes in a certain claim are, in themselves, meaningless.[3]

With this in mind, in 1999 I set out to re-examine the question of public belief in astrology from a sociological perspective, issuing questionnaires and conducting interviews not to establish levels of belief, but to establish various attitudes to astrology as expressed either through opinions, aspirations or behaviour. Whether these results are then used to infer levels of belief is another matter. However, for the sake of comparison I did invite respondents to rate their belief in astrology. I collected simple quantitative data but, rather than entering into statistical analysis, I looked to my interview data to provide the personal testimony, which might shed light on the figures. It is a truism that the answer to any question is dependent on the way in which the question is asked, but one which is widely ignored. Russell McCutcheon's words, however obvious, still deserve to be more widely heard: 'Our choice of question shapes the answer we will receive; a researcher's

---

[1]   Tony Walter and Helen Waterhouse, 'A Very Private Belief: Reincarnation in Contemporary England', *Sociology of Religion*, 60/2 (1999), p. 192.

[2]   John D. Miller, 'The Public Acceptance of Astrology and other Pseudo-Science in the United States', paper presented to the 1992 annual meeting of the American Association for the Advancement of Science, 9 February 1992.

[3]   Walter and Waterhouse, 'A Very Private Belief', p. 192.

presuppositions and biases regarding who counts in a society as it tells us about the society under question'.[4] It is important to remember at all times the generally recognised but too-often ignored truism that different types of questions elicit different types of answer, and to this end I made the maximum use of the handful of previous studies which had attempted to move beyond the simple quantification of belief.[5] The obvious points of concern are the extent to which individuals may give apparently contradictory replies within the same questionnaire and whether the results in previous surveys may be replicated. The headline results are discussed in this chapter and should be seen as indicative rather than definitive and may be used as the basis for further studies within the field. I need to explain why I am cautious about simple quantification, especially when small samples are converted into statistical probabilities. The notion that we can count the number of people who believe is a persistent one; witness the need in some quarters, both scientific and theological, to put a precise figure on the number of people who believe in astrology. However, the quantification of belief is highly problematic, and there are substantial problems with both the collection and interpretation of statistical data concerning religious affiliation, practice and attitude. These were well defined by Dale Caird and Henry Law, who made seven criticisms of previous research into religious affiliation.[6] Amongst the issues they identified were a failure to define religion, a lack of differentiation between the different levels at which religion may be viewed, a failure to investigate multiple affiliations, a reliance on items of belief which are not representative of the whole domain and inadequate scaling methods. By asking similar questions in different ways I have tried to recognise the unstable nature of attempts to establish fine definitions for religious affiliation. Although Caird and Law itemised the weaknesses involved in attempts to quantify belief, their concern was hardly new. Back in 1913 Edmund Husserl criticised deductive, quantitative investigations for their tendency to reach grand conclusions based on little evidence or, as he put it, resting either on 'an infinitude of axioms' or, at the other extreme, 'a very few axioms'.[7] More recently, Charles

---

[4] Russell T. McCutcheon, 'General Introduction', in Russell T. McCutcheon, *The Insider/Outsider Problem in the Study of Religion: A Reader* (London, 1999), p. 10. See also Hadley Cantril, 'Foreword', in Stanley L. Payne, *The Art of Asking Questions* (Princeton, 1980), p. x.

[5] Kurt Pawlik, and Lothar Buse, 'Self-Attribution as a Moderator Variable in Differential Psychology: Replication and Interpretation of Eysenck's Astrology/Personality Correlations', *Correlation*, 4/2 (1984), pp. 14–30; John Bauer and Martin Durant, 'British Public Perceptions of Astrology: An Approach from the Sociology of Knowledge', *Culture and Cosmos*, 1/1 (1997), pp. 55–7; Susan Blackmore and Marianne Seebold, 'The Effect of Horoscopes on Women's Relationships', *Correlation*, 19/2 (2000–1), pp. 14–23.

[6] Dale Caird and Henry G. Law, 'Non-Conventional Beliefs: Their Structure and Measurement', *Journal for the Scientific Study of Religion*, 21/2 (1982), p. 161.

[7] Edmund Husserl, *Ideas: General Introduction to Pure Phenomenology* (London, 1972), p. 6.

Glock attributed the contradictory results of studies of religion in the US to the conceptualisation of religion in universal terms and a failure to recognise its other dimensions.[8] As Milton Yinger pointed out,

> We cannot quantify without precise measurement. But what are we going to measure? So long as there are disagreements over the definition of religion we shall design different measuring instruments and apply them to different bodies of data. Almost certainly, as a result, we will arrive at different views of the religious situation.[9]

Most of this was understood perfectly well in the 1970s, yet public narratives on astrology continue to be dominated by naive expectations that belief in it can somehow be fixed to the nearest percentage point and that astrologers' relationship with organised religion is somehow easily defined. The flaw in most studies of astrology is a complete failure to understand the diversity in astrologers' truth claims and practices and this failure, in turn, results from a tendency to ignore astrologers, the nature of their practice, their varying truth claims and their literature. Simply, they ignore the primary sources. It is a little like exploring Christianity without reading the scriptures or investigating Christians. In addition, for the anthropologist, quantification is, in its very nature, likely to be misleading. To quote John Beattie: 'It is very much less feasible to make quantitative statements … about people's beliefs and values; their ideas about sorcery, for example, or their standards of filial piety'.[10]

The problematic nature of attempts to define religious affiliation are well known. For example, Charles Glock and Rodney Stark proposed the existence of five universal dimensions in all world religions: ideological (belief), intellectual (knowledge), ritualistic (behaviour traditionally defined as religious), experiential (inner emotional experiences which may be defined as spiritual) and consequential (the effects of the first four dimensions on the secular world).[11] Although Glock and Stark's efforts represented recognition that existing measures of religious affiliation were inadequate, and that their scale provided a means for differentiating different levels of religiosity or commitment to religion, they were overtly concerned with examples drawn from Christianity.[12] Yet Richard Clayton

---

[8]   Charles R. Glock, 'On the Study of Religious Commitment', *Religious Education*, 37/4 (1962), p. 100; see also J. Milton Yinger, *The Scientific Study of Religion* (New York, 1970), p. 32.

[9]   J. Milton Yinger, 'A Structural Examination of Religion', *Journal for the Scientific Study of Religion*, 8 (1969), p. 88.

[10]   John Beattie, *Other Cultures: Aims, Methods and Achievements in Social Anthropology* (London, 1989), p. 39.

[11]   Glock, 'Religious Commitment', pp. 98–9; Charles R. Glock and Rodney Stark, *Religion and Society in Tension* (Chicago, 1966), pp. 20–1.

[12]   Glock, 'Religious Commitment', p. 100.

and James Gladden observed that many people involved in 'non-conventional religions', including those characterised as New Age, in which they included theosophy and spiritualism, 'tend to have multiple group memberships'.[13] The search for simple group identities is therefore flawed at the outset and research which has assumed that individuals have one religious affiliation may therefore be unreliable. Clayton and Gladden suggested that the key element of religiosity is primarily defined by commitment to an ideology, and that Glock and Stark's other dimensions are merely expressions of the strength of that commitment. The crucial task in the study of religiosity is then to pinpoint the belief system, or ideology, with which the believer identifies. A preferable term, perhaps, rather than the problematic 'ideology' and 'belief system', is the more neutral, value-free, 'worldview'.[14] Such scales are useful, but their goal – to identify the true religiosity of any individual – is dubious in a context in which, as Quine and Ullian so delightfully put it, 'one's repertoire of beliefs changes with every waking moment'.[15] A worldview may be fluid rather than fixed, and be characterised by internal contradictions rather than consistency.

The result of such debates is a widespread scepticism concerning previous attempts to demonstrate such phenomena as secularisation. Sociologists, as Grace Davie has observed, are now often suspicious of statistics.[16] However, the appeal of simple quantification based on inadequate data remains strong, as we have seen from the repetition of data on astrology, but Davie's point is well made and we can agree that sociologists *should* be sceptical. For example, church membership may be both an unreliable guide to belief and a poor measure even of attendance. Indeed, Davie reports, the 'disjunction between practice and "belief" characterises much of British religious life since 1945'. Obviously we can apply this statement directly to astrology, so why should we expect a connection between practice and belief? In addition, how much can declining church attendance tell us about religiosity as a state of mind? And then how much can practical engagement with astrology tell us about astrologers' states of mind? Perhaps very little. Dean Shiels and Philip Berg provided support for Davie's claim, reporting that 'Church attendance appears to be a grossly inadequate indicator of religiosity'; they found that, while many of their respondents (63 per cent) scored medium to high on orthodox beliefs, 60 per cent of the respondents attended church only once or not at all during a four-week period, and only 20 per cent attended church four or

[13]   Richard R. Clayton and James W. Gladden, 'The Five Dimensions of Religiosity: Toward Demythologizing a Sacred Artefact', *Journal for the Scientific Study of Religion*, 13 (1974), pp. 135–43.

[14]   Ninian Smart, *Dimensions of the Sacred: An Anatomy of the World's Beliefs* (Berkeley and Los Angeles, 1996), pp. 10–12.

[15]   W.V. Quine and J.S. Ullian, *The Web of Belief*, 2nd edn (New York, 1978), p. 9.

[16]   Grace Davie, *Religion in Britain since 1945* (Oxford, 1994), p. 15.

more times in a month.[17] Thus, levels of stated belief were high, but the expected corresponding activity was low. As Michael Hill recognised, there is no certainty whatsoever that inner commitment will take a social or institutional form.[18] The converse is that levels of activity – church attendance, let us say – are not a reliable indicator of belief. In relation to astrology, then, Plug found that readership of horoscope columns is not necessarily an indication of belief, which throws some of Gallup's conclusions into doubt.[19] In other words, any attempt to infer belief in astrology from readership of horoscope columns is bound to be suspect. In addition, belief in one thing does not necessarily suggest belief in another, so that, for example, 'to believe that witches do exist does not make one a "believer in witches", that is, a disciple or a follower of witchcraft'.[20]

To look at 'belief' as if it were a single, monolithic state of mind and acceptance of a defined set of dogma is therefore just misleading, Here, Michael Hornsby-Smith set the precedent when he argued in his study of modern English Catholic belief patterns that each item of dogma, from teachings on contraception to papal infallibility, and each activity from church attendance to pilgrimage, may be a different indicator of belief or, to use a more socially functional word, 'commitment'.[21] Thus, astrologers' differing attitudes and commitment may be distinguished by opinions on whether astrology can forecast the future or transform the soul, by attendance at classes or conferences, or opinions about whether horoscopes are accurate or whether the stars influence life on earth.

Ronald Belter and Erwin Brinkmann, meanwhile, took this scepticism concerning the measurement of belief to its ultimate conclusion: they even wondered whether the attempt to quantify belief, as opposed to non-belief, was so epistemologically flawed as to be utterly pointless. They found that the results obtained when testing whether believers in God placed the locus of control in their lives externally or internally were inconsistent, and concluded that there was a general 'problem in conceptualizing and measuring belief in God', adding that 'it is apparent that such a belief is more complex than a simple belief–disbelief dimension' and that therefore to contrast belief with disbelief as if the two were mutually exclusive opposite positions would not 'relate adequately to the individual's locus of control orientation'; that is, a simple belief/disbelief dichotomy cannot reveal the true complexity of an individual's worldview or

---

[17]   Dean Shiels and Philip Berg, 'A Research Note on Sociological Variables Related to Belief in Psychic Phenomena', *Wisconsin Sociologist*, 14 (1977), p. 27.

[18]   Michael Hill, *A Sociology of Religion* (London, 1979), p. 14.

[19]   C. Plug, 'An Investigation of Superstitious Belief and Behaviour', *Journal of Behavioural Science*, 2/3 (1975), p. 174.

[20]   Richard N. Williams, Carl B. Taylor and Wayne J. Hintze, 'The Influence of Religious Orientation on Belief in Science, Religion, and the Paranormal', *Journal of Psychology and Theology*, 17/4 (1989), p. 358.

[21]   Michael Hornsby-Smith, *Roman Catholic Beliefs in England: Customary Catholicism and Transformations in Religious Authority* (Cambridge, 1991), p. 3.

meaning system.[22] We should stress the finality of the word 'cannot': simply, attempts to quantify belief are doomed to failure. The result, then, is an understanding that quantitative results have little significance in isolation from phenomenological considerations, particularly the understanding that belief may be a highly flexible phenomenon. Having thoroughly critiqued the whole notion of quantified data, I then set out to collect it. However, my complaint is not with quantification *per se*, but with the unquestioned assumption that quantified information can be taken out of the context of the question which produced it. Within context, and always treated with caution, quantified data can indicate trends and provide a starting point for analysis and comparison. What I am rejecting is blind acceptance of quantified data: I am instead advocating a sufficient cautious approach, which takes into account all the criticisms made of its application to human behaviour.

I conducted two surveys as part of my research in the early 2000s, one of astrologers which I summarise in Chapter 12, and one on public attitudes which I deal with here. My own questionnaire combined direct with indirect questions, was designed to replicate the previous quantitative studies by Gallup, and by Sue Blackmore and Marianne Seebold and, as will be clear, obtained significantly higher figures than Gallup, suggesting that Blackmore and Seebold's nuanced and varied style of questions will offer a better model. The groups I investigated were small, and I interviewed individuals where they were willing. My concern was with Robert Stake, who has identified 'the uniqueness of individual cases and contexts', and I used unique cases in the sense of small, transient groups.[23] My public survey was therefore fairly limited and my samples were small, following the model set by Gillian Bennett, on whose experience in folklore studies I have relied: she argued that, 'folklore study is unlike social sciences such as sociology in that it prefers small-scale studies to large-scale surveys. What it loses in universal significance by this approach, it gains in understanding'.[24]

The figures I obtained are indicative 'snapshots', a starting point for discussion rather than definitive results. I do not wish to generalise about society as a whole, but rather attempt to illuminate questions surrounding the quantification of belief; and I would suggest that future, larger surveys follow this example. The consequence of small samples, though, is that small variations in the number of responses can result in substantial variations in percentage results. I have included percentages in most of my results for consistency and for comparison, so that different samples can be matched and common patterns identified. I am confident that the results both indicate real trends and illustrate the methodological problems that afflict attempts to measure belief.

---

[22]   Ronald Belter and Erwin H. Brinkmann, 'Construct Validity of the Nowicki-Strickland Locus of Control Scale for Children', *Psychological Reports*, 48 (1981), p. 431.

[23]   Robert E. Stake, *The Art of Case Study Research* (London, 1995).

[24]   Gillian Bennett, *Traditions of Belief: Women, Folklore and the Supernatural Today* (London, 1987), p. 11.

The questionnaires were distributed in seven small batches, and 286 were returned. Five of the samples were local to my academic location at the time – Bath Spa University – and I was concerned to identify comparisons rather than absolute figures. Rather than expecting absolute figures, in view of my scepticism about their value, my concern was to see exactly how different questions asked of different groups allowed conclusions to be drawn. I then followed what I would call a spontaneous network distribution, as personal contacts volunteered to distribute my questionnaire. The links led from one network to another, connected by networks with multiple affiliations. All my questions were culled from, or referred back, to previous studies. The questions listed below begin with number 4 as they followed preliminary questions about personal information.

4. Do you read horoscope columns (a) every day (b) once a week (c) once a week (d) once a month (e) never.
5. Do you value the advice given by the astrologer (a) always (b) often (c) sometimes (d) never.
5a. If offered the opportunity, would you like to have your personal horoscope drawn up?
6. Have you ever purchased a computerised horoscope reading?
7. Have you ever visited an astrologer for a private consultation?
8. Do you know your sun-sign (i.e. star-sign or birth-sign)?
9. Do you know your moon-sign?
10. Do you know your Rising Sign (Ascendant)?
11. Do you think that your sun-sign description accurately reflects your personality?
12. Would you consult an astrologer before getting married or settling down with a partner?
13. Have you ever read a 'Teach Yourself' astrology book?
14. Have you ever taken an astrology course?
15. Do you think that the stars influence life on earth?
16. Do you think astrology is just superstition?
17. Do you think that astrology can make accurate forecasts about the future?
18. Would you alter your behaviour due to material that you read in your horoscope?
19. Do you find out the sun-signs of people that you're having relationships with?
20. Have you ever read a book concerning your star-sign in love or the year ahead for your sun-sign?
21. Would you consider yourself to be a spiritual person?
22. Do you use astrology as a spiritual tool?

The distribution was as follows:

1. Forty-eight questionnaires were distributed to undergraduate students in the Study of Religions Department at Bath Spa University College in November 2002 (coded SR1).
2. The questionnaire was then adapted and distributed to a further 59 undergraduate students in the Study of Religions Department at Bath Spa University College in November 2002 (SR2).
3. For comparison 51 questionnaires were distributed to undergraduate students in the Food Technology Department at Bath Spa University College in November 2002 (FT).
4. The questionnaire was further adapted and around 40 copies were distributed at the Long Ashton Golf Club, near Bristol, in March 2003; 29 replies were received (GC).
5. The questionnaire was further adapted and around 200 copies were distributed at the MAJMA Middle Eastern dance festival in Glastonbury on 4–6 April 2003; 46 replies were received (MJ).
6. The questionnaire was further adapted and around 100 copies were distributed by one individual who had been present at the MAJMA festival to her Arabic dance classes in Manchester (AD); 19 replies were received. The number is small but they can be compared to the MAJMA group and, in any case, conform to Gillian Bennett's view that folklore studies thrives on small samples.
7. Thirty-four copies were distributed at the AGM of the local branch of the National Federation of Spiritual Healers in 2004 at Glastonbury (NSFH).

Each of these groups constitutes what we might call an 'identity community', held together by webs of shared attitudes, values and activities. Such groups consist of individuals with multiple affiliations, and so the raw figures always represent an average within the group, rather than a picture to which each individual conforms. I obtained a response rate of 100 per cent amongst the student groups who completed the questionnaires as a class exercise, even though they were informed that it was voluntary. In the other distribution groups responses were much lower as I was dependent on various 'gate-keepers' to persuade respondents to complete the questionnaires. That said, it was individuals in each group who volunteered to distribute the questionnaires in a self-generating process.

The first problem is to test for self-declared belief in astrology and either confirm or challenge the widely quoted Gallup poll figures. These, usually based on direct questions, are generally located between 20 per cent and 29 per cent, as we saw in Chapter 10. However, the more nuanced studies by Pawlik and Buse and by Bauer and Durant arrived at much higher figures as a result of inference based on indirect questions. It therefore seems apparent that individuals may deny belief, yet give favourable answers which may, in themselves, be used to suggest belief, to other questions. As has been suggested, the connection between 'belief' and practice is tenuous, at best. That said, the results for self-declared belief in astrology from my study (summarised in Tables 11.1 and 11.2) varied considerably, ranging from

Table 11.1   Belief in astrology: comparison of strong and moderate, belief and disbelief (percentages)

	Strong belief	Moderate belief	No opinion	Moderate disbelief	Strong disbelief
FT	2	21.6	25.5	27.5	23.5
SR2	5.1	37.3	18.6	27.1	10.2
GC	3.4	27.6	17.2	31	17.2
MJ	10.9	58.7	4.3	13	0
AD	5.3	57.9	5.3	15.8	10.5
NFSH	23.5	67.6	0	0	0

Note: Author's data.

Table 11.2   Belief in astrology: comparison of author's data with other studies, illustrating minimum and maximum figures based on different types of question

Place and date of survey	Percentage of belief in astrology	Source
UK 1975	14	Gallup 1976a (vol. 2, p. 1417)
US 1975	22	Gallup 1978 (vol. 1, p. 572)
US 1978	29	Gallup 1979 (p. 184)
UK 1978	20	Gallup 1980 (p. 329)
Germany 1980s	70	Pawlik and Buse 1984
US 1995	23	Gallup 1996 (p. 10)
US 1996	25	Gallup 1997 (p. 205)
UK 1990s	73	Bauer and Durant 1997
US 2003	26	Harris 2009
US 2005	25	Lyons 2005
UK 2005	22.5	Lyons 2005
UK 2002	23.6	Campion (FT)
UK 2002	52.4	Campion (SR2)
UK 2003	31	Campion (GC)
UK 2003	69.6	Campion (MJ)
UK 2003	63.2	Campion (AD)
UK 2004	91.1	Campion (NFSH)

Note: The figures from Pawlik and Buse, Bauer and Durant and Campion combine different levels of belief into one figure.

23.6 per cent for the Bath Spa University Food Technology students to 69.6 per cent for respondents at the MAJMA festival and 91.1 per cent for NFSH members.

There are a number of points which are immediately apparent from these figures. The first is the huge gap between the highest and the lowest. The second is that both Pawlik and Buse and Bauer and Durant obtained similar total figures, suggesting that quantification can yield useful data. That one set of data was gathered in Germany, the other in the UK, also suggests that similar figures may be obtained across the Western world. The lowest figures for self-declared belief were obtained from Food Technology students and members of the Long Ashton Golf Club. Given that over 60 per cent of the former were aged under 30 and 100 per cent of the latter were aged over 50, we may conclude that age in itself is not a determining factor; that is, that young people are no more likely to state belief in astrology than older people. On the other hand, Stuart Rose noted that the average demographic profile of participants in his research into New Agers who had ever had an astrological reading was between 35 and 55.[25] Thus the MAJMA group is within the target age range and has the greatest figure for the purchase of personal horoscopes. Following Geoffrey Dean, then, who argued that belief in astrology may follow a successful visit to an astrologer, the MAJMA group's high level of belief might be sustained by positive experiences of such visits.[26] But then the question becomes one of cause and effect: is a visit to an astrologer a cause or consequence of belief?

It is noticeable that the Study of Religions students scored almost twice as much for belief in astrology as the Food Technology students, even though they represent a similar demographic, while MAJMA festival dancers scored three times as much, the latter statistic confirmed by the figure obtained from the smaller sample of Arabic dancers (a vindication of the usefulness of small samples), and the NFSH sample higher still. The figures therefore indicate a clear contrast between undergraduates taking a vocational course and Golf Club members aged over 50 on the one hand, as opposed to NFSH members and women who take up Arabic dance on the other. The former may, perhaps, be considered more conventional, the latter less conventional, and age is irrelevant. This contrast may, then, be confirmation of Robert Wuthnow's marginality hypothesis: his 'type 2' marginal individuals are adventurous and possess an ability to think independently.[27] In this sense, attendees at the MAJMA festival may be defined as marginal (as long as the term has no pejorative associations), whereas the Food Technology students and the members of the Golf Club are not.

There may also be a connection between these varying figures for belief and religious affiliation. If it is assumed that those professing both Christianity (and attending a regular church service) and atheism are likely to be hostile to astrology, while those defining themselves as pagan or 'spiritual but non-aligned' are more likely to be sympathetic, then the headline result for religious affiliation may indeed

---

[25]   Stuart Rose, 'Transforming the World: An Examination of the Roles played by Spirituality and Healing in the New Age Movement', PhD thesis, Department of Religious Studies, Lancaster University, 1996, p. 389.

[26]   Geoffrey Dean, 'Discourse for Key Topic 4: Astrology and Human Judgement', *Correlation*, 17/2 (1998/99), pp. 26–8, 47–51.

[27]   Robert Wuthnow, *The Consciousness Revolution* (Berkeley, 1976), p. 173.

Table 11.3   Religious affiliation of Campion respondents (percentages)

	Christian	Atheist	Pagan	Spiritual but non-aligned	Attend service regularly
FT	41.1	23.5	0	15.7	15.7
SR	40.7	8.5	8.5	25.4	18.6
GC	96.5	3.4	0	0	27.5
MJ	34.8	8.7	15.2	37	15.2
AD	36.9	0	10.5	5.3	5.3
NFSH	23.5	0	0	61.8	26.5

Note: 'Christian' includes Protestant, Roman Catholic and non-denominational Christian.

support this hypothesis (Table 11.3). Thus the MAJMA sample produced the lowest figure for Christian affiliation, a low figure for atheism and the highest for paganism and 'spiritual but non-aligned'. Its headline figure for belief in astrology was the second highest, at 69.8 per cent. The Food Technology group produced the highest figure for atheism, a low figure for 'spiritual but non-aligned' and, like the Golf Club group, had no pagans at all. Accordingly it had the lowest figure for belief in astrology. The Study of Religions group, meanwhile, produced almost exactly the same figure as the Food Technology sample for Christian affiliation, but a much lower figure for atheism and higher ones for paganism and 'spiritual', and accordingly produced a higher level for belief in astrology. The second lowest figure for belief in astrology was produced by the Golf Club group, which also was 96.5 per cent Christian with no positive responses for pagan or 'spiritual' and the highest level of church attendance.

Having posed direct questions about belief in astrology, we can then move on to elicit information from a range of other questions which have, in the past, been used to infer belief. Pawlik and Buse and Bauer and Durant both inferred belief in astrology from readership of horoscope columns while Gallup poll figures on readership of columns are used in the secondary literature to infer belief. As I have argued, to suggest that such figures can infer levels of belief is to engage in a category error. However, they are a form of evidence, as Michael Hornsby-Smith would suggest, on individual items of behaviour.

All these figures, including those from my own research, are summarised in Table 11.4. The Gallup questions are vague and the figures variable. For example, in the UK in 1975 15 per cent claimed to read a horoscope column 'regularly' and 38 per cent 'from time to time', a total of 52 per cent; in the same year in the US 23 per cent claimed to read columns 'regularly'.[28] Both 'regularly' and 'time to time', though, are periods which invite widely differing interpretations; they might be presumed to be anywhere between once a day and once a month, or even longer.

---

[28]   George H. Gallup, *The Gallup International Public Opinion Polls: Great Britain 1937–1975*, 2 vols (New York, 1976), vol. 2, p. 1417.

Table 11.4   Comparison of readership of horoscope columns: author's data compared with other studies (percentages)

	Every day	Once a week	Once a month	Ever	Never	Total readers
B and D	21	23	29	n/a	27	73
B and S	n/a	n/a	n/a	70	n/a	70
FT	13.7	29.4	27.5	n/a	27.5	70.6
SR1	4.2	37.5	35.4	20.8	n/a	77.1
SR2	3.4	33.9	35.6	22	n/a	87.7
GC	3.4	24.1	34.5	37.9	n/a	62
MJ	6.5	26.1	54.3	13	n/a	86.9
AD	3.4	24.1	34.5	37.6	n/a	62
NFSH	5.9	20.6	52.9	5.9	n/a	85.3
Gallup[a]	n/a	n/a	n/a	52	n/a	52
Gallup[b]	n/a	n/a	n/a	23	n/a	23
Miller	n/a	n/a	n/a	16–22	n/a	16–22

Notes: [a]Gallup, *Great Britain 1937–1975.* [b]George Gallup, *The Gallup Poll: Public Opinion 1972–1977,* 2 vols (Wilmington DE, 1978). 'B and D' denotes Bauer and Durant; 'B and S' Blackmore and Seebold.

Jon Miller found that between 16 per cent and 22 per cent of respondents read columns (or 'personal reports') on an unspecified timescale, while for Blackmore and Seebold the figure of 'regular' readers was 70 per cent.[29] This higher figure has been supported by other recent research. Alan Orenstein, for example, found that 57.6 per cent of his sample answered 'yes' to the question, 'Do you ever read a horoscope or tour personal astrology report?'[30]

Pawlik and Buse did not publish their raw data but Bauer and Durant attempted to refine the readership of horoscope columns into four frequencies: often, fairly often, not often and not at all. Table 11.4 compares these figures with those from my survey. The results are surprisingly similar, given that Bauer and Durant's general definitions of time periods may not coincide with my specific ones. The totals also correspond with Blackmore and Seebold's figures. It should be noted, though, that the numbers reading horoscope columns every day are tiny and that the Food Technology students, low on belief, scored the highest percentage for daily readership. The dislocation between declared belief on the one hand and activity on the other is exactly as Plug anticipated. The first simple conclusion is that an activity, in this case readership of horoscope columns, may have little relationship

---

[29]   Miller, 'The Public Acceptance'; Blackmore and Seebold, 'The Effect of Horoscopes', pp. 14–23.

[30]   Alan Orenstein, 'On Evolution, Abortion and Astrology', *Skeptical Inquirer*, 33/4 (2009), p. 49.

Table 11.5   Headline figures for questions on astrology: author's data compared with Gallup and Blackmore and Seebold (2000–01) (percentages)

Q	G	B and S	FT	SR	GC	MJ	AD	NFSH
5	–	39	51	56.7	31	73.9	68.4	76.4
5A	38[a]	–	–	–	–	69.6	68.4	79.4
6	–	15	7.8	17.4	3.4	19.6	5.3	38.2
7	–	–	7.8	9.7	17.2	26.1	5.3	29.4
8	57[b]/76[c]	100	98	88.8	100	82.6	84.2	91.1
9	–	22	3.9	12.4	0	26.1	10.5	26.5
10	–	–	5.9	13.8	3.4	23.9	10.5	35.3
11	37[d]	85	45.1	52.7	44.8	63	79	44.1
12	–	13	0	3.6	3.4	13	5.3	23.5
13	–	24	11.8	27	6.9	37	15.8	26.5
14	–	24	2	2.5	0	17.4	0	5.9
15	23[e]/25[f]	–	19.6	44.9	17.2	50	36.8	70.6
16	–	28	62.7	40.4	69	43.5	42.6	17.7
17	15[g]	–	25.5	32.3	6.9	28.3	21.1	52.9
18	–	15	2	8.9	10.3	17.4	5.3	17.6
19	–	89	45.1	57.5	17.2	67.4	57.9	61.8
20	–	78	31.4	56.9	17.2	59.4	63.2	64.3
21	–	–	33.3	67.3	41.4	69.6	63.2	88.2
22	–	–	5.9	14.3	6.9	30.4	15.8	14.7

Note: Question 5 combines figures for 'always', 'often' and 'sometimes'. Questions 16 and 17 were a single question in Blackmore and Seebold's questionnaire (no. 8); data for the two groups SR1 and SR2 are combined. [a]Data for the UK 1975: Gallup, *Great Britain 1937–1975*, vol. 2, p. 1417. [b]Data for France 1962: George H. Gallup, *The Gallup International Public Opinion Polls: France 1939. 1944–1975* (2 vols, New York, 1976), vol. 1, p. 309. [c]Data for US 1975: Gallup, *Public Opinion 1972–1977*, vol. 1, p. 572. [d]'Do you think that the character traits attributed to individuals according to their signs contain a good deal of truth, a moderate degree of truth or none at all?': 'Good deal' 6; 'Moderate degree' 31 (Gallup, *Great Britain 1937–1975*, vol. 2, p. 1417). [e]'Which, if either, of the following do you believe in? In astrology, or that the positions of the stars and planets can affect people's lives?'. Data for US 1995: George Gallup Jr., *The Gallup Poll: Public Opinion 1995* (Wilmington DE, 1996), p. 10. [f]'Do you believe in astrology, or that the positions of the stars and planets can affect people's lives?'. Data for US 1996: George Gallup Jr., *The Gallup Poll: Public Opinion 1996* (Wilmington DE, 1997), p. 205. [g]'Do you think it is possible to see the future in the stars?'. Data for Sweden October 1978: George H. Gallup, *The International Gallup Polls: Public Opinion 1978* (Wilmington DE, 1980), p. 329.

with self-declared belief in an apparently related area, in this case astrology. This was exactly my experience of the Central Television audience, the vast majority of whom read horoscopes yet refused to admit belief in astrology. In short, the results of direct questions about belief may, in themselves, be misleading.

I then asked a further series of questions replicating those asked by both Gallup and Blackmore and Seebold. Questions 5 to 22 are summarised in Table 11.5. It is immediately apparent that the Gallup poll figures are, in general, low, and that of my seven groups the Golf Club results are the most cautious and the MAJMA group the most sympathetic to astrology. The difference between questions which apparently require an objective judgment (questions 18–20) about the real state of the world and those which ask for a subjective response (questions 7–8) are evident in the differing replies. For example, in the MAJMA group 50 per cent think the stars influence life on earth and 28.3 per cent think astrology can make accurate forecasts, yet 69.6 per cent would like to have a personal horoscope cast and 73.9 per cent value the astrologer's advice when they read a horoscope column. The discrepancy between these figures is apparent in all my seven samples. Blackmore and Seebold's survey, though, did not show this pattern. The possible reason may be that their question on whether the astrologer's advice is valued asked for a simple yes/no answer, whereas mine allowed for 'always', 'often' and 'sometimes': whereas behaviour, such as the purchase of books or computerised horoscope reports, may be subject to yes/no answers, attitudes, opinions and aspirations are not.

The wording of questions and the options offered as answers are crucial to the final figures. A dramatic example was provided by the amendment of question 14, on the accuracy of sun-sign character descriptions, in the amended questionnaire distributed to the Arabic dancers. Previously this question only allowed for a yes/no answer. In response to feedback following the MAJMA festival though, I added a third option, 'partly', and whereas 47.4 per cent said their sun-sign was accurate, a figure in line with other groups, when the positive answers for 'partly' were added, the resulting figure rose to 79 per cent, the highest in any of my samples. Again, a slight change in wording appears to result in a substantially changed response.

We should also ask which of these questions, if any, should be taken as indicating belief in astrology. For the MAJMA group is it the 73.9 per cent who value the astrologer's advice, the 63 per cent who regard their sun-sign as an accurate description of their character or the 28.3 per cent who consider that astrology can make accurate forecasts about the future? It may be possible to discern different levels of involvement in astrology between, for example, those for whom astrology consists solely of sun-sign delineations and columns on the one hand, and the greater involvement indicated by a personal visit to an astrologer on the other. Other indications of greater involvement might be the reading of a teach-yourself book, the taking of a course, knowledge of moon or rising signs (the so-called 'ascendant', the zodiac sign rising over the eastern horizon at birth) the use of astrology as a spiritual discipline or a willingness to alter behaviour. Figures for all these questions rarely rise above 20 per cent, except amongst the MAJMA sample, together with the 35.4 per cent of the first Study of Religions sample (SR1) who had purchased a teach-yourself book. Amongst the MAJMA sample 19.6 per cent had purchased a computerised horoscope, 26 per cent knew their moon-sign and 23.9 per cent their rising sign, and 17.4 per cent had taken an astrology course. The positive answers in the MAJMA group may have been boosted by the fact that respondents were self-selecting, unlike those in the three student groups. Yet the Golf Club group was also self-selecting and produced the least positive answers. It is clear that it is difficult to generalise across the population as a whole and that the nature of the sample is crucial. In addition, generalisation on the basis of large samples may conceal sharp variations between different groups, such as between the Golf Club and MAJMA groups.

The difficulty of generalisation is evident from the NFSH group. They produced the largest figure for belief in astrology (91.1 per cent believing and nobody ticked no opinion of disbelief), and 70 per cent (almost three times the Gallup figure) believe that the stars influence events on earth, yet only 17.6 per cent would alter their behaviour on the basis of a horoscope. It is clear, then, that the latter question is not an indicator of belief in astrology but an indicator of an attitude towards it; that it may be used for advice in combination with other factors but can not be used alone. Again, we reinforce the point that simple questions on belief are misleading.

Regarding astrology's presumed identity as a New Age discipline, the personality profiles represented by the sun-signs are Alan Leo's most significant contribution to astrology: his view was that they were essential to the increase in self-awareness which, in turn, was necessary for each individual to play their full part in bringing the New Age into manifestation. Sun-sign astrology as a general cultural phenomenon, as was argued in Chapter 7, may be considered part of the New Age *sensu lato*: there is no necessary connection between knowledge of the zodiac sign's psychological personality profiles and strict belief in the coming of the New Age, but they were only constructed as a consequence of Leo's belief that the New Age was imminent. The evidence from previous studies indicates that between 82 per cent and 100 per cent of adults know which sun-sign they were born under, and anywhere between 37 per cent and 85 per cent think that their sun-sign describes their character, depending on the group and how the question is asked. Knowing the key characteristics of one's sun-sign indicates how far knowledge of this form of astrology has penetrated the modern mentality, but reveals nothing about attitudes to it. What is more important is whether people act on this information, in which respect the question piloted by Blackmore and Seebold asked simply, 'Do you find out the zodiac sign of someone you are having a relationship with?' Here, the results are most interesting.

Leaving out the older Golf Club group (who are less likely than students to be changing partners), between 45 per cent and 67 per cent of my samples made a point of discovering the sun-sign of people they are having relationships with, a sure indication that it is understood that the information gleaned will be practically useful. Between 31 per cent and 64 per cent also brought a book about their sun-sign for the year ahead, suggesting at least that there is a personal use in astrology. If Michael York argued that astrology was the *lingua franca* of the 1960s counter-culture and New Age movement, then my samples indicate that it has also become an essential part of the language of popular culture and mass psychology.[31]

The four groups most sympathetic to astrology (SR2, MJ, AD, NSFH) each showed a strong tendency to admit to moderate belief in astrology. In two groups (MJ and AD) close to 60 per cent chose this option. In all five groups levels of 'moderate belief' were far greater than levels of 'strong belief', while the gap between the two options was much greater than that between 'moderate disbelief' and 'strong disbelief'. This suggests that, in general, respondents were happier to admit to strong disbelief than strong belief and that, when they did admit to belief, moderate belief was the chosen option, suggesting an underlying bias against the notion of 'belief'. When figures for self-declared belief in astrology are lower than those for practical engagement with it, this points to an unwillingness to admit to 'belief' in certain topics which are likely to be ridiculed. This is exactly as Gillian Bennett suggested and this observation would seem to chime very well with Jahoda and Bennett's contentions that there is a general reluctance to admit to belief in anything which has been labelled as superstitious.[32] And, as David Hufford suggested, 'disbelief' is prioritised over 'belief'. However, there is a further implication with significance for the general view that belief in astrology presents peculiar methodological problems. For example, as I pointed out in Chapter 10, Dean and Mather, drawing primarily on opinion poll figures, commented that 70 per cent of the adult population read horoscopes while only 20 per cent 'believe that there is something in it'.[33] This raises the problem of why 50 per cent of the adult population does something it regards as meaningless. There is a clearly a 'belief' gap: half the adult population of the US and the UK perform an act which, most commentators insist, is concerned with 'belief', without 'believing' in it. One standard answer – that people read horoscope columns for a laugh – is unconvincing: as Richard Dawkins pointed out, horoscope columns are not funny.[34] Yet, if we forget the opinion polls and take the maximum figures for belief obtained by Pawlik and Buse (70 per cent) and Bauer and Durant (73 per cent), the discrepancy between the headline figures for belief (both moderate and strong belief) and readership of horoscope columns (daily, weekly and monthly) shrinks. However, this does not really deal with the problem, for all these authors did was convert readership of horoscope columns into presumed belief. The removal of the 'belief gap' is therefore achieved by altering the way in which belief is measured from the answer to a direct question to an inference based on behaviour; namely the readership of horoscope columns translates directly into intensity of belief.

[31]   Michael York, *Historical Dictionary of New Age Movements* (Lanham MD, 2003), pp. 25–6.

[32]   Gustav Jahoda, *The Psychology of Superstition* (London, 1969), pp. 25–6; and Bennett, *Traditions of Belief*, p. 27.

[33]   Geoffrey Dean and Arthur Mather, *Recent Advances in Natal Astrology: A Critical Review 1900–1976* (Subiaco, Australia, 1977), pp. 79, 83.

[34]   Richard Dawkins, 'Newsnight', BBC2, 3 January 1996.

That the relationship between positive answers to questions on astrology correlates only weakly with stated levels of belief supports Plug's proposition that readership of horoscope columns may be a poor indicator of belief. When looked at individually, the MAJMA cohort produced some interesting results. One respondent gave indications of strong belief: had visited an astrologer for a private consultation, would alter behaviour depending on astrological advice and used astrology as a spiritual tool, but never read horoscope columns and declared a level of 'moderate belief'. Another 'moderate believer', though, had also been to an astrologer for a consultation, read horoscope columns once a month and sometimes valued the advice given, but was uniformly negative in all other answers. A third 'moderate believer' read horoscope columns once a month, sometimes valued the advice and would have liked to have a personal horoscope but was otherwise uniformly negative. Between the range of these three respondents, it is apparent that the answers to specific questions have only a loose relationship with stated levels of belief. Further, the answers given by one of the few 'strong believers' were actually slightly less positive than those given by the moderate believer, while another 'moderate disbeliever' sometimes valued the advice given in horoscope columns and found out the sun-signs of people with whom s/he was having relationships. Thus, the theory that the wide discrepancy between figures for belief in astrology and the readership of horoscope columns may be explained by the claim that many readers do not take astrology seriously is contradicted by the generally high figure for actions such as finding out partners' sun-signs.

A similar lack of clarity was found amongst the other groups. For example, in the Golf Club group one respondent classed themselves as a 'strong believer' and had visited an astrologer, but did not wish to have a personal chart cast. Another 'moderate believer' would alter their behaviour on astrological advice, but read horoscope columns only once a month. When respondents were allowed to rate their belief on a line scale, two others chose 'not at all', but, of the five levels of belief, the former chose 'moderate disbelief' while the latter chose 'no opinion'. That is, asked to choose between levels of belief on different scales, individuals choose substantially different options. The same patterns are found in the student samples. For example, one 'moderate believer' amongst the Food Technology students was a Roman Catholic, answered 'yes' to all the religious questions, read horoscope columns every day and gave very positive answers to most of the other questions on astrology. Clearly, there is no absolute and necessary reason for Christian conviction to conflict with deep acceptance of astrology.

The major interest in astrology from Christian commentators, whether hostile or just mildly concerned, is with its presumed status as a rival to Christianity, as if the two are somehow fundamentally incompatible. Here again, though, the evidence is contradictory: depending on how the figures are read, belief in Christian dogma correlates positively with belief in astrology.[35] Of course, we

---

[35]   Erich Goode, 'Two Paranormalisms or Two and a Half? An Empirical Exploration', *Skeptical Inquirer*, 24/1 (2000), pp. 29–35.

do not know if the figure results from Christian believers accepting astrology, or astrologers being open to Christianity. In either case, the figures are a warning against simple assumptions. I posed three questions with a view to establishing whether evangelical Christianity correlates inversely with belief in, or attitudes to, astrology, based on research done in Northern Ireland in the 1970s.[36] These were: 'Jesus Christ is the divine Son of God', 'The Bible is the word of God' and 'God really does answer prayer'. The presumption is that positive answers to these questions indicate evangelical Christianity. If the theory that Christianity and astrology are inherently incompatible holds true, then positive answers to these questions should indicate hostility to Christianity and vice versa. However, the picture is by no means clear. In the Golf Club group it is apparent that a high level of Christian affiliation correlates with a low level of acceptance of astrology. However, when individual responses are considered, this conclusion is questioned. For example, of the five who had visited astrologers, one answered 'yes' to all three religious questions, two answered 'yes' to two, one to one and one did not answer. There is in these examples no sense in which attitudes to astrology necessarily correlate with religious affiliation. Another, who read horoscopes every day, answered 'yes' to all three religious questions, adding to the statement that Jesus was the divine son of God that 'that is our teaching as Christians'. The apparent relationship between religious belief and attitude to astrology therefore disappears when individual responses are considered. Instead it seems not to be an issue. In addition, amongst this group the answers to the three questions can be a mixture of 'yes' and 'no'. For example, one 'non-denominational Christian' amongst the MAJMA group agreed that the Bible is the word of God but disagreed that Jesus is God's divine son or that God answers prayer. Such individual answers completely demolish the notion of Christianity as a heterogeneous set of beliefs: here is a Christian who believes that the scriptures are God's work but denies two fundamental tenets of Christian faith and practice.

Also significant is the extent to which non-Christians may give positive answers to the tests for evangelical Christianity. For example, amongst the MAJMA group two respondents, both answered yes to all three religious questions while the former's religious affiliation was 'spiritual but non aligned' and the latter's was 'Buddhist'. Another who was 'spiritual but non-aligned' denied that Jesus is the divine son of God or that the Bible is the word of God, but agreed that God answers prayer and added, so do 'Jesus and Mary, because they seem to have more time to spare'. Clearly, individual testimony points to a tenuous relationship between Christian affiliation and core items of Christian dogma, a phenomenon we might associate with privatisation.

I would therefore suggest that, as Charles Glock and Rodney Stark observed, the traditional questions to test for religious affiliation may be inappropriate in an

---

    [36]   Independent Television Authority, *Religion in Britain and Northern Ireland: A Survey of Popular Attitudes* (London, 1970).

increasingly pluralistic context.[37] In order to investigate the problem of apparently inconsistent answers on religious affiliation and attitude to astrology I conducted a number of interviews with students from the Study of Religions group. One respondent I spoke to had previously completed a questionnaire in which s/he gave religious affiliation as Protestant, ticked 'yes' to Jesus as the divine son of God and God answering prayer, but 'no' to 'the Bible is the word of God'. S/he then gave very strong positive answers for astrology, but picked a level of belief in the middle of the line scale, claiming neither belief nor disbelief. In a follow-up interview the respondent gave further details, giving a picture of deep religiosity, though low attachment to the church, an interest in New Age or paranormal phenomena, and a sense that these are valuable, even though they are condemned by fundamentalist Christians:

I was raised in a Church of England home and I went to Church regularly as a child … I am in the Church choir and you know … as I got older I got more interested in religion and especially through studying religion … I am not devout Christian … but … I agree with the statements that Jesus is the Son of God. I ticked the Protestant box for which denomination I am but I don't think the Bible is solely the word of God. I think it is the product of the time it was written in … I have practised meditation. Not just on my own. I have some books on yoga and I like to practise yoga. I am not, I am not really, you know, solely into it but I do find it interesting. I have done also … meditation. I have done candlegating – that's kind of meditating if you are looking at a candle. I am also very interested in psychics and life after death, mediums, that kind of thing. What happens when we die, that kind of stuff and also, it is very conflicting. Christians would say that mediums is a no-go area. It does say in the Bible that you shouldn't visit mediums but I am quite interested in that and I think I have read things on that by people who are Christians but also are mediums and how that works. So yes, I am in to it, all that kind of stuff.

I do read [horoscope columns] and … they are almost like a bit of a help to how to just go about life and stuff and that is kind of, kind of spiritual, it is almost like guidance from what I read … I don't take it literally but I do I do take it to heart a bit, what I read … it says oh 'You are going to have … um … Your relationship with this person is going to become more involved this week.' So, if I have been spending a lot of time with this particular person, then I think 'Oh well it must mean, must mean this person and um' and then I think that that would affect how I behave with that person that week and do, they do stick in my head. I don't just read them and forget about them.

I think about [Christian opposition to astrology] a lot because obviously it is, it is a big conflict, especially with one of my housemates who if we are speaking

37   Glock and Stark, *Religion and Society in Tension*, p. 93.

about it she will say that I shouldn't read them and that that it is hard to reconcile the two ... But at the same time I can't deny that I am interested in it so that even though I do say that I am Christian, I wouldn't go so far as to say that I wouldn't read them.

Lastly, the respondent stated her belief in astrology as 'middle' (in the middle of the line scale), that is, neither belief nor disbelief, because

[even though] I do say that I believe in it, I am still very sceptical of everything and I could never, I could never completely believe in it. There is always a part of me, I don't know for certain that it is true and that is the same with Christianity. That's the thing of always holding back.

When, therefore, the personal feelings behind the answers are investigated, the apparent confusion of the questionnaire results is replaced by a situation of multiple affiliations and the individual reconciliation of competing worldviews. Caird and Law's observation that 'a substantial proportion of persons involved in non-conventional religion tend to have multiple group memberships' seems to be confirmed.[38] Most researchers in the past have simply asked subjects their religion, thus missing this complexity. Nelson and his colleagues pointed out, additionally, that 'non-doctrinal or invisible religion does not form a unitary belief system'.[39] Again, the proposition is confirmed and complexity is therefore to be expected. Moreover, as Roof et al. argued, the 'multidimensional' aspects of 'non-doctrinal' religion are shared with 'traditional, church religion'.[40] So we should not be surprised to observe self-declared Christians denying key aspects of Christian dogma, while non-Christians accept them. It is clear that the debate on both astrology's popularity and its religious affiliation is deeply flawed. First, attempts to quantify belief on the basis of either direct questions or through inference on the basis of behaviour are deeply flawed, both because the concept of belief is so problematic and because of the methodological problems arising from the assumptions behind the questions.

There are two main, general conclusions arising out of this discussion. First, opinion poll data dramatically underestimates interest in astrology and may, I suggest, be inaccurate in all questions of belief, problematic as that word is. Second, we can ask direct questions about belief, but the results are misleading unless asked in combination with questions concerning specific items of behaviour and opinion. The specific conclusion we can draw concerning astrology are that

---

[38]　Caird and Law, 'Non-Conventional Beliefs', pp. 161–2.

[39]　Nelson et al., 'A Test of Yinger's Measure of Non-Doctrinal Religion: Implications for Invisible Religion as a Belief System', *Journal for the Scientific Study of Religion*, 15/3 (1976), p. 267.

[40]　Roof et al., 'Yinger's Measure of Non-Doctrinal Religion: A Northeastern Test', *Journal for the Scientific Study of Religion*, 19/4 (1977), p. 407.

its penetration into popular culture is much broader than previous figures suggest, and the issues are much more complex than simple dichotomies of astrology versus science or astrology versus Christianity suggest. And, *if*, astrology is indeed a New Age discipline, then the penetration of New Age thought into Western society, or at least the UK and US, is equally wide, and premature notions of the New Age culture's demise can safely be dismissed. Indeed, it has truly gone mainstream. Further, in that New Age culture is emphatically *not* inherently hostile to Christianity, only to the mainstream churches, there is no sense in which astrology, as a New Age discipline, can be considered hostile to Christianity. Evangelical hostility to astrology therefore appears to be a replication of similar antipathy to other Christian groups. Additionally, the theory that people desert the churches partly because they are attracted to a range of New Age disciplines, such as astrology, is misplaced, and the notion that, as belief in God declines, so people believe in anything is without foundation.

Chapter 12

In Their Own Words: The Astrologers' Universe of Discourse

Karen Hawkwood … says it makes her laugh when people ask, 'Do you believe in astrology?' Because that's like asking, 'Do you believe in biology?' Of course this thing exists.[1]

As we have seen, figures on the presumed levels of belief in astrology generally make no distinction between astrologers and the general public, between producers and consumers, we might say. Only the two studies by Paulik and Buse and Bauer and Durant attempted to distinguish 'intensity' of belief, which they assumed might then be related to a scale moving from casual horoscope reading, representing weak belief, to professional engagement with astrology, indicating intense belief. As far as astrology's nature is concerned, there is, as we have noted, the widespread assumption that it is a religion or that it is New Age in nature. As we have also seen, these inferences should be questioned. In some senses astrology may seem to be New Age, in others not.[2]

With this in mind, I conducted qualitative research, along with the collection of simple numerical data from 1999 to 2011. Initially I attended a series of astrology conferences, including three in the US, one in the UK and two on mainland Europe. After conducting a pilot study at the Northwest Astrology Conference (NORWAC) in Seattle in May 1999, which received 82 responses out of around 200 distributed, I issued a revised questionnaire at the Astrological Association Conference of Great Britain (AA) in Plymouth in August 1999, and at the United Astrology Congress (UAC) in Orlando, Florida, in July 2002. I distributed 500 questionnaires at the AA conference, of which 159 (31.8 per cent) were returned. The return rate at UAC was much lower: 152 (12.6 per cent) out of a total of 1,200 distributed. I distributed a simplified questionnaire at the International Society for Astrological Research (ISAR) conference at Anaheim, California, in October 2003; around 400 questionnaires were distributed and 54 returned. I also distributed an earlier, fuller version of this simplified questionnaire at two conferences outside the English-speaking world, the First Balkan Astrology Conference in Belgrade in March 2001 and the Norwegian Astrological Conference in Oslo in November 2001. Ninety-

---

[1] Mark D. Fefer, 'Learning with the stars: inside the country's first college of astrology', *Seattle Weekly*, 23–29 August 2001, <http://www.seattleweekly.com/features/0134/news-fefer.shtml>, accessed 6 September 2001.

[2] Nicholas Campion, 'Astrology's Role in New Age Culture: A Research Note', *Culture and Cosmos*, 13/2 (2009), pp. 87–94.

six questionnaires were returned at the former (almost everyone at the conference participated) and 30 at the latter. While some of my samples, such as that from the ISAR conference, are small, and need to be taken cautiously, the total number returned, 573, is enough to develop a reasonably reliable picture. Also, that the results show a fair level of consistency across the samples, regardless of size, suggests that this is not a critical factor. I have converted even small numbers into percentages, even though at low levels this can be misleading, purely for consistency.

In 2011 I gathered a new set of data from three gatherings: the British Astrological Association Conference in September (76 questionnaires out of around 100 distributed), a meeting of the Fundacion Centro Astrologico de Buenos Aires in Argentina in November (105 returned out of around 150 distributed), and the annual conference of SINARJ, the Brazilian astrological association, in Rio de Janeiro, also in November (83 returned out of around 200 distributed). My full data has been published by the British Astrological Association.[3] This brought my total responses to 837.

I followed a number of principles in gathering my data. First, I asked similar questions in a variety of ways in order to account for the problem that, ultimately, the answer to any question is shaped by the assumptions which are either inherent in the question, or perceived in the question by respondents. Second, I allowed feedback on each survey to influence my design of the next one. Throughout, there were essentially two strands to my research: first, astrologers' religious affiliation and, second, their opinions about astrology. I asked a wide range of questions, but what I am concerned about here are astrology's millenarian character, and astrologers' New Age affiliation and religious identity.

My questions on religious affiliation asked for information on original and current religious affiliation, attendance at religious services, attitudes to the nature of divinity and scripture, and whether prayer works. I was interested in general religious attitudes as well as items of New Age and theosophical lore such as whether God is a 'supreme consciousness' or, rather, a Goddess; whether the soul is subject to the laws of karma and reincarnation; and whether New Age identity is compatible with articles of Christian dogma. This data is summarised in Tables 12.1–12.4

To deal with astrologers' religious affiliation first, Marcia Moore had included questions on religious identity in her 1960 survey of 198, mainly American, astrologers.[4] Moore found that 96 (41 per cent) of her sample were self-declared Christians but she also proposed one ill-defined category, 'Universal' (15 people, or 6 per cent) and 'Esoteric-Occult-Metaphysical' (43 individuals, or 17 per cent). I would regard both these as, in some sense, theosophical-spiritual, or what we

---

[3]   Nicholas Campion, 'What do Astrologers Believe about Astrology?', *Astrological Journal*, 54/2 (2012, forthcoming).

[4]   Marcia Moore, *Astrology Today: A Socio-Psychological Survey* (New York, 1960), p. 91.

Table 12.1   Astrologers' religious affiliation (1): author's data compared with Moore (1960) (M)

Religion	M 1960	N 1999	AA 1999		UAC 2002		AA 2011	
			Upb.	Cur.	Upb.	Cur.	Upb.	Cur.
a. Prot	74 30%	20 24%	75 47%	6 3.8%	67 44%	3 2%	32 42.1%	4 5.3%
b. RC	18 7%	See a	20 12.6%	8 5%	45 29.6%	9 5.9%	16 21%	4 5.3%
c. O	n/a	See a	0	0	0	0	0	0
d. NDC	11 4%	See a	23 14.5%	28 17.6%	12 7.9%	6 3.9%	9 10.5%	2 2.6%
e. Jew	3 1%	n/a	3 1.9%	3 1.9%	12 7.9%	7 4.6%	2 2.6%	0
f. M	n/a	n/a	0	0	1 0.6%	1 0.6%	0	0
g. B	7 3%	15 18%	0	5 3.1%	1 0.6%	5 3.2%	3 3.9%	6 7.9%
h. H	3 1%	9 11%	0	1 0.6%	0	2 1.3%	0	1 1.3%
i. P	n/a	18 22%	10 6%	12 7.5%	1 0.6%	11 7.2%	0	4 5.3%
j. Ag	n/a	3 3.6%	10 6.3%	12 7.5%	3 2%	11 7.2%	7 9.2%	4 5.3%
k. Ath	n/a	5 6%	3 1.9%	9 5.6%	3 2%	2 1.3%	1 1.3%	1 1.3%
l. Other	n/a	46 56%	3 1.9%	9 5.6%	7 4.6%	25 16.4%	6 7.9%	n/a
m. SNA	n/a	n/a	n/a	n/a	n/a	91 60%	n/a	45 60.5%

Note 1: Data from Marcia Moore (M) (1960) and from Campion at Norwac (N), UAC and the British AA Conferences 1999 and 2011.

Note 2: Figures for Upbringing (Upb.) and Current (Cur.) affiliation analysed as Protestant (Prot), Roman Catholic (RC), Orthodox (O), Non-denominational Christian (NDC), Jew, Muslim (M), Buddhist (B), Hindu (H), Pagan (P), Agnostic (Ag), Atheist (Ath), Other, Spiritual but non-aligned (SNA).

Note 3: The Protestant figure for the Norwac (N) conference in 1999 includes all Christians.

might generally term as New Age. In this case, the total New Age figure is 23 per cent, a substantial number, but around half the number of self-declared Christians. The results are given in Tables 12.1 and 12.2. Like Moore, my initial questionnaire at the NORWAC conference asked only about current religious affiliation, but the figures are not inconsistent with the more detailed versions at the AA and UAC where I asked for both original and current affiliation. For example, over 24 per

Table 12.2   Astrologers' religious affiliation (2): author's data from Serbia, Norway, Argentina and Brazil

Religion	Serbia 2001		Norway 2001		Argentina 2011		Brazil 2011	
	Upb.	Now	Upb.	Now	Upb.	Now	Upb.	Now
a. Prot	1 1%	0	21 70%	7 23.3%	1 1%	2 1.9%	4 4.8%	0
b. RC	16 16.7%	10 10.4%	2 6.7%	1 3.3%	69 65.7%	18 17.1%	54 65%	7 8.4%
c. NDC	21 21.9%	21 21.9%	5 16.7%	1 3.3%	12 11.4%	14 13.3%	9 10.8%	6 7.2%
d. O	31 32.3%	34 35.4%	0	0	0	0	0	0
e. Jew	3 3.1%	1 1%	0	0	6 5.7%	2 1.9%	4 4.8%	1 1.2%
f. M	0	0	0	0	0	0	0	0
g. B	1 1%	2 2.1%	0	4 13.3%	1 1%	2 1.9%	2 2.4%	1 1.2%
h. H	0	1 1%	0	1 3.3%	0	0	1 1.2%	2 2.4%
i. P	0	1 1%	0	2 6.7%	0	0	1 1.2%	1 1.2%
j. Ag	2 2.1%	0	6 20%	3 10%	0	1 1%	0	2 2.4%
k. Ath	7 7.3%	4 4.2%	2 6.7%	0	8 8.4%	1 1%	1 1.2%	1 1.2%
l. Other	19 19.8%	21 21.9%	5 16.7%	14 46.7%	n/a	n/a	n/a	n/a
m. SNA	n/a	n/a	n/a	n/a	15 14.3%	63 60%	8 9.6%	56 67.5%

cent of the NORWAC delegates gave their religious affiliation as Christian, close to the total of 26 per cent at the AA, but substantially more than the figure of almost 12 per cent at UAC. Both figures were less than Moore's result of forty years earlier, suggesting a drift away from formal Christian affiliation in the forty years which included the counter-cultural 1960s and the popular spread of New Age ideology in the 1970s. Two other interesting features arose from the NORWAC survey. One was the variety of terms which delegates relied on to describe their Christian upbringing from the expected (Congregational, Episcopalian, Catholic, Methodist, Lutheran, Presbyterian, Latter Day Saints) to the more idiosyncratic (Sunday School, Detached Christian, Tacky Christian, Christian-Varied, Greek

Orthodox and Atheist, Holy Roller, Standard and Christian-Wicca). Simply, the term 'Christian' as a catch-all phrase to describe religious affiliation is of limited value.

Given that the demographics at all three conferences, NORWAC, AA and UAC, were similar, the smaller figure for Christian affiliation at UAC is intriguing, especially as the NORWAC and AA figures are similar. It is possible that the lower figure at UAC might be due the inclusion of a category of 'spiritual but non-aligned' which might, I suggest, appeal to certain of those who have been exposed to Christian rhetoric via Alice Bailey and Rudolf Steiner, but might feel more comfortable with a general rather than a Christian label. I suggest that this category is not unlike Moore's 'Universal' and 'Esoteric-Occult-Metaphysical'. Dick Houtman and Stef Aupers considered the 'spiritual turn' in Western culture, which they related to better-educated people who are attracted to New Age culture and are more susceptible to detraditionalisation.[5] The figure for 'spiritual but non-aligned', 60 per cent, was far greater than any other, and may be taken as supporting evidence for the 'privatisation' hypothesis – the theory that modernity is accompanied not by a decline in religious affiliation but in much greater pluralism. The figure was repeated at the British Astrological Association conference in 2011. It also supports the common contention that, increasingly, to be spiritual is seen as far preferable to being religious.[6] Repeatedly, in my interviews I found that 'religion' is perceived as old-fashioned and requires individual subordination to values which are restrictive, dogmatic and oppressive, while 'spirituality' is experienced as individual, enlightening, liberating and life-affirming.

Given the difficulties of using 'Christian' as a single, meaningful category, the dramatic collapse of Christian affiliation was striking in the AA and UAC surveys, a pattern shared by the Norwegian sample. (The Balkan sample is an exception and we may read the stability in the figure for Christian affiliation as, in part, a nationalist and anti-communist statement, with identification with the Orthodox Church becoming, as in Russia, a means of asserting a new identity and rejection of the immediate past.) At the AA in 1999, 74.1 per cent declared an original family Christian affiliation, a figure which drops to 26.4 per cent as adults. When non-denominational Christianity (the rise in which merits further investigation) is excluded, the figure drops from 59.6 per cent to 8.8 per cent. The UAC figure is still more dramatic: a steep decline in stated Christian affiliation from 81.5 per cent as children to 11.8 per cent as adults. The shift, though, is not to atheism, which remains so weak as to be almost insignificant: just 5.6 per cent at the AA in 1999 and 1.37 per cent (just two individuals) at UAC declared themselves to be atheists. Even when agnosticism and atheism are added together

---

[5]   Dick Houtman, Dick and Stef Aupers, 'The Spiritual Turn and the Decline of Tradition: The Spread of Post-Christian Spirituality in 14 Western Countries, 1981–2000', *Journal for the Scientific Study of Religion*, 46/3 (September 2007), pp. 305–20.

[6]   Wade Clark Roof, *A Generation of Seekers: The Spiritual Journeys of the Baby Boom Generation* (San Francisco, 1993), pp. 123–2, 194–200.

it is found that 86.9 per cent at AA in 1999 and 85 per cent at UAC still declared a religious or spiritual affiliation. In all my samples the number of atheists is very low, both by upbringing and current affiliation, in the latter case smaller than in the population as a whole, figures which were reinforced by the evidence from the 2011 AA Conference. There are, then, very strong similarities between the UK and US figures and consistency over the 12 years from 1999 to 2011. Each survey, for example, shows a small but similar rise in the number of pagans and Buddhists. The virtual absence of Hindus and Muslims is unsurprising in a mainly white, Western sample. That these trends are shared in the Norwegian sample suggests that we might find similar results in the Western world as a whole. Indeed, the same trends were evident in the data I obtained from my repeat visit to the British AA conference in 2011, as well as the Argentinian and Brazilian data I gathered in the same year, suggesting that the collapse of traditional Christian affiliation within the astrological milieu is as evident within South America as in North America and Europe. I need to make one other comment on the validity of small samples: the shift towards Buddhism concerns only a handful of individuals, but the pattern is found in the US, UK and Norway, suggesting that tiny results can be confirmed by multiple data sets.

We should compare these figures to wider statistics for religious membership in the US and UK. The percentages of religious affiliation in the US in 2002 were 79 per cent Christian (of whom 2 per cent were Catholic), 12 per cent 'none', 7 per cent 'other' and 1.3 per cent Jewish.[7] (The figure for 'none' was around 2 per cent in 1948–57, climbed to 9 per cent from 1966–87, and has been relatively stable since then. The figure for Christian affiliation stood at 91 per cent in 1948, when Gallup started collecting data).[8] From this perspective, American astrologers appear to be substantially less Christian than expected. However, they are not necessarily less religious than the population as a whole, given the general gap between declared religious affiliation and religious behaviour, as the UK example demonstrates. In 2001 the UK Office for National Statistics gave the percentage of Christians in the UK as 71.69 per cent, while the 2000 figure cited in *Religious Trends*, the *UK Christian Handbook*, was 63 per cent.[9] However, *Religious Trends* reported that only 7.4 per cent attended a Sunday church service, leaving 55.6 per cent of the adult population who were at the same time self-declared Christians but non-church attendees. Again, we meet the same gap between belief and practice in general religious activity as that between the lowest and highest figures for

[7]   Figures for 2001 from Religious Tolerance, at <http://www.religioustolerance.org/chr_prac2.htm>, accessed 5 November 2009.

[8]   Frank Newport, 'This Easter, smaller percentage of Americans are Christian: Americans more likely now than in previous decades to say they have no religious identity', 10 April 2009, at <http://www.gallup.com/poll/117409/Easter-Smaller-Percentage-Americans-Christian.aspx>, accessed 5 November 2009.

[9]   Peter Brierly (ed.), *UK Christian Handbook: Religious Trends no 3, 2002/3* (London, 2001), pp. 2.3, 2.23.

belief in astrology. At 7.4 per cent, the UK figure for church attendance amongst Christians is actually similar to the percentage of UK astrologers (my sample of Astrological Association conference delegates), 9.4 per cent in 1999, and 10.5 per cent in 2011, who attend a religious service regularly. So, what may be happening with the astrologers? First, they may be less inclined to declare Christian affiliation if their religiosity can be satisfied by other options which may be unfamiliar to many people and, secondly, they may be as diligent in their church attendance as the rest of the population. The other problem, of course, is that it is possible to have multiple affiliations, such as agnostic/spiritual, for example, which are obscured when individuals choose just one designation.[10]

At the ISAR conference in 2003 I asked further questions, replicating those tests for fundamentalist Christianity which I posed in my public surveys. The answers were instructive. Asked whether Jesus is the divine son of God, 18 (40 per cent) agreed, 11 (24.4 per cent) disagreed and 15 (33.3 per cent) had no opinion. But, when faced with the statement, 'The Bible is literally true', the overwhelming majority, 41 (91.1 per cent) disagreed, only 3 (6.7 per cent) agreed and one had no opinion. This is about as exact a picture of levels of theosophical Christianity, as propagated by Rudolf Steiner and Alice Bailey, with their belief in the cosmic Christ, as we could wish for: around 40 per cent of the ISAR sample thought that Jesus was the divine son of God, but considered that the Bible is not literally true. That is, a willingness amongst a substantial minority to accept Jesus' divinity is not matched by an acceptance of the truth of scripture as a whole. We could see this as a Gnostic position in which direct contact with the divine is elevated over reliance on the written word as a source of truth. Further, 35 (77.7 per cent) agreed that 'there are spiritual beings in the universe who can guide us' (only 4 people disagreed) suggesting the prevalence of the kind of angelology promoted by Blavatsky and Steiner and the theosophical astrologers Alan Leo and Dane Rudhyar. The numbers who believe in a personal God who answers prayer was also instructive, ranging from a low of 22 per cent at the AA to around half at ISAR and the Norwegian conference. This point needs emphasising: between a quarter and a half of astrologers believe in a personal God who answers prayer. This number may be significantly less than it might have been a century ago – we lack the data – but is substantial enough to suggest that astrology is not a threat to religion, seen conventionally as belief in a personal God. Again we see a picture of diversity with different items of religious dogma being combined. At the ISAR conference, then, a quarter of the delegates declared themselves as Christians, but a half agreed that there is a personal God who answers prayer. At the UAC conference the position was reversed, with 10 per cent less agreeing that God answers prayer than believe in God.

---

[10]   Luke W. Galen, 'Profiles of the Goddess: Results from a Survey of the Nonreligious', *Free Inquiry*, 29/5 (2009), pp. 41–5, at <http://www.secularhumanism.org>, accessed 11 September 2011.

Easier to identify, perhaps, is astrology's possible New Age identity. The question is to what extent astrologers accept certain key tenets of New Age ideology, along with the esoteric astrology developed by the devout New Age astrologers Alan Leo and Dane Rudhyar. This suggests a belief in the inner divine derived from Gnosticism, personal transformation, the individual as the source of ultimate truth, cultural relativism, the coming of the New Age, an increase in spirituality and Christ Consciousness, syncretism, karma and reincarnation, along with Popperian activism. My first set of questions (Tables 12.3 and 12.4) combined questions concerning religious affiliation and activity with karma and reincarnation. My intention was to establish different attitudes to divinity, the extent of theosophical Christianity and attitudes to karma and reincarnation, without which Alan Leo regarded astrology as effectively pointless.

The numbers who attend a church or religious service regularly is small but, in the case of the UAC figure, larger than the total who declares Christian affiliation. This suggests that in the US it may be more common for those who have a broader spiritual affiliation to attend a service of any religious character than in the UK. The number declaring belief in the Goddess is also higher in the US than the UK and, at 36 per cent, indicates a substantial penetration of feminist theology into astrological circles. An element of continuity was demonstrated by the almost exact same percentage of those believing in the Goddess at the 2011 British Astrological Association conference as in 1999: there was no change over 12 years. More striking though, is the deeply negative response to belief in the Goddess in the Argentinian and Brazilian data, even though the high level of belief in a Supreme Consciousness and in reincarnation and karma was similar to that in the other astrological groups. Clearly, local conditions can counter general international trends.

The high figures declaring belief in a supreme consciousness indicate the popularity of the Neoplatonic creator, an indicator of New Age culture discussed in Chapter 4, although New Culture has deep historic roots. The very high figures claiming belief in reincarnation and, to a lesser extent, karma, attests to the success of Alan Leo's argument that astrology is meaningless without reincarnation, discussed in Chapter 6, and hence to the penetration of his New Age astrology *sensu stricto* into the wider astrological world. Actually, if we combine the positive answers for belief in reincarnation and karma, the figures are higher than at first sight: at NORWAC, for example, only 9 individuals (10.9 per cent) denied belief in either reincarnation or karma. In Norway only one person denied belief in reincarnation. The figure of at least 90 per cent who can therefore be said to be profoundly influenced by Alan Leo, and so by theosophy, is supported by the AA and UAC samples. If Alan Leo is, then, the key New Age astrologer, and his reform of astrology was explicitly intended to promote the coming of the New Age, then this is powerful testimony that most astrologers operate within the context of New Age spirituality. Other figures are more variable and, again, we see the Balkan sample being more conservative; even on belief in a God who answers prayer their agreement (18.7 per cent) was low in view of their declared Christian affiliation.

Table 12.3   Astrologers' religious behaviour and attitudes (1): author's data
            compared with Moore (1960) (M)

	M 1960	N 1999	AA 1999	UAC 2002	ISAR 2003	AA 2011
Attends service regularly	n/a	n/a	15 9.4%	26 17.1%	n/a	8 10.5%
Believes in God	n/a	40 48.8%	42 26.4%	74 48.6%	n/a	16 21%
Believes in Goddess	n/a	29 35.4%	19 11.9%	36 23.6%	n/a	8 10.5%
Believes in Supreme Consciousness	n/a	46 56.1%	83 52.2%	74 48.6%	n/a	52 68.4%
Personal God who answers prayer	n/a	36 43.9%	35 22%	58 38.2%	23 51.1%	17 22.4%
Astrology influenced by religion	27 10%	20 24.3%	52 32.7%	58 38.2%	n/a	17 22.4%
Believes in reincarnation	186 74%*	62 75.6%	164 78%	125 82.2%	n/a	53 69.7%
Believes in law of karma	n/a	64 78%	101 63.5%	119 78.2%	n/a	44 57.9%

Note: *Moore, *Astrology Today*, p. 123.

Table 12.4   Astrologers' religious behaviour and attitudes (2): author's data
            from Serbia, Norway, Argentina and Brazil

	Serbia 2001	Norway 2001	Argentina 2011	Brazil 2011
Attends service regularly	8 8.3%	6 20%	18 17.1%	30 36.1%
Believes in God	35 36.5%	17 56.7%	49 46.7%	39 47%
Believes in Goddess	4 4.2%	6 20%	2 1.9%	3 3.6%
Believes in Supreme Consciousness	53 55.2%	19 63.3%	58 55.2%	46 55.4%
Personal God who answers prayer	18 18.7%	15 50%	37 35.2%	45 54.2%
Astrology influenced by religion	11 11.5%	12 40%	6 5.7%	22 26.5%
Believes in reincarnation	43 44.8%	29 96.7%	66 62.8%	63 75.9%
Believes in law of karma	61 63.5%	19 63.3%	73 68.5%	40 48.2%

That around a third of the both the 1999 AA and UAC samples stated that their practice of astrology is influenced by their religion indicates that a high proportion of those who selected non-Christian options regard themselves as religious. However, the high number, particularly at UAC, declaring belief in God (48.6 per cent) and a personal God who answers prayer (38.1 per cent) far exceeds those declaring conventional Christian affiliation. It may be that a residual Christian belief remains strong, perhaps supported by Bailey and Steiner's emphasis on Christ-consciousness. But we also appear to be facing a customary religion, similar to Hornsby-Smith's customary Catholicism, in which a completely different picture is obtained, depending on which items of practice or affiliation are asked about.[11] As suggested in Chapter 4, then, New Age culture may be hostile not to Christianity, only to the institutional church; the two are regarded as entirely distinct. The other interesting feature of this question is that all three US samples, NORWAC and UAC, produced a higher figure for belief in God, including a personal God who answers prayer, than did the UK survey, suggesting that the language of traditional religion (which most evidence suggests remains stronger there) is evident amongst astrologers, a group regarded with suspicion by main Christians.

We should draw attention to one other feature of these surveys, which has wider implications for questionnaire-based research as a whole. When people are offered the chance to choose multiple answers, they often do so; 26 (31.7 per cent) of the respondents at NORWAC stated that they believed in both God and the Goddess, while 6 (7.3 per cent) chose all four options – 'God', 'Goddess', 'Supreme Consciousness' and 'Other', suggesting a notion of deity which defies attempts at categorisation. Again, this is evidence of a theosophical or, if we prefer, New Age Christianity. It also suggests that research based on the need to choose single categories is bound to be inaccurate.

Analysis of the annotations made on questionnaires, or choice of multiple answers, also indicates an element of diversity. At the AA conference in 2011 four respondents declined to choose a religious upbringing, of whom one specified 'None at home and basic Christian at school' – a clear case of a multiple affiliation. Four chose two categories: one was Protestant plus Agnostic, one Protestant plus Roman Catholic, one Roman Catholic and Jew, and one Buddhist plus Other. Such choices may represent the absence of personal religiosity and, instead, self-definition according to a division of religious affiliation amongst the parents. Suppose, then, that the mass of those who declare an early religious affiliation do so for social and family reasons rather than through personal devotion: in this case the huge move to 'spiritual but non-aligned' might actually point to a rise in religiosity. When it came to choice of a current affiliation, four declined to choose any option, of whom one wrote in 'Pantheist', clearly feeling that no other choice matched this description.

---

[11]   Michael Hornsby-Smith, *Roman Catholic Beliefs in England: Customary Catholicism and Transformations in Religious Authority* (Cambridge, 1991).

Other, indirect questions were posed in order to establish how many astrologers would select 'New Age' definitions of astrology – bearing in mind that certain features of New Age astrology may have deep philosophical roots in European esotericism (Tables 12.5 and 12.6). These are largely based on Dane Rudhyar's exposition of the correct practice of astrology required to assist personal transformation and the entry to the New Age.[12] My question was 'How would you define astrology?', and I allowed respondents both to offer their own definitions and to choose as many definitions from a prescribed list as they liked, or none. The self-created definitions were instructive and overwhelmingly emphasised the spiritual and psychological. Where there was an appeal to science, it was of the theosophical variety, with reference to energies and vibrations. The following list is a fair sample:

> A helpful guide to the centre of one's life.
> A system of meaning derived from planetary positions in space and time.
> As above, so below.
> A blueprint of psycho/emotional etc. make-up.
> The science of the relation between the bodies of our planetary system and life on earth and the art of interpreting the results of the same.
> A tool for those who want to attune themselves to the continuing creation of the universe and particularly those who want to take as constructive a part in it as possible.
> A hermetic system containing all the different psychological combinations.
> Use of natural energy forces, possibly magnetic, given out by the planets.
> A sort of 'glasses' through which you can see the true reality of the world.
> A means by which we can observe spiritual law.
> The study and practice of the dynamic, intelligent interconnectedness of all things, through the macrocosmic language of frequency – or! – god's film-script!
> A form of communication with unseen minds.

The prescribed definitions are summarised in Tables 12.5 and 12.6 and draw on standard astrological works, with a special attention to the New Age literature. Dane Rudhyar, for example, rejected prediction using astrology, and scientific approaches to astrology, but would have understood the concept of 'divine science' familiar to Blavatsky and Alice Bailey. His astrology was a psychological tool, a path to spiritual growth and a means of healing the soul which could be achieved through counselling. In Tables 12.5 and 12.6 I have indicated those questions which reflect Rudhyar's influence with an asterisk. The question concerning divination is difficult to place: divination tended to be anathema to astrologers who regard astrology as a demonstrable science, but could have an identifiable place in the astrological tradition represented by magical practitioners. Similarly, while astrology is often

---

[12]   Dane Rudhyar, *Person Centered Astrology* (New York, 1980), p. 126.

Table 12.5   Astrologers' definitions of astrology (1)

Definition	N 1999	AA 1999	UAC 2001	AA 2011
A science	36 43.9%	39 24.5%	55 36.1%	35 46%
A divine science*	44 53.6%	67 42%	79 52%	33 43.4%
A psychological tool*	64 78%	103 64.8%	92 60.5%	67 88.2%
A form of divination	32 39%	53 33.3%	61 40.1%	55 72.4%
A religion	10 12.2%	11 6.9%	12 7.9%	6 7.9%
A path to spiritual growth*	64 78%	105 66%	85 55.9%	61 80.3%
A form of counselling*	68 82.9%	92 57.8%	99 65.1%	64 84.2%
A healing art*	58 70.9%	85 53.4%	88 57.9%	59 77.6%
A means of predicting the future	36 43.9%	67 42%	66 43.4%	48 63.2%

Note: Asterisks indicate questions which reflect Rudhyar's influence.

Table 12.6   Astrologers' definitions of astrology (2)

Definition	Serbia 2001	Norway 2001	Argentina 2011	Brazil 2011
A science	84 87.5%	17 56.7%	83 79%	46 55.4%
A divine science*	62 64.6%	21 70%	44 41.9%	42 50.6%
A psychological tool*	77 80.2%	25 83.3%	91 86.7%	70 84.3%
A form of divination	70 72.9%	20 66.7%	16 15.2%	20 24.1%
A religion	14 14.6%	3 10%	2 1.9%	1 1.2%
A path to spiritual growth*	91 94.8%	25 83.3%	93 88.6%	73 87.9%
A form of counselling*	89 92.7%	23 76.6%	93 88.6%	71 85.5%
A healing art*	56 58.3%	23 76.6%	82 78.1%	54 65.1%
A means of predicting the future	85 88.5%	17 56.6%	68 65%	53 63.8%

identified as a healing art in a New Age context, there is no reason why any 'Old Age' astrologer should object to its medical uses. On the other hand, to describe astrology as a divine science is distinctly theosophical, and to label it a psychological tool, a path to spiritual growth and a form of counselling is Rudhyarian and therefore shows the influence of his New Age ideology. As a matter of comparison, delegates at the NORWAC, AA and UAC conferences were asked a factual question – 'How is astrology defined?' – whereas at the Balkan and Norwegian conferences they were asked to rate agreement with particular statements. At the NORWAC conference, for example, delegates were essentially asked 'Is astrology divination' whereas at the Balkan conference they were asked to express an opinion on whether it is divination. I return to the implications of this below.

Respondents were invited to tick multiple options. The results indicate a clear resistance to the definition of astrology as science (although slightly higher than recent results from a survey of the public[13]), although not as a 'divine science', in theosophical terminology, and a profound hostility to the categorisation of astrology as religion across all my samples. In 1960 Moore had found that 70 per cent of her sample agreed that astrology 'is or can be' a science.[14] If the figures are reliable, astrologers may have shared the widespread public disillusion with science which is said to have been prompted by such incidents as the Three Mile Island nuclear accident and the controversy over GM crops. Of the 11 who chose religion at the AA, five selected every option, reducing the number for whom religion might be considered a meaningful category. Astrology, for these people, transcends any specific label and includes everything.

It is noticeable that all the definitions indicating Leo and Rudhyar's New Age legacy receive high scores, with 'path to spirituality' receiving the highest score, 66 per cent, at the AA, and receiving 55.9 per cent at UAC. Rudhyar's legacy is also evident in the 65.1 per cent who chose 'a form of counselling' as a definition of astrology at UAC, while the broader field of psychological astrology fares well at both AA (64.8 per cent in 1999, rising to 88.2 per cent in 2011) and UAC (60.5 per cent). The pervasive influence of Leo and Rudhyar's astrology in this sample, though, is indicated by a small number, under five in each case, who failed to choose any New Age options. Under half of all three samples agree that astrology is a means of predicting the future, echoing Leo and Rudhyar's emphasis on the present, and on alterations in one's behaviour as a means of changing the future, thereby rendering prediction useless. The message of these figures was confirmed by other responses at NORWAC where, when asked about the purpose of an astrological reading, 14 (17 per cent) said that it is to make accurate predictions but 74 (90 per cent) to 'enable the client to understand themselves/ make their own choices'. Only 32 (39 per cent) agreed that it is even possible

---

[13]   In a recent sample 33.3 per cent of those interviewed defined astrology as 'very' or 'sort of' scientific: see Alan Orenstein, 'On Evolution, Abortion and Astrology', *Skeptical Inquirer*, 33/4 (2009), p. 50, and <www.sda.berkeley.edu> for the raw data.

[14]   Moore, *Astrology Today*, p. 86.

to make accurate predictions about an individual's future as against the 40 (48 per cent) who disagreed. On this all three surveys agree: astrology is concerned with self-responsibility, personal understanding and development, rather than predicting a fixed, or even indeterminate, future. This is not to say that astrology is unambiguously New Age. Rather, there is a dominant New Age discourse. And this, we must remember, is heavily Gnostic and Neoplatonic (even if filtered through Blavatsky) in its emphasis on the inner divine and the sense that the inner person, rather than the precision of technical astrology, should be the primary focus of the astrological mentality.

At the ISAR conference I asked further questions designed to test for relativity, on the grounds that this is a New Age attribute. A total of 31 (68.9 per cent) agreed that there are no inherently good or bad 'aspects' in a horoscope, meaning that, as good or bad fortune is not established at birth, individuals are responsible for their own destinies.[15] As a point of interest, and to stress the point that New Age ideology need not be new, this argument is derived from the fourth-century Neoplatonic philosopher Plotinus.[16] The same number approved of the statement 'All forms of astrology are a path to the truth', although 11 (24 per cent) disagreed. In spite of the substantial minority against the proposition, this suggests majority approval for Rudhyar's position that the rules and regulations of astrological interpretation have no objective validity and instead achieve meaning only in the hands of an astrologer who can then reveal one's real, spiritual destiny.

I then asked a series of other questions designed to elicit New Age attitudes, asking similar questions in different ways which recognised, again, that the answer to any question is shaped by the phrasing of the question.[17] Whereas, in the questions summarised in Tables 12.5 and 12.6, I had asked for a statement of fact – how astrology is defined – in those summarised in Tables 12.7 and 12.8 I asked for opinions – agreement or disagreement with particular statements. Questions iii, v and vii are designed to elicit 'Old Age' opinions, the others (marked with an asterisk) to indicate New Age attitudes (given, as I have stressed, that such opinions may be deeply rooted in classical philosophy). I interpreted 'New Age' in this sense as locating the individual in the centre of the astrological process, rather than a series of external pressures or determining factors. Questions i and ii emphasised the astrologers' selection of the method of astrological interpretation at the expense of any idea that particular rules have to be followed in order to reach a cosmically defined conclusion. Dane Rudhyar also emphasised astrology's function as a language – rather than a rule-based system – (question iv), the use

---

[15]   An aspect is the angular distance between any two points, usually planets, measured in degrees. Different types of aspect are traditionally seen as representing either difficulties or advantages.

[16]   Plotinus, 'On Heaven', 'On Whether the Stars are Causes', *Ennead*, II, 2, vol. 2, trans. A.H. Armstrong (Cambridge MA and London, 1966), 1.5–10, 2.15–20.

[17]   Russell T. McCutcheon, *The Insider/Outsider Problem in the Study of Religion: A Reader* (London, 1999), p. 10.

Table 12.7   Attitudes to astrology (1)

	N 1999	AA 1999	UAC 2001	ISAR 2003	AA 2011
i. *Each astrologer finds the techniques which suits them	70 85.4%	153 96.2%	148 97.3%	42 93%	66 86.8%
ii. *The right house system is 'the one which works for you'	62 75.6%	113 71%	106 69.7%	n/a	n/a
iii. The planets exert a physical influence on events on earth	40 48.8%	81 50.9%	92 60.5%	n/a	35 46%
iv. *Astrology is a language	74 90%	139 87.4%	141 92.7%	42 93%	61 80.3%
v. Astrology can make accurate predictions	48 58%	94 54.1%	110 72.3%	n/a	n/a
vi. *Signs of the zodiac are archetypes	70 85%	120 75.5%	129 84.9%	n/a	60 80%
vii. Astrology should take other factors, e.g. environment and heredity, into account	50 61%	120 75%	109 71.7%	n/a	n/a
viii. *The birth chart contains our potential, and it's up to us how we use it	68 83%	139 87.4%	133 87.5%	44 97.7%	n/a
ix. *Intuition is necessary for a good astrological reading	n/a	129 81.1%	98 64.5%	n/a	60 80%
x. *Astrology enables people to control their lives	n/a	n/a	n/a	n/a	44 57.9%
xi. The future is fated	n/a	n/a	n/a	n/a	27 35.5%

Note: A house is a division of the diurnal circle. Every horoscope contains 12 houses.

of the Platonic-Jungian concept of archetypes (question vi), the birth chart as a map of developmental potential (question x) and the use of intuition – again at the expense of fixed astrological rules (question xi). Questions viii (on divination) and vii (on the use of non-astrological factors to reach an astrological judgement) are ambiguous, being rooted in non-New Age tradition, without being incompatible with New Age ideas. Question iii on whether the planets exert a physical influence is located in naturalistic Aristotelian cosmology, and indicates respect for a materialistic cosmology without being necessarily incompatible with New Age spirituality.

Each question was conceived as a test for theosophical influence, primarily from Dane Rudhyar, but also Alan Leo and C.G. Jung: questions i and ii were designed to test the relativistic consequences of Rudhyar's astrology; question iv tested for Leo's argument that astrology is a language; question vi tests for C.G Jung's influence

Table 12.8   Attitudes to astrology (2)

	Serbia 2001	Norway 2001	Argentina 2011	Brazil 2011
i. *Each astrologer finds the techniques which suits them	75 78.1%	23 76.7%	59 56.2%	39 46.7%
iii. The planets exert a physical influence on events on earth	79 82.3%	18 60%	80 76.1%	45 54.2%
iv. *Astrology is a language	82 85.4%	17 56.7%	93 88.6%	77 92.8%
vi. *Signs of the zodiac are archetypes	76 79.2%	25 83.3%	89 84.8%	74 89.1%
ix. *Intuition is necessary for a good astrological reading	85 88.5%	23 76.7%	85 80.1%	62 74.6%
x. *Astrology enables people to control their lives	71 72.4%	16 53.3%	47 44.7%	38 45.78%
xi. The future is fated	54 55.1%	10 33.3%	45 42.8%	10 12%

(which was popularised by Rudhyar); question vii reflects Rudhyar's statement that astrology is divination (but received a relatively low score); question x expresses the Rudhyarian view which has become the basic proposition of psychological astrology; and question xi expresses a widely held argument in New Age circles that, as discussed in Chapter 4, one should listen to the inner divine. The high figures for approval of all these questions suggests a substantial uptake of Dane Rudhyar's ideas. The logic of Rudhyar's ideology, in which astrology had to be reformed in order to save souls of the New Age, suggests again that the large majority of astrologers operate in a New Age context. They may not be dedicated New Agers but the astrology they use, and their attitude towards it, is.

Question v tests for attitudes to prediction, which Leo and Rudhyar argued was irrelevant in natal astrology. As in Table 12.3, it receives a relatively low score compared to some other questions. It is still high enough, though, to indicate that prediction remains one of astrology's core purposes and that the need to predict the future overwhelms both Leo and Rudhyar's insistence that it is not an appropriate use of astrology (at least, not for individuals – both predicted the coming of the Aquarian Age). It may be that the question is itself inadequate and needs to be refined to account for specific contexts. The score for question iii on planetary influence was much higher than expected as my personal experience indicates that most astrologers reject this concept, and it is rare to find it discussed in modern astrology books. It indicates a perhaps surprising persistence of a natural, mechanical rationale for astrology.

However, there was huge support, varying from 65 per cent to 97 per cent, for the propositions that astrologers use the techniques which work for them,

Table 12.9   The New Age and the Age of Aquarius

New Age is beginning	N 1999	AA 1999	UAC 2001	ISAR 2003	AA 2011
Yes	52 63.4%	97 63%	73 52%	30 67%	14 18%
No	4 4.9%	36 23%	34 24%	4 9%	32 42%
Don't know	16 9.5%	21 14%	33 24%	10 22%	30 40%
Age of Aquarius is beginning					
Agree	46 55.3%	88 76%	78 56%	n/a	n/a
Disagree	n/a	15 13%	16 12%	n/a	n/a
No opinion	n/a	12 11%	45 32%	n/a	n/a

Note: Figures are rounded off to the nearest percent.

Table 12.10   Belief in the beginning of the New Age

New Age is beginning	Serbia 2001	Norway 2001	Argentina 2011	Brazil 2011
Yes	53 55%	7 23.%	77 73%	33 40%
No	7 7%	2 7%	5 5%	15 18%
Don't know	31 32%	16 53%	21 20%	31 37%

Note: Figures are rounded off to the nearest percent.

that astrology is a language, that zodiac signs are archetypes, that the birth chart contains the individual's potential and that intuition is necessary for a good astrological reading. These statements stand at the heart of the Rudhyarian project – to prepare humanity for the dawn of the New Age.

At the same time, we need to draw attention to certain variations arising from the phrasing of questions. When, for example, UAC delegates were asked whether astrology *is* a means of predicting the future, 43.4 per cent agreed, but when they were asked whether it *can* make accurate opinions, 72.3 per cent answered in the affirmative. In other words, when the question was phrased in a hypothetical manner far more astrologers agreed. This is an important methodological issue, and an illustration of the difficulties of accurately quantifying attitudes to astrology. Possibly far more astonishing, though, is the conclusion that not only did over half of the delegates at the world's biggest gathering of astrologers reject the definition of astrology as a predicting device, 27.7 per cent, almost a third, rejected any possibility that astrology can make accurate predictions. Of course, accuracy in this sense was not defined. That would require further work. We do not know whether these astrologers believe that loose and negotiable predictions can be made, or whether they think prediction is either completely useless or impossible. Whatever the case, public perceptions of astrology as invariably a tool for prediction are completely demolished. I would conclude, then, that almost a third of the delegates at the UAC gathering might be classed, in their attitudes to prediction, as deeply Rudhyarian. Does this mean they are New Age? In a simple sense, yes. True, they are also Neoplatonists, but their Neoplatonism is largely filtered from Blavatsky via Rudhyar and other theosophical astrologers.

As we have seen, the term 'New Age' is both a description of a contemporary cultural phenomenon and of a future historical period, which may or may not be identical with the astrological Age of Aquarius. The Aquarian Age can be either just the next historical phase, or a new Age of spiritual enlightenment. I also asked a series of direct questions in order to establish levels of agreement with the notion that the New Age and Age of Aquarius are currently beginning, or are about to begin (see Tables 12.9 and 12.10). The imminence of the arrival of the next age, as was noted in Chapter 2, is a key feature of millenarian belief. Separate questions were asked about the New Age and the Age of Aquarius in order to allow for those astrologers who might believe that the Age of Aquarius is beginning, but that this does not necessarily indicate the coming of the New Age as a time of spiritual evolution; that is, that the New Age and the Age of Aquarius are not identical. As a comparison, Stuart Rose found that 69 per cent of his respondents believed that 'we are entering a new era'.[18]

The percentage stating that the New Age is beginning were significantly higher at the AA Conference than at UAC, but those stating that the Age of Aquarius is beginning were roughly comparable. Nevertheless, these figures indicate that around half, or over half, of all astrologers operate within a millenarian context. However, only 22 per cent at both AA and UAC claimed that the New Age is *not* beginning and only around 10 per cent stated that the Age of Aquarius is not beginning. Such low figures may reflect a reluctance to agree to statements of fact, rather than report personal opinions. Apart from indicating that a minority accept the Age of Aquarius while resisting the New Age, this suggests that a low positive figure might result from the phrasing of the question, which appears to call for a statement of objective fact, as I discussed in Chapter 11. Interestingly, a sizeable percentage in Belgrade agreed that the New Age is coming but a much lower figure in Oslo although in each case the levels of uncertainty and disagreement were sufficiently high to indicate a resistance to the term 'New Age'.

---

[18]   Stuart Rose, 'Transforming the World: An Examination of the Roles Played by Spirituality and Healing in the New Age Movement', PhD thesis, Department of Religious Studies, Lancaster University, 1996, p. 365.

Having established levels of millenarian affiliation amongst astrologers, at the ISAR conference we can obtain a more nuanced picture. The statement, 'The Age of Aquarius will see a significant leap in spiritual evolution', designed to test for devotion to the theosophical millennium prophesied by Leo, Rudhyar, Steiner and Bailey, elicited approval from just half of the small number who answered, 17 (46.7 per cent). On the other hand, only 7 (15.5 per cent) expressed disagreement, the remainder being undecided. Additionally a relatively low number, 12 (26.6 per cent) thought that 'In the New Age we will all recognise the divine within us'. Again, the phrasing of the question calls for an objective perspective (will others apart from the respondent recognise the inner divine?) and resulted in a lower result than the previous comparable question. 42 delegates (93.3 per cent) agreed with the statement 'We all contain the divine within us', so this item of adherence to New Age Gnosticism is not at issue; it is almost universally accepted.

Much clearer was the level of approval to the question 'Astrology is a vital tool in the preparation for the New Age'; 35 people (77.8 per cent) agreed with this, echoing Leo and Rudhyar and their activist tendencies. Most striking of all, though, was the response to the statement, 'The transition to the New Age will be smooth and peaceful'. Thirty delegates (66.7 per cent) disagreed with this statement, and only 5 (11.1 per cent) disagreed, suggesting a strong pre-millennial tendency: the transition to the New Age will be violent. The most notable finding, though, of my return to the British AA conference in 2011 was of a collapse in anticipation of an imminent beginning of the New Age from 63 per cent to 14 per cent. Even given the uncertainty in all quantified data, to which I have already drawn attention, this is striking, and points to a sharp move away from belief in cosmic salvation during the 1990s, even while New Age culture as a whole remains strong. The New Age *sensu stricto* appears to have fallen out of favour amongst this distinct group, even while the New Age *sensu lato* retains its appeal.

More dramatic though, is the profound influence of Leo and Rudhyar's New Age philosophy in astrology as a whole. An overwhelming relativism in relation to astrological technique suggests that, as Rudhyar argued, astrology is just a technique for gaining understanding into the 'real', spiritual world. Even while they weave grand narratives, many astrologers are, true to their New Age context, epistemological individualists.[19] The emphasis on 'spiritual path' as a definition of astrology points directly to Leo's legacy, while its definition as a form of counselling and a psychological tool points to the success of Rudhyar's ideas and is suggestive of Heelas's idea that the 'self-ethic' lies at the heart of New Age philosophy. These findings do not, however, support the proposition that all contemporary astrology is New Age any more than 'New Age' can itself be defined a single phenomenon. There is also evidence for a strong millenarian, historicist framework for contemporary astrology which, along with the activism noted in the

---

[19]   Paul Heelas, *The New Age Movement* (Oxford, 1996), p. 21; Christopher H. Partridge, 'Truth, Authority and Epistemological Individualism in New Age Thought', *Journal of Contemporary Religion*, 14/1 (1999), pp. 289–313.

popularity of self-empowerment, justifies the use of Popper's historicism/activism model as a rationale for astrology. On a more general level, the privatisation theory of spiritual pluralism has been supported. The proposition that yes/no questions on belief do not yield useful information was supported and the notion that either the New Age or astrology are necessarily anti-Christian, as opposed to anti-church, cannot be sustained. This was as Marcia Moore found in 1960 – 80 per cent of her sample regarded astrology as compatible with 'doctrines of established religions'.[20]

We begin to see that, as with attitudes to astrology (or religion) in general, there are different ways to measure New Age discourse in astrology. Do we take the 54 per cent at UAC who felt more spiritual after using astrology, the 52 per cent who think the New Age is coming, or the 82 per cent who believe in reincarnation? The position, as we can see, is complex, and subject to multiple, overlapping narratives. We can identify major trends. There is clear evidence of the privatisation hypothesis in which secularisation becomes not the decline of religiosity but the move from Christian dominance to pluralism. There is profound evidence of insistent New Age affiliation amongst astrologers in the sense that the individual, as a source of authority, displaces the rules and regulations of an externally based astrology from the astrological process. Heelas's self-spirituality is much in evidence in the numbers who regard themselves as 'spiritual but non-aligned' and the extent of 'detraditionalisation' in astrology is evident in the extent of rejection of the notion of fixed astrological rules. The prediction that the Aquarian Age is coming is evidence of the general popularity of an 'invented tradition', even if one deeply rooted in the millennia-old lineage of astrological millenarianism. We can identify, perhaps, Hanegraaff's two New Age cultures, *stricto* and *lato*, in differing levels of interest in the New Age: the millennial belief in the imminent arrival of the New Age achieves majority support but is not universally held and a persistent number disagree even that the Age of Aquarius is coming. The majority, though (55 per cent to 67 per cent), with the unexplained exception of the Norwegian contingent, agree that the New Age is imminent. Is astrology, then, New Age? The answer is: 'it can be'. Yet, even then, firstly the 'New Age' label should not be used unless its Gnostic and Neoplatonic roots are understood. Further, the narratives amongst astrologers about what astrology is and how it should be used are diverse, which puts astrology into the same class as most other ways of analysing the world, especially in the humanities and social sciences – from history and economics to anthropology and sociology. That said, the most striking result from the entire survey is the high level of choice of 'spiritual but non-aligned' as current religious affiliation, and the consequent support for the privatisation hypothesis: astrologers in general define themselves as spiritual, but reject what they see as the out-of-touch dogma of established Christian religion, without necessarily abandoning articles of Christian faith.

---

[20]   Moore, *Astrology Today*, p. 111.

Chapter 13

With Their Own Voices: Interviews with Astrologers

I had had my chart done once or twice. I was kind of impressed by what they were able to see.[1]

In all the published studies of astrology so far, there has been almost no interest in what astrologers themselves actually say: there is just one published volume of interviews with astrologers.[2] This chapter draws on 39 interviews with astrologers conducted between 1999 and 2003, mainly at astrological conferences, including the Astrological Association of Great Britain Conference in Cirencester in September 2001, and the United Astrology Conference in Orlando, Florida, in July 2002. I decided to inquire into the religious interests of astrological 'opinion formers' defined as teachers, lecturers and writers.[3] I was also very influenced by Susan Greenwood's research into modern pagans, in the sense of listening clearly to my interviewees.[4] I also report on two interviews conducted with the clients of one astrologer; again, the first time that the views of users of astrology at this level have been included in research. The resulting discussions were wide-ranging but my main concern was to investigate attitudes to the relationship between astrology, religion, Christianity, New Age culture and belief in the Age of Aquarius. I was also interested in the distinction that is made between the terms 'spiritual' and 'religious'.[5] My approach was open-ended and I did not set out with a prearranged list of interviewees or a category of astrologer. Instead, I approached those amongst conference speakers who were known as writers, teachers or organisers in the astrological community, and who were willing and available.

This was the first time that astrologers had been asked to speak for themselves academically, rather than being spoken for, and I found them generally open and responsive. I maintained, as far as I could, my phenomenological approach: no

---

[1]   Author's interview with Jonathan Cainer, *Daily Mail* astrologer.

[2]   Garry Phillipson, *Astrology in the Year Zero* (London, 2000).

[3]   I was influenced by Dyer P. Bilgrave and Robert H. Deluty, 'Religious Beliefs and Therapeutic Orientations of Clinical and Counselling Psychologists', *Journal for the Scientific Study of Religion*, 37/2 (1998), pp. 329–49, who inquired into the religious affiliations and beliefs of clinical and counselling psychologists in the US.

[4]   Susan Greenwood, *Magic, Witchcraft and the Otherworld: An Anthropology* (Oxford, 2000).

[5]   See, for example, Wade Clark Roof, *A Generation of Seekers: The Spiritual Journeys of the Baby Boom Generation* (San Francisco, 1993), pp. 123–2, 194–200.

academic study will ever do justice to astrologers unless they are allowed to have their say, exactly as with any other tribe, group, sub-culture or society. Although my discussions included a wide range of issues such as number of clients (see Chapter 8) or belief in astrology (see Chapter 12), the extracts in this chapter focus on astrologers' backgrounds and relationship with Christianity and the New Age, the core of my entire study. At the heart of the matter, then, is astrology's millenarian nature. That said, of the 39 astrologers I interviewed only one, Alan Oken, was happy to agree to belief in astrology. For almost all the others belief was an inappropriate concept to apply to a practice validated by daily experience.

I asked the interviewees how their interest in astrology developed as a means of reflecting on the reasons for belief discussed in Chapter 8. The means by which the interviewees discovered astrology was often circumstantial; exposure to a book, a horoscope reading, or to counter-cultural influences in the 1960s or all three. According to Alan Oken, a follower of Alice Bailey and the author of a series of influential books in the 1970s, 'it was the early sixties and so you had this wave that was coming in through young people about experimenting with all sorts of alternative belief systems'. Ronnie Dreyer, an American author known for her expertise in Indian astrology, was similarly exposed to astrology through a cultural milieu. She was studying drama in New York in the early 1970s and encountered astrology through her theatrical connections. She told me:

> I had always been into astronomy and I really loved the sky and the stars and all that and my father would take me to the planetarium when I was a kid. And I was also studying drama in New York and a lot of the people who were involved in the theatre were going to astrologers. They were going to astrologers to find out whether they were going to be successful. I thought 'Oh, that's interesting'. And at the same time that I started hearing a lot about astrology and people going to astrologers, my father brought home a book, because he would bring home a lot of books that came out from McGraw-Hill [where he worked as Marketing Director] and he brought home a book called the *Compleat Astrologer* by Derek and Julia Parker … He gave it to me and he said, 'Maybe you will find this interesting'. I opened it up and it taught you how to calculate your chart and everything and I couldn't put it down. I opened the book up and read it cover to cover and I was hooked.

Dreyer's interest was deepened through study in India. The Eastern connection is persistent: Greg Bogart, an author and teacher at the California Institute of Integral Studies, and Bob Mulligan, Chair of the Organisation for Professional Astrology (OPA), both reported that experiences with Indian teachers were significant and Demetra George's introduction to astrology, like that of Alan Oken, was directly through counter-cultural experiences. She told me that

> I had two friends who were going to the city every week to study with an astrologer that I thought was so exotic, but that wasn't my thing. Then I went travelling in the East for a year after that, so my whole belief system really

got loosened up after that. I spent about six months in Afghanistan. When I came back to the States a number of my friends from college were living on a commune in Southern Oregon, so I decided to go out and visit them and see what they were up to. They were in the middle of the woods and there was a group of people and there was a library of almost 1000 esoteric books that somehow people had brought with them. All of the Bailey books were there and the Theosophical books and books on astrology and Krishnamurti, and that is what we would spend our time doing – reading books and chopping wood and scrubbing clothes on the washboard and having conversations, and there were several people doing astrology ... So I became interested in someone doing astrology and then taught myself out of Llewellyn George's *ABC Horoscope Maker and Delineator*. Then my first two books that I read were Alice Bailey's *Esoteric Astrology* and Rudhyar's *Astrology of Personality*, and then did a year of correspondence at least with the Rosicrucians where I could just send a dollar donation and get a lesson.

Shelley von Strunckel, well known as the astrologer for the London *Evening Standard*, happened to live in the right place, Los Angeles, where she was exposed to New Age thought through her family. She said that

When I was a kid in LA there was a very metaphysical context to life ... the theosophical society was around, the Dante Society was around, the self-realisation fellowship was around. We used to go, my Mom, my Aunt and I used to go to meals sitting under a portrait of Yogananda when he was a kid. So I grew up in an environment where it was perfectly natural to be interested in Eastern thought and philosophy ... Also, however, I remember, as a kid, I must have been about 10, being given a diary ... I tore out the horoscope pages and threw away the diary. So I was interested in it from a young age.

Melanie Reinhart, a teacher and writer known for her inclusion of recently discovered solar-system bodies into astrology, also encountered astrology as a child. She told me, 'I discovered astrology when I was ten and, when I did, it felt like a rediscovery of something very familiar. When I think of it now it seems odd because I was only ten. At the time it felt perfectly normal.' Once she found it, though, it satisfied a deeper purpose, providing a sense of meaning:

I think it was a desire to understand life and the human psyche more deeply and the pale reflection of that that I got in this one initial book that I found simply served to whet my appetite and to want to go deeper ... I see it very much set in a cosmic context and I think that one of the things that appeals greatly to me about astrology is that it is actually possible to contextualise an individual life or a collective process, anything to do with human life individually or collectively. It is possible to contextualise that in such a way as to arrive intuitively at a sense of participation in something greater.

Liz Greene, who is famous for her use of depth psychology in order to frame astrological symbolism, had a similarly early introduction. Like von Strunckel, astrology had been a familiar feature of her early years. She told me:

> I don't remember a time when I wasn't conscious of it, going back to childhood,
> I think it was always there. I had no issue about it but when I was at university I
> went to an astrologer to have my own chart done and that was really the kick-off.
> It intrigued me and I wanted to know how it worked, so I started teaching myself
> … I had some friends who were going to see Isabel Hickey and they said 'Why
> don't you go and get your chart done?'

Jonathan Cainer, one of the most successful media astrologers of recent times (having written for a series of British newspapers – *Today*, the *Daily Mail*, the *Daily Mirror* and the *Daily Express*), told a similar story. He reported that

> Astrology had always been in my life … I was a teenage musician and fan of the
> alternative, and astrology had always been knocking around and I knew lots of
> people who were into birth signs and that sort of thing. But it was while I was in
> America … about 1980 … I had had my chart done once or twice. I was kind of
> impressed by what they were able to see and I was at a real crossroads in my life.

One common pattern, then, is of early exposure to astrology, which creates an atmosphere of acceptance, followed by an encounter with a book on the subject or an astrologer, often via friends, which confirms that astrology is a real source of valuable information. Another narrative, less common but still frequent, is of the sceptic who comes to astrology after a dramatic encounter with it. For example, Mavis Klein, a psychotherapist, was initially a sceptic, but was convinced after hearing the tape of a client's readings. She told me how

> I was an ordinary educated sceptic, thought it was all a load of bullshit or
> didn't really think about it at all until a man who had been in one of my therapy
> groups, psychotherapy groups, for two years came one night and said 'I have
> just consulted an astrologer, made a tape recording. Will you please listen to
> it?' I said, 'Yes of course' indulgently, and without really paying any attention
> I turned the tape on while the kids were screaming around me, I was doing
> the ironing and the television was on and within five minutes everything it had
> taken me three years to find out about the man is on that tape, and more, and
> I thought I would have to be blocking my eyes and ears very, very hard not to
> inquire further.

At first sight, my questions about religious affiliation told a similar story to my questionnaires – the progressive rejection of traditional Christianity in favour of Eastern and theosophical alternatives which is said to be a feature of privatisation and New Age culture. My interviewees came from a wide range of backgrounds, but a drift towards eclecticism and an interest in Eastern philosophies was evident. Maria Kay Simms, former Chair of the US-based National Council for Geocosmic Research (NCGR) was brought up a Methodist but moved through Catholicism and Unitarianism and was a high Episcopalian before becoming a Wiccan priestess, a step which for her was natural in view of what she saw as the strong pagan identity of Catholic and high Anglican ritual. Rick Tarnas, a professor at the California Institute of Integral Studies, comes from a devout Catholic family and retains Christian influences, but with the addition of Buddhism, Taoism, shamanism and the philosophies of Rudolf Steiner and C.G. Jung, a combination typical of New Age syncretism. Arlan Wise, who was to become Chair of the US-based Organisation of Professional Astrologers, grew up in a conservative Jewish household and was drawn to Tibetan Buddhism, as are Jessica Adams (who writes horoscope columns as well as teenage fiction), whose background is Roman Catholic, and Demetra George, whose family was originally Greek Orthodox. Melanie Reinhart came from a 'religiously neutral' background, went to a convent school and was confirmed Roman Catholic but became, as she told me,

> very distressed by this idea that the interpretation of the 'I am the way, the truth and the light', meaning that anyone who wasn't a Christian was basically condemned ... for posterity. This had me, like, weeping in my bed as a child. I was just frantic with distress and feeling somehow it couldn't be right. So, having got confirmed and so on, I set myself a task; at thirteen years old, I set myself a task of finding out what everybody else did. My first port of call was the Spiritualist Church who I stayed with for a number of years, and there I apprenticed to a healer learning all kinds of stuff, transforming, the whole business. I had a very, very, very wonderful teacher.

> Then ... eventually [I encountered] Eastern imports, Hinduism, Buddhism and so on, were intriguing me very deeply. The whole notion of life as a quest not just for personal enlightenment but the unfolding of consciousness that took root very deeply in me and I came over to England to find a teacher and I linked up with a Sufi Master. I am still linked with that tradition and I consider it something of a root and in that tradition is a very strong emphasis on unity and in their exoteric church service – it is called the Church of All – they have a table on which is a candle for every one of the world's major religions, including one for everything else, with an acknowledgement that, although the paths be many, the source is one. And that appealed endlessly to me and still does. That unifying intent or process found, for me, a perfect reflection in astrology because we all, on earth, everybody lives as it were, under the same sky.

Reinhart's syncretism echoes Tarnas's and is representative of a trend to broaden the childhood religion rather than reject it. Such a finding puts a new gloss on my questionnaire findings, suggesting that the dramatic decline in declared Christian affiliation is less a rejection of Christianity than an attempt to place it within a wider context informed by the theosophical notion that all religions share a core of truth, a fact obscured by the dogma and ritual of rival churches: the privatisation hypothesis is seen to be clearly supported. Alan Oken argued, from his Baileyite perspective, that all religions should be respected, with the sole exception of fundamentalist Christianity, while Arlan Wise retains respect for her own Jewish roots. In keeping with what we might see as a residual Christianity of a Neoplatonic hue, views of God, when expressed, were primarily deist. For Ronnie Dreyer, God is 'a concept ... something higher to aspire to'. For Glenn Perry, a major advocate of the combination of astrology and psychotherapy in the style of Dane Rudhyar, God is 'a transcendent ineffable intelligent principle that orders the cosmos and regulates its affairs ... It is the essence of all.' Demetra George maintains respect for God as an aspect of her respect for the Goddess, and experiences a direct and symbiotic relationship between her religious beliefs and her practice of astrology. She told me that

> When I was a very young astrologer, before each reading I would still, by and large, light a candle. I have a journal of prayers that I would make to God before I knew about the goddess and I would go, 'Dear Lord, Father in Heaven, please give me the guidance and words I need that this will be of benefit to this client coming in', and date it and sign it before each reading. At that point, I see now, I was going back to that direct, natural divination of understanding that I was a vehicle for some higher celestial power to use me in order to give counselling and advice to a person who comes to that oracle for advice. I wasn't consciously thinking that that was what I was doing. That's just what I did. So, again, I try to keep that connection now by lighting the candle before a reading. At that point I am alone in myself, getting some of that direct or natural flow of energy. As a young woman it was my connection with astrology that brought me very close to a belief in God or a creed of intelligence when I saw the perfection of the patterning that seemed to exist. That nothing was an accident. The impeccable timing. I knew that there was something going on out there that was a lot bigger than I was. That's what brought me – it is interesting that it was astrology that brought me into a belief system of divine reality.

George is representative of a minority, although a sizeable one (see Chapter 12) who agreed that their religion influenced their astrology. Others place less emphasis on spiritual beliefs. Sean Lovatt, who practised as an astrologer near Glastonbury in the 1980s and 1990s, 'had no religious background at all apart from morning prayers at school which for me, and I think everybody else, had no religious significance at all ...'. He was influenced in his life as a whole by his reading of mystical traditions, but declared that it 'has no effect on his astrological work'.

I asked the interviewees how they responded to the definition of astrology as a religion. The response confirmed my questionnaires in its overwhelming negativity. Typical was Bob Mulligan, who told me that 'The word religion has a very negative connotation for most thinking people these days because it means subservience to something that you do not understand and, sort of, relinquishing any sense of power and living in an atmosphere of fear.'

Ronnie Dreyer was put off organised religion by what she perceived as its exclusivity and intolerance. She told me that

> Kindness, forgiveness, charity, compassion. Those are the qualities that I think religion should encourage. Really. That's really the basis. The reason I really turned away from a lot of religions was that most of them did the opposite. They were elitist, judgmental, punishing rather than forgiving. So I find religion itself very contradictory.

To an extent the question of whether astrology is a religion is meaningless for astrologers like Ronnie Dreyer and Komilla Sutton, founder of the UK-based British Association of Vedic Astrologers (BAVA). Both practise Indian astrology and may describe astrology in terms which may appear religious in Western terms – namely that it is a practice which is integral to the Hindu worldview, but they understand that the separation of religion as a distinct activity from the rest of daily life is a peculiarity of the modern West. But, for the majority of Western astrologers, the definition of astrology as a religion is unacceptable. When I asked Arlan Wise if astrology is a religion she replied, 'No. I just wouldn't think of it as a religion … I don't see how [it can be]'. Alan Oken used an exclusivist definition of religion, stating that 'astrology is not a religion for me. I don't worship astrology and I don't worship through astrology'. Similarly Melanie Reinhart told me that

> Astrology is not a religion in any formal sense because you know there isn't a church and there aren't a whole set of prescribed rituals and moral codes and hierarchy of officials and all the rest of it. So in that sense, it is not a religion. But I do feel it can be if one wants to take it this way. It can be a very powerful accompaniment to one's spiritual path in the sense that it provides the reflection of – of not only oneself but life. And it can take you as deep as you want to go.

Reinhart identified spirituality as a complement to astrology, but was adamant that astrology and religion are entirely distinct, a view shared by Bob Mulligan. He told me that

> My spiritual practice is to love God and that influences everything that I do including anything in my personal life or professional life [including astrology]. Always in the back of my mind is that when I am talking to somebody that this person is a soul or a whole soul and that infinite intelligence is inside of them and if I can do anything that unleashes that infinite intelligence, the person knows what the right thing is about. There is an inherent embedded value system not so much in astrology as a technical discipline but in the cosmos. There is a moral order to the way that things happen. There is a moral equivalent of cause and effect. Creation sprang into existence for love to experience itself and souls go

through creation for the development of consciousness so they can consciously experience that love that sums up the entire meaning of everything.

Glenn Perry elaborated on the religion/spirituality dichotomy, stating that

> [R]eligion [is] doctrine ... ideology ... embodied in various conventional, orthodox, positions ... but spirituality ... is an experience of the divine ... a more mystical kind of participation in something numinous that you can experience through prayer or some other kind of spiritual discipline [or] meditation.

He went on to tell me how astrology is part of his spiritual practice and how,

> when I think about the chart in a natal sense, I think of it sort of as a set of instructions, a particular kind of fate, a character that I am which is reflected in the chart, which I believe is in some ways a meaningful consequence of whatever the history of my soul is. I believe in reincarnation so I think that the particular birth chart that I have in some way is purposeful and derives out of whatever actions and effects I have set in motion on the basis of my past lives. So in that regard it is kind of a growth model. It is a particular chart that is uniquely organised in such a way to maximize or actualise whatever it is that I need to further develop.

Of those who mentioned spirituality, only Robert Zoller was adamant that the separation of spirituality and religion resulted from a misunderstanding of the nature of both. Zoller, though, is untypical. He was unique in practising medieval astrology in the 1970s, years before this became fashionable; he has never been influenced by the New Age astrology of Leo and Rudhyar, and is a Lutheran who is very much influenced by the mystical cosmology of Jacob Boehme,
I then asked about attitudes to Christianity. The general response was that there is no necessary contradiction between astrology and Christianity. Neither was any hostility expressed towards Christianity, only to fundamentalism, and then unanimously because the fundamentalists were blamed for rejecting ideas which they do not understand. This position was espoused by Lee Lehman, who was later Dean of Kepler College and, like Zoller, has never subscribed to any form of New Age astrology. In her view, 'astrology was, was always understood by Christianity or Islam as being competitive.' Rob Hand, the respected author of a series of influential books, enlarged on this theme, telling me that

> There is definitely a rivalry between astrology and their sort of religion for the very simply reason than their sort of religion is rival – rivals every alternate belief system. Fundamentalist Christianity disbelieves actively in fundamentalist Judaism which disbelieves actively in fundamentalist Islam and if you go into a Christian bookstore in the States you will find, you will find treatises and books against Mormonism, against Jehovah's Witnesses, people you would think that

they would be associated with. They despise all deviations from their own point of view with equal enthusiasm. Astrologers are simply one of the groups with which they disagree.

According to Ken Irving, 'if you are a fundamentalist, an evangelical Christian, there are competitors on every street corner.' Jonathan Cainer agreed, arguing that, 'So religion doesn't like astrology in much the same way as religion doesn't like other religions. That's all. And astrology is, to some extent, a belief system.' For Jessica Adams, the problem came down to a fundamental incompatibility between Christianity's (particularly Roman Catholicism's) social conservatism, for example on the abortion issue, and most astrologers' liberalism. Lynda Hill, an astrologer and teacher from Australia, resents the Christian allegation that astrology is a 'crutch', arguing that it is the Catholic church that becomes the crutch, but pointed out that there are plenty of people who cross the Christianity/astrology divide. Robert Zoller acknowledges Christian hostility to astrology but denies its theological basis and argues that, instead, the secular humanists are astrology's real enemies. Glenn Perry, meanwhile, distinguished the message of Christianity from the institution, arguing that

> If you can eliminate all the dogma and all the kind of political overlay of Christianity and just get down to the heart, the essence of what Christ embodied and represented, I think it is very interesting. I think that, you know, the story of Christ in and of itself is a wonderful model for striving to actualise one's spiritual attributes. But all the, you know, all the political overlay that occurred, the encrusted on the top of the religion is something that I don't have much patience with.

Sean Lovatt, whose general position is non-religious, admitted that 'It is obvious some astrologers – I mean myself … don't have many good feelings about Christianity', but could see no reason for the rivalry: 'I would say that astrology, belief in astrology is fundamentally compatible with Christianity if you were to take the view that the mechanism by which divine will is delivered to the earth is through the planets.' Greg Bogart took a more sympathetic view of religion, but from a theosophical perspective. He argued that 'One needs to adopt some kind of a religious viewpoint, whether it is Christian or not; but it has to do with the relationship of the individual with the creator, the Absolute, the source.' Von Strunckel is unusual in being a member of a Christian church, but her belief exists within the context of her theosophical background. She told me that

> As it happens I go to Church. I mean my philosophy is very broad, obviously. I would be as happy observing a Hindu approach, a Buddhist approach but in this life I was born as a Christian, but anyway, that's the Church I go to, which is very high Church of England.

Rick Levine, an author who is one of the directors of the StarIQ website, pointed out that astrology exists within Christianity. He told me, 'The short answer is this: if astrology is so threatening to Christianity, then why, if Jesus only invited three people to his birth, were they all astrologers?' Bernadette Brady who, like Zoller and Lehman, has never been influenced by New Age astrology, relied on sun-as-god theory[6] to argue that Christianity and astrology are

> the same inherently and in essence ... The crisis comes from the delineation of the power base in mainstream Catholicism and the power structure and the need to control the thinking of the people within that framework ... but actually at the essence Christ was a solar god who died at a solar eclipse, nailed to a cross of matter which we have in the middle of our [astrological birth] charts.

Rick Tarnas took a balanced view, arguing that the problem exists on both sides: astrology's Christian critics are ignorant of its nature while astrologers themselves still carry 'archaic memories of the deterministic fatalism of the late Hellenistic, late Classical period'. He sees a positive future though:

> I think, well understood, Christianity will actually see astrology as being a profound ally in Christianity's deeper mission, which is to mediate the incarnational transformation of the divine, of the human being and the cosmos. Astrology can profoundly support that motive or mission that is essential I think to the Christian vision.

When I asked about the religious affiliation of clients, Melanie Reinhart told me that there is no pattern, and that her clients are from all affiliations: atheist, pagan, New Age, Buddhist and Christian. However, there was a universal hostility to the definition of astrology as New Age, almost as much as to its inclusion as a religion. This was partly because, as Liz Greene said, astrology cannot be New Age because it is old. However, Greg Bogart accepted that, although astrology is old, it is a characteristic of New Age culture to revive old systems of thought but Jonathan Cainer was more typical. He asked, 'Well how can it be new age? It is as old age as they bloody get. It is a bit of a funny one that, isn't it? Hey, we know that astrology is older than Christianity so how come it is suddenly New Age?'

Some even doubt that 'New Age' exists. For Liz Greene it's a 'buzzword' (similar, perhaps, to Sutcliffe's 'emblem') and, for Rick Tarnas, a phenomenon which has become too easy to 'caricature'. Ken Irving, the editor of *American Astrology* claimed that

---

[6]   Nicholas Campion, 'Prophecy, Cosmology and the New Age Movement: The Extent and Nature of Contemporary Belief in Astrology', PhD thesis, University of the West of England, 2004, p. 52.

I don't think there is any such thing as a New Age system. The New Age is just a ragbag of things that people believe or things that people like or things that are fun to believe ... New Age as you will find it commercially, things sold as 'New Age'. If you go into a bookstore nowadays, instead of having an astrology section or a 'this' section, they will have New Age and everything semi-weird goes in the New Age section. It is just a ragbag.

He also identified hostility to astrology from within a certain quarter of New Age culture:

But there are people, particularly I think in America, there is this class of these sort of – Ken Wilbur types with these PhDs and minds and this very, this sort of sixties baby-boomer attitude towards life and the universe and they have developed something which I would call New Age just totally apart from that. Those people don't seem to like astrology at all. They consider astrology as a wretched subject.

Sean Lovatt was likewise cynical about New Age culture. He said that

There is a particular danger and a particularly strange relationship between New Age philosophy and astrology that I personally don't understand but most astrologers would probably, I think, align themselves with a perceived rebirth of spirituality in our culture which they may describe as the Age of Aquarius, as it often is. I don't necessarily believe that but New Ageism is really a religion. It is a religion without a formal structure. It is a religion because there are certain tenets that are held by a significant proportion of New Age followers.

Jonathan Cainer confirmed the distinction between New Age and astrology, pointing out that, just because New Agers do astrology, that does not mean astrology is New Age. For Liz Greene, New Age ideology is no better than any other sort of religious authority. She said that

I have always liked John Cooper Powys' line that the devil is any god who requires exact obedience. I think that any authority, whether it is New Age spiritual in the form of a guru, or orthodox religious in the form of the Pope, or scientific in the form or a high-powered academic, or political, that's when we start giving away our capacity to discriminate.

Lee Lehman also took a sceptical line, arguing that,

If astrology ever becomes an exclusively New Age discipline we are in deep doodoo ... Because first of all the New Age movement is merely this particular New Age movement, because both you and I know perfectly well there have been multiple New Age movements historically, and you simply call the one of your current era the new one because you are part of it. So this is actually expressing a cyclic phenomenon.

A similar scepticism was expressed about the idea of the Age of Aquarius. The reality of precession is accepted by all (although Perry found it astrologically irrelevant) but only in the sense that, as Bob Mulligan commented, it means another stage in an ongoing process of change. According to an anonymous interviewee,

> This precessional age thing is so vague, the timing, as you point out, is so vague, and also I don't believe though in astrology there is a big change. Today is one age, tomorrow is another age. We are moving from one to another anyway over hundreds of years timescale. So I think the whole idea of that is not a useful analysis content. We should just do today.

Rick Levine spoke about the Aquarian Age, like the New Age, as 'a PR guy's dream. It's perfect. It is just what we need to promote what we are doing'. Reinhart considered that the Aquarian Age might be a helpful model, arguing that

> Perhaps the Age of Aquarius and its incoming energy help people to understand the world from a point of view that is congruent with the discipline of astrology. That's how I would understand it. The other manifestations of change, you know like the computer age and the shift in New Physics and all that, they are all part of the same thing in a way that sort of loosens up people's mental framework sufficiently so that they can – they have a context.

Liz Greene elaborated the same point, arguing that

> It could be and that may have more to do with our potentials rather than with some grand design or evolution. But it is a bit like a human life. By the time you get to a certain age, your experiences are beginning to have become cyclical and you start recognising that you have been in that sitting room before. That could actually produce something better in terms of wisdom in terms of navigating things better or handling them more creatively, or it may just make people bitter and make them more destructive because they get frenzied when they realise they have been there before. I think there is potentially a genuine evolution possible, but I don't think that it's a given and I am not at all convinced that it is a plan. It is something that we could actually do ourselves if we are intelligent enough to manage it.

Certain strong patterns emerged from these interviews. Religious eclecticism was notable, though with a preference for spirituality above religion. There was a pronounced move away from Christianity, though not a rejection of it. Rather there was a rejection of the church, but with a sense that the church had begun the process by ignorantly rejecting astrology and failing to offer the wisdom and self-understanding available from other religions or spiritualities. A few interviewees, though, maintained a Christian affiliation if they felt they would experience a sympathetic welcome or supportive theological context. Opposition to the notion of astrology as a New Age discipline, scepticism about the Aquarian Age's apocalyptic associations and hostility to the definition of astrology as a religion were almost universal, to a much stronger degree than was found in the questionnaires. To put these conclusions into context, I have argued that the range of expressions of religious or spiritual attitudes expressed in these interviews are New Age, emerging from astrology's encounter with theosophy, but some are clearly not. The rejection of 'New Age' as a label, though, goes to the heart of whether contemporary New Age culture is any more than an 'emblem' or 'etic [outsider] formulation', and parallels opposition to the label from other groups who feel they are wrongly subjected to the 'New Age' label.

I also conducted two interviews with clients. This was not a main feature of my research but when Melanie Reinhart mentioned to me that a few of her clients were priests and nuns, the logic of the phenomenological approach – following the data wherever it leads – suggested that I should take the opportunity of talking to them. In order for me to pursue the question of whether Christianity and astrology are necessarily opposed, Melanie agreed to put me in touch with some of her clients. I spoke to two, both of whom were involved in the Guild for Pastoral Psychology, the London-based organisation which treats Jungian psychology in a spiritual context.

Diana appreciates the fact that Melanie herself has a spiritual practice and visits her periodically, perhaps every few years, when she feels that she needs an outside voice to put her life into context. I asked Diana about her then Christian practice (she has since left the Church of England):

> I would say that for me the Christian myth still informs my, my sense of ritual and what I enjoy in ritual and my sense of worship … I find the Eucharist really gives me a sense of mystery … I go to a Church which is fairly High Church of England but not really high, high, high. But I also go to a Christian monastery where it is Anglican and it is monks and nuns. An experimental community and I go there because … there is more an inner sense of meditation … I have found a few fellow travellers in the Church, yes. And it is difficult … I am not a very good congregant member of the Church, nor would I just in general congregation go to Bible reading classes or whatever. I study, if I do, the Bible either with rabbis who have been some fellow travellers or with people – but I still often can't find people – I would like to study the Gospel more but I can't find too many fellow travellers who don't, when it comes really down to the nitty gritty, interpret the gospels at some level very literally. There was the Bishop of Durham who tried to say, didn't he, that you know you didn't have to believe in the bodily resurrection of Christ and practically got hounded out of the Church.

The other interviewee had been a Roman Catholic nun for 25 years before leaving her order and discovering the Guild. She retains her Catholic faith but meets privately with friends for the Eucharist rather than attending a church. Her testimony describes her current vision, a theology reintegrated with a cosmology in which all parts of the universe are interdependent.

> I spent twenty-five years in a Roman Catholic convent and had a breakdown and left and the challenge was there, how do I come to terms with giving up my vows? Because that for me felt the most awful thing to have to do. So that confronted me with putting into question everything that I thought I believed in and, um, I needed then a new language for my spirituality, for my Christianity and for my understanding of what life was for and about. And so I began to wonder how I could deal with this and the first language that made sense was psychology because I met a therapist who helped me. And the second language I met which was cosmology which was linked very much to astrology … I began to get an understanding of the inter-connectedness of all things. If that is really the case, then I must be affected by how and what is going on in the universe. I can't be just a little separate person which I thought before. Then I began to feel a huge affinity to the Moon and believe that the cycles of the Moon must have something to do with who I am and then I bumped into Melanie in the Guild of Pastoral Psychology and … I knew she had something that I needed, not that I was quite clear what that was or why that was. And my first session with her was an extraordinary experience of her saying things that I would hardly have dared say yet I knew were true and how she presented how I might be was totally true, and that really won me.

> I work with clients now and a lot of it is that we all have this unique, very special contribution to make to the universe now, not just as a preparation for hereafter, whatever hereafter might mean. So the context is huge and yet tiny at the same time. Everybody's contribution is minute, is my belief, but it's in this huge picture of the stars and the galaxies and the planets and the earth and our planet and in us in our tiny way and if I don't do it, nobody will do my bit for me. I remember realising that for the first time and being quite awed by what that might mean. In that sense, at the time I'm born and what is happening in the planetary world when I am born makes a difference. That's how I would make the big picture important.

It is clear from both testimonies that their Christianity is deep but their relationship with the church verged from the uncomfortable to the non-existent (since my interview, Diana no longer describes herself as Christian). Both interviewees use astrology for purely pragmatic purposes; because it is useful, and neither can see any theological reason why the church should condemn it. The issue for them would seem to be the church's exclusivity; that, with no real justification, it rejects a practice which has helped them both. From this perspective, rivalry between the church and astrology therefore originates with the church, not with astrology.

These interviews are really just the beginning of a long-term project, to fulfil Tristan Platt's 1991 suggestion that we are in need of an 'anthropology of astronomy', using 'astronomy' here, as Claudius Ptolemy did in the second century, and as was common until the seventeenth century, to include astrology.[7] The conclusion of these preliminary interviews, I suggest, is that the existing work on astrology as a New Age discipline, is substantiated in some respects, if we consider New Age ideology in the broad sense. However, there is a distinct resistance to simple notions of an imminent entry into a New Age and an insistence that those features of astrology which are defined as New Age by New Agers, academics and Christian critics, are no more than deeply embedded features of an ancient practice. We see a high acceptance of theosophy, with a small 't', in the sense of a belief that all religions share universal truths, but a scepticism regarding the rigid historical prophecies of Blavatsky, as well as Alan Leo and Dane Rudhyar. The secularisation hypothesis, as a decline of religion, may at first be justified by a wholesale move away from Christianity, but qualified in others: the move is not away from Christianity as such, but from the rigidity of dogma and the conservatism of the church. Privatisation theory, though, is thoroughly supported. What is clear though, above all, is that many leading astrologers talk in terms identified by academics as both religious and New Age, while simultaneously and unequivocally rejecting any identification with either.

---

[7]   Tristan Platt, 'The Anthropology of Astronomy', in *Archaeoastronomy*, suppl. to *Journal of the History of Astronomy*, 16 (1991), p. S83; Claudius Ptolemy, *Tetrabiblos*, trans. F.E.Robbins (Cambridge MA, 1940), I.1.

Chapter 14
Conclusion: Modernity and Normality

Paradoxical as it may seem, therefore, we conclude that popular belief in astrology may be part and parcel of late modernity itself.[1]

The question we come to, then, is essentially twofold. First there is the matter of astrology's nature, particularly whether it is a New Age discipline or new religious movement? To follow this line of inquiry also requires that we touch on its religious nature in general (although I have only done this peripherally, through public attitudes rather than in terms of astrology's intrinsic nature), its relationship with Christianity, and its millenarian context (which I hope I have covered in sufficient detail). Second is the issue of belief in astrology. This is, if anything, the more problematic of the two questions and I have questioned the entire notion that belief can be measured. The methodological difficulty, though, is not the only one. The conceptual problem is probably greater: the notion of belief as a peculiar cognitive state is a nonsense, an artefact arising out of post-Enlightenment sceptical rhetoric, the assault on religion as uniquely false, and the pseudohistorical narrative of evolutionary cultural theory.

My starting point for discussion throughout has been the existing body of literature, primarily sociological and historical works. However, as Michael Hill acutely observed, all academic disciplines 'which pursue the goal of a rigorous and systematic investigation of the empirical world sooner or later come up against the "pure" and "applied" dichotomy'.[2] I have found this to be true in the case of astrology. Those sociological works which refer to contemporary astrology tend to ignore the actual theory and practice of modern astrologers and its 'applied' nature, and assume *a priori* that astrology should be categorised in 'pure' terms, as a religion, new religious movement, New Age discipline or superstition, and that its claims are false. It is also assumed that astrology can be treated as a single entity, as if all astrologers think the same and work according to a single code. Astrologers themselves are not immune from the same conceptual trap. They often classify astrology as a symbolic language in which the future may be negotiated, while talking and behaving as if it is both literal, rather than metaphorical, and a matter of determinism, rather than choice.[3] Yet astrology, taken as a whole, is, like any other discipline, marked as much by its diversity as by its uniformity. As David Hufford

---

[1]   John Bauer and Martin Durant, 'British Public Perceptions of Astrology: An Approach from the Sociology of Knowledge', *Culture and Cosmos*, 1/1 (1997), p. 69.

[2]   Michael Hill, *A Sociology of Religion* (London, 1979), p. 6.

[3]   Nicholas Campion, 'Is Astrology a Symbolic Language?', paper presented to the Ninth Annual Sophia Centre Conference, Bath, 4–5 June 2011.

remarked, when arguing that belief cannot be considered in isolation from disbelief, 'we must be prepared to tolerate some theoretical uncertainty and even dissonance while we develop a comfortable theoretical consistency primarily by selectively avoiding pertinent information and by forcing that information into appropriate, preconceived patterns'.[4] In this respect Festinger's notion of cognitive dissonance removes the need to look for consistency of thought or practice amongst astrologers any more than within any other discipline.[5] My goal, as Primiano put it, has been to 'do justice to belief and lived experience'.[6] So, to tackle the thorny question of 'belief', I have pointed out that, as applied to matters of presumed superstitious or religious significance, the word frequently carries pejorative overtones, the result of which is to distort research into the extent of belief. For this reason the very notion of belief in astrology amongst both astrology's detractors and its supporters is bound up with the view that astrology is necessarily false. However, if the word's core meaning, 'to have confidence', is taken as the principal definition, then the issue becomes one of confidence in astrology. But, in view of the diversity of astrological claims, which aspect of astrology might any 'believer' have confidence in? As I have shown, there are sharply polarised differences of view amongst professionals and students of astrology concerning, for example, the use of astrology for prediction as opposed to counselling, or the value of sun-sign columns as against the interpretation of the individual birth chart. Additionally, as I argued, lay attitudes to astrology can be shown to be inconsistent, once the nature of the questions asked is modified, as can those of astrologers.

My argument therefore supports the doubts expressed by Davie, Hill and Shiels and Berg in relation to attempts to quantify belief based on outward behaviour or institutional affiliation.[7] Simply, the problems are complex and the results uncertain. Attempts to derive a single figure for belief in astrology therefore lack credibility, and it may well be that measures based on behaviour (such as readership of horoscope columns) or opinion (such as whether it can predict the future) are best left as they are, rather than be converted into scales of belief. If we wish to understand astrology's penetration of society, it is useful to know how many people read horoscope columns and how often, but there is no logic that leads from there to an assumption about belief in astrology. We can adapt Tony Walters and Helen Waterhouse's conclusion from their study of belief in reincarnation (that to quantify belief in it may be meaningless) to astrology.[8] My research indicates that

---

    [4]   David Hufford, 'Traditions of Disbelief', *Talking Folklore*, 1/3 (1987), p. 27.

    [5]   Leon Festinger, *A Theory of Cognitive Dissonance* (Stanford, 1968).

    [6]   L. Primiano, 'Vernacular Religion and the Search for Method on Religious Folklife', *Western Folklore*, 54/1 (1995), p. 41.

    [7]   Grace Davie, *Religion in Britain since 1945* (Oxford, 1994), p. 45; Dean Shiels and Philip Berg, 'A Research Note on Sociological Variables Related to Belief in Psychic Phenomena', *Wisconsin Sociologist*, 14 (1977), p. 27; and Hill, *A Sociology of Religion*, p. 14.

    [8]   Tony Walter and Helen Waterhouse, 'A Very Private Belief: Reincarnation in Contemporary England', *Sociology of Religion*, 60/2 (1999), p. 192.

the statement that '*x* percent of the population believes in astrology' is actually close to being meaningless. However, it is equally clear that quantification should not be rejected altogether, for the data on belief in, and attitudes to, astrology does indicate trends and patterns. The data, though, can only be understood if it is recognised that belief and disbelief do not exist as discrete categories, that the very notion of belief as a distinct cognitive state is problematic, and that individual responses to questions on belief are shaped by social and ideological pressures.

Moreover, the popular assumption that belief in astrology is increasing is difficult to demonstrate. Quite simply, the available primary data do not suggest an increase in belief in astrology in recent decades – even if we could measure belief: perhaps 'acceptance' of astrology, or 'interest' in it, would be better terms. Even then, there is no sure way to measure any increase or decline in interest. In addition the continuation of a tradition of popular astrology from the seventeenth to nineteenth centuries suggests that interest in astrology never actually died out following the scientific revolution. The popularity of newspaper astrology columns after 1930 may therefore be a symptom of acceptance of astrology, rather than a cause of it: as we have seen, the positive public response to R.H. Naylor's *Sunday Express* article on Princess Margaret in 1930 was immediate.[9] This suggests that, rather than creating an interest in astrology as Bart Bok, an implacable opponent of astrology, thought, the new sun-sign columns catered to an existing interest, one which can be traced back to the nineteenth century and earlier, through the traditions of 'low' astrology.[10] Modern popular astrology may therefore be seen as a part of what Grace Davie has identified as the 'common religion' of Britain', the sum total of people's opinions, attitudes and behaviour, one which has direct and continuous links with the seventeenth century and hence with early modern Britain.[11] We find elements of both continuity and innovation. Core New Age ideas such as Gnosticism and the importance of astrology to the soul are rooted in classical Neoplatonism, while astrological millenarianism can be traced back to the ancient Near East. Yet innovation, which may contain elements of detraditionalisation, is represented by the invention of the Age of Aquarius in the late eighteenth century, the location of the sun-sign as key to personality analysis dates to the early twentieth century and the horoscope column to the 1930s.

The reasons for belief in astrology given in the published literature so far are, frankly, inadequate. These reasons are generally based on the assumption that, from a positivist perspective, not only are astrology's claims false, but the information that this is the case is so widely available that belief in astrology must result either from psychological inadequacy or from social marginality in the sense of poverty, low educational attainment or membership of an ethnic minority,

---

[9]   Ellic Howe, *Urania's Children: The Strange World of the Astrologers* (London, 1967), p. 66.

[10]   Bart J. Bok and Margaret W. Mayall, 'Scientists Look at Astrology', *Scientific Monthly*, 52 (1941), pp. 237–9.

[11]   Davie, *Religion in Britain since 1945*, p. 77.

or some other condition which prompts a perverse refusal to acknowledge the evidence. No educated, psychologically balanced, socially integrated person, the argument runs, could possibly believe in it. Therefore, reasons for belief need to be sought and solutions recommended. For example, if scientific illiteracy is the cause, the solution is better science education.[12] One response, often made by astrologers, to the positivist position is the argument that, in a context of epistemological pluralism there are domains of human experience and knowledge which lie outside the territory of modern science. The same argument may equally made, though, by some scientific critics of astrology, as it was by Jacqui Boivin in her response to Pat Harris. However, for the current discussion it is perhaps more important to point out that there is in the public domain literature which accepts the right of contemporary science to comment on astrology and which both details positive scientific evidence for astrology and criticises the scientific attitude which attacks astrology. For the purposes of the present discussion it is not necessary to comment on the veracity of that work, only to observe that it exists, and therefore that explanations for belief in astrology based on its obvious falsity are themselves derived from a false premise. The starting point for the investigation is flawed. There *is* positive scientific evidence for astrology for those who need it. And for those that do not, personal experience provides all the evidence that is required. As Richard Gregory observed, 'Anyone who has taken even the most casual interest in astrology will have noticed that, contrary to all common sense, it seems to work.'[13] He did not say that it *does* work, but that it *seems* to, and this is all we need to explain 'belief' in astrology. No psychological theory or social construct is necessary.

Then we have to consider the claims that astrology is a religion, or even a cult. The first, and frequently ignored, problem is that definitions of what constitutes a religion are many and varied. Neither do such claims recognise the diversity of astrology. There is a profound difference between astrologers who forecast financial futures or the outcome of sporting contests, on the one hand, and those who may be counselling clients or pursuing their own spiritual development on the other. For current purposes I am considering only the latter forms of astrology, together with sun-sign horoscopes and sun-sign personality delineations, those varieties of astrology which I have classified as New Age. We may observe with Milton Yinger that some groups labelled as religious reject the description.[14] Perhaps this is true of some astrologers. But it is not true of all. However, whatever we conclude concerning the identity of *some* astrology, to define economic forecasting as religious stretches even the most inclusivist definition of religion to

---

[12]   Jon D. Miller, 'The Public Acceptance of Astrology and other Pseudo-Science in the United States', paper presented to the 1992 annual meeting of the American Association for the Advancement of Science, 9 February 1992.

[13]   Richard L. Gregory, *The Oxford Companion to the Mind* (Oxford, 1998), p. 50.

[14]   J. Milton Yinger, 'A Structural Examination of Religion', *Journal for the Scientific Study of Religion*, 8 (1969), p. 90.

breaking point. To define *all* astrology as religion, or as a new religious movement, runs counter to the evidence.

Neither does astrology conform to strict exclusivist definitions of religion. It has no organised church, set of dogma or priestly hierarchy in the sense required by Emile Durkheim, nor a creator God, nor any necessary belief in any kind of divinity, angel or spirit. Neither does it have a recognised moral code. All it has is a set of rules for interpreting life on earth. This is precisely why some cuneiform scholars identify Mesopotamian astrology, from which Western astrology is descended, as a science.[15] However, let us consider those components of astrology which may be religious. Esoteric astrology, as developed by the ardent theosophists Alan Leo and Dane Rudhyar, does posit the existence of supernatural beings, although there is no personal creator. It may therefore correspond to Tylor's key requirement of a religion: belief in supernatural beings. Leo certainly predicted that astrology was to be the religion of the twentieth century, and the millenarian New Age astrology *sensu stricto* of Leo and Rudhyar can therefore be legitimately considered religious. However, there is no place for supernatural beings in those forms of psychological astrology derived from Dane Rudhyar, which have become detached from their overtly theosophical roots. Psychological astrology owes as much to depth psychology as to theosophy, and more to astrology's Neoplatonic lineage than to Blavatsky's syncretic combination of Eastern and Western teachings. The same point may be made of sun-sign delineation and forecasting. It may have been born of Leo's move of the Sun to the centre of the astrological interpretation, and perhaps of Rudhyar's invention of the 12-paragraph horoscope column, and some leading columnists may be theosophists, but there is no reason why they should be: R.H. Naylor, who wrote the first regular horoscope column in the British press, certainly was not.

It is inevitable that inclusivist definitions of religion may encompass many forms of astrology, just as they include science and Marxism. Michael York defined religion as the 'shared positing of the identity of any relationship between humanity, the world and the supernatural in terms of meaning assignment, value allocation and validating enactment'.[16] Here, again, problems of definition are encountered. Astrology takes no consistent position on the supernatural. Indeed, some explanations of it are entirely naturalistic.[17] However, if it is considered that astrology's explanatory models, such as Jungian synchronicity, are beyond natural explanation then they are by definition 'super-natural', and astrology may be a religion, along with Marxism and scientism, which also take explicit positions

---

[15]   Francesca Rochberg, *The Heavenly Writing: Divination and Horoscopy, and Astronomy in Mesopotamian Culture* (Cambridge, 2004).

[16]   Michael York, 'A Report', *Journal of Contemporary Religion*, 10/2 (1995), p. 107.

[17]   See, for example, Percy Seymour, *Astrology: The Evidence of Science*, 2nd edn, rev. (London, 1990).

in relation to the supernatural.[18] In that case astrology may also be described as what Yinger called 'hidden' and Luckmann called 'invisible' religion; one which is generally not recognised or respected by other religions. It may also be considered what Michael Hill defined as a 'God of the Gaps'; that is, one of many popular responses to the 'disenchantment', or the loss of sacred character, which is characteristic of the modern world.[19]

This opens up an alternative approach that bypasses those exclusivist definitions which insist that religion requires supernatural dogma and institutional hierarchies. Astrology may then be regarded as a series of 'perspective realms', 'meaning systems' or 'symbolic universes' which flourish at a popular level but are not officially recognised. Indeed they may be widely condemned, or subject to official restriction, as in the case of the ITC code. Thus James Lewis described astrology's survival until modern times as being 'at the level of "folk religion"'.[20] This relates to what, in turn, Grace Davie has identified as 'the "common religion" of Britain' as opposed to what Hornsby-Smith referred to in the title of his study of modern English Catholics as 'customary', that is, traditional mainstream religion.[21] Davie considered the diversity of 'common religion' which

> at one end of the spectrum ... [has] some link to Christian teaching, ... [and at] the other ... is extremely diverse ... ranging through a wide range of heterodox ideas; for example ... healing, the paranormal, fortune telling, fate and destiny, life after death, ghosts, spiritual experiences, prayer and meditation, luck and superstition.[22]

Popular astrology may also reasonably be added to this list. Davie herself observes that these beliefs and practices are now generally included within the overall category of 'New Age', the popularity of which counters the proposition that the UK is becoming more secular (in the sense that religiosity is in decline). In any case, as we have seen, the term 'secular' has a series of meanings which are not well defined but which are sufficiently different to confuse the issue: if for

---

[18]   C.G. Jung, 'Richard Wilhelm: In Memoriam', in *The Spirit in Man, Art, And Literature*, vol. 15, trans. R.F.C. Hull (London, 1971).

[19]   Hill, *A Sociology of Religion*, p. 247. See also Roy Willis and Patrick Curry, *Astrology, Science and Culture: Pulling Down the Moon* (Oxford, 2004); Alex Owen, *The Place of Enchantment: British Occultism and the Culture of the Modern* (Chicago, 2004); Christopher Partridge, *The Re-Enchantment of the West*, vol. 1 (London, 2004).

[20]   James Lewis, 'Introduction', in James Lewis (ed.), *The Beginnings of Astrology in America: Astrology and the Re-Emergence of Cosmic Religion* (London and New York, 1990).

[21]   Davie, *Religion in Britain since 1945*, p. 77; Michael Hornsby-Smith, *Roman Catholic Beliefs in England: Customary Catholicism and Transformations in Religious Authority* (Cambridge, 1991).

[22]   Davie, *Religion in Britain since 1945*, p. 83.

Hanegraaff New Age esotericism is itself a kind of secularity, the notion of what is or is not secular becomes almost impossible to discuss in a meaningful sense. An alternative to the terms 'folk' and 'popular' religion is what Primiano described as 'vernacular' religion, which Bowman and Sutcliffe follow Yoder in defining as 'the totality of all those views and practices of religion that exist among the people apart from, and alongside, the strictly theological and liturgical forms of the official religion'.[23] They include New Age culture as a sub-type of 'popular religion' and add that,

> If social religion [is] defined as religion founded on authoritative documents and propagated by religious specialists, priests or hierarchy, then the term 'popular' can apply to any layperson, whether peasant or ruling-class, who adopts beliefs and practices which may be at odds with the religious specialist's views.[24]

However, the overwhelming majority of astrologers are keen to remove astrology from the religious sphere, while supporting the definition of astrology as a spiritual path. In relation to this problem Bowman and Sutcliffe wrote: 'That converts to belief systems as varied as Buddhism, Islam, and Paganism consistently say "It's not a religion, it's a way of life" speaks volumes about a previously impoverished understanding of what "religion" is'.[25] The evidence suggests that astrologers' attitudes to the word 'religion' are indeed 'impoverished', to judge by their thorough rejection of religion as a definition of astrology, compared to their high acceptance of spirituality. Such negative attitudes amongst astrologers are evident in the literature on the Age of Aquarius, in which there is an overwhelming assumption that the traditional religion of the Christian church is oppressive and is to be overthrown when the Age of Aquarius begins. Astrologers' general resistance to the definition of astrology as religion is, as the Aquarian Age literature demonstrates, itself based on an understanding of Christianity as normative. This assumption, as Ninian Smart observed, was shared by much of the literature on sociology of religion.[26] In addition, astrologers' overwhelmingly pragmatic, rational justifications for their interest in astrology may be seen both as an attempt to locate a place for astrology outside religion, and as a rhetorical answer to astrology's scientific and religious critics' external definitions of astrology as 'superstition', 'substitute religion' or 'alternative belief'. In this sense, if astrology is a religion then it is a matter of practice rather than belief, of orthopraxy rather than orthodoxy: astrologers do not 'believe' in astrology, they 'do' it.

---

[23]   Primiano, 'Vernacular Religion'; Marion Bowman and Steven Sutcliffe, *Beyond New Age: Exploring Alternative Spirituality* (Edinburgh, 2000), p. 6; D. Yoder, 'Towards a Definition of Folk Religion', *Western Folklore*, 33/1 (1974), p. 14.

[24]   Bowman and Sutcliffe, *Beyond New Age*, p. 11.

[25]   Bowman and Sutcliffe, *Beyond New Age*, p. 5.

[26]   Ninian Smart, *The Phenomenon of Religion* (London, 1973), pp. 10, 34–5.

For the sake of argument, if astrology may be defined as a 'common', 'vernacular' or 'folk' religion then it may be the most popular of popular religions, to judge from the higher figures given for horoscope readership. I should make it clear, though, that I am not including in this definition what is commonly known as 'natural' astrology. I am therefore not considering any astrology, the rationale for which is derived primarily from the concept of physical relationships between humanity and the cosmos, and which is not based on the complex procedures of horoscope interpretation.[27] The boundaries between judicial astrology – in which the astrologer's judgement is central – and natural astrology are not watertight and may overlap, but the distinction is one which has to be recalled whenever conclusions are reached about what astrology as a whole is or is not: all such conclusions refer only to a part of the phenomenon of astrology. If we talk about astrology as New Age or as a form of religion, then, we are only talking about *some* astrology. Similarly, if astrologers' religious views and opinions about astrology provide support for the theory of 'privatisation', this only concerns *some* astrologers.

The question is raised, then, as to whether astrology, as a vernacular religion or as a New Age discipline, is a rival to Christianity. There were two schools of thought within theosophy after the 1890s, the 'Eastern' and the 'Western'.[28] The former was truer to Blavatsky's profound hostility to the Christian church but the latter, inspired by traditions of esoteric Christianity, emphasised Blavatsky's Gnosticism and respect for Christ as a great teacher. Most of the Aquarian Age and New Age literature forecasts the collapse of traditional church structures yet, for astrologers such as Rudhyar, influenced by the two most prominent Westerners, Bailey and Steiner, the coming of the New Age will bring a reform of Christianity rather than its destruction. According to this account, and true to the tradition of Swedenborgianism, the *parousia* will not take place as Christ's literal return, but as the triumph of 'Christ-consciousness' within every human being. It is this essentially humanistic Christianity which alarms astrology's evangelical Christian critics. It is arguable, therefore, that, while there is clear antipathy from astrologers to the established institutions both of the church and mainstream Christianity, the rivalry between the two may be seen within the broader historical context as a revival of the two-thousand-year-old clash between two Christianities, Gnostic and Catholic.[29] I need at this point to turn to my title, *Astrology and Popular Religion in the Modern West*, the 'modern West' being the operative words. Even though the bulk of my literature review and data is from the English-speaking world, the

---

[27]   See, for example, Michel Gauquelin, *Cosmic Clocks* (London, 1969; San Diego, 1982).

[28]   Joscelyn Godwin, *The Theosophical Enlightenment* (New York, 1994), p. 344.

[29]   By 'Catholic' I mean that form of Christianity whose dogma was outlined at the Council of Nicaea in 325 and subsequent church councils, accepting the doctrine of the Trinity and Christ's divine/human status. See Rosemary Goring (ed.), *Chambers Dictionary of Beliefs and Religions* (London, 1992), pp. 90, 370.

lineage of astrological ideas and theosophical context is thoroughly international. While, therefore, I have focused on the English-speaking theosophical astrologers Alan Leo and Dane Rudhyar, by the early 1900s the Theosophical Society was a global force. Certain striking similarities in my data showing common attitudes in Norway and Argentina, Serbia and Brazil, the UK and the US, point to a shared ideology, or at least a common pool of ideas. Only certain striking differences, such as the completely negative responses to the concept of the 'Goddess' in Argentina and Brazil, showed profound local variations.

Popper's historicist/activist model as applied to millenarianism also permits discussion of astrology's potential function. Astrology allows the prediction of a promised or threatened future, together with the possibility that the future is simultaneously determined and open to negotiation. If, following Malinowski, we wish to identify such intervention as magical, then we need to be sure that magic is not an endeavour set aside from daily life, but integral with it. Also, as we have seen, astrology's millenarian function is grounded in the Old Testament as well as classical cosmology, particularly Platonism and Stoicism. In this sense, under no circumstances is it 'new'. However, whether astrology is old or new has no bearing on its function. As an activist discipline its purpose may be to encourage individual decision-making within a framework which posits that the future both has a purpose and that, at least for New Age astrology *sensu stricto*, it is bound to represent an improvement over the present. As Hall argued, 'When fully manifest, whatever their contents, apocalyptic narratives work against the grain of existing social orders. They hold the power to reorganise cultural meanings.'[30] Raymond Williams, meanwhile, claimed that religion provides a source and shape for ideology and culture, and hence for social movements.[31] In turn, social experimentation, Robert Wuthnow claimed, has a strategic social value in encouraging innovation.[32] Astrology, with its dual historicist/activist emphasis on personal responsibility within a much greater context, in which individual character and destiny is linked to the changing qualities of time and the heavens, may then, as Michael York suggested, be not only the lingua franca of the New Age but a key organising philosophy of it.[33] However, in view of Irving's point that there are some intellectual 'New Agers' who are deeply hostile to astrology, astrology should be better called *a*, not *the*, organising principle.

The cultural context of astrology may therefore be considered in relation to other contemporary 'millenarianisms'. The hostility expressed by evangelical Christians to astrology may be seen as an objection to New Age views of the *parousia*, particularly the rejection of the Second Coming as a literal event, while

---

[30]   John R. Hall, *Apocalypse Observed: Religious Movements and Violence in North America, Europe, and Japan* (London and New York, 2000), p. 7.

[31]   Rhys H. Williams, 'Religion as Political Resource: Culture or Ideology?', *Journal for the Scientific Study of Religion*, 35/4 (1996), p. 377.

[32]   Robert Wuthnow, *The Consciousness Revolution* (Berkeley, 1976), p. 203.

[33]   Michael York, *Historical Dictionary of New Age Movements* (Lanham MD, 2003).

Aquarian Age literature, on the other hand, regards the established church as a failed symptom of the Piscean Age. Hostility to astrology from secular quarters may also be seen as a clash between different views of the future. For example, the positivist worldview has adopted the evolutionist theory of religion, which is, in turn a manifestation of the theory of progress. Following Bury and Baillie, belief in progress may consequently be defined as a modern species of millenarianism.[34] In addition, positivism itself originated in the revolutionary millenarian ideology of August Comte.[35] Karl Popper argued on similar lines, pointing out that the emphasis on prediction in the social sciences may be interpreted as a variety of historicism.[36] Positivism's hostility to New Age astrology can therefore be based on its competing views of evolution and humanity's future development. Christian, New Age and positivist models of history may all, therefore, be forms of what Collingwood defined as quasi-history; each has its own prophecy of the future to champion and proceeds partly by attacking its rivals.[37] This clash of millenarianisms may itself be a feature of modernity. As Baldwin et al. argued,

> It is one of the great paradoxes of modernity that, on the one hand, time is organised according to an objective, scientific model, and, on the other, everyday life fragments into multiple cultures of time. This is perhaps explained by the revolutionary nature of modernity, which sweeps away old orders in the name of the new, but which is constantly creating new forms of culture which contest a single, normative standard.[38]

The question arises then, as to whether astrology's survival in the modern world is anachronistic. This question was addressed by challenging the positivist argument that 'belief' as a whole, and hence belief in astrology, is itself anachronistic. The argument is fundamentally an epistemological one and concerns the issue of who has the right to pronounce on matters of truth. The positivist view that only modern science can make such declarations is deeply flawed. I have also argued that contemporary popular astrology should be understood in terms of continuity with the early modern period, the seventeenth century, rather than a revival of a lost tradition. In this sense then, popular astrology is a defining condition of the vernacular modern worldview rather than an eruption into it of an extinct superstition.

---

[34]   J.B. Bury, *The Idea of Progress: An Inquiry into its Growth and Origins* (London, 1932), pp. 1–36; John Baillie, *The Belief in Progress* (London, Glasgow and Toronto, 1951), pp. 64–5.

[35]   Nicholas Campion, *The Great Year: Astrology, Millenarianism and History in the Western Tradition* (London, 1994), pp. 429–34.

[36]   Karl Popper, *The Open Society and its Enemies*, rev. edn (2 vols, London and New York, 1986), pp. 12–13.

[37]   R.G. Collingwood, *The Idea of History* (Oxford, 1946), pp. 14–15, 18.

[38]   Elaine Baldwin et al., *Introducing Cultural Studies* (London, 1999), pp. 155–6.

This takes us into a consideration of astrology's location in the modern world. Now, there is a prevailing assumption by both academic commentators and some astrologers that astrology belongs to the postmodern, a proposition which may be relevant in some instances but is certainly not appropriate in all cases.[39] But the connection is more usually assumed than argued with evidence. For example, looking at the context within which astrology thrives, Hess considers the New Age movement as a whole to be postmodern although he offers no explanation for this.[40] Paul Heelas, meanwhile, considered the New Age movement in its counter-cultural aspects, and hence astrology, which he includes as New Age, as an aspect of 'modernity in crisis'.[41] However, he neither defines modernity nor explains why the New Age might not in fact be an aspect of modernism. Robert Bellah, however, did point to the crisis in modernity and the consequent shift in spirituality, which he identified as arising, in the US at least, from 'the massive erosion of the legitimacy of American institutions – business, government, education, the churches, the family'.[42] The sociologists of science John Bauer and Martin Durant discussed the matter in their study of astrology, agreeing with Heelas's view that astrology is encouraged by the crisis of late modernity.[43]

Of course, by 'late modernity' Bauer and Durant mean, as did Heelas, that phase of modernity-in-crisis which is sometimes synonymous with postmodernism. The problem, though, is that modernity, modernism, postmodernity and postmodernism are not clear-cut concepts: are they chronological periods and, if so, of what duration, or are they ideological positions and, if so, what are their claims? Unfortunately, the very use of terms such as 'modern' and 'postmodern' encourage scholars to fall into the trap of categorisation: this thing is modern, that is post-modern, as if such distinctions can possibly be made in any other than a rigidly binary universe. When we look at human society with all its rich, messy complexity, such theoretical boxes reduce clarity rather than enhance it. New Age culture may therefore be postmodern in some respects, modern in others. As Hexham and Poewe pointed out, the counter-culture of the 1960s contained elements of both modernism and postmodernism.[44] And so it is with astrology.[45]

---

[39] Nicholas Campion, 'Astrology's Place in Historical Periodisation: Modern, Premodern or Postmodern?', in Nicholas Campion and Liz Greene (eds), *Astrologies* (Lampeter, 2010), pp. 217–54.

[40] David J. Hess, *Science in the New Age: The Paranormal, Its Defenders and Debunkers and American Culture* (Madison WI, 1993), p. 36.

[41] Paul Heelas, *The New Age Movement* (Oxford, 1996), pp. 23, 34, 138.

[42] Robert N. Bellah, 'New Religious Consciousness and the Crisis in Modernity', in Charles Glock and Robert N. Bellah, *The New Religious Consciousness* (Berkeley, 1976), p. 333.

[43] Bauer and Durant, 'British Public Perceptions', p. 69.

[44] Irving Hexham and Karla Poewe, *New Religions as Global Cultures* (Boulder CO, 1997), pp. 149–51.

[45] Campion, 'Astrology's Place'.

Then, we should turn our attention to the historiography of modernism, the attempt to show that the postmodern, including alternative spiritualities, is at fault for deviating from the Enlightenment inheritance. First we need to demolish, as R.G. Collingwood did, the over-simplified view of eighteenth-century intellectual culture as characterised by brave scientists or cool, rational encyclopaedists.[46] As Antoine Faivre and Karen-Claire Voss argued, belief in astrology was rather more a part of an historical 'continuation of trends of thought and spirituality, rather than a reaction against modernity'.[47] Joscelyn Godwin inferred, in the use of the term 'Theosophical Enlightenment', that the eighteenth-century advocates of 'alternative spiritualities' were outside the mainstream Enlightenment, so we can turn to Dorinda Outram, who has argued that the paganism of the French Enlightenment, which is so important to the foundation of Aquarian and New Age ideas, is part of the Enlightenment, not separate from it.[48] As Gillian Bennett argued, the notion that astrology's existence in the modern world is somehow incompatible with post-Enlightenment rationalism is based on a misunderstanding of popular belief.[49] In the sense that New Age astrology is a peculiarly twentieth-century innovation, then, following Hanegraaff's arguments on New Age culture's intellectual lineage, it may be seen in part as a product of Enlightenment secularisation. Some who are sympathetic to astrology encourage its definition as postmodern on the grounds that postmodernism's espousal of multiple truths accommodates astrology's pluralistic nature.[50] Some astrologers who have addressed the matter agree, finding in postmodernism liberation from the reliance on restrictive, reductionist and positivist science which is supposedly a feature of modernity and which makes it difficult for astrology's voice to be heard.[51] If modernism is characterised by the self-confident creation of the future and if modernists think 'compulsively about the New ... [try] to watch its coming into being and look for "new worlds"', as Jameson put it, then astrologers such as Alan

---

[46]   R.G. Collingwood, *An Essay on Metaphysics*, rev. edn (Oxford, 1998).

[47]   Antoine Faivre and Karen-Claire Voss, 'Western Esotericism and the Science of Religions', *Numen*, 42/1 (1995), p. 53.

[48]   Godwin, *The Theosophical Enlightenment*; Dorinda Outram, *The Enlightenment* (Cambridge, 1995), pp. 31–46.

[49]   Gillian Bennett, *Traditions of Belief: Women, Folklore and the Supernatural Today* (London, 1987), pp. 24–5.

[50]   Patrick Curry, 'Astrology: From Pagan to Postmodern?', *Astrological Journal*, 36/1 (1994).

[51]   Gerry Goddard, 'Beyond a Post-Modern Astrology', at http://www.islandastrology. net/resp-can.html>, accessed 20 January 2007; Robert Hand, 'Towards a Post-Modern Astrology', AstroDienst, at <http://www.astro.com/astrology/in_postmodern_e.htm>, accessed 20 January 2007; Candy Hillenbrand, 'An Archaic Astrology Cast Adrift in a Post-Modern World', at <http://www.aplaceinspace.net/Pages/CandyPostmodern.html>, accessed 20 January 2007; Glenn Perry, 'The New Paradigm and Postmodern Astrology', International Forum on New Science, University of Fort Collins, Colorado, 27 September 1991, at <http://www.aaperry.com/index.asp?pgid=21>, accessed 20 January 2007.

Leo and Dane Rudhyar were thorough-going modernists.[52] And in this sense, we should point out, modernism is post-millennial in its assumption that the promised utopia is emerging out of the present without any requirement for an apocalyptic catastrophe.

Patrick Curry took a similar line, writing of the esoteric and psychological astrology which was developed at the beginning of the twentieth century that, 'Far from being an irrational aberration, the new occult astrology was perfectly suited to the capitalism and individualism of the age'.[53] But then he also argues that astrology is postmodern in that, in the astrological consultation, pluralism reigns: 'The astrologer and/or the client', he wrote, 'bring a complex set of values, assumptions, problems and strategies to *every* situation, a situation which can never be repeated and so cannot represent an absolute truth'.[54] Zygmunt Bauman recognised the problem of defining postmodernism when he claimed that the term means different things to different people and 'perhaps more than anything else [it is] a state of mind'.[55] Bauman lets us out of the modern/postmodern trap. Just as 'New Age' as an emblem can be applied to ideas and behaviour without implying anything about their essential nature, so can 'postmodern'. The question largely depends on our particular viewpoint. We might stand back from astrology as a whole and be struck by the diversity of competing voices, of multiple narratives, and this may look postmodern. However, Jean-François Lyotard, who did so much to define modernism, and characterised it as marked by 'grand narratives', the belief in universal truths, comes closer to describing modern astrology.[56] But, if each school of astrology is proclaiming a grand narrative in which astrology can explain or, at least, comment on, absolutely everything known to humanity, and some of those schools assume that they are engaged in creating a better world, we see unabashed modernism: one of modernity's key features, aside from a belief in the creation of a new world, is the belief in a set of absolute criteria by which judgements can be made and certainty arrived at.[57] It is difficult to find grander, more confident, narratives than those set out by Alan Leo and Dane Rudhyar. And then we can turn to a variety of sociological argument, promoted by Grace Davie and others, that religious pluralism is not a postmodern reaction to modernity but is actually a feature of modernity. However we phrase the question, astrology is not part of a postmodern aberration, a symptom of a failure to cope with modernity, a

---

[52] Frederic Jameson, *Postmodernism, or, the Cultural Logic of Late Capitalism* (London and New York, 1991), p. ix.

[53] Patrick Curry, *A Confusion of Prophets: Victorian and Edwardian Astrology* (London, 1992), p. 132.

[54] Willis and Curry, *Astrology, Science and Culture*, p. 97.

[55] Zygmunt Bauman, *Intimations of Postmodernity* (London, 1992), p. vii.

[56] Jean-François Lyotard, *The Postmodern Condition: A Report on Knowledge* (Manchester, 1985), p. xxiii.

[57] Steven Best and Douglas Kellner, *Postmodern Theory: Critical Interrogations* (London, 1991), p. 161.

bizarre relic from a superstitious past, as the scientific modernists would put it, but a normal part of the modern world. The evidence for the proposition that astrology is at odds with the modern world is just is not there.

That astrology maybe modern, at least in its New Age guise, tells us nothing about the truth of its claims, only that there is no necessary contradiction between it and modernity. But it does enable us to begin to find a position when we can at least assess what its practitioners are doing, and how they relate to contemporary culture. When we consider the examination of astrology I have set out in this book, then there is indeed a certain postmodern relativism in astrologers' rhetoric – the widespread assertion, for example, that the techniques of astrological interpretation are purely matters of convenience with no intrinsic, objective value. Yet time and time again, with a few notable examples, the representatives of particular schools of thought in astrology, whether the 'traditionalists', supporters of divination, or advocates of science or psychology, assert the absolute truth of their positions. Theirs is the grand narrative of cosmic truth. And how much more true this is of those followers of Leo and Rudhyar for whom the creation of a new world, to which everyone, with no exceptions, will be subject, is the overwhelming priority. If we have to reach a conclusion, we could concede that astrology's existence is evidence of a certain postmodern worldview in which grand narratives such as progress and science are no longer taken for granted. However, how do we then explain that astrology flourished when modernity, supposedly, was at its height, or that it is impossible to demonstrate that the alleged advent of postmodernity has resulted in an increase in its popularity? Even if we accept the doubtful concept of a shift from modernity to postmodernity, there is no demonstrable correlation with any supposed increase in astrology's popularity. Besides, in spite of astrologers' epistemological individualism, there is no greater grand narrative than the proposition that astrology can explain *everything*.

But if some astrologers are overwhelmingly modernists in their promotion of the modern and their adherence to the metanarrative of cosmic truth, my research also shows significant subtexts which can clearly be described as postmodern, such as the finding that a significant number regard the techniques of astrological interpretation as a matter of subjective convenience ('each astrologer uses the techniques which work for them'). The New Age in this sense is far more than the emblem which can be used, almost at random, to describe cultural ideas and behaviour. It is immediate, important and urgent. Dane Rudhyar's New Age astrology presupposes an eschaton *of* history in that eventually the entire material cosmos will disappear and become pure spirit, but both he and Leo were more concerned with the imminent eschaton *in* history – the transition to the Aquarian New Age. And both saw as essential for this an eschaton *of the mind*, an internal transformation, necessary for this historical shift to proceed peacefully.

Astrology exists within a view of modernity in which religion and spirituality are not dying out, as traditional secularisation theory claims, but diversifying. Its survival in the twenty-first century is therefore not an anomaly to be explained, but an aspect of the modern world to be examined on its own terms. As Bowman and Sutcliffe wrote of New Age culture, the 'alternative' may be now better seen as 'mainstream'.[58] And as Christopher Partridge has pointed out, it is no longer enough to consider a range of practices such as astrology as exotic or deviant.[59] The major part of the astrology of the modern West is not part of the supposed crisis of late modernity. It is an integral part of modernity itself. The implications are wider than the narrow concerns of modern astrology, though. On the broader level, we should abandon any notion that practitioners or 'believers' in the esoteric, 'alternative spiritualities' or New Age disciplines are somehow excluded from the modern world, standing outside the general flow of history. This is essential if we are to understand the diversity of contemporary spiritual culture. As it is, an over-emphasis on labels allows evidence to be missed, manipulated or misinterpreted. We are in need of a dose of genuine classical scepticism; we should cultivate more doubt concerning the easy acceptance of emblems such as New Age and astrology, science, religion and secularity, or modernity and postmodernity.

---

[58] Bowman and Sutcliffe, *Beyond New Age*, p. 11.

[59] Partridge, *The Re-Enchantment of the West*, vol. 1, p. 25.

Bibliography

Abell, George O., 'Astrology', in George O. Abell and Barry Singer (eds), *Science and the Paranormal: Probing the Existence of the Supernatural* (London: Junction, 1981).

Abu Ma'shar, *On Historical Astrology: The Book of Religions and Dynasties (On the Great Conjunctions)*, eds and trans. Keiji Yamamoto and Charles Burnett (2 vols, Leiden: Brill, 2000).

Addey, John, *Astrology Reborn* (London: Faculty of Astrological Studies, 1971).

Adorno, Theodor, *The Stars Down to Earth* (London: Routledge, 1994 [1953]).

——, Else Frenkel-Brunswick, Daniel J. Levinson and R. Nevitt Sanford, *The Authoritarian Personality*, abr. edn (New York and London: Norton, 1982 [1950]).

Alcock, James E., *Parapsychology: Science or Magic? A Psychological Perspective* (Oxford: Pergamon, 1981).

Allchin, Douglas, 'Pseudohistory and Pseudoscience', *Science and Education*, 13 (2004): 179–95.

Amano, J. Yutaka, and Norman L. Geisler, *The Infiltration of the New Age* (Wheaton IL: Tyndale House, 1989).

Amis, Martin, *The Information* (London: HarperCollins, 1996).

Anderson, Benedict, *Imagined Communities* (London: Verso, 2006).

Anderson, Peter, *Satan's Snare: The Influence of the Occult* (Welwyn, Hertfordshire: Evangelical Press, 1988).

Ando, Clifford, *The Matter of the Gods* (Berkeley: University of California Press, 2008).

Appleyard, Brian, 'Divide and rule', *Sunday Times*, Culture section, 29 November 2009, pp. 8–9.

——, 'Bryan Appleyard meets Steven Pinker', *Sunday Times*, News Review, 14 October 2007, p. 5.5.

Arroyo, Stephen, *Astrology, Karma and Transformation: The Inner Dimensions of the Birth Chart* (Davis CA: CRCS, 1978).

——, *Astrology, Psychology and the Four Elements: An Energy Approach to Astrology and its Use in the Counselling Arts* (Davis CA: CRCS, 1975).

Astrological Association, 'AA Response to Anti-Astrology Propaganda', at <http://astrologicalassociation.blogspot.com/2011/01/aa-response-to-anti-astrology.html>.

Astrology (Richmond: Reachout Trust, n.d.).

Atkins, Anne, 'The Message', BBC Radio 4, 4 June 1999.

Augustine (Saint), *City of God*, trans. Henry Bettenson (Harmondsworth: Penguin, 1972).

Babbage, D.R., and H.R. Ronan, 'Philosophical Worldview and Personality Factors in Traditional and Social Scientists: Studying the World in our own Image', *Personality and Individual Differences*, 28 (2000): 405–20.

Bailey, Alice A., *Esoteric Astrology* (London: Lucis Press, 1973 [1951]).

——, 'The Coming World Order', in Alice A. Bailey, *The Externalisation of the Hierarchy* (New York: Lucis, 1957 [1940]).

——, 'Seed Groups in the New Age', in Alice A. Bailey, *The Externalisation of the Hierarchy* (New York: Lucis, 1957 [1937]).

——, 'The Period of Transition', in Alice A. Bailey, *The Externalisation of the Hierarchy* (New York: Lucis, 1957 [1934]).

——, *Education in the New Age*, 2nd edn (London: Lucis, 1954).

——, *The Unfinished Autobiography* (London; Lucis, 1951).

——, *The Destiny of the Nations* (New York: Lucis, 1949).

——, *The Reappearance of the Christ* (New York: Lucis, 1948).

——, *Initiation, Human and Solar* (London: John M. Watkins, 1933 [1922]).

——, *A Treatise on Cosmic Fire* (London: Lucis, 1925).

Baillie, John, *The Belief in Progress* (London, Glasgow, Toronto: Oxford University Press, 1951).

Baldwin, Elaine, Brian Longhurst, Scott McCracken, Miles Ogborn and Greg Smith, *Introducing Cultural Studies* (London: Prentice Hall Europe, 1999).

Bann, Stephen, *The Inventions of History: Essays on the Representation of the Past* (Manchester: Manchester University Press, 1990).

Barclay, Olivia, 'Memoirs of a Horary Astrology. Chapter 4', *Astrology Quarterly*, 70/1 (1999/2000): 42–50.

——, 'Will the Astronauts have to Abandon the Mir Space Station?: A Horary Judgement', *Astrological Journal*, 41/6 (1999): 30–2.

——, 'Memoirs of a Horary Astrology. Chapter 3', *Astrology Quarterly*, 69/4 (1999): 23–8.

——, 'Memoirs of a Horary Astrology. Chapter 2', *Astrology Quarterly*, 69/3 (1999): 36–44.

——, 'Memoirs of a Horary Astrology. Chapter 1', *Astrology Quarterly*, 69/1 (1998/99): 6–11.

——, *Horary Astrology Rediscovered* (West Chester PA: Whitford, 1990).

Barker, Eileen, 'New Religions and New Religiosity', in Eileen Barker and Margot Warburg (eds), *New Religions and New Religiosity* (Aarhus: Aarhus University Press, 2001).

Basil, Robert, 'New Age Thinking', in Gordon Stein (ed.), *The Encyclopaedia of the Paranormal* (Amherst NY: Prometheus, 1996).

Bastedo, Ralph W., 'An Empirical Test of Popular Astrology', *Skeptical Inquirer*, 3/1 (1978): 17–38.

Bauer, John, and Martin Durant, 'British Public Perceptions of Astrology: An Approach from the Sociology of Knowledge', *Culture and Cosmos*, 1/1 (1997): 55–72.

Bauman, Zygmunt, *Intimations of Postmodernity* (London: Routledge, 1992).

Beattie, John, *Other Cultures: Aims, Methods and Achievements in Social Anthropology* (London: Routledge, 1989).

Bellah, Robert N., 'New Religious Consciousness and the Crisis in Modernity', in Charles Glock and Robert N. Bellah, *The New Religious Consciousness* (Berkeley: University of California Press, 1976).

Belter, Ronald, and Erwin H. Brinkmann, 'Construct Validity of the Nowicki-Strickland Locus of Control Scale for Children', *Psychological Reports*, 48 (1981): 427–32.

Bennett, Gillian, *Traditions of Belief: Women, Folklore and the Supernatural Today* (London: Penguin, 1987).

Berger, Peter, *The Sacred Canopy: Elements of a Sociological Theory of Religion* (New York: Anchor, 1969).

Besant, Annie, 'An Appreciation', in Bessie Leo, *The Life and Work of Alan Leo* (London: Modern Astrology, 1919).

Best, Steven, and Douglas Kellner, *Postmodern Theory: Critical Interrogations* (London: Macmillan, 1991).

Bilgrave, Dyer P., and Robert H. Deluty, 'Religious Beliefs and Therapeutic Orientations of Clinical and Counselling Psychologists', *Journal for the Scientific Study of Religion*, 37/2 (1998): 329–49.

Bird, Alison, 'Astrology in Education: An Ethnography', DPhil thesis, University of Sussex, 2006.

Blackmore, Susan, *The Meme Machine* (Oxford: Oxford University Press, 1999).

—— , 'Are Women More Sheepish? Gender Differences in Belief in the Paranormal', in E. Coly and R. White (eds), *Women and Parapsychology* (New York, 1994), pp. 68–89.

—— and Marianne Seebold, 'The Effect of Horoscopes on Women's Relationships', *Correlation*, 19/2 (2000–01): 14–23.

Blake, William, 'Milton', in Geoffrey Keynes (ed.), *Complete Writings* (Oxford: Oxford University Press, 1971).

Blavatsky, H.P., *The Secret Doctrine* (2 vols, Los Angeles: The Theosophy Company, 1982, facs. of 1888 edn).

—— , *Isis Unveiled* (2 vols, Pasadena: Theosophical University Press, 1976, facs. of 1877 edn).

Bloom, William, *The New Age: An Anthology of Essential Writings* (London: Rider, 1991).

Bogart, Greg, 'Rudhyar's Astrology in Plain Language', *International Astrologer*, 31/4 (2002): 18–31.

Boivin, Jackie, 'Pat Harris, "Astrology and Fertility: Where is the Evidence?"', *Sexuality, Reproduction and Menopause*, 7/2 (2009), available online at <http://www.srm-ejournal.com/>, accessed 3 September 2011.

Bok, Bart J., and Margaret W. Mayall, 'Scientists Look at Astrology', *Scientific Monthly*, 52 (1941): 233–44.

Bok, Bart J., Lawrence E. Jerome and Paul Kurtz, 'Objections to Astrology: A Statement by 186 Leading Scientists', *Humanist*, 35/5 (1975): 4–6.

Bonatti, Guido, 'The One Hundred and Forty-Six Considerations of the Famous Astrologer Guido Bonatus', trans. Henry Coley, in *The Astrologer's Guide* (London: Regulus, 1986 [1886]).

Bowles, John A., 'Astrology and the Skeptics', *AFAN Newsletter*, Winter (2001): 9–19.

Bowman, Marion, and Steven Sutcliffe, *Beyond New Age: Exploring Alternative Spirituality* (Edinburgh: Edinburgh University Press, 2000).

Boyce, Mary, *Zoroastrians: Their Religious Beliefs and Practices* (London and New York: Routledge & Kegan Paul, 1987).

Braden, William, *The Age of Aquarius: Technology and the Cultural Revolution* (London: Eyre & Spottiswoode, 1971).

Brau, Jean-Louis, Helen Weaver and Allan Edmunds, *Larousse Encyclopaedia of Astrology* (New York: Plume, 1982).

Brierly, Peter (ed.), *UK Christian Handbook: Religious Trends no 3, 2002/3* (London: Christian Research, 2001).

British Astrological and Psychic Society, Facebook, accessed 15 June 2011.

Broch, Henri, 'Save our Science: The Struggle for Reason at the University', *Skeptical Inquirer*, 24/3 (2000): 34–9.

Brooke, John L., *The Refiner's Fire: The Making of Mormon Cosmology, 1644–1844* (Cambridge: Cambridge University Press, 1996).

Bruce, Steve, *Religion in Modern Britain* (Oxford: Oxford University Press, 1995).

Bryman, Alan, *Quantity and Quality in Social Research* (London and New York: Routledge, 2001 [1988]).

Bunge, Mario, 'Absolute Skepticism Equals Negative Dogmatism', *Skeptical Inquirer*, 24/4 (2000): 34–6.

Burkeman, Oliver, 'New age America is entranced by Obama's electoral aura', *The Guardian*, G2, 3 July 2008, p. 2.

Burnett, Charles, 'The Certitude of Astrology: The Scientific Methodology of al-Qabīṣī and abū Ma'shar', *Early Science and Medicine*, 7/3 (2002): 198–213.

Bury, J.B., *The Idea of Progress: An Inquiry into its Growth and Origins* (London: Macmillan, 1932).

Caird, Dale, and Henry G. Law, 'Non-Conventional Beliefs: Their Structure and Measurement', *Journal for the Scientific Study of Religion*, 21/2 (1982): 152–63.

Campbell, Bruce H., *Ancient Wisdom Revived: A History of the Theosophical Movement* (Berkeley: University of California Press, 1980).

Campion, Nicholas, *Astrology and Cosmology in the World's Religions* (New York: New York University Press, 2012).

——, 'What do Astrologers Believe about Astrology?', *Astrological Journal*, 54/2 (forthcoming, 2012).

——, 'The Extent of Contemporary Belief in Astrology in the UK and USA: A Literature Review', *Correlation* (forthcoming, 2012).

——, 'The 2012 Mayan Calendar Prophecies in the Context of the Western Millenarian Tradition', in Clive Ruggles (ed.), *Archaeoastronomy and Ethnoastronomy: Building Bridges between Cultures*, Proceedings of International Astronomy Union Symposium 278 (Cambridge: Cambridge University Press, 2011), pp. 249 54.

——, 'Is Astrology a Symbolic Language?', paper presented to the Ninth Annual Sophia Centre Conference, Bath, 4–5 June 2011.

——, 'Astrology's Place in Historical Periodisation: Modern, Premodern or Postmodern?', in *Astrologies: Plurality and Diversity*, eds Nicholas Campion and Liz Greene (Lampeter: Sophia Centre, 2010), pp. 217–54.

——, *A History of Western Astrology* (2 vols, London: Continuum, 2009).

——, 'Astrology's Role in New Age Culture: A Research Note', *Culture and Cosmos*, 13/2 (2009): pp. 87–94.

——, 'Horoscopes and Popular Culture', in Bob Franklin (ed.), *Pulling Newspapers Apart: Analysing Print Journalism* (Oxford: Routledge, 2008).

——, *What do Astrologers Believe?* (Oxford: Granta, 2006).

——, 'Prophecy, Cosmology and the New Age Movement: The Extent and Nature of Contemporary Belief in Astrology', PhD thesis, University of the West of England, 2004.

——, 'Do Astrologers Have to Believe in Astrology?', *Sceptic*, 15/2 (2002): 20–2.

——, 'The "Mars effect" that refuses to go away', *Independent*, Thursday Review, 21 October 1999, p. 7.

——, *The Great Year: Astrology, Millenarianism and History in the Western Tradition* (London: Penguin, 1994).

——, 'Editorial', *Astrological Journal*, 36/1 (1994): 1–5.

—— and Liz Greene, *Astrologies: Plurality and Diversity*, Proceedings of the Eighth Annual Sophia Centre Conference, June 2010 (Lampeter: Sophia Centre, 2011).

Cantrill, Hadley, 'Foreword', in Stanley L. Payne, *The Art of Asking Questions* (Princeton: Princeton University Press, 1980 [1951]).

Capp, Bernard, *Astrology and the Popular Press: English Almanacs 1500–1800* (London and Boston: Faber & Faber, 1979).

Carey, Hilary, *Courting Disaster: Astrology at the English Court and University in the Later Middle Ages* (London: Macmillan, 1992).

Carlson, Shawn, 'A Double-Blind Test of Astrology', *Nature*, 318 (1985): 419–25.

Carter Charles, *An Encyclopaedia of Psychological Astrology* (London: Theosophical Publishing House, 1977 [1924]).

——, *An Introduction to Political Astrology* (London: Fowler, 1951).

——, *The Zodiac and the Soul* (London: Theosophical Publishing House, 1948).

——, 'Editorial', *Astrology*, 21/2 (1947): 111–13.

——, 'Editorial', *Astrology*, 13/1 (1939): 1–3.

——, 'Editorial', *Astrology*, 12/1 (1938): 1–3.

Cassidy, (Rev.) Lawrence, 'The Believing Christian as a Dedicated Astrologer', *Astrology Quarterly*, 64/3 (1994): 3–13.

Cassirer, Ernst, *The Myth of the State* (New Haven and London: Yale University Press, 1967).

Catechism of the Catholic Church 1994: Divination and magic. Online at <http://www.usccb.org/catechism/text/pt3sect2chpt1.shtml>, accessed 30 July 2011.

Caton, Gary, 'Uranus in Pisces: Birthing the New Age', *NCGR Memberletter*, August/September (2002): 4–5, 20.

Chance, J. Bradley, *Jerusalem, the Temple, and the New Age in Luke-Acts* (Macon GA: Mercer University Press, 1988).

Chandler, Russell, *Understanding the New Age* (Milton Keynes: Word 1989).

Cheiro, *The Book of World Predictions* (London: Herbert Jenkins, 1931 [1925]).

——, *When Were You Born?* (London: Herbert Jenkins, 1913).

Christiansen, Arthur, *Headlines all my Life* (London: Heinemann, 1961).

Chryssides, George, *Exploring New Religions* (London: Cassell, 1999).

Clayton, Richard R., and James W. Gladden, 'The Five Dimensions of Religiosity: Toward Demythologizing a Sacred Artefact', *Journal for the Scientific Study of Religion*, 13 (1974): 135–43.

Cohn, Norman, *Cosmos, Chaos and the World to Come: The Ancient Roots of Apocalyptic Faith* (New Haven and London: Yale University Press, 1993).

——, *The Pursuit of the Millennium* (London: Paladin, 1970).

Cole, Michael, Jim Graham, Tony Higton and David Lewis, *What is the New Age?* (London: Hodder & Stoughton, 1990).

Collingwood, R.G., *An Essay on Metaphysics*, rev. edn (Oxford: Clarendon Press, 1998).

——, *The Idea of History* (Oxford: Clarendon Press, 1946).

Collins, J.E., and Carole Wilson, 'Astrology and Extra-Corporeal Fertilization', *Astrological Journal*, 21/3 (1980): 124–33.

Condorcet, Marquis de, *Sketch for a Historical Picture of the Progress of the Human Mind*, trans. June Barraclough (London: Weidenfeld & Nicholson, 1955 [Paris, 1795]).

Connor, Steve, 'Scientists identify "the sweet tooth gene"', *Independent*, 23 April 2001, p. 3.

——, 'Human evolution is heading in a new direction claims study into childbirth', *Independent*, 23 April 2001, p. 9.

Costello, Bridget, 'Astrology in Action: Culture and Status in Unsettled Lives', PhD thesis, University of Pennsylvania, 2006.

Cox, Brian, 'Science: A Challenge to TV Orthodoxy', Huw Wheldon Lecture 2010, <http://www.youtube.com/watch?v=QPrdK4hWffo>, accessed 3 September 2011.

Cox, David, *'I Don't Need to Believe in God – I Know'* (London: Guild of Pastoral Psychology, 1985).

Crowe, Richard A., 'Astrology and the Scientific Method', *Psychological Reports*, 67 (1990): 163–91.

Culver, Roger B., and Philip A. Ianna, *Astrology: True or False? A Scientific Evaluation*, rev. edn (Buffalo NY: Prometheus, 1988).

Cumont, Franz, *Astrology among the Greeks and Romans* (New York: Dover, 1960 [1912]).

Cunningham, Donna, *An Astrological Guide to Self-Awareness* (Reno: CRCS, 1978).

Curry, Patrick, 'Astrology: From Pagan to Postmodern?' *Astrological Journal*, 36/1 (1994): 69–75.

——, *A Confusion of Prophets: Victorian and Edwardian Astrology* (London: Collins & Brown, 1992).

——, *Prophecy and Power: Astrology in Early Modern England* (Oxford: Polity, 1989).

——, Nicholas Campion and Jacques Halbronn, *La vie astrologique il y a cent ans* (Paris: Edition Guy Trédaniel, 1992).

Curtiss, Frank Homer, *The Message of Aquaria: The Significance and Mission of the Aquarian Age* (San Francisco: Curtiss Philosophic Book Co., 1921).

Dambrun, Michael, 'Belief in Paranormal Determinism as a Source of Prejudice Towards Disadvantaged Groups: "The Dark Side of Stars"', *Social Behaviour and Personality*, 32/1 (2004): 627–36.

Davie, Grace, *Religion in Britain since 1945* (Oxford: Blackwell, 1994).

Dawkins, Richard, *Unweaving the Rainbow* (London: Penguin, 1998).

——, 'Newsnight', BBC2, 3 January 1996.

Dean, Geoffrey, 'Does Astrology need to be True?', in Kendrick Frazier (ed.), *The Hundredth Monkey and Other Paradigms of the Paranormal* (Amherst NY: Prometheus, 1992).

——, 'Discourse for Key Topic 4: Astrology and Human Judgement', *Correlation*, 17/2 (1998/99): 24–71.

—— and Ivan Kelly, 'Is Astrology Relevant to Consciousness and Psi?', *Journal of Consciousness Studies*, 10/6–7 (2003): 175–98.

—— and Arthur Mather, 'Sun Sign Columns: An Armchair Invitation', *Astrological Journal*, 38/3 (1996): 143–55.

—— and Arthur Mather, *Recent Advances in Natal Astrology: A Critical Review 1900–1976* (Subiaco, Australia: Analogic, 1977).

——, Ivan Kelly and Arthur Mather, 'Astrology', in Gordon Stein (ed.), *The Encyclopaedia of the Paranormal* (Amherst NY: Prometheus, 1996).

'A Degree in Astrology: A Long-Standing Dream Comes True', *The Kepler College of Astrological Arts and Sciences, Notes*, 1/4 (1994).

Desroche, Henri, *The Sociology of Hope* (London: Routledge & Kegan Paul, 1979).

Devlin, Hannah, 'School finds the secret of exam success: let teenagers have a lie-in', *Times*, 27 August 2011, p. 4.

Douglas, Ed, 'Stephen Pinker: the mind reader', *Guardian*, Saturday Review, 6 November 1999, pp. 6–7.

Doward, James, 'Church attendance "to fall by 90%"', *Observer*, 21 December 2008, at <http://www.guardian.co.uk/world/2008/dec/21/anglicanism-religion>, accessed 5 November 2009.

Downing, Mary, 'Media Watch – "Astrology is rubbish, says new research"', 18 August 2003, *AFAN email digest*, 530 (2003).

Draper, Derek, 'I used to live a shallow life', *Times*, 21 February 2001, p. 3.

Durkheim, Emile, *The Elementary Forms of Religious Life*, trans. Karen E. Fields (New York: Free Press, 1995 [1912]).

Eccles, Bernard, 'Astrology in England in the Twenty-First Century', *Journal for the Study of Religion, Nature and Culture*, 1/2 (2007): 237–58.

——, 'The Death of Astrology', paper presented to the Astrological Association of Great Britain conference, Plymouth, August, 1999.

——, 'The Radical Nature of Sun-Sign Astrology', *Astrological Journal*, 38/6 (September/October 1996): 306–10.

Edwards, Allen L., *Techniques of Attitude Scale Construction* (New York: Appleton-Century-Crofts, 1957).

Eliade, Mircea, *Occultism, Witchcraft and Cultural Fashions* (Chicago: University of Chicago Press, 1976).

——, *The Sacred and the Profane: The Nature of Religion* (New York: Harcourt, Brace Jovanovich, 1959).

——, *The Myth of the Eternal Return or, Cosmos and History* (Princeton: Princeton University Press, 1954).

Elliot, Roger, 'Notes', *Astrological Journal*, 32/2 (March/April 1990): 87–8.

Elwell, Dennis, *Cosmic Loom: The New Science of Astrology* (London: Unwin Hyman, 1987).

——, 'Astrology: An Alternative Reality', *Astrological Journal*, 28/4 (1986): 143–9.

Ertel, Suitbert, and Kenneth Irving, *The Tenacious Mars Effect* (London: Urania Trust, 1996).

'Esther', Esther Rantzen Discussion programme, BBC1, 1997, n.d.

Evans-Pritchard, E.E., *Social Anthropology* (London: Cohen & West, 1967 [1951]).

Eysenck, Hans, and David Nias, *Astrology: Science or Superstition?* (London: Pelican, 1982).

Faivre, Antoine, and Karen-Claire Voss, 'Western Esotericism and the Science of Religions', *Numen*, 42/1 (1995): 53.

Farnell, Kim, *Flirting with the Zodiac* (Bournemouth: Wessex Astrologer, 2007).

——, *The Astral Tramp: A Biography of Sepharial* (London: Ascella, 1998).

Fefer, Mark D., 'Battle of the stars: if religion is, why isn't astrology a legitimate subject for study?', *Seattle Weekly*, 23–29 August 2001, at <http://www.seattleweekly.com/features/0134/news-fefer2.shtml>, accessed 6 September 2001.

——, 'Learning with the stars: inside the country's first college of astrology', *Seattle Weekly*, 23–29 August 2001, at <http://www.seattleweekly.com/features/0134/news-fefer.shtml>, accessed 6 September 2001.

Feher, Shoshanah, 'Who Holds the Cards? Women and New Age Astrology', in James R. Lewis and J. Gordon Melton, *Perspectives on the New Age* (Albany: State University of New York Press, 1992).

——, 'Who Looks to the Stars? Astrology and its Constituency', *Journal for the Scientific Study of Religion*, 31/1 (1992): 88–93.

Festinger, Leon, *A Theory of Cognitive Dissonance* (Stanford: Stanford University Press, 1968 [1957]).

Finkbeiner, Ann, 'What Newton gave us', review of Edward Dolnick, *The Clockwork Universe: Isaac Newton, the Royal Society, and the Birth of the Modern World*, San Francisco, Harper Collins, 2011, in *New York Times*, Sunday Book Review, p. BR19, 27 March 2011, at <http://www.nytimes.com/2011/03/27/books/review/book-review-the-clockwork-universe-by-edward-dolnick.html?nl=books&emc=booksupdateema4>, accessed 3 September 2011.

Fiske, John, *Understanding Popular Culture* (London: Routledge: 1989).

Fitzgerald, Robert, 'Astrological Ages as an Accurate and Effective Model of History', *Astrological Journal*, 51/5 (2009): 55–62.

Forrest, Steven, and Jeffrey Wolf Green, *Measuring the Night: Evolutionary Astrology and the Keys to the Soul* (Boulder CO: Daemon, 2000).

Fowden, Garth, *The Egyptian Hermes: A Historical Approach to the Late Pagan Mind* (Princeton: Princeton University Press, 1986).

Freud, Sigmund, 'Psychoanalysis and Telepathy', in James Strachey (trans.), *The Complete Psychological Works of Sigmund Freud*, vol. 28 (London: Hogarth, 1955 [1921]).

Gadd, C.J., *Ideas of Divine Rule in the Ancient East*, Schweich Lectures of the British Academy (Munich: Kraus Reprint, 1980 [1945]).

Galen, Luke W., 'Profiles of the Godless: Results from a Survey of the Nonreligious', *Free Inquiry*, 29/5 (2009), pp. 41–5, at <http://www.secularhumanism.org/index.php?section=library&page=galen_29_5>, accessed 11 September 2011.

Gallup, George H., *The International Gallup Polls: Public Opinion 1978* (Wilmington DE: Scholarly Resources, 1980).

——, *The Gallup Poll: Public Opinion 1978* (Wilmington DE: Scholarly Resources, 1979).

——, *The Gallup Poll: Public Opinion 1972–1977* (2 vols, Wilmington DE: Scholarly Resources, 1978).

——, *The Gallup International Public Opinion Polls: Great Britain 1937–1975* (2 vols: vol. 1, 1937–64; vol. 2, 1965–75; New York: Random House, 1976a).

——, *The Gallup International Public Opinion Polls: France 1939. 1944–1975* (2 vols: vol. 1, 1939, 1944–67; vol. 2, 1968–75; New York: Random House, 1976b).

Gallup, George Jr., *The Gallup Poll: Public Opinion 1996* (Wilmington DE: Scholarly Resources, 1997).

——, *The Gallup Poll: Public Opinion 1995* (Wilmington DE: Scholarly Resources, 1996).

Garin, Eugenio, *Astrology in the Renaissance: The Zodiac of Life* (London, Boston: Routledge, 1976).

Garrett, Clarke, 'Swedenborg and the Mystical Enlightenment in Late Eighteenth-Century England', *Journal of the History of Ideas*, 45 (1984): 67–81.

Gauquelin, Michel, *Written in the Stars* (Wellingborough, Northamptonshire: Aquarian Press, 1988).

——, *The Cosmic Clocks* (London: Peter Owen, 1969; San Diego: Astro-Computing Services, 1982).

Gaynard, T.J., 'Young People and the Paranormal', *Journal of the Society for Psychical Research*, 58/826 (1992): 165–80.

Gelfer, Joseph (ed.), *2012: Decoding the Countercultural Apocalypse* (Sheffield: Equinox, 2011).

Geneva, Ann, *Astrology and the Seventeenth-Century Mind: William Lilly and the Language of the Stars* (Manchester and New York: Manchester University Press, 1995).

Gill, Robin, *Churchgoing and Christian Ethics* (Cambridge: Cambridge University Press, 1999).

Gleadow, Rupert, *Your Character in the Zodiac* (London: Phoenix House, 1968).

Glick, Peter, and Mark Snyder, 'Self-Fulfilling Prophecy: The Psychology of Belief in Astrology', *Humanist*, 46/3 (1986): 20–5, 50.

'Global Transformation: The Evolution of Consciousness through Mythology and Planetary Archetypes', at <http://www.royalroads.ca/continuing-studies/CYGLEL1820-Y09.htm>, accessed 23 September 2009.

Glock, Charles R., 'On the Study of Religious Commitment', *Religious Education*, 37/4 (1962): 98–110.

—— and Robert N. Bellah (eds), *The New Religious Consciousness* (Berkeley: University of California Press, 1976).

—— and Rodney Stark, *Religion and Society in Tension* (Chicago: Rand McNally, 1966).

Goddard, Gerry, 'Beyond a Post-Modern Astrology', at <http://www.islandastrology.net/resp-can.html>, accessed 20 January 2007.

Godwin, Joscelyn, *The Theosophical Enlightenment* (New York: State University of New York Press, 1994).

Goode, Erich, 'Education, Scientific Knowledge, and Belief in the Paranormal', *Skeptical Inquirer*, 26/1 (2002): 24–7.

——, 'Two Paranormalisms or Two and a Half? An Empirical Exploration', *Skeptical Inquirer*, 24/1 (2000): 29–35.

Goodman, Linda, *Linda Goodman's Sun Signs* (London: Pan, 1970).

Gorer, Geoffrey, *Exploring English Character* (London: Cresset, 1955).

Goring, Rosemary (ed.), *Chambers Dictionary of Beliefs and Religions* (London: BCA, 1992).

Grasse, Ray, 'Cinema and the Birth of the Aquarian Age', *Mountain Astrologer*, 108 (2003): 9–18.

——, 'Drawing Down the Fire of the Gods: Reflections on the Leo/Aquarius Axis', *Mountain Astrologer*, 89 (2000): 12–21.

Greeley, Andrew M., *The Sociology of the Paranormal* (London: Sage, 1975).

——, *Unsecular Man: The Persistence of Religion* (New York: Dell, 1974).

Greene, Liz, *Astrology for Lovers* (London: Unwin, 1986).

——, *Relating: An Astrological Guide to Living with Others on a Small Planet* (London: Coventure, 1977).

—— and Howard Sasportas, *The Dynamics of the Unconscious: Seminars in Psychological Astrology* (London: Arkana, 1988).

—— and Howard Sasportas, *The Development of the Personality: Seminars in Psychological Astrology* (London: Arkana, 1987).

Greenwood, Susan, *Magic, Witchcraft and the Otherworld: An Anthropology* (Oxford: Berg, 2000).

Gregory, Richard L., *The Oxford Companion to the Mind* (Oxford: Oxford University Press, 1998).

Groothuis, Douglas R., *Unmasking the New Age: Is there a New Religious Movement Trying to Transform Society?* (Downer's Grove IL: Intervarsity, 1986).

Grossman, Wendy, 'Bang!', *Skeptic*, 22/3 (2011): 9.

——, 'Skeptic at Large', *Skeptic*, 15/3 (2002): 7.

Guide to Worldwide Astrology 2002/3 (London: Urania Trust, 2002).

Gummerman, George J., and Miranda Warburton, 'The Universe in a Cultural Context: An Essay', in John W. Fountain and Rolf M. Sinclair (eds), *Current Studies in Archaeoastronomy: Conversations Across Time and Space* (Durham NC: Carolina Academic Press, 2005).

Hale, Beth, 'Is astrology bunk?', *Daily Mail*, 18 August 2003.

Hall, John R., *Apocalypse Observed: Religious Movements and Violence in North America, Europe, and Japan* (London and New York: Routledge, 2000).

Hall, Stuart. 'Cultural Studies: Two Paradigms', *Media, Culture and Society*, 2 (1980): 57–72.

Hamblin, David, 'Astrology as Religion: The Spiritual Dimension of Astrology', from his letter in *The Astrological Journal*, 32/6 (1990): 406–7, at <http://www.rudolfhsmit.nl/p-reli1.htm>, accessed 6 July 2008.

Hand, Robert, 'Towards a Post-Modern Astrology', *AstroDienst*, at <http://www.astro.com/astrology/in_postmodern_e.htm>, accessed 20 January 2007.

——, 'Foreword', in Olivia Barclay, *Horary Astrology Rediscovered* (West Chester PA: Whitford, 1990).

Hanegraaff, Wouter J., *New Age Religion and Western Culture* (Leiden, New York: Brill, 1996).

Hankinson, R.J., *The Sceptics* (London: Routledge, 1995).

Hanson, Paul, *The Dawn of Apocalyptic: The Historical and Sociological Roots of Jewish Apocalyptic Eschatology* (Philadelphia: Fortress, 1983 [1975]).

Haraldsson, E., 'Representative National Surveys of Psychic Phenomena: Iceland, Great Britain, Sweden, USA and Gallup's Multinational Survey', *Journal of the Society for Psychical Research*, 53 (1975): 145–58.

Harding, Michael, 'Response to Roger Elliot's Views in "Notes"', *Astrological Journal*, 32/2 (1990): 89–91.

Harris, Doug, *Occult Dangers Explained – Safely* (Richmond: Reachout Trust, 2000).

——, *Occult Overviews and New Age Agendas: A Comprehensive Examination of Major Occult and New Age Groups* (Richmond: Reachout Trust, 1999).

Harris, Pat, 'Response to Jacki Boivin, "Pat Harris, 'Astrology and fertility: Where is the evidence?'"', *Sexuality, Reproduction and Menopause*, 7/2, May 2009, at <http://www.srm-ejournal.com>.

——, 'Managing Fertility Treatments and Stress with Astrology', *Sexuality, Reproduction and Menopause*, 6/3 (2008): 43–4, at <http://www.srm-ejournal. com>.

Harris Poll, 'What People Do and Do Not Believe in', at <http://www.harrisinteractive. com/vault/Harris_Poll_2009_12_15.pdf>, accessed 1 September 2011.

Harvey, Charles, 'Town v Gown', *Astrological Journal*, 16/1 (1973–74): 28–40.

Harvey, Ronald, 'Scientists and Sun-Signs', *Astrological Journal*, 38/5 (September/ October 1996): 339–40.

Hastings, James (ed.), *A Dictionary of the Bible* (2 vols, Edinburgh: T. & T. Clark, 1910 [1898]).

Hawking, Stephen, *The Universe in a Nutshell* (London: Bantam, 2001).

Heath, Robin, 'To Sun Sign or not to Sun Sign? (Is that Really the Question?)', *Astrological Journal*, 38/3 (1996): 129–32.

Heelas, Paul, *Religion, Modernity and Postmodernity* (Oxford: Blackwell, 1998).

——, *The New Age Movement* (Oxford: Blackwell, 1996).

——, Linda Woodhead, Benjamin Seel, Karin Tusting and Bron Szerszynski, *The Spiritual Revolution: Why Religion Is Giving Way to Spirituality* (Oxford: Blackwell, 2005).

Heenan, Edward F. (ed.), *Mystery, Magic and Miracle: Religion in a Post-Aquarian Age* (Englewood Cliffs NJ: Prentice Hall, 1973).

Heindel, Max, *The Rosicrucian Cosmo-Conception* (London: Fowler, 1929 [1909]).

——, *The Message of the Stars* (London: Fowler, 1929).

Herbrechtsmeier, William, 'Buddhism and the Definition of Religion: One More Time', *Journal for the Scientific Study of Religion*, 32/1 (1993): 1–18.

Hess, David J., *Science in the New Age: The Paranormal, Its Defenders and Debunkers and American Culture* (Madison: University of Wisconsin Press, 1993).

Hexham, Irving, and Karla Poewe, *New Religions as Global Cultures* (Boulder CO: Westview, 1997).

Higgins, Godfrey, *Anacalypsis, an Attempt to Draw Aside the Veil of the Saitic Isis; or an Inquiry into the Origins of Languages, Nations and Religions* (2 vols, London: Longman, Res, Orme, Brown, Green and Longman, 1836).

Hill, Michael, *A Sociology of Religion* (London: Heinemann, 1979 [1973]).

Hillenbrand, Candy, 'An Archaic Astrology Cast Adrift in a Post-Modern World', at <http://www.aplaceinspace.net/Pages/CandyPostmodern.html>, accessed 20 January 2007.

Hinnells, John R. (ed.), *A New Dictionary of Religions* (Oxford: Blackwell, 1995).

Hobsbawm, Eric, and Terence Ranger (eds), *The Invention of Tradition* (Cambridge: Cambridge University Press, 1983).

Holden, James Herschel, *A History of Horoscopic Astrology* (Tempe AZ: American Federation of Astrologers, 1996).

Holm, Nils G., 'The Indian Factor in New Religious Movements: A Religio-Psychological Perspective', in Eileen Barker and Margot Warburg (eds), *New Religions and New Religiosity* (Aarhus: Aarhus University Press, 2001).

Hone, Margaret, *The Modern Textbook of Astrology* (London: Fowler, 4th edn repr. 1973 [1951]).

Hoopes, John, 'A Critical History of 2012 Mythology', in Clive Ruggles (ed.), *Archaeoastronomy and Ethnoastronomy: Building Bridges between Cultures*, Proceedings of International Astronomy Union Symposium 278 (Cambridge: Cambridge University Press, 2011), pp. 240–8.

Hornsby-Smith, Michael, *Roman Catholic Beliefs in England: Customary Catholicism and Transformations in Religious Authority* (Cambridge: Cambridge University Press, 1991).

Houlding, Deborah, 'The Backstory of the AA's Petition and how Twitter-Chums Stick Together when the Beeb makes a Boob, 07/02/2011', at_<http://www.astrologicalassociation.com/pages/bbc/petition.pdf>, accessed 28 July 2011.

Houtman, Dick, and Stef Aupers, 'The Spiritual Turn and the Decline of Tradition: The Spread of Post-Christian Spirituality in 14 Western Countries, 1981–2000', *Journal for the Scientific Study of Religion*, 46/3 (September 2007): 305–20.

Howe, Ellic, *Urania's Children: The Strange World of the Astrologers* (London: William Kimber, 1967).

Hufford, David, 'Traditions of Disbelief', *Talking Folklore*, 1/3 (1987): 19–29.

Hunt, Stephen J., *Religion and Everyday Life* (London: Routledge, 2005).

——, *Alternative Religions: A Sociological Introduction* (Aldershot: Ashgate, 2003).

Huntley, Janice, *The Elements of Astrology* (Shaftsbury: Element, 1990).

Husserl, Edmund, *Ideas: General Introduction to Pure Phenomenology* (London: Collier-Macmillan, 1972 [1913, Eng. trans. 1931]).

Hutton, Ronald, 'Astral Magic: The Acceptable Face of Paganism', in Nicholas Campion, Patrick Curry and Michael York (eds), *Astrology and the Academy*, papers from the inaugural conference of the Sophia Centre, Bath Spa University College, 13–14 June 2003 (Bristol: Cinnabar, 2004).

Independent Television Authority (ITA), *Religion in Britain and Northern Ireland: A Survey of Popular Attitudes* (London: ITA, 1970).

Independent Television Commission (ITC), *Paranormal Programming, Consultation Paper*, Programme Code Consultation, 2003.

'The Infinite Monkey Cage', Series 5, 'A Balanced Programme on Balance', BBC Radio 4, 28 November 2011.

'Inquisition', Grampian TV, c. 1995.

Introvigne, Massimo, 'After the New Age: Is There a Next Age?', in Mikael Rothstein (ed.), *New Age Religion and Globalization* (Aarhus: Aarhus University Press, 2001).

Irwin, Harvey J., *The Psychology of Paranormal Belief: A Researcher's Handbook* (Hatfield: University of Hertfordshire Press, 2009).

Isidore of Seville, *The Etymologies*, trans. Stephen A. Barney, W.J. Lewis, J.A. Beach and Oliver Berghof (Cambridge: Cambridge University Press, 2007).

Jahoda, Gustav, *The Psychology of Superstition* (London: Allen Lane, 1969).

Jameson, Frederic, *Postmodernism, or, the Cultural Logic of Late Capitalism* (London and New York: Verso, 1991).

Janis, I.L., 'Anxiety Indices related to Susceptibility to Persuasion', *Journal of Abnormal and Social Psychology*, 51 (1955): 663–7.

——, 'Personality Correlates of Susceptibility to Persuasion', *Journal of Personality*, 22 (1954): 505–18.

Jerome, Lawrence E., 'Astrology: Magic or Science?', *Humanist*, 35/5 (1975): 10–16.

Jevons, Frank, *Introduction to the History of Religions* (London: Methuen, 1896).

Jones, Steve, 'A Review of the Impartiality and Accuracy of the BBC's Coverage of Science', in *BBC Trust Review of Impartiality and Accuracy of the BBC's Coverage of Science; With an Independent Assessment by Professor Steve Jones and Content Research from Imperial College London* (London: BBC, 2011).

Jung, C.G., 'Jung to Freud, 12 June 1911', in Gerhard Adler et al. (eds), *Letters 1906–1950* (Princeton: Bollingen, 1992).

——, 'Richard Wilhelm: In Memoriam' in *The Spirit in Man, Art, And Literature*, in *The Collected Works of C.G. Jung*, vol. 15, trans. R.F.C. Hull (London: Routledge & Kegan Paul, 1971).

——, 'The Sign of the Fishes', in *Aion*, in *The Collected Works of C.G. Jung*, vol. 9, part 2, trans. R.F.C. Hull (London: Routledge & Kegan Paul, 1959).

——, 'Gnostic Symbols of the Self', in *Aion*, in *The Collected Works of C.G. Jung*, vol. 9, part 2, trans. R.F.C. Hull (London: Routledge & Kegan Paul, 1959).

Kanitscheider, Bernulf, 'A Philosopher Looks at Astrology', *Interdisciplinary Science Reviews*, 16/3 (1991): 258–66.

Kelly, Aidan, 'Dane Rudhyar', in James R. Lewis, *The Astrology Encyclopaedia* (Detroit, London, Washington: Visible Ink, 1994).

Kelly, Ivan W., '"Debunking the Debunkers". A Response to an Astrologer's Debunking of Skeptics', *Skeptical Inquirer*, 23/6 (1999): 37–43.

——, 'Why Astrology Doesn't Work', *Psychological Reports*, 82 (1998): 527–46.

——, 'The Concepts of Modern Astrology: A Critique', at <http://www.astrology-and-science.com/a-conc2.htm>, 2005, accessed 3 September 2011, orig. publ. in *Psychological Reports*, 81 (1997): 1035–66.

Kemp, Daren, *New Age: A Guide* (Edinburgh: Edinburgh University Press, 2004).

Kempton-Smith, Debbi, *Secrets from a Stargazer's Notebook: Making Astrology Work for You* (New York: Bantam, 1982).

Kennedy, E.S., and David Pingree, *The Astrological History of Masha'Allah* (Cambridge MA: Harvard University Press, 1971).

Kennedy, James E., 'The Roles of Religion, Spirituality and Genetics in Paranormal Beliefs', *Skeptical Inquirer*, 28/2 (2004): 39–42.

Kirk, C.S., J.E. Raven and M. Schofield, *The Presocratic Philosophers*, 2nd edn (Cambridge: Cambridge University Press, 1983).

Knowles, Elizabeth (ed.), *The Oxford Dictionary of Quotations* (Oxford: Oxford University Press, 2004).

Koch, Walter, 'Vernal Point and Era of Aquarius', *In Search*, Winter 1958/59 and Spring 1959, 2/1 and 2 (1959).

Koch-Westenholtz, Ulla, *Mesopotamian Astrology: An Introduction to Babylonian and Assyrian Celestial Divination* (Copenhagen: Museum Tusculunum Press, Carsten Niebuhr Institute of Near Eastern Studies, University of Copenhagen, 1995).

Krippner, Stanley, and Michael Winkler, 'The "Need to "Believe"', in Gordon Stein (ed.), *The Encyclopaedia of the Paranormal* (Amherst NY: Prometheus, 1996).

Krupp, E.C., 'Night Gallery: The Function, Origin and Evolution of Constellations', *Archaeoastronomy: The Journal of Astronomy in Culture*, 15 (2000): 43–63.

Lacey, F.W., 'Early Days in Astrology', in Bessie Leo (ed.), *The Life and Work of Alan Leo* (London: Modern Astrology, 1919).

Lamb, Terry, *Born to be Together: Love Relationships, Astrology, and the Soul* (Carlsbad CA: Hay House, 1998).

Latour, Bruno, *We Have Never Been Modern* (Cambridge MA: Harvard University Press, 2006 [1991]).

Lawson, Nigella, 'Astrology and the need to believe: why are we going to New Age cranks for old-style cures?', *Times*, 13 November 1996, p. 17.

Leigh, James, 'Editorial', *Prediction*, 1/3 (1936): 98.

Lemesurier, Peter, *Gospel of the Stars: The Mystery of the Cycle of the Ages* (London: Vega, 2002 [1st edn 1990]).

——, *This New Age Business: The Story of the Ancient and Continuing Quest to Bring Down Heaven on Earth* (Forres: Findhorn, 1990).

Leo, Alan, *The Art of Synthesis* (London: Modern Astrology, 1936 [1st edn as *How to Judge a Nativity*, pt 2, 1904]).

——, *Esoteric Astrology: A Study in Human Nature* (London: Modern Astrology, 1925 [1913]).

——, *How to Judge a Nativity* (London: Modern Astrology, 1922 [1903]).

——, 'An Historic Event': *Modern Astrology*, New Series, 8/10 (1911): 402–5.

——, 'The Editor's Observatory': *Modern Astrology*, New Series, 8/10 (1911): 397–9.

——, 'The Editor's Observatory: Modern Astrology's Coming-of-Age', *Modern Astrology*, New Series, 8/8 (1911): 265–312.

——, 'The Editor's Observatory', *Modern Astrology*, New Series, 8/5 (1911): 177–82.

——, 'The Age of Aquarius', *Modern Astrology*, New Series, 8/7 (1911): 272.

——, 'The Editor's Observatory', *Modern Astrology*, New Series, 8/5 (1911): 133–5.

——, 'The Editor's Observatory', *Modern Astrology*, New Series, 8/3 (1911): 89–96.

Lerner, Mark, editorial comments in *Welcome to Planet Earth*, 14/10 (1995).

Levi (Levi Dowling), *The Aquarian Gospel of Jesus the Christ* (Chadwell Heath: Fowler, 1980 [1907]).

Levine, Joyce, 'Entering the Age of Aquarius', *Horoscope*, February (1997): 2–4.

Lewis, James, 'Introduction', in James Lewis (ed.), *The Beginnings of Astrology in America: Astrology and the Re-Emergence of Cosmic Religion* (London and New York: Garland, 1990).

—— and J. Gordon Melton (eds), *Perspectives on the New Age* (New York: State University of New York Press, 1992).

Lilly, William, *Christian Astrology* (London, 1647 [facs. edn London: Regulus, 1985]).

Lind, Ingrid, *Astrology and Commonsense* (London: Hodder & Stoughton, 1962).

Lindsay, James, *The Psychology of Belief* (Edinburgh and London: Blackwood, 1910).

Linklater, Magnus, 'An academic dispute that is out of this world', *Times*, 30 August 2001, p. 12.

Lipton, Bruce H., *The Biology of Belief: Unleashing the Power of Consciousness, Matter and Miracles* (London: Hay House, 2008).

Lister, Johnny, *The New Age: How Entering the Aquarian Age Affects You and the World Today* (San Francisco: Entheos, 1984).

The Llewellyn Journal, website, at <www.llewellyn.com>, accessed 10 March 2009.

Lowe, Oliver, 'Astrology as an Aid in the Education of Children', *Modern Astrology*, New Series, 8/10 (1911): 406–13.

Luckmann, Thomas, *The Invisible Religion* (New York: Macmillan, 1967).

Lynch, Gordon, *Understanding Theology and Popular Culture* (Oxford: Blackwell, 2005).

Lyndoe, Edward, *Plan with the Planets* (London: Herbert Jenkins, 1949).

Lyons, Linda, 'Paranormal beliefs come (super)naturally to some: more people believe in haunted houses than other mystical ideas', Gallup, 1 November 2005, at <http://www.gallup.com/poll/19558/Paranormal-Beliefs-Come-SuperNaturally-Some.aspx>, accessed 24 September 2009.

Lyotard, Jean-Francois, *The Postmodern Condition: A Report on Knowledge* (Manchester: Manchester University Press, 1985).

McCann, Maurice, *The Sun and the Aspects* (London: Tara Astrological Publications, 2002).

McCulloch, Gillian, *The Deconstruction of Dualism in Theology: With Special Reference to Ecofeminist Theology and New Age Spirituality* (Carlisle: Paternoster, 2002).

McCutcheon, Russell T. (ed.), *The Insider/Outsider Problem in the Study of Religion: A Reader* (London: Cassell, 1999).

——, 'General Introduction', in Russell T. McCutcheon, *The Insider/Outsider Problem in the Study of Religion: A Reader* (London: Cassell, 1999).

McDevitt, Theresa H., 'Sharon and Arafat: Axis of Closure to the Pisces-Virgo Age', *NCGR Memberletter*, June/July (2002): 1, 16–17.

——, 'USA and Serbia: The Composite', *NCGR Memberletter*, June/July (1999): 1, 9.

McGervey, John D., 'A Statistical Test of Sun-Sign Astrology', *Zetetic*, 1/2 (1977): 48–55.

MacKinnell, Terry, 'A New Look at the Old Ages', *NCGR Memberletter*, June/July (2002): 10–11, 19–20.

McMillan, Penelope, 'Horoscopes: fans bask in sun sign', *Los Angeles Times*, 5 July 1985, pp. 1, 3, 18.

McRitchie, Ken, 'Support for Astrology from the Carlson Double-Blind Experiment', *International Astrologer*, 40/2 (2011): 33–38, at <http://www.theoryofastrology.com/carlson/carlson.htm>.

Magnay, Keith, 'New Flight in the Age of Aquarius', *Astrological Journal*, 37/3 (1995): 162–7.

Main, Roderick, *Jung on Synchronicity and the Paranormal* (London: Routledge, 1997).

Malinowski, Bronislaw, *Magic, Science and Religion* (New York: Doubleday, 1954).

Manuel, Frank E., *Shapes of Philosophic History* (London: Allen & Unwin, 1965).

—— and F.P. Manuel, *Utopian Thought in the Western World* (Oxford: Blackwell, 1979).

Marks, David, and John Colwell, 'Fooling and Falling into the Feeling of Being Stared At', *Skeptical Inquirer*, 25/2 (2001): 62–3.

Marsh, Stefanie, 'Testing positive', *Times*, Review section, 2 January 2010, p. 9.

Marsom, F.B., 'Astrologers and Astronomers', *Astrology Quarterly*, 13/1 (1939): 20–7.

Martens, Ronny, and Tim Trachet, *Making Sense of Astrology* (Amherst NY: Prometheus, 1998).

Martin, Walter, *The New Age Cult* (Minneapolis: Bethany House, 1989).

Massey, Gerald, *The Hebrew and Other Creations* (London: Williams & Norgate, 1887).

Mather, Arthur, 'Correlation', *Astrological Journal*, 18/1 (1975/76): 26–33.

Matthews, Margaret, 'Dogmatism', *Modern Astrology*, New Series, 8/6 (1911): 263–4.

Matthews, Robert, 'Astrologers fail to predict proof they are wrong', *Sunday Telegraph*, 17 August 2003, p. 9.

Mayo, Jeff, *Teach Yourself Astrology* (London: Hodder & Stoughton 1981 [1964]).

Mee, Arthur, 'The Divine Use of Astrology', in Bessie Leo, *The Life and Work of Alan Leo* (London: Modern Astrology, 1919).

Melton, J. Gordon, 'The Emergence of New Religions in Eastern Europe Since 1989', in Eileen Barker and Margot Warburg (eds), *New Religions and New Religiosity* (Aarhus: Aarhus University Press, 2001).

——, 'The Future of the New Age Movement', in Eileen Barker and Margot Warburg (eds), *New Religions and New Religiosity* (Aarhus: Aarhus University Press 2001).

——, Jerome Clarke and Aidan A. Kelly, *New Age Almanac* (London and New York: Visible Ink, 1991).

'The Message of the Stars', *American Astrology*, March, 1/1 (1933): 6.

Miller, Elliot, *A Crash Course on the New Age Movement* (Eastbourne: Monarch, 1990).

Miller, Jon D., 'The Public Acceptance of Astrology and Other Pseudo-Science in the United States', paper presented to the 1992 annual meeting of the American Association for the Advancement of Science, 9 February 1992.

Mitton, Jacqueline, *The Penguin Dictionary of Astronomy* (London: Penguin, 1993).

Moore, Marcia, *Astrology Today: A Socio-Psychological Survey*, Astrological Research Associates Research Bulletin no. 2 (New York: Lucis, 1960).

Morey, Robert A., *Horoscopes and the Christian: Does Astrology Accurately Predict the Future? Is it Compatible with Christianity?* (Minneapolis: Bethany House, 1981).

Mosher, Donald L., 'Approval Motive and Acceptance of "Fake" Personality Test Interpretations Which Differ in Favorability', *Psychological Reports*, 17 (1965): 395–402.

Myers, David G., *Social Psychology*, 3rd edn (New York: McGraw-Hill, 1990).

National Science Foundation, 'Science and Technology: Public Attitudes and Public Understanding Science Fiction and Pseudoscience', at <http://www.nsf.gov/sbe/srs/seind02/c//c/s5.htm>, accessed 6 May 2002.

Naylor, R.H., 'Star-Lore (1)', *Prediction*, 8/8 (1943): 24.

——, 'Horoscopes for all Months', *Prediction*, 1/7 (1936): 16–17.

——, 'What is the Future of Astrology', *Prediction*, 1/4 (1936): 151, 157.

——, 'Born in February?', *Prediction*, 1/1 (1936): 12–13.

——, 'What the stars foretell for this week', *Sunday Express*, 26 October 1930, p. 12.

——, 'Were you born in October?', *Sunday Express*, 5 October 1930, p. 11.

——, 'Were you born in September?', *Sunday Express*, 31 August 1930, p. 7.

——, 'What the stars foretell for the new Princess and a few hints on the happenings of this week', *Sunday Express*, 24 August 1930, p. 11.

Nederman, Cary J., and James Wray Goulding, 'Popular Occultism and Critical Social Theory: Exploring Some Themes in Adorno's Critique of Astrology and the Occult', *Sociological Analysis*, 42/4 (1981): 325–32.

Nelson Hart, M., Robert F. Everett, Paul Douglas Mader and Warren C. Hamby, 'A Test of Yinger's Measure of Non-Doctrinal Religion: Implications for Invisible Religion as a Belief System', *Journal for the Scientific Study of Religion*, 15/3 (1976): 263–7.

Ness, Lester, *Written in the Stars: Ancient Zodiac Mosaics* (Warren Center PA: Shangri La, 1999).

The New Age Store, website, at <http://www.newagestore.com/>, accessed 25 August 2011.

Newport, Frank, 'This Easter, smaller percentage of Americans are Christian: Americans more likely now than in previous decades to say they have no religious identity', 10 April 2009, at <http://www.gallup.com/poll/117409/Easter-Smaller-Percentage-Americans-Christian.aspx>, accessed 5 November 2009.

Newport, John P., *The New Age Movement and the Biblical Worldview: Conflict and Dialogue* (Grand Rapids MI: Eerdmans, 1998).

Nobel, Steve, 'Age of Transition', *Prediction*, 68/7 (2002): 28–30.

O'Hear, Anthony, *Experience, Explanation and Faith: An Introduction to the Philosophy of Religion* (London: Routledge & Kegan Paul, 1984).

Office for National Statistics, 'Religion in the UK Census shows 72% Identify as Christians', at <http://www.statistics.gov.uk/cci/nugget.asp?id=293>, accessed 5 November 2009.

Oken, Alan, *Soul-Centred Astrology: A Key to Your Expanding Self* (New York: Bantam, 1990).

——, *Alan Oken's Complete Astrology*, rev. edn (New York: Bantam Dell, 1988).

——, *Astrology; Evolution and Revolution, a Path to Higher Consciousness through Astrology* (New York: Bantam, 1976).

——, *The Horoscope, the Road and its Traveller: A Manual of Consciousness Expansion through Astrology* (New York: Bantam, 1974).

——, *As Above, So Below: A Primary Guide to Astrological Awareness* (New York: Bantam, 1973).

Oliphant, John, *Brother Twelve: The Incredible Story of Canada's False Prophet and His Doomed Cult of Gold, Sex and Black Magic* (Toronto: McClelland & Stewart, 1991).

Orenstein, Alan, 'On Evolution, Abortion and Astrology', *Skeptical Inquirer*, 33/4 (2009): 48–52.

Origen, *The Philocalia of Origen*, trans. George Lewis (Edinburgh: T. & T. Clark, 1911).

Orr, Marjorie, *The Astrological History of the World: The Influence of the Planets on Human History* (London: Vega, 2002).

Otto, Rudolf, *The Idea of the Holy* (Oxford: Oxford University Press, 1958 [1923]).

Outram, Dorinda, *The Enlightenment* (Cambridge: Cambridge University Press, 1995).

Owen, Alex, *The Place of Enchantment: British Occultism and the Culture of the Modern*, (Chicago: University of Chicago Press, 2004).

Park, Robert, *Voodoo Science: The Road from Foolishness to Fraud* (Oxford: Oxford University Press, 2000).

Parker, Derek, *The Question of Astrology. A Personal Investigation* (London: Eyre & Spottiswoode, 1970).

—— and Julia Parker, *The Compleat Astrologer* (London: Mitchell-Beazley, 1971).

Partridge, Christopher H., *The Re-Enchantment of the West*, vol. 1 (London: T. & T. Clark International, 2004).

——, 'Truth, Authority and Epistemological Individualism in New Age Thought', *Journal of Contemporary Religion*, 14/1 (1999): 289–313.

Pawlik, Kurt, and Lothar Buse, 'Self-Attribution as a Moderator Variable in Differential Psychology: Replication and Interpretation of Eysenck's Astrology/Personality Correlations', *Correlation*, 4/2 (1984): 14–30.

Pearce, Alfred, *The Text Book of Astrology* (2 vols, London: Cousins, 1879), vol. 1.

Pearson, Joanne, 'Assumed Affinities: Wicca and the New Age', in Joanne Pearson, Richard H. Roberts and Geoffrey Samuel, *Nature Religion Today: Paganism in the Modern World* (Edinburgh: Edinburgh University Press 1998).

Pels, Peter, 'Spirits of Modernity: Alfred Wallace, Edward Tylor and the Visual Politics of Fact', in Birgit Meyer and Peter Pels (eds), *Magic and Modernity: Interfaces of Revelation and Concealment* (Stanford: Stanford University Press, 2003), pp. 141–271.

Perkins, Maureen, *Visions of the Future: Almanacs, Time, and Cultural Change* (Oxford: Clarendon Press, 1996).

Perry, Glenn, 'The New Paradigm and Postmodern Astrology', International Forum on New Science, University of Fort Collins, Colorado, 27 September 1991, at <http://www.aaperry.com/index.asp?pgid=21>, accessed 20 January 2007.

Persinger, M.A., and Makarec, K., 'Exotic Beliefs may be Substitutes for Religious Beliefs', *Perceptual and Motor Skills*, 71 (1990): 16–18.

'Personal Forecast', *American Astrology*, March, 1/1 (1933): 11–15.

Phillips, Melanie, 'The False Faith of Scientific Reason', *Jewish Chronicle*, 17 October 2008, at <http://www.melaniephillips.com/the-false-faith-of-scientific-reason>, accessed 30 July 2011.

———, 'The Age of Unreason', *Daily Mail*, 6 August 2007, at <http://www.melaniephillips.com/the-age-of-unreason>, accessed 30 July 2011.

Phillipson, Garry, *Astrology in the Year Zero* (London: Flare, 2000).

Phipps, Kelly Lee, 'How Not to Collectively Lose our Minds', *ISAR Newsletter*, 212 (2002).

Piedmont Psychiatric Clinic, 'Patient's Check List', at <http://www.piedmontpsychiatricclinic.com/forms.html>, accessed 30 November 2009.

Pilcher, Helen, 'Beware Witchdoctors: Are you a Victim of Placebo's Evil Twin', *New Scientist*, 202/2708 (2009): 30–9.

Pinker, Steven, *How the Mind Works* (New York: Norton, 1997).

Plato, *Republic*, trans. Paul Shorey (2 vols, Cambridge MA and London: Harvard University Press, 1937).

———, *Timaeus*, trans. R.G. Bury (Cambridge MA and London: Harvard University Press, 1931).

Platt, Tristan, 'The Anthropology of Astronomy', in *Archaeoastronomy*, suppl. to *The Journal of the History of Astronomy*, 16 (1991): S76–S83.

Plotinus, 'On Heaven', 'On Whether the Stars are Causes', *Ennead*, II, 2, vol. 2, trans. A.H. Armstrong (Cambridge MA and London: Harvard University Press, 1966).

Plug, C., 'An Investigation of Superstitious Belief and Behaviour', *Journal of Behavioural Science*, 2/3 (1975): 169–78.

Popper, Karl, *The Open Society and its Enemies*, rev. edn (2 vols, London and New York: Routledge, 1986 [1945]).

Primiano, L., 'Vernacular Religion and the Search for Method on Religious Folklife', *Western Folklore*, 54/1 (1995): 35–56.

Ptolemy, Claudius, *Tetrabiblos*, trans. F.E. Robbins (Cambridge MA: Harvard University Press, 1940).

——, 'Centiloquium', in John Partridge, *Mikropanastron, or an Astrological Vade Mecum, briefly Teaching the whole Art of Astrology – viz., Questions, Nativities, with all its parts, and the whole Doctrine of Elections never so comprised nor compiled before, &c.* (London: William Bromwich, 1679), pp. 305–21.

Pugh, Judy F., 'Astrological Counseling in Contemporary India', *Culture, Medicine and Psychiatry*, 7 (1983): 279–99.

Quine, W.V., and J.S. Ullian, *The Web of Belief*, 2nd edn (New York: McGraw-Hill, 1978).

Rael, Layla, 'Happy Birthday, Rudhyar, and Thanks', *Astrological Journal*, 27/2 (1985): 76–83.

Reid, Vera W., *Towards Aquarius* (New York: Arco, 1944).

Reinhart, Melanie, 'In the Shadows of the Age of Aquarius', *Astrological Journal*, 29/3 (1987): 108–14.

Religious Tolerance, website, at <http://www.religioustolerance.org/chr_prac2.htm>, accessed 5 November 2009.

Rice, Tom W., 'Believe It or Not: Religious and Other Paranormal Beliefs in the United States', *Journal for the Scientific Study of Religion*, 42/1 (2003): 95–106.

Ringgren, Helmer, 'Akkadian Apocalypses', in David Hellholm (ed.), *Apocalypticism in the Mediterranean World and the Near East, Proceedings of the International Colloquium on Apocalypticism, Uppsala, 12–17 August 1979* (Tübingen: Mohr, 1989).

Robbins, Martin, 'Astrologers angered by stars', *Guardian*, 24 January 2011, at <http://www.guardian.co.uk/science/the-lay-scientist/2011/jan/24/1>.

Robinson, James M., 'Introduction', in James M. Robinson (ed.), *The Nag Hammadi Library in English* (Leiden and New York: Brill, 1988).

Rochberg, Francesca, *The Heavenly Writing: Divination and Horoscopy, and Astronomy in Mesopotamian Culture* (Cambridge: Cambridge University Press, 2004).

Roof, Wade Clark, *A Generation of Seekers: The Spiritual Journeys of the Baby Boom Generation* (San Francisco: HarperCollins, 1993).

——, Christopher Kirk Hadaway, Myrna L. Hewitt, Douglas McGaw and Richard Morse, 'Yinger's Measure of Non-Doctrinal Religion: A Northeastern Test', *Journal for the Scientific Study of Religion*, 19/4 (1977): 403–8.

Rose, Stuart, 'Transforming the World: An Examination of the Roles Played by Spirituality and Healing in the New Age Movement', PhD thesis, Department of Religious Studies, Lancaster University, 1996.

Rudhyar, Dane, *The Astrology of Transformation: A Multilevel Approach* (Wheaton IL: Theosophical Publishing House, 1984 [1980]).

——, *Person Centered Astrology* (New York: Aurora, 1980 [1976]).

——, *The Planetarisation of Consciousness* (New York: Aurora, 1977 [1970]).

——, *The Practice of Astrology as a Technique in Human Understanding* (New York: Penguin, 1975 [1968]).

——, *Occult Preparations for a New Age* (Madras and London: Theosophical Publishing House, 1975).

——, *An Astrological Mandala: The Cycle of Transformation and its 360 Symbolic Phases* (New York: Vintage, 1974).

——, *Astrological Timing: The Transition to the New Age* (San Francisco, New York and London: Harper & Row, 1972 [1969]).

——, *The Astrology of Personality* (New York: Lucis and Aurora, 1970 [1936]).

——, *Fire out of the Stone: A Reinterpretation of the Basic Images of the Christian Tradition* (The Hague: Servire, 1963).

——, *New Mansions for New Men* (New York: Lucis, 1938).

Ruggles, C. and Saunders, J., *Astronomies and Cultures* (Boulder CO: University of Colorado Press, 1993).

Ruperti, Alexander, 'Dane Rudhyar (March 23, 1895 – September 13, 1985): Seed-Man for the New Era', *Astrological Journal*, 33/2 (1986): 55–60.

Russell, D.S., *The Method and Message of Jewish Apocalyptic: 200 BC–AD 100* (Philadelphia: Westminster, 1964).

Sagan, Carl, *The Demon-Haunted World: Science as a Candle in the Dark* (New York: Random House, 1995).

——, *Cosmos: The Story of Cosmic Evolution, Science and Civilisation* (London: Warner, 1994).

St Aubyn, Lorna, *The New Age in a Nutshell: A Guide to Living in New Times* (Wellow: Gateway, 1990).

St Clair, Michael J., *Millenarian Movements in Historical Context* (New York and London: Garland, 1992).

Saliba, John A., *Perspectives on New Religious Movements* (London: Geoffrey Chapman, 1995).

Sancho, Jane, *Beyond Entertainment? Research into the Acceptability of Alternative Beliefs, Psychic and Occult Phenomena on Television* (London: Broadcasting Standards Commission and Independent Television Commission, 2001).

Sasportas, Howard, *The Gods of Change: Pain, Crisis and the Transits of Uranus, Neptune and Pluto* (London: Arkana, 1989).

'Science and Technology: Public Attitudes and Public Understanding Science Fiction and Pseudoscience', at <http://www.nsf.gov/statistics/seind02/c7/c7s5. htm>, accessed 6 May 2002.

Scott, Walter (trans.), *Hermetica: The Ancient Greek and Latin Writings which contain Religious or Philosophic Teachings Ascribed to Hermes Trismegistus* (4 vols, Boulder CO: Shambala, 1982).

The Search for Faith and the Witness of the Church: An Exploration by the Mission Theological Advisory Group (London: Church House, 1996).

Seifer, Nancy, and Martin Vieweg, 'Aquarius Rising: Obama and the Aquarian Age', at <http://newagejournal.com/2007/new-age-articles/aquarius-rising-obama-and-the-aquarian-age>, accessed 27 July 2009.

Seymour, Percy, *Astrology: The Evidence of Science*, 2nd edn, rev. (London: Penguin-Arkana, 1990 [1988]).

Sheaffer, Robert, 'UFOlogy 2009: A Six-Decade Perspective', *Skeptical Inquirer*, 33/1 (2009): 22–9.

Sheldrake, Rupert, 'Research on the Feeling of Being Stared At', *Skeptical Inquirer*, 25/2 (2001): 58–61.

Sherriff, Lucy, 'Women are NOT from Gullibull', *Skeptic*, 14/3 (2001): 7.

Shiels, Dean, and Philip Berg, 'A Research Note on Sociological Variables Related to Belief in Psychic Phenomena', *Wisconsin Sociologist*, 14 (1977): 24–31.

Shumaker, Wayne, *The Occult Sciences in the Renaissance: A Study in Intellectual Patterns* (Berkeley, Los Angeles, London: University of California Press, 1972).

Sibbald, Luella, *The One With the Water Jar: Astrology, the Aquarian Age and Jesus of Nazareth* (San Francisco: Guild for Psychological Studies, 1978).

Silber, John, 'Silliness under Seattle stars', *Boston Herald*, 16 May 2001, at <http://www.bostonherald.com/news/columnists/silber05162001.htm>, accessed 1 June 2001.

Smart, Ninian, *Dimensions of the Sacred: An Anatomy of the World's Beliefs* (Berkeley and Los Angeles: University of California Press, 1996).

——, *The Phenomenon of Religion* (London: Macmillan, 1973).

Smit, Rudolf, 'Moment Supreme: Why Astrologers Keep Believing in Astrology', trans. and updated from orig. Dutch article in *Skepter*, March 1993, at <http://www.rudolfhsmit.nl/a-mome2.htm>, accessed 6 July 2008.

Smith, Daniel Naylor, 'Astrology and Theosophy', *Modern Astrology*, New Series, 8/9 (1911): 396.

Smith, Jonathan Z., *Imagining Religion: From Babylon to Jonestown* (Chicago: University of Chicago Press, 1982).

Smith, Wilfred Cantwell, *Faith and Belief* (Princeton: Princeton University Press, 1998 [1979]).

Snow, Theodore P., and Kenneth R. Brownsberger, *Universe: Origins and Evolution* (London and New York: University of Colorado, Wadsworth, 1997).

Snyder, C.R., and Glenn R. Larson, 'A Further Look at Student Acceptance of General Personality Interpretation', *Journal of Consulting and Clinical Psychology*, 38/3 (1972): 384–8.

Solté, David A., 'Millennium Watch: The Outer Planets and the Aquarian Age', *Mountain Astrologer*, 85 (1999): 77–8.

Somerfield, Barbara, 'To Dane Rudhyar, Who Inspired my First Steps on the Path, With Loving Gratitude for his Sustainment, In Memoriam', *Welcome to Planet Earth*, 14/10 (1995): 55–7.

Spangler, David, *A Pilgrim in Aquarius* (Forres: Findhorn, 1996).

——, 'The New Age: The Movement Toward the Divine', in Duncan S. Ferguson, *New Age Spirituality: An Assessment* (Louisville KY: Westminster John Knox Press, 1993).

——, 'Revelation – Birth of a New Age', in William Bloom, *The New Age: An Anthology of Essential Writings* (London: Rider, 1991).

——, *The Rebirth of the Sacred* (London: Gateway, 1984).

——, *Explorations: Emerging Aspects of the New Culture* (Forres: Findhorn, 1980).

——, *Revelation: The Birth of a New Age* (Forres: Findhorn, 1976).

——, *Festivals in the New Age* (Forres: Findhorn, 1975).

Sparks, Glenn G., 'The Relationship between Paranormal Beliefs and Religious Beliefs', *Skeptical Inquirer*, 25/5 (2001): 50–6.

Spencer, Neil, *True as the Stars Above: Adventures in Modern Astrology* (London: Victor Gollancz, 2000).

Stake, Robert E., *The Art of Case Study Research* (London: Sage, 1995).

Stanley, Michael W., 'The Relevance of Emanuel Swedenborg's Theological Concepts for the New Age as it is Envisioned Today', in Robert Larson (ed.), *Emanuel Swedenborg: A Continuing Vision* (New York: Swedenborg Foundation, 1988).

Stark, Rodney, 'Atheism, Faith, and the Social Scientific Study of Religion', *Journal of Contemporary Religion*, 14/1 (1999): 41–62.

—— and William Simms Bainbridge, *A Theory of Religion* (New Brunswick NJ: Rutgers University Press, 1987).

—— and William Simms Bainbridge, *The Future of Religion: Secularization, Revival and Cult Formation* (Berkeley: University of California Press, 1985).

Steiner, Rudolf, *The Reappearance of Christ in the Etheric* (Spring Valley NY: Anthroposophic, 1983).

Stenmark, Mikael, *Scientism: Science, Ethics and Religion* (Aldershot: Ashgate, 2001).

Stone, Jon R., *Expecting Armageddon: Essential Readings in Failed Prophecy* (London: Routledge, 2000).

Strachan, Gordon, *Christ and the Cosmos* (Dunbar: Labarum, 1985).

'Strange Days', BBC2, 18 June 1996.

Strohmer, Charles, *What Your Horoscope Doesn't Tell You* (Wheaton IL: Tyndale House, 1988).

Strinati, Dominic, *An Introduction to Theories of Popular Culture* (London: Routledge, 1995).

'Supernatural Investigator: It's in the Stars', Sorcery Films, 2009.

Sutcliffe, Stuart, *Children of the New Age: A History of Spiritual Practices* (London: Routledge, 2003).

——, 'Between Apocalypse and Self-Realisation: "Nature" as an Index of New Age Spirituality', in Joanne Pearson, Richard H. Roberts and Geoffrey Samuel (eds), *Nature Religion Today: Paganism in the Modern World* (Edinburgh: Edinburgh University Press, 1998).

Svensen, Stuart, and Ken White, 'A Content Analysis of Horoscopes', *Genetic, Social and Psychological Monographs*, 12/1 (1995): 7–38.

Swedenborg, Emanuel, *The Apocalypse Revealed Wherein are Disclosed the Arcana Foretold Which Have Hitherto Remained Concealed*, Eng. trans. of the Latin edn of 1766, n.d., The Swedenborg Digital Library, at <http://www.swedenborgdigitallibrary.org/contets/AR.html>, accessed 20 June 2009.

Tambiah, Stanley Jeraraja, *Magic, Science, Religion and the Scope of Rationality*, Lewis Henry Morgan Lectures, 1984 (Cambridge: Cambridge University Press, 1990).

Taylor, Robert, *The Diegesis; being a Discovery of the origin, Evidences, and Early History of Christianity* (London: Richard Carlile, 1829).

Tester, Jim, *A History of Western Astrology* (Woodbridge: Boydell, 1987).

Thompson, William Irwin, 'Sixteen Years of the New Age', in David Spangler and William Irwin Thompson, *Reimagination of the World: A Critique of the New Age, Science, and Popular Culture* (Santa Fe: Bear, 1991).

Thorndike, Lynn, *History of Magic and Experimental Science* (8 vols, New York: Columbia University Press, 1923–58).

Thrower, James, *Religion: The Classical Theories* (Edinburgh: Edinburgh University Press, 1999).

Tobacyk, Jerome, and Gary Milford, 'Belief in Paranormal Phenomena: Assessment Instrument Development and Implications for Personality Functioning', *Journal of Personality and Social Psychology*, 44/5 (1983): 1029–37.

Trevelyan, (Sir) George, *A Vision of the Aquarian Age: The Emerging Spiritual World View* (London: Coventure, 1984).

Truzzi, Marcello, 'On Pseudo-Skepticism', *The Anomalist*, repr. from the *Zetetic Scholar*, 12–13 (1987), at <http://www.anomalist.com/commentaries/pseudo.html>.

——, 'Astrology as Popular Culture', *Journal of Popular Culture*, 8 (1975): 906–11.

Tuchman, Gaye, 'The Symbolic Annihilation of Women by the Mass Media', in Lane Crothers and Charles Lockhart, *Culture and Politics: A Reader* (New York: St Martin's, 2000), pp. 150–74.

Tylor, Edward Burnett, *Primitive Culture* (London: John Murray, 1873), vol. 1.

Ulansey, David, *The Origins of the Mithraic Mysteries: Cosmology and Salvation in the Ancient World* (New York and Oxford: Oxford University Press, 1989).

Ullman, Leonard P., and Leonard Krasner, *A Psychological Approach to Abnormal Behaviour*, 2nd edn (Englewood Cliffs NJ: Prentice Hall, 1969).

Underwood, Peter, *Into the Occult: A Survey for the Seventies* (London: Harrap, 1972).

Valens, Vettius, *Anthologarium*, ed. David Pingree (Leipzig: B.G. Teubner Verlegsgsellschaft, 1986).

Vaughan, Valerie, 'Debunking the Debunkers: Lessons to be Learned', *Mountain Astrologer*, 80 (1998): 35–42, 122.

Vertovec, Steven, 'Inventing Religious Traditions', in Armin W. Geertz and Jeppe Sinding Jensen (eds), *Religion, Tradition and Renewal* (Aarhus: Aarhus University Press, 1991).

Volney, Constantin François, *The Ruins, or A Survey of the Revolutions of Empires* (London: 1795).

Wallis, Robert J., *Shamans/Neo-Shamans: Ecstasy, Alternative Archaeologies and Contemporary Pagans* (London: Routledge, 2003).

Walter, Tony, and Helen Waterhouse, 'A Very Private Belief: Reincarnation in Contemporary England', *Sociology of Religion*, 60/2 (1999): 187–97.

Webb, James, *The Harmonious Circle: The Lives and Work of G.I. Gurdjieff, P.D. Ouspensky, and their Followers* (Boston: Shambhala, 1980).

Weber, Max, *The Sociology of Religion*, trans. Ephraim Fischoff, 4th edn (Boston: Beacon, 1963).

Webster, Charles, *From Paracelsus to Newton: Magic and the Making of Modern Science* (Cambridge: Cambridge University Press, 1982).

Welsh, Lorraine, 'Fear Abandonment, Use Astrology, Cut Wrist', *AFAN Newsletter* Winter (2000): 13.

Wessinger, Catherine, 'Millenialism with and without the Mayhem', in Thomas Robbins and Susan J. Palmer, *Millennium, Messiahs and Mayhem: Contemporary Apocalyptic Movements* (London: Routledge, 1999).

West, John Anthony, and Jan Gerhard Toonder, *The Case for Astrology* (London: Penguin, 1973).

Williams, Raymond, *Culture and Society 1780–1950* (London: Pelican, 1971).

Williams, Rhys H., 'Religion as Political Resource: Culture or Ideology?', *Journal for the Scientific Study of Religion*, 35/4 (1996): 368–78.

Williams, Richard N., Carl B. Taylor and Wayne J. Hintze, 'The Influence of Religious Orientation on Belief in Science, Religion, and the Paranormal', *Journal of Psychology and Theology*, 17/4 (1989): 352–9.

Willis, Roy, and Patrick Curry, *Astrology, Science and Culture: Pulling Down the Moon* (Oxford: Berg, 2004).

Wilson, Bryan, *Contemporary Transformations of Religion* (Oxford: Clarendon Press, 1979 [1976]).

——, *Religion in Secular Society: A Sociological Comment* (Harmondsworth: Pelican, 1969 [1966]).

Wilson, Colin, 'Why I now believe astrology IS a science', *Daily Mail*, 22 March 2001, p. 13.

'Witness', Channel 4, 18 June 2000.

Woodwell, Donna, 'Marketing Astrology 2.0', *ISAR Memberletter*, 637 (2011).

Wunder, Edgar, 'Erfahrung, Wissen, Glaube – ihr Beziehungsgeflecht bezuglich der Astrologie', *Zeitschrift fur Anomalistik*, 2/3 (2002): 275–87.

Wuthnow, Robert, *Experimentation in American Religion: The New Mysticisms and their Implications for the Churches* (Berkeley: University of California Press, 1978).

——, *The Consciousness Revolution* (Berkeley: University of California Press, 1976).

Wynne, Dee, 'Astrology as a Religion', *AFAN Interactive Digest*, 1281 (2010).

Yates, Frances, *The Rosicrucian Enlightenment* (London: Routledge & Kegan Paul, 1986 [1972]).

——, *The Occult Philosophy in the Elizabethan Age* (London and Boston: Routledge & Kegan Paul, 1983 [1979]).

Yinger, J. Milton, *The Scientific Study of Religion* (New York: Macmillan, 1970).

——, 'A Structural Examination of Religion', *Journal for the Scientific Study of Religion*, 8 (1969): 88–99.

Yoder, D., 'Towards a Definition of Folk Religion', *Western Folklore*, 33/1 (1974): 2–15.

York, Michael, *Historical Dictionary of New Age Movements* (Lanham MD: Scarecrow, 2003).

——, *The Emerging Network*: *A Sociology of the New Age and Neo-Pagan Movements* (London: Rowan & Littlefield, 1995).

——, 'A Report', *Journal of Contemporary Religion*, 10/2 (1995): 197.

Zadkiel, *Lilly's Astrology* (London: George Bell & Sons, 1882).

——, *The Grammar of Astrology* (London: Cornish, 1849).

Ziesler, John, *Pauline Christianity* (Oxford: Oxford University Press, 1991).

Zinnbauer, Brian J., Kenneth J. Pargament, Brenda Cole, Mark S. Rye, Eric M. Butter, Timothy G. Belavich, Kathleen M. Hipp, Allie B. Scott and Jill L. Kadar, 'Religion and Spirituality: Unfuzzying the Fuzzy', *Journal for the Scientific Study of Religion*, 36/4 (1997): 549–64.

Zoller, Robert, 'The Use of the Archetypes in Prediction', *Astrological Journal*, 44/6 (2002): 6–16.

Interviews

Adams, Jessica, 8 September 2001.
Brady, Bernadette, 19 April 2001.
Cainer, Jonathan, 8 September 2001.
Dreyer, Ronnie, 17 June 1999.
George, Demetra, 29 May 1999.
Grace-Jones, Diana, 14 April 2003.
Greene, Liz, 14 August 2001.
Hand, Robert, 6 September 2002.
Hill, Lynda, 20 July 2002.
Irving, Ken, 8 September 2001.
Klein, Mavis, 12 September 2001.
Lehman, Lee, 6 December 2002.
Levine, Rick, 22 July 2002.
Lovatt, Sean, 16 March 2001.

Mulligan, Bob, 7 September 2001.
Nobel, Steve, 25 March 2003.
Oken, Alan, 21 July 2002.
Perry, Glenn, 10 October 2003.
Quigley, Kathleen, 25 March 2001.
Reinhart, Melanie, 8 September 2001.
Simms, Maria Kay, 23 July 2002.
Strunckel, Shelley von, 31 October 2002.
Sutton, Komilla, 8 September 2001.
Tarnas, Rick, 21 July 2002.
Wise, Arlan, 7 September 2001.
Zoller, Robert, 19 July 2002.

Personal communications

Blake, Lois, 14 November 2003.
Boggia, Margueritte dar, 5 November 2003.
Boggia, Margueritte dar, 16 July 2011.
Clynes, Frances, 3 January 2012.
Curry, Patrick, 18 April 2001.
Ellis, Mick, 7 April 2008.
Fei, Linda, 13 November 2003.
Gillett, Roy, 26 October 2003.
Gray, Andy, 15 December 2003.
Hudson, Gill, 21 March 2000.
Irving, Ken, 10 October 2003.
Martin, Clare, 28 October 2003.
Ridder-Patrick, Jane, 5 December 2000a.
Ridder-Patrick, Jane, 5 December 2000b.
Ridder-Patrick, Jane, 8 December 2000.
Stacey, Wendy, 17 July 2011.
Weschke, Carl Llewellyn, 3 May 2002.
Weschke, Carl Llewellyn, 4 May 2002.

Other

George, Demetra, Kepler College first-year draft syllabus notes, email, 5 April 2001.

Index